Palgrave Advances in Behavioral Economics

This ground breaking series is designed to make available in book form unique behavioral economic contributions. It provides a publishing opportunity for behavioral economist authors who have a novel perspective and have developed a special ability to integrate economics with other disciplines. It will allow these authors to fully develop their ideas. In general, it is not a place for narrow technical contributions. Theoretical/conceptual, empirical, and policy contributions are all welcome.

More information about this series at
http://www.palgrave.com/gp/series/14720

Gary D. Lynne

Metaeconomics

Tempering Excessive Greed

palgrave
macmillan

Gary D. Lynne
University of Nebraska–Lincoln
Mesa, AZ, USA

ISSN 2662-3846 ISSN 2662-3854 (electronic)
Palgrave Advances in Behavioral Economics
ISBN 978-3-030-50600-1 ISBN 978-3-030-50601-8 (eBook)
https://doi.org/10.1007/978-3-030-50601-8

This Palgrave Macmillan imprint is published by the registered company Springer Nature Switzerland AG.
The registered company address is: Gewerbestrasse 11, 6330 Cham, Switzerland

To John Tomer, who gave substantive meaning to a humane economics.
And, to the Grandchildren: May they experience a more empathy-based,
and, thus, a more humane and good capitalism.

Preface

The path to Metaeconomics has been very much a personal path, going back to my early experience on a grain and livestock farm in northern North Dakota, only 100 miles or so south of the Canadian border, way up north. Because of challenging climate and weather conditions, including a short growing season, it was not easy to make wealth. It was (and still is) a high-risk part of the Spaceship Earth in which we were trying to farm and raise livestock. It was essential to recognize the interdependence and jointness in market&community. Farmers in the local, state, and regional setting had to work together, while still working individually, in order to economically survive. Seeing the jointness in market&community, and, then, in Market&Government, was very much a part of being able to prosper. It was about a kind of jointness, nonseparability, interdependence at work, each reinforcing and essential to the other.

Early Experiences Pointed to a Metaeconomics

Early experience involved our heavy participation in cooperatives of various kinds. Farmers who generally cherish their independence, liberty, and freedom to pursue their Self-interest could join with other farmers (and consumers: there were also grocery store and rural electricity coops) to amass the capital essential to make a good capitalism work. It was through joining in with the wider, shared Other-interest of a larger, cooperative venture, that a viable Market-based community became possible. That is, while most capital (including the equipment, buildings, farmland itself) was owned by a person, there was also considerable benefit arising out of the shared Other-interest in owning some capital, together.

Said capital included jointly owning capacity to produce oil products (gasoline, diesel fuel) in a shared refinery; cooperatives selling seeds, fertilizers, tools, fencing materials, and farm equipment; cooperatively owned local grain elevators buying the grain, as well as terminal elevators on the Great Lakes for moving the grain to Market, and livestock terminals to move animals to the processing facilities; and, yes, even insurance companies owned cooperatively; and the rural electric cooperative that produced and distributed the electricity so essential to the production on a farm.

Also, the nature of altruism became clear to me, as it was a matter of sacrifice, now in two dimensions. If one did buy or sell outside the coop business circle, then one was sacrificing the Other-interest of the coop to gain in the Self-interest in a lower cost or higher price outside the coop. Keeping business efforts primarily, but not completely, within the circle of coop business meant maximizing a balanced Self&Other-interest. Thinking back, now with my Metaeconomics lens, it is also apparent how a bit of sacrifice in both domains of interest gave more resilience and viability to that farming community.

So, working together, it was all about using both money capital and social capital, to facilitate more productive ways to achieve Self-interest. It was a Self-interest in accumulating money capital tempered by the Other (shared with others within the coop-community)-interest, the latter representing the essential social (both money and non-money value including social) capital, too. It was all about finding the way to building a good capitalism.

Intriguingly, I also recall high school experiences where disparaging remarks were made about the cooperatives, as though they were somehow communist or socialist in their way of doing business. It was amazing at the time, and even more so now after reflecting on the nature of an economy&community in many decades of formal study, how underinformed and uninformed such comments really were, and, intriguingly, we still hear such empty platitudes to this day.

I also came to understand that community also encompassed more than just the people: It included the livestock on the farm, and the wildlife and other living creatures (even the microorganisms in the soil) in the ecosystem. It was all about interdependence with other Humans, as well as with all the other creatures and systems on the Spaceship Earth.

It also became clear that it was about building effective institutions and organizations which gave context to the Market, represented most generally in the notion of a progressive Government. Yet, it was also becoming apparent of the need for conservative Government, too. It really was more about finding the balance in Conservative and Progressive Government, than about one or the other.

Such experiences stirred me to educate myself, both formally and in finding out on my own, seek the facts, on how best to build Market&Government, a good capitalism. It would also become a search for the best combination of private&public (shared with others)-property, too, as cooperatives always reflected and pointed to finding good balance in the kind of property. It would also become clear that a moral dimension, a moral community, an ethics-based doing-the-right thing, was in the background of the balance. And, while I did not have a term for describing it at the time, it all took a lot of Empathy: It was not just about the Ego.

Eventually, it started to become clear that it was about finding balance in a joint Ego&Empathy, in a joint and balanced Self&Other-interest. It was about finding balance in a joint Market&Government. Metaeconomics emerged from the effort to find better ways to think about and make sense of said balance. It was developed through an integration across a wide array of sciences, while bringing attention to the moral and ethical dimension of a balance. It was to become an integration across science&ethics.

Intended Audience

Metaeconomics integrates across such diverse scientific fields as Evolutionary Biology and Psychology; Ecological Economics; Neuroscience and Neuroeconomics; Economic Psychology; Economic Sociology, Sociology; Political Science; business, especially Marketing; Psychological Economics; and, most importantly on Behavioral (including Experimental) Economics. It integrates across mainstream Neoclassical and Neoinstitutional Economics, including the many subfields within each. It also rests on a foundation built in Thermodynamics: The latter points to the inherent interdependence among physical, biological, cultural, governmental, and economic systems all embedded within the Spaceship Earth on which we Travel, together, around the Sun. So, persons with any of said backgrounds will potentially find Metaeconomics intriguing.

Yet, the language is economics. So, no matter your favorite school of economic thought, Metaeconomics will look familiar. And, one does not need a great deal of advanced training to gain something: Only a basic course in Microeconomics is necessary to handle most of the book without any extraordinary effort. And, if you are a bit rusty with, or have never been introduced to the basics, perhaps the best ever microeconomics text, to provide a commonsense understanding, and, it is still available, is McCloskey (1985).

Metaeconomics will be helpful to staff economists for Government entities in all the branches, including the Administrative, Legislative, and Judicial. Administrative agencies like the US Department of Agriculture, US Department of the Interior, US Environmental Protection Agency, US Natural Resource Conservation Service, US Department of Health, US Department of Energy, US Department of Justice, US Department of Commerce, among many others, can all benefit. It will be useful to staff economists and others in the US State Agency counterparts. The reason is straight forward: Metaeconomics sees a key role for the Government in the Market, and for the Market in the Government. Market&Government are joint, interdependent, nonseparable, with each essential to the other.

People running for election in the Administrative Branch (President, Governor) and Legislative Branches (Senators, Representatives) often have people on their election staffs concerned with economics and economic policy. Metaeconomics can be used and be especially productive in such situations, as it is all about the content of the shared Other-interest, and each Political Isle has at least one. Metaeconomics can also help staff working with Judges and others in the Judicial Branch. And, hopefully, the politicians and judges, themselves, will also consider reading and learning about Metaeconomics.

Metaeconomics is also intended for people in business and industry who just naturally, through their training and experience, have some understanding of economic principles. Business people naturally think about supply and demand, while working to make solid investment, management, and marketing decisions for their companies. Metaeconomics will especially resonate with people in marketing, which is about Empathy, about "walking-in-the-shoes" of the customer. Businesses have also been admonished for being too focused on just the shareholders, with not enough Empathy with suppliers, customers, employees, and the Spaceship Earth System within which business and industry is embedded. Metaeconomics shifts attention to Empathy.

And, finally, it is hoped that the general reader, anyone trying to make sense of the turmoil in the Markets and in the Government, might also find Metaeconomics intriguing. The turmoil is not peaceful, and is not contributing to making very many happy. Metaeconomics is all about trying to bring peace and happiness back into both, through seeing the potential for both a humane and efficient integration in Market&Government.

Mesa, AZ, USA Gary D. Lynne

References

McCloskey, D. N. 1985. *The Applied Theory of Price*. 2nd Ed. New York: Macmillan. Available for download at https://www.deirdremccloskey.com/docs/price.pdf.

Acknowledgments

Starting in high school, an agricultural education teacher by the name of Gerald Wagner saw a future for me I could not imagine at the time. He kept nudging. Moving into the university years, an early influence was from mentor Dale Anderson: Go, do a PhD, he said. And, then, there was my PhD advisor, Emery Castle, who encouraged me to explore widely, including reading philosophy, which was his hobby. Albert Halter, too, for his skills in mathematical economics, about which we were always encouraged to check against the reality of the complex system it was to represent. And, most importantly, he observed that picking a good PhD dissertation topic would ensure that one had something to work on their entire career: Right on. It was about multiple objective planning for water development: After three to four decades of considering the matter, always in the background of what I was working on, it turned out to be all about nonallocable inputs and nonallocable goods, the inherent jointness. It was also about the dual interest serving both each person and the people which came with the large dams for water development. Metaeconomics gives the framework and theory I was lacking when working on that dissertation.

While at the University of Florida, I really appreciated the productive interactions with Chris Andrew, and his observing, after an extended conversation, "Ok," he said, "what you are telling me is that: The We needs a Me to Be, and without a Me there is no We." I said, "Yes, that is it." I am also indebted to Clyde Kiker, especially on his teaching me thermodynamics, principles of sustainability. And, then, in more recent years, at the University of Nebraska-Lincoln, a special thanks to John Hibbing, for working jointly in running a seminar in Behavioral Economics and Behavioral Political Science. Another special thanks to Emie Yiannaka, especially for supporting the development of a Behavioral Economics group in the Department, and in working jointly to develop the Experimental and Behavioral Economics Laboratory. I owe a special debt of gratitude to Natalia Czap, first a graduate student, and then a colleague, and a reader with good suggestions for several parts of this book. I am especially indebted to her efforts in the design and operation of the laboratory experiments, as well as helping me make sense of experimental techniques and methods. Others involved in the laboratory effort included Hans Czap and Mark Burbach, as well as Marianna Khachaturyan. The result was a substantive, empirical foundation for Metaeconomics.

Major insights also evolved in working with a number of graduate students. Leandro Rola, who had a degree in sociology, and, who made it clear during my very first attempt to make sense of what drove farmer conservation behavior that there was a sociology at work among farmers. Other students who helped a great deal include Phyllis Saarinen, Frank Casey, John Sautter, and Robert Sheeder.

And, then, on a larger scale, I have interacted with so many in the Society for the Advancement of Behavioral Economics, especially as represented in Morris Altman and John Tomer. Gerald Cory is another. Lindon Robison also needs a mention: We worked as one in stirring the formation of the Institutional and Behavioral Economics Section of what is now the Agricultural and Applied Economics Association. We had both come to the realization that something fundamentally was missing in the frame and theory of economics. Lindy called it social capital; I called it shared Other-interest; and, we overlapped a great deal. Another academic, with whom I have had productive interactions while we were department heads at the University of Nebraska-Lincoln, is Earl Russell, with whom I have continued to have good dialogue during our Professor Emeritus years. He provided publishing advice, in addition to serving as a reader with many helpful suggestions. And, thank you to Larry Van Tassell, Professor and Head of the Department of Agricultural Economics at the University of Nebraska-Lincoln, for providing encouragement, as well as some word processing and other technical support, continuing well after my becoming a Professor Emeritus. I also wish to thank Palgrave Macmillan, specifically Elizabeth Graber, Commissioning Editor, Economics, and Sophia Siegler, Editorial Assistant, Economics and Business, for their patience, understanding, and help on many fronts. I also appreciate the help from Sudha Soundarrajan, Project Manager, and others in editorial and publishing roles at SPi Content Solutions – SPi Global. Also, most importantly, my thanks to John Tomer, Behavioral Economics Series Editor, who suggested I write this book, and, unfortunately, he passed before it was finished. It would not exist except for his nudge.

And, then, there are many friends and relatives. My father, Gordon, who arguably knew more about what would comprise a pragmatic, useful set of agricultural policies than most experts. He fundamentally understood the play of the farmer&community, writ even larger in the Market&Government. And, my mother, Dorothy: Empathy was her starting point, leading to sympathy with, and compassion for, everything that lived on this Spaceship Earth. I have also appreciated interacting with brothers Ryan and Richard. Ryan is the empath, who demonstrates the essential connection we have with our Spaceship Earth. And, Richard, the politically oriented thinker, who encouraged me to keep trying to communicate Metaeconomics to a wider audience, including the farmers like himself. Our daughters, too, Jill and Erica, have given substantive feedback, especially in reminding Dad that he needs to get to the point. And, many friends have had the patience to interact, stirring new ideas, especially Mike Gordon, with many productive conversations.

And, to my companion and wife of 50+ years: Thank you for the patience to put up with my perhaps too frequent shifts in conversation toward the notion of balance in I&We, the Self&Other of life. And, for putting-up with my impatience, and sometimes intolerance, for those around me and in the political realm, for not understanding the subtlety of jointness, and the need for that balance.

Praise for *Metaeconomics*

"This is an important and original contribution to economics and is well situated in the emerging literature in behavioral and institutional economics. Well-positioned in current theoretical and policy debates, through the prism of Lynne's interdisciplinary Metaeconomics, this book engages with existing scholarship and moves us forward analytically by providing us with a broader and more informed analytical framework, going beyond the parameters of traditional neoclassical economics."

—Morris Altman, Dean, *School of Business, University of Dundee*

"Lynne's focus is a sharper, more constrained one than my consilience approach. Both are needed. It represents the top of contributors to dual motive theory, even though we proceed from different perspectives. The contribution to dual motive theory is significant and undeniable."

—Gerald A. Cory, Jr., Senior Fellow, *San Jose State University*

"Economics has traditionally focused on self-interest, but it has more recently progressed by broadening its theories to recognize that the interests we share with others can also motivate us. Metaeconomics proposes a unique take, proposing that both self-interest and the other (shared with others, but internalized within)-interest are jointly represented in our own-interest. A person seeks to maximize the own-interest which includes a balance in the two interests. Metaeconomics contributes to this progress in a way that should be comfortable to economists: Just as our self-interests imply that we face tradeoffs in our world where resources are scarce, so our interests in others generate tradeoffs. This book provides many thought-provoking illustrations of why it is useful to recognize our shared interests with others. It helps us explain many observations that economic theory focused on self-interest alone cannot explain, and it broadens the reasonable scope of economic policy."

—Mark Pingle, *Professor of Economics, University of Nevada, Reno*

"This book reminds us that on so many fronts success and survival require an integration of self and other interests. I have long admired Lynne for pointing out that the emperor of greed focused economics is missing an important part of his wardrobe. Metaeconomics offers to complete the emperor's attire. Convincingly, Lynne instructs that on so many fronts, understanding and remediation requires that we account for and integrate self-interest and the interest we share with others. As evidence, Lynne applies his Metaeconomics paradigm to issues of voting, stable food supplies, pandemics, community sustainability, and taxation and others while embracing the empirically-based insights of behavioral economics. By writing this book, Lynne has demonstrated his interest in the well-being of others even though self-interest didn't require it."

—Lindon Robison, Professor Emeritus, *Michigan State University*

Contents

About the Author

Gary D. Lynné is Professor Emeritus at the University of Nebraska-Lincoln, USA. Lynne earned BS and MS degrees from North Dakota State University and a PhD from Oregon State University, all in Agricultural Economics. He specialized in Natural Resource Economics. He worked mainly in research, holding positions at the University of Florida and the University of Nebraska-Lincoln. Lynne has published over 180 journal papers, book chapters, reviews, reports, and articles—all connected into the related science that gave form and substance to the empirical foundation for Metaeconomics. It also led to coining the notion of Empathy Conservation. For further information about the research program and the author, see the website https://www.metaeconomics.info.

List of Figures

List of Tables

Advanced Organizers and Conventions

Books used at every university and high school to teach economics use the linking "and" to talk about such things as individuals and community; economy and society; economy and community; economy and government; and, the most important in Metaeconomics, market and government. Everything is presumed independent. Metaeconomics, in contrast, points to everything on the Spaceship Earth on which we Travel together as interdependent. The "&" is used regularly to bring the interdependence to the top.

It is also the convention in standard economics books to refer to an individual, as though we are individual. Metaeconomics sees instead a person, who is interdependent with every other person, and with every part of the Spaceship Earth System.

It is also true of the political isles: The standard framing is about Conservative (Right) OR Progressive (Left), and Conservative (Right) VS. Progressive (Left). Again, no. The point is: What really works is seeing the interdependence of Conservative&Progressive, Right&Left.

An even more fundamental reason for the "&" is that every person has both an Ego and a capacity for Empathy (different parts, but overlapping within the brain) jointly at work in the brain and mind, as represented in Ego&Empathy, Self&Other. It is said interdependence that is at the core. So, dear reader, patience and understanding: Every time you see an "&" connecting two descriptors, please think jointness, interdependence, non-separable, overlapping, with each term describing something essential to the other. Also, think Empathy: It is the main driver in finding the balance represented in the "&."

Now having pointed to the interdependence, Metaeconomics is still about the behavior of a person. The focus is on what "turns the crank" of each person, not the collective, the market, the community, or the government. The "&" also means, then, "present within each person."

And, on Capitalization: "Capitals are useful word-changers ... You can make a word into a concrete and Proper Noun by capitalizing it, which makes it concrete. It's easy to point at a named Thing. That's why arguments in economics and mathematics go by names, even by names of people..." (McCloskey 2019, p. 72). But, like McCloskey also says, use it Sparingly. I try to do so.

So, another related matter: How I refer to a Human and a human. I use Human as a human different from the human who is an Econ. The Econ from mainstream economics as represented in Microeconomics is totally focused on Self-interest—arrogant self-love—with little if any attention to that which others will go along with. Metaeconomics introduces the Other-interest which represents what others, including the Human in question, can go along with: A Human tempers Self-interest with that Other-interest.

Finally, Metaeconomics is a coined word. It is not yet in the dictionary, or in an encyclopedia. And, it is good in the sense that "New words suggest new thoughts" (McCloskey 2019, p. 106).

References

McCloskey, D. N. 2019. *Economical Writing: Thirty-Five Rules for Clear and Persuasive Prose*. Chicago: University of Chicago Press.

CHAPTER 1

Introduction

Metaeconomics is fundamentally about the problem of having too much emphasis on the Market or too much emphasis on the Government. It is about the essential need to bring empirical reality and ethics into finding balance: It is essential to achieving a good capitalism. Why? Well, because of the natural tendency to excessive Greed. As DeWaal (2009) would have it, we live in an age of Empathy: Ego based Greed is out. The Greed needs to be tempered, balanced, and perhaps bounded, with Empathy-based ethics. And, as Metaeconomics makes clear, it is because there is a dual nature of human nature, but it is an old story, from Smith (1759/1790):

> How selfish so ever man may be supposed, there are evidently some principles in his nature, which interest him in the fortune of others, and render their happiness necessary to him, though he derives nothing from it except the pleasure of seeing it. Of this kind is pity or compassion, the emotion which we feel for the misery of others [Smith 1759/1790, *The Theory of Moral Sentiments*, quoted in Solomon 2007, p. 64, who adds: Without compassion (sympathy), there would be no foundation and no motivation for ethics].

As it suggests, expressing the moral sentiments is all about Empathy as the starting point, perhaps leading to Sympathy with (not for, but with), and then possibly to compassion (or not). Solomon (2007) agrees: There is something (empathy-sympathy-compassion based ethics, the moral and ethical dimension) beyond mere Self-interest at work. Yet, Self-interest is

G. D. Lynne, *Metaeconomics*, Palgrave Advances in Behavioral Economics, https://doi.org/10.1007/978-3-030-50601-8_1

still the key feature of a viable and good capitalism, as Smith (1776/1789) made clear. And, reality, please.

As the story about Metaeconomics unwinds, the case will be made that the something essential to tempering mere Self-interest is an Empathy (and ethics)-based Other-interest. And, that a viable and good capitalism requires balance in Ego&Empathy, selfish&selfless, person&people, person&community, Self&Other (the latter shared with others, but internalized within Own-self)-interest. Remember: Metaeconomics is about the person. At a larger scale, the balance needs to be in Market&Government. An integrated Smith (1776/1789) & Smith (1759/1790) represents it. As Smith tried to teach us, it is about seeking a way for each person to maximize their Own-interest in their own (humane and liberal) way, which includes both Self&Other-interest. It cannot be emphasized enough. The goal, the possibility for happiness (and peace), depends on Own-interest, not Self-interest only. Said Own-interest involves humanely including others, represented in the underlying ethic that gives content to the shared Other-interest. For the early analysis and claim that interdependency, jointness, and nonseparability of a dual interest is represented in Smith (1776/1789) & Smith (1759/1789), see Lynne (2006). For the latest claims about Adam Smith and dual interest, especially on how the moral sentiments relate to Empathy and Sympathy, leading to the moral and ethical dimension of the economy, see Lynne et al. (2016, esp. pp. 245–250).

Dual interest reasoning can be used to provide new insights into solving old economic puzzles, resolving paradoxes and anomalies. It can be used to suggest and guide new empirical testing on a way to a more reality-based economics. So, hang on, here we go, on a potentially fun and productive ride toward an ethics-based, and, yes, a reality-based, economics.

After going through the formal model and several demonstrations and applications showing how it works, the book turns to proposing new insights into resolving the irritation (and outrage) surrounding current policy issues when balance is missing. And, we feel it often. We eventually move, in the last chapter, to speculation on how Metaeconomics could play a substantive role in saving a liberal and humane democracy-based capitalism, through balancing. The current version is doing badly, and, is under fire from several quarters: See Deneen (2019a, b); Fukuyama (2006); Goldberg (2018); Hedges (2018); Hirschfeld (2018); MacLean (2017); McCloskey (2019); Stanley (2018); and Stiglitz (2019), to list a few. We need to first develop and explain Metaeconomics to make sense of the fire, and to develop the new analytical machinery on how to put it out, or, at least manage it, before we can fix it: So, hang on.

Metaeconomics Represents Both Dimensions of Adam Smith

Adam Smith was quite aware of the duality and jointness within Own-self, which perhaps has not been enough appreciated. In fact, the seeming disparity in focus of the two books at one point came to be characterized as being "das (the) Adam Smith problem (as suggested by the German historical school)," as though Adam Smith did not know the need for, or how to, balance the two tendencies. Wrong.

In fact, he not only understood it but also had a kind of subtle sense of humor about it. Smith (1759/1790) saw the Empathy-based Other (shared with others and internalized within Own-self)-interest:

> (a Human) naturally desires, not only to be loved, but to be lovely. (Smith 1759/1790, cited in Roberts 2014, loc 282)

As Smith said it, Be Lovely: Humor. We really want to be liked by others, and to be part of the community. Smith (1776/1789) saw the Ego-based Self-interest, too: Be Loved. More humor. We want to achieve high status, otherwise be held in high regard, and become wealthy, respected, and admired, perhaps even envied: People are fascinated with the wealthy and their lifestyle. So, how do we achieve both, in good balance?

Well, Smith (1759/1790) clarifies it is about the moral dimension, the moral and ethical rules (see Samuels, Johnson, and Perry 2011, loc 3391), the moral community and ethical system widely shared. Each person, through paying attention to the moral community, tempers, and conditions works at tempering the pursuit of Self-interest. It is done within each person, through going to the Station of the Impartial Spectator: We go to the Station and reflect, ponder, and consider what is in the shared Other-interest. Just like Adam Smith, Metaeconomics sees the essential need to temper (we decide what to temper, at the Station) the more primal urges in the Self-interest, which is all about self-love. As Smith and Wilson (2019, p. 8) say it, seeing it as a key part of their Humanomics: "For (Adam) Smith, 'self-love' is necessarily at the core of our being... (but with maturation) conduct is shaped by learnt ... rules of social order originating in our capacity for mutual sympathetic fellow-feeling." It is through empathy-sympathy we form that fellow-feeling in a shared Other-interest with our fellows: We then form a more lovely Own-self. Also, the social order, the mutual sympathetic fellow-feeling has nothing to do with social preference: There is no such thing. It is only about the Own-self, but with a shared Other-interest at play within.

So, Humanomics, a close relative of Metaeconomics, is also about the interplay of self-love (Self-interest) and fellow-feeling (shared Other-interest) in Smith (1776/1789) & Smith (1759/1790). The interplay of the two dimensions in Adam Smith was first proposed in Metaeconomics in the 1990s. In Metaeconomics, using modern terms, self-love reflects the Ego-based Self-interest and fellow-feeling reflects the expression of Empathy-based Other-interest. Also, by the time of Lynne et al. (2016), Metaeconomics had made the connection with ethics, the moral and ethical dimension of the economy arising in the Empathy-based Other-interest. The key role of ethics, also made clear in Smith (1759/1790), has recently been emphasized by McCloskey (2019), in pointing to the need to return to the (ethics based) humane liberalism of Adam Smith. Metaeconomics brings all of said threads together into one analytical system. It sees the essential role of balance in the Ego-based Self-interest and Empathy (ethics)-based Other-interest in finding the way to a truly humane and liberal economic system, a good capitalism.

Also, in modern terms, Metaeconomics points to the fact that we need to become mindful. We empathize, projecting Own-self into the situation of the other. Empathy takes us to Station of the Impartial Spectator. At the Station, in that frame of mind, we consider the possibility of joining in sympathy with, and perhaps even act on compassion for, the other. Yet, as Adam Smith makes clear, it is all still within the Own-self; it really has little to do with the other, per se. We seek to maximize our Own-interest. It is good for the person, and for capitalism, for a good and humane capitalism.

We all know the urges, and the need to temper same, as in eating too much; wanting sex too often; wanting way more material goods and pleasures than we really need: Excessive Greed is not beyond any of us, right? Yachts and way too many houses and cars at the high end; not enough money left to field a $400 essential at the lower end. So, Metaeconomics brings the moral and ethical dimension, as in Smith (1759/1790), back into view within the framework of the economics about the person, now better representing the real economic picture, the real nature of a Human. And, while Microeconomics gets it partly right, each person is partly an Econ, Metaeconomics clarifies we can be far more fun and interesting. We really are better characterized as a Human, after all. The distinction between the Econ and the Human is borrowed from Thaler and Sunstein (2008).

Smith also, then, saw the nature of true happiness (and, it was to be the essential feature of a good capitalism) requiring balance. Achieving balance in Self&Other was to Be Loved & Be Lovely. Metaeconomics clarifies, in a formal mathematical framework, and some nice-looking figures with curves, that happiness means we have achieved good balance in Ego&Empathy, Self&Other-interest, jointly achieved. Are you feeling happier, already, knowing we have a way to characterize it in formal economic terms? Hoping so.

Other philosophers have been well-aware of the possible duality, and allude to the jointness, going back at least to Plato (see Hayes and Lynne 2004, 2013), with the metaphor of the black stallion of passion, the Ego-based Self-interest. The white mare has the role to temper the passion through the Empathy-based Other-interest. The chariot driver brings reason, rationality to bear with Self-control, choosing the best path for the dual horses to jointly travel. As Elster (1979) would have it, bind me to the mast, else I crash my ship on the rocks, as the sirens call. Hard work, here, temper our passions? Slow down and guide our hedonistic drives?

As Fukuyama (2006) would have it, in a similar idea, drawing on Hegel as philosopher, using the Kojève interpretation as he explains it, there is desire&thymous at work within. A kind of "dialectic" is at work, with the real possibility for a synthesis through reason. Desire is hedonism. Thymous is the need to temper it, for our own-good and the good of others in our lives. Actually, it is good for everyone on Spaceship Earth on which we travel together around the Sun, and through the Universe. Metaeconomics sees it much the same way, seeing Ego&Empathy as a kind of dialectic, going in both directions. Too much Ego (Empathy) leads to a new synthesis in better balance, joint with Empathy (Ego). It is resolved through reason, to the extent it can be brought to bear through adequate Self-control. Ever experienced it, where you have tempered your Ego (and hedonistic) drives with a bit of Empathy from within, and directed through mindfulness with others, and, as a result arrived on a Higher Plane, at peace? Bet you have, as Humans do it, regularly, lest they crash from the imbalance. Metaeconomics clarifies the economic, psychological, and philosophical (and a bit, but not much, on related religious) notions as we go.

As is also made clear in the development of the story about Metaeconomics, quite a number of social scientists of various backgrounds and scientific inclinations have over the years written both deeply and extensively about the possibility of duality in Humans. So, we are about to go through the first-ever Metaeconomics book, together, and some parts are not at all original. But, then, again doing what we can to integrate across ideas is hard work. And, just maybe hard work can lead to a unique integration, and then the MetaEcon (those who do the Metaeconomics) can yet lay claim to be a bit original?

Duality is in us, as Humans. It is especially made visible in the dual-self, multiple-self arena of psychology, as pointed to in Lester (1987, 1995): Most people point to multiple selves, in a range of three to seven. Maslow (1954) is all about fusing the dichotomous tendencies between Self&Other. Berne (1961) characterizes the Ego-driven child, the Empathy-driven parent, and the rational chooser, the adult in charge of balancing the two forces. With both a nurturing and critical parent, as well as an adapted and free child, counting the adult: That makes five sub-selves. We could turn it into ten sub-selves by putting valence on each segment, as in negative and positive thinking. We could even make it 12, with 2 adults, as in the algorithmic (thinking, analyzing, calculating) mind and rational mind (in effect, managing own-mind, choosing the best, balanced, rational path) after Stanovich (2011).

Some other economists have also recognized the real possibility of a multiple-self (Elster 1979, 1986). Ainslie (1986, p. 133) points to the visceral self and the ideal self. Buber (1923/1958) points to the I&Thou, the Ich&Du, and the person&community. Etzioni (1986) suggests two kinds of utility, represented in the pleasure utility (Ego-based hedonism, again) and the moral utility (yes, we need to do the right thing, through Empathy, the moral sentiments, the ethics, as Adam Smith would have it). It is where Metaeconomics also started, as represented in the first paper about duality (Lynne 1995). And, again, we are Humans, so maybe we need a more Humanistic Economics, as Tomer (2012, 2017, Chapter 13) has called for. An Ego&Empathy, Self&Other-interest based Metaeconomics fits the bill. And, the dual self with a (self) controller captures the essence of the complexity.

Lutz and Lux (1988) tried to bring a Humanistic Economics into play, and no one much listened, seeing the need to temper Self-interest by what we share. Frank (2004), too, sees how the moral dimension can and often needs to influence the Self-interest only tendency. In fact, university students studying (or, is it brain-washed?) Self-interest only Microeconomics results in students becoming more selfish. We probably do not need the kind of encouragement and confirmation of it somehow being scientific, as Microeconomics claims to be, as being selfish is already deep in the brain, primal, from birth.

Marglin (2008) also sees the dual tendency in his lamenting the fact Neoclassical Economics, and the Microeconomics single interest analytical engine, has extracted community (the Other-interest in Metaeconomics) from the economic framework. Psychology professor turned clinical psychologist, focused on neurosis, Angyal (1941, 1965) points to dealing with the duality as essential to getting healthier, being better, and achieving mental stability. The focus on what leads to mental stability in the sense of being a better Own-self clarifies the inherent overlap and potential conflict in the autonomous (Ego-based) & homonomous (Empathy-based) personality, and it sometimes needs help.

In particular, the dual Own-self often needs help in Self-control, when the internalized Other-interest, as Angyal (1965) calls it, the homonomy, fails to restrain the Self-interest. It results in not achieving balance. When the internal nudging fails, the control sometimes must come from outside the person, in the notion of a heteronomous (outside controlling) influence. Please think about your own experiences of trying your best to manage your own drives, and how difficult it is to bring Self-control (like pushing away from the table before the plate is empty) online?

Cory (1999), especially, sees the duality within the Own-self, building on the triune brain construct coming out of Neuroscience, as represented in MacLean (1990). The case is made for how evolution has led to a natural tension between the proto-reptilian core in the brain (the Ego) and the paleo-mammalian (the Empathy) over-layer in the brain. The tension is resolved through actions of the over-layer represented in the rational part of the brain, which seeks to find balance in Ego&Empathy. Sounds complicated. Not really. We just have the two evolved tendencies, deep in the folds of our brain, and, we, using our rational mind, must balance them. That is all, but it is not easy.

Metaeconomics is consistent with Cory (1999). Metaeconomics also rests in more recent Neuroscience- and Neuroeconomics-based findings

about the brain and the mind, which sees, in even greater detail, the complexity of the human brain, with different functional areas: Ego drives the main tendency, which is often tempered by the Empathy parts of the brain (Singer 2009). For an overview, in a brain science for dummies, embedded within the well-done *Behavioral Economics for Dummies* book, see Altman (2012, Chapter 3, loc 1179).

Metaeconomics as a kind of Behavioral Economics builds upon the empirical reality being developed throughout many branches of Behavioral Economics (for overviews, demonstrations see Altman 2012; Tomer 2017). In another sense, Metaeconomics can influence the direction of Behavioral Economics research, especially with respect to the role of the shared Other-interest. It especially reflects and contributes to the Humanistic Branch of Behavioral Economics (a point made in Tomer 2012, see esp. p. 139).

Overall, Metaeconomics is offered in the spirit of *Consilience: The Unity of Knowledge*, after Wilson (1998). Metaeconomics works to bring various pieces and arguments together to capture the essence of the many different proposals. Big word, *Consilience*, but it just means thinking, framing, done within one's Own-self, after doing a lot of reading. Metaeconomics strives to be a truly integrated, empirically based economics, also building upon fundamental principles of how Spaceship Earth Systems work, as described in thermodynamics: It is another big word, but, for a wonderful explanation of it, see Söllner (1997). Metaeconomics also builds upon ecology and the idea of resilience: Just think about how you have bounced through life, finding a way to adjust, to make it work (see Walker and Salt 2006; Perrings 1987). Metaeconomics also draws upon, and builds upon Microeconomics, with the focus on a single interest, prudence the only virtue, maximization theory. It also builds upon Sociology; Economic Sociology; and Socioeconomics, all of which see the Other-interest. It builds and draws upon Psychology, Economic Psychology, and Psychological Economics, which see the Self-interest. It draws upon various subfields of economics, too, like Marxian economics; Austrian economics; Buddhist, Humanistic, Humane, and Feminist Economics. Metaeconomics is a specific integration across a wide range of knowledge. And, most importantly, it brings Empathy, and the moral and ethical system it produces, back into view within a Metaeconomics Framework and Dual Interest Theory.

So, *Consilience*, is it good? Like Lester (1995, p. 161) would have it, in commenting on the parallel need for such a *Consilience* project to unify the theories in psychology:

> Researchers await a new theorist who will assimilate the old theories and present an integrated theory incorporating previous concepts and propositions. A cynical colleague of mine once said that such a task requires the

services of someone in marketing because the ideas will not be new ones, but merely old ones presented in new packaging.

Metaeconomics is in many ways a marketing project, integrating many old ideas into one framework and theory. Yet, maybe there are just a few new ideas in Metaeconomics, especially as related to the role of Empathy and ethics in the economy? You will have to be the judge.

Metaeconomics Solves Old Puzzles While Suggesting New Arenas for Testing

Neoclassical Economics, referred to herein as Self-interest only economics, has the Ego-based part of economic choice well in hand. It leaves out Empathy-based ethics, and, the moral dimension, and, what we will learn, the shared Other-interest representing it. Also, in case you had not noticed, Self-interest only economics is well developed and touted as the truth, and nothing but the truth, in Microeconomics. It is represented in hundreds of books and thousands of journal papers. Neoclassical Microeconomics is the mainstream, period. The only other, albeit distant contender for mainstream status, is Neoinstitutional Economics. It is referred to as Other-interest economics herein.

Now, we think Neoinstitutional (and the older Institutional Economics) framing needs to be paid more attention to, and, we very much do so in Metaeconomics, but also see it as largely atheoretical. One does not generally see a mathematical model or figure, like an indifference curve, or an isoquant, in a Neoinstitutional Economics framed argument. Generally, Neoinstitutional Economics does not use theory as much as in Neoclassical Economics. Metaeconomics holds potential to be said theory. Metaeconomics also integrates across both Neoclassical and Neoinstitutional Economics. Really, you say, how audacious, how presumptuous? Well, think of it as marketing: People who market sometimes are quite so.

Metaeconomics for the Grandchildren

During the first round of review organized by the publisher, a reviewer suggested: "Just tell me—what is the main take away from Metaeconomics. Can you describe it to your wife, grandchildren, to your seatmate on a plane?" So, before we go any further, let me try the takeaway, realizing it depends on the current frames of reference, but also the personalities of said people.

For My Wife of 50+ Years First, I sometimes remind you that "you are town and I am gown." Second, do you recall the marriage counselor who asked, "how did you two ever find each other," in that your personality type is commonly found in the Hollywood community and mine hidden away in a philosophy department in some University? Well, the answer is, empirical: Small towns in North Dakota are really small. And, to top it off, you as my wife of 50+ years (ok, I already said it, but it has been going on for a long time) have always preferred, well before Twitter, 140-character descriptions. It is not likely you will read this book: So, no acknowledgement along the lines of an appreciation for all your edits, albeit your listening to me for over 50 years about the I&We, Self&Other, Market&Government, has been priceless.

So, here is the Twitter version, to start the conversation: "Remember the three candles in our wedding ceremony? We each used our Self-interest candle to jointly light the shared Other-interest candle?" Ok, so it took 138 characters: Pushing it. Metaeconomics is about the three candles, and especially about the third one, the one we lit together. Lighting the third candle, together, was a way to express a certain community and commitment, there, in the act, to a set of shared interests in making the marriage work, "until death do us part." The "shared with each other" part represents an ethical, moral commitment, a moral community, the moral dimension of our marriage. Also, others at the ceremony we might expect also overlapped with our commitment, a shared Other-interest writ much larger than the two of us. Make sense? Now, take a sip of wine, a deep breath, and stay with me a bit more, so we can look further into what role the third candle plays.

The candle we lit, using our individual candles, says that as a couple we would no longer be independent; we are now joint, interdependent, non-separable (if we work at it, and, it is hard work, as we now know, represented in the empirical data, over-50 years, and the hard work continues). Also, the burning single candle is still within each of us. And, I cannot know what the burn means within you. It is just my best guess, my walking-in-your-shoes and trying to understand what the burn feels like, as we can never know (for the Microeconomics-trained reader: There is actually no such thing as interdependent utility, no such thing as an other-regarding preference. Flawed theory). The third candle is also now both mine and yours, inside, internalized, interdependent, and joint, with our single candles.

Also, it means we must be Self-disciplined, in Self-control, and, when it does not work, help each other to be more disciplined, nudging each other back to Self-control, especially basing the nudge in the shared, good ethic. And, if it does not work, call the police, and bring in the courts to slap a restraining order, put in place some controls. Or, if both nudging and control fails, we part ways. The divorce snuffs out the third candle: So much for the "until death" frame.

Also, it is about a bit of sacrifice: Every person in a relationship with a significant other knows it, and sometimes it is more than a bit? A marriage, a relationship between people, always requires a bit of sacrifice in each domain of interest, a bit of sacrifice in the "I" as represented in "Self-interest." The sacrifice is essential in order to achieve the gains in the unity of the "We," the "shared Other-interest." It also means a bit of sacrifice in the shared Other-interest, or else we cannot, ironically, be our Own-self. The Own-self, to be happy, needs to sacrifice a bit in both domains of interest. Make sense?

Metaeconomics is about the fact we cannot separate I&We, Self&Other into unique, separable, nonjoint, independent accounts: Want empirical evidence? Well, we know it does not work well for each having our own bank accounts. It also does not work to separate out our mental accounts. It is more productive, contributing to Own-interest, better to put the accounts together into one account, with each still having access for "I" use. The joint account produces more interest. The "sum is greater than the sum of the parts." Only 47 characters.

I went over 140 characters too many times, and it took too long, but we enjoyed sipping faster and faster, through an entire bottle of wine. And, I can now say it even more concisely, even with a wine tongue: "The Me needs a We to Be, but without a Me there is no We." And, that is only 59-characters. Do I get a gold star?

Now, for the Grandchildren Well, they are each unique, so let me try it from youngest to oldest, the numbers only meaning their relative ages, in that they are all #1, each being Grandpa's favorite. And, for every one of them, the main thing is: Work at staying on the side of doing the right thing. Grandpa's Metaeconomics is about working hard to ensuring we are doing the right thing, bringing the moral dimension, the ethical system, into view in our day-to-day lives, and especially in economic choice. It is, writ large, about the golden rule: Do unto others what you would have them do unto you. Life is about balance within: About what you want, what turns your crank, and about what you share with others. And, achieving said balance will be a challenge, as it is hard to stay in Self-control, to stay disciplined, to not go to excesses in what turns our (selfish) crank.

#1, Grandson You ask what Grandpa thinks of the idea of multi-universes; wonder out loud about space and space travel; read lots of books; can be very social but you like your own space. You see the big picture. So, first, you likely already know that Einstein believed the thermodynamic laws were the scientific laws least likely to ever be repealed. The 1st Law, the conservation law, says we cannot destroy energy and matter, only changing the form of each. The 2nd Law, the entropy law, says we are on a one-way path to maximum entropy. So, low entropy fuels like the carbon fuels (the gasoline in the car that takes you to Karate lessons) need careful and serious conservation, as we may want a bit of that kind of fuel down the road to do the heavy lifting. It runs the big trucks and road building machinery, with ease. Also, we may want to have a few of the fuels around on the way to the time our fusion reactor, the Sun, around which our Spaceship Earth flies, burns out. So, it is time for you and your friends to start building our own fusion reactor.

#2, Granddaughter The dancer, and singer, and likely someday a counseling psychologist for youth and families, we would start in pointing to how dancing and singing is about both Self&Other (shared with others), within your Own-self, In ballet, your favorite, you as a dancer are connected with the shared interest in dancing as an art form, which will affect how you dance, and your enjoyment from doing so. If you move to dancing with another, in a couple styled dance, you will not be able to dance well together unless each of you sacrifice a bit of yourself in order to make a bit more gain in the shared other, better ensuring moving in unity as one. At the same time, there may need to be a bit of sacrifice in the shared other in order to gain enough payoff in the self to motivate the hard work of dancing well, individually and as a couple. Dance is all about balance in the self and the other.

In singing, the shared Other-interest is the beauty of the sound, the words put to tune, meaningful words that work together. Yet, it is your beautiful voice, and the payoff from doing it, hearing it for your Own-self, that is also at work.

Now, on youth and family counseling psychology: In counseling, you will be dealing with the Child of your patient, which is in the core of everybody's brain: Reptilian, it is said. It is a part of everyone's personality, the part that wants to do as they please, starting at about age two, and lasting through the teen years. You will also learn as you go that many people want their Child to be more tempered, as in problems with sexual drives, as well as drug addictions, the latter especially common in families at the current time. In effect, many of your patients never did grow-up, never getting much beyond age two, not developing enough Self-control. The child wants to be free to do as they wish, without bounds.

As counselor, you will especially come to know about the parent, another part of everyone's brain, which is what Grandpa refers to as the Other (shared with others, on what is the right thing to do)-interest. Source of the capacity in the brain for Empathy? Mammalian, it is said, especially when the Parent is nurturing. And, as counselor, you will have to do lots of that, including teaching the patient how to nurture Own-self, nurture one's own Child.

#3, Grandson You as the sports enthusiast, who wants to work in the sports industry, perhaps even involved in scouting, recruitment, and pay. You will need to understand that paying athletes is clearly a problem in balance in the Ego&Empathy, Self&Other-interest of every athlete on the playing field. You will find that paying individual athletes, feeding their Ego based Self-interest too much, reduces team morale, and team performance. The challenge is to be a bit more oriented to Empathy-based Other-interest, leading to a reasonable, more optimal, inequality. If you pay the better players a bit more, it can give better overall team performance, in that the best athletes on the team will respond to higher pay. On the other side of it, if you pay the better players too much, the resulting extreme inequality leads to resentment by others, counterproductivity, lower overall team performance.

Fans, too, tolerate and want some degree of inequality, but when taken to extremes, they quit supporting the team. It is all about balance in the Self&Other-interest, and there is an optimal, best level of inequality in paying athletes, which as a sports person, you will have to address. It is the only way to ensure the team, and each person on the team, will be successful.

Also, how about all the games of monopoly we have played, ever since you were old enough to throw a set of dice, and count the money? It is a game bent on claiming all the property, and profits it can produce. It is all Greed.

Grandpa's Metaeconomics sees Greed as normal, the more basic driver. It is also clear, though, as you and I have learned, that to win one must carefully work to find mutual gains from trade of the property we have accumulated, else we never will obtain sets (recall your favorite set, Boardwalk and Park Place) essential to winning. It always takes a bit of sacrifice in the trade in order to achieve a gain in the shared Other-interest in the trade, the win-win of the Market. Yet, the shared Other-interest was also reduced, a bit, for each of us to achieve a point where we could perhaps move toward greater payoff in the Self-interest from owning the same colored set of property, with houses and hotels built on same.

So, monopoly is about the balance. Without it, bad capitalism is the outcome, as the winner is isolated, living alone behind the locked gates and high walls on Boardwalk and Park Place. Only by starting over (high estate taxes, anyone?), can we once again work toward achieving good capitalism. All the money and property go back to the bank and we roll the dice again, with the hope that perhaps Empathy will better temper the Ego, in the next round of the game.

Intriguingly, we then sometimes shift to masterpiece, the art trading game, with all the grandchildren joining in, which is not only about push-pins (like monopoly, and the dollar value of the piece of art in masterpiece), but also about poetry (the grandpa&grandma–painting sometimes commands a premium price, demonstrating value way beyond what would be deemed rational in Microeconomics, but it is quite rational in Metaeconomics). We also start to observe that #5 Granddaughter tends to win most frequently, as she plays a game of Empathy-tempered pursuit of the Ego-driven quest for the wealth from owning more paintings. So, what is going on? Well, again, it is all about maximizing Own-interest, not just the Self-interest. Masterpiece tilts toward Empathy; monopoly tilts toward Ego. Balance is the best.

#4, Granddaughter Ok, so you are quite social, and also the one who has a passion for elementary education, but also likes to take her dad's credit card to the mall, which means the income from teaching will probably not work. So, your passion for teaching, which is more about what is shared with the students than about self, which is to be applauded, does not pay well. Value exceeds price. Such sharing is part of the notion in Grandpa's Metaeconomics that is referred to as the Other (shared with others, internalized within Own-self, about public education)-interest. So, what do?

Well, join and be active in the teacher's union, walk-out on the street to get the politician's attention, especially the attention of people who do not want to pay taxes for educating the public, and vote for politicians who do support it. Working in private sector education is also an option (have to get close to the money to make money, and the private sector has almost all of it right now), but working in private education can only work for you if the shared Other-interest within the private school system is a good Other-interest, one that works for you. And, in the meantime, have a plan B.

And, on your social side: Well, you clearly understand Grandpa's shared Other-interest, as in members of your sorority having such an interest. Your sorority has a shared Other-interest to help the community writ large, as well as the community within. You, and me, and everyone we know, need balance in I&We, Self&Other, and student&sorority.

#5, Granddaughter You as the scientist, a laboratory researcher and academic, looking to unlock the genome to enable precision medicine, will face special challenges because of the current environment with all the skepticism about the role of science in both the Market&Government. So, much like your sister who is oriented to the shared Other-interest in education, you will face special challenges. Saying it again more directly: Science has fallen from favor. Too many current political leaders do not believe in science. Fascist Politics and Fascist Religion, sometimes blended, are working to discount all reputable sources of facts and information, including the universities. Even the science of pandemics is not to be trusted: Coronavirus, anyone?

We might guess that some believe the electronics to send meaningless tweets just magically appeared, not realizing it was public tax dollars funding public research that created the key pieces of the technology. So, I guess we will have to go back to living in caves, or, perhaps mighty stone towers, symbols to the anti-science gods who focus on egoistic-hedonistic drives. Yet, without science, there may not be any water and electricity, and carbon-based fuels (as we are using them entirely too fast), nor any technology to run them. We will have to deal with pandemics using verses from old religious books, as the science budgets are cut to shadows of their former selves, and scientists are discounted.

On a positive front: Extreme income and wealth inequality on the Spaceship means some who have amassed huge amounts of wealth (a dozen families on the Spaceship Earth now control more wealth than over one-half of the entire wealth on the Spaceship) may help? Hopefully, at least a few of said people will come to realize the foundation of the wealth is in science, understandings on which good wealth is made, not just taken, and kept. So, there will be a few who are investing in science and research, albeit they are generally unwilling to pay taxes to do it in public universities (e.g., not adequately funding the Land Grants, which have filled the supermarkets with high quality food, but now scramble to keep their doors open). So, go to work in a private university, as it is where the money is.

For the Seat Mate on an Airplane Who Is a Business Person, or Is Otherwise in the Market It is a weekday, so, because of the substantive amount of business travel during the week, odds are the seat mate is a person from the business world, working in the Market, so we will start here.

Ever heard of Milton Friedman (as in Friedman and Friedman 1980)? Well, he is the guy, an economist, a Chicago school, Neoclassical, Microeconomist with a Libertarian bent, who focused on the Self-interest only. Friedman believed the business manager has no social responsibility to the suppliers, customers, communities, or the Spaceship Earth System. In fact, the only responsibility is to maximize the Self-interest of the Econ, measured in shareholder value, and, we might surmise, because they go together, also maximize CEO pay (typically meaning the Chief Executive Officer, but often acting like the Chief Ego Officer, about which Friedman would have approved). Metaeconomics starts with the shared Other-interest, the moral dimension, the moral community, the ethic in play, and asks the CEO to act more like a Chief Empathy Officer.

Metaeconomics still recognizes the key, primal role of Self-interest (it is in our genes, in our reptilian core, the cold-blooded snake in each of us). It sees the essential need to focus, too, on the returns to shareholders (to keep investment flowing) and on adequate CEO pay (to retain the incentives to keep costs down and profits high, to pay higher share prices). But, shift the balance a bit away from Ego to Empathy: Makes sense?

Metaeconomics also suggests, as an empirical question, that the extreme inequality virtually ensured by bad capitalism is a public health problem, which business really does have a social responsibility to address. Did Friedman get it wrong? Probably. Like baseball teams, business is more productive with ideal amounts of inequality, not extreme inequality (and, if the seatmate is a baseball fan, we could go further into the well-researched reality about extreme inequality reducing both each person's and the team performance, alluded to in the conversation with #3 Grandchild).

In fact, rather than to encourage the current sense of entitlement, we see at both the lower and upper rungs of the income and wealth ladder, Metaeconomics suggests the business managers' task is to find the best level of inequality; in effect, reduce prices to consumers; pay both raw produce and processors, the input suppliers, employees and middle-managers more; contribute to the community; and pay the costs of Spaceship Earth sustainability. Specifically, reduce CEO pay, relatively speaking. Support minimum wages, at levels sufficient to give a living, and not depend on the Government safety-net. With sufficient pay, individuals could perhaps even save money for retirement, so social security could be reduced. And, let the shareholder/stock prices find their best level, after the best balance is achieved. What think?

For the Airplane Seat Mate Who Is a Politician, Political Appointee, Bureaucrat, Manager, Employee in the Government The main charge of someone in Government is to represent the shared Other-interest, as represented in the constitution; law produced through legislation; administrative rules and regulations, and the efforts of the administrative agencies, like the US Environmental Protection Agency, US Department of Agriculture, US Food and Drug Administration, and US Department of the Interior, to list a few; and Common (ethics based) Law arising out of, and interpreted by, the judicial system, widely applied and not to serve a narrow Other-interest of only a few. And, there is no such thing as a deep state: Conspiracy theory, only, to avoid paying the price of Government, which is about the shared Other-interest, writ large, when it is good. So, it also means being careful to not represent just the narrow, special (narrow other) interests, the factions, the political tribes, which naturally arise. And, especially, the person in Government needs to avoid that which arises whenever capitalism founders a bit, represented in always reappearing Fascism. It is especially important to be wary of the Fascist Politicians (and their Fascist Religious supporters) who promise to fix everything.

As a Government person, watch out that you do not encourage bad rent seeking: And, be aware, it is common to find rent seeking at both ends of the spectrum. It is found among the lowest-income (e.g., welfare programs, fraud and deception in disability programs) and among the highest-income people (e.g., trade restrictions, giving renewals on patents that are not justified, bank bailouts with bonuses to the bankers who created the mess in the first place). Both ends tend to think they are entitled. One reason the middle-class is essential: It seems persons in the more nearly optimal middle ground of inequality often seek balance? At least it is an intriguing empirical question to ask. Also, extreme inequality registers with resentment in the middle-class, who tends to pay for the entitlement at both ends of the income and wealth ladder.

Also, as a Government person, it is essential to understand that good balance in Market&Government is still about liberty and freedom for each person, including you, to pursue Own-interest. As McCloskey (2019) would have it, encourage the humane liberal pursuit of income and wealth; encourage a humane, ethical, and empirical science–based Economy.

Now, the reviewer did not mention my Political Isle friends. It seems it would also be a good idea to have a chat with them, especially given the tendency to form into tribes, like the Conservative Isle Tribe and the Progressive Isle Tribe.

So, First to My Conservative Friends Just as you generally do as Conservatives, in the Conservative Tribe, Metaeconomics starts with recognizing Ego-based Self-interest is more primal, wired into our human nature. Manipulating, nudging, and otherwise trying to change it is likely futile. So, I know that you as Conservatives say, "forget Government, even if science based," as a tool to mold and change human nature. Accept human nature for what it is, and use the Market for its expression; use an unfettered, free Market, to unleash the entrepreneurial spirit, paying people with the creativity and work ethic to bring about new products, markets, and economies. Inequality is inherent in human nature, and unequal outcomes, such as in extreme income and wealth inequality, is presumed the right thing to do, the right outcome. The emphasis is on nature rather than on nurture, on Ego rather than on Empathy.

Metaeconomics acknowledges the nature&nurture frame, but sees each as interdependent with the other, not in competition. It does not make economics a kind of untested ideology or theology, instead subjecting it to empirical testing. For example, is extreme inequality in practice a good thing, or does it just lead to bad capitalism, which seems to be the outcome (indicated by populist and Fascist responses to it)? And, if it is bad capitalism, what do we do about it?

Conservative thinking is also more prone to focus on the short term, without perhaps enough regard for both the current and longer-term costs on others? Am I understanding it is short-term thinking? There seems to be far less concern for sustaining the environment on Spaceship Earth, which is essential for long-term viability: Why? Why do you as a Conservative, even though on average, a fearful bunch (suggest you read Hibbing, Smith, and Alford 2014, for the empirical evidence) not concern yourself with the tragedy of the excess? Ever hear of Garrett Hardin (1968)?

Ironically, however, as easily explained in Metaeconomics, your Conservative frame does see a role for the Other-interest, too, just like do your Progressive friends; it is a more narrowly defined Other-interest, however, as represented in the traditional family, religion, and local community (as argued in Deneen 2019a, b). I understand that you do not want either nudges or outside controls to come from the Government, albeit you allow, encourage religious controls (like anti-abortion controls placed on women and their bodies), and demand the Government does it? It seems you stand for minimal Government, until maximum Government serves your needs better? For Metaeconomics, it is more of an empirical question, looking for what works best, rather than asserting controls, especially when the church&state is being brought back into joint control? It is essential to remember that the founding fathers separated church and state. Metaeconomics does not see an "&" as a good thing for church and state.

Also, Metaeconomics understands that the Legislative Branch is to play the larger role, as the Conservative Isle sees it. Well, fine, but then we must ensure the Legislative Branch represents all the people: Ensure everyone can vote, anyone?

Now, to the Progressive Well, also much like Metaeconomics, Progressive thinking in the Progressive Tribe sees the role of an Empathy-based Other-interest and sees a role for Empathy in Tempering and otherwise influencing Ego-based Self-interest. You are not as sure as your Conservative friends that it will happen on its' own, so Government plays a larger role.

Also, in general, Progressives have a stronger belief in science, in the empirical reality, it can bring to addressing complex problems. It is also a main feature of Metaeconomics: Go and do fact finding, the empirical testing. As a result, it comes to positing that human nature is not a given, and, indeed can be influenced, perhaps behaviors changed (become a recycler, anyone?) with good (often defined as science based) policy. Government is to play a role in influencing human nature.

So, the Progressive Isle is more about nurture than nature, more focused on Empathy than Ego. While people are given freedom and liberty to grow the Market, Government must also grow in order to deal with the inherent excess of the Market, and to help the Market keep within bounds. It generally requires science-based nudges and controls, the latter as represented especially in administrative regulation and law. In the Progressive frame, the Administrative Branch grows in relative influence over time, while the Legislative Branch works to bring in law that can be elaborated and put to work in the Administrative Branch. The Judicial Branch is expected to facilitate progress (Progressive) in that which is the content of the shared Other-interest, widely shared, for every Traveler, not just a narrow few.

To Both my Conservative and Progressive Friends So, who has it more correct, the nature version of humans as Econ touted in the Conservative Isle, or the nurture version of humans as Human (which includes the Econ tendencies, too) as touted in the Progressive Isle? Well, as Metaeconomics makes clear, there is an element of fact in each realm. It is about nature&nurture, Self&Other, and, to both sets of friends, about Conservative&Progressive-politics, looking for the best outcomes from integration across the Isles.

Brain Biology: The Triune Brain

As alluded to at the outset, the three forces of Ego-based Self-interest, Empathy-based Other (shared, but internal to Own-self)-interest and Self-control (see Fig. 1.1) reflect the fundamental biology of the triune brain as posited by Maclean (1990) and developed further by Cory (1999). The theory is based in Paleontology, Evolutionary Biology, profoundly recognizing the evolution of our beings, and as such is an evolutionary theory. It also needs to be understood: The Triune Brain Theory faces some controversy, as highlighted by Reiner (1990). Yet, the review had several problems in it, as Cory (1999) makes clear. We draw heavily on the Lynne (2002) review of Cory (1999) in the next few paragraphs.

Cory (1999) starts with a call for *Consilience*, "a concerted effort toward unifying the natural and social sciences" (as developed in the companion book, Cory 2000). It is also about integrating across science&ethics, which is the plan and driver of the Metaeconomics book, too. Cory seeks a higher-level generalization of the brain (Cory 1999, p. 26), arguing that we continue to evolve toward a triune brain, a "triality" (Cory 1999,

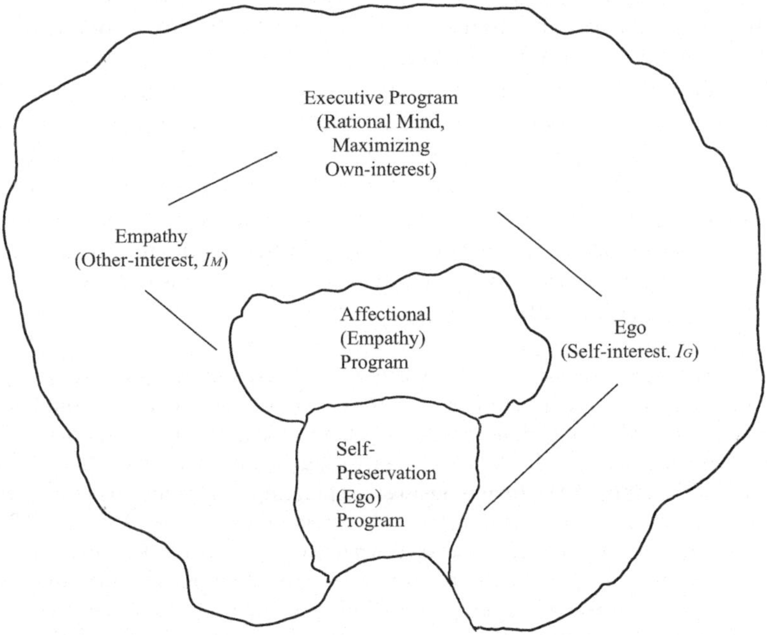

Fig. 1.1 Conflict systems model of the triune brain suggesting the need to balance the Ego-based Self-interest (I_G) and the Empathy-based Other-interest (I_M) in order to maximize the Own-interest. (Source: Author's creation, inspired by Cory 1999, p. 33)

p. 34), building upon propositions in MacLean (1990). We need to recognize an egoistic Self-interest; an empathetic Other-interest; and a dynamic, cognitive, rational balancing of the two semi-autonomous tendencies, the "Executive Program" as Cory (1999) refers to it, doing the balancing. All three dimensions are represented in Metaeconomics.

Building on MacLean (1990), Cory (1999) argues that the structure of the human brain rests on the proto-reptilian core, which is the source of the Ego-based Self-interest, dating back to the dinosaurs, the source of such terms as "cold blooded" or "a snake" and other descriptions: Disparaging characterizations of humans, for sure. The terms actually better describe the Econ represented in Neoclassical Microeconomics (Cory did not use such characterizations, which as noted come from Thaler and Sunstein 2008, the Econ and the Human, but are useful ways to represent the framing in Cory 1999, who well understood the differences). And, as Hedges (2018, p. 90) says it "...the state of egoism is in contradiction with human nature and hence to precarious to endure." Being just an Ego-based Econ is not an easy life.

Intriguingly, while the dinosaurs were the dominant species on Spaceship Earth for millions of years "they never developed a society or civilization of any kind" (Cory 1999, p. 112). It took the paleo-mammalian overlayer, which is the source of the Empathy-based Other-interest. Empathy brought the human into civilization as we now know it. The Market, being driven primarily by Ego, needs to be tempered by the Empathy of the community, generally represented in a good Government. As stated in Lynne (2002, p. 583):

> The egocentric, selfish, greedy, mastering, self-expanding and 'self-interest practiced with guile' (from Cory 1999, p. 74), part of humans ... could not have led to anything even partially resembling what we now experience in modern life because this core lacks nurturing. We needed to see the evolution of the empathetic, loving, giving, cooperating, nurturing structure represented in the paleo-mammalian, other-maintaining (Cory 1999, p. 27), other-interested overlayer to evolve what we know as modern experience and society. This part of the brain provides the "biological glue" and the "moral consciousness" of life (Cory 1999, p. 27). So, in reality the reptilian core that holds the self-interested autonomous tendency is counter-balanced by the other-interest, causing humans to be at best "semi-autonomous creatures" submerged in a "pervasive social context" (Cory 1999, p. 45), the latter arising due to the mammalian over-layer. This also suggests there is no

such thing as a "positivist, value-free human politics, economics … society" (Cory 1999, p. 59), in that empathy, or lack of it, is always an influence.

As Cory (1999) makes clear, there is an on-going reciprocity, encouraged by Empathy, resulting in a kind of inherent struggle and conflict between the forces of Self-interest and Other-interest. The goal is to achieve balance. Because the brain is intertwined, the two forces, interests are jointly arising, being nonseparable and interdependent. The challenge is to find a way to represent the jointness, the reality in a formal economic framework and theory.

Cory (1999), probably because of having some background in computers, uses computer terminology and framing to propose how the balancing is accomplished. There is a kind of programming, software if you like, in each domain of interest. It needs to be reconciled in the software in a third area of the brain, a "dynamic range (Cory 1999, p. 37)," working to deal with the algorithms in the "egoistic range" with its "self-preservation programming" (Cory 1999, p. 30) and in the "empathetic range" with its "affectional programming" (Cory 1999, p. 30). It is the latter that makes the Human (not the Econ) mindful, sensitive to the decision context, the community, the moral community as it were, in the background. Cory (1999) claims the Human experiences inordinate stress if there is not a reasonable balance achieved in the Ego&Empathy, and Self&Other-interest.

Metaeconomics builds said ideas into the Metaeconomics Framework and especially into Dual Interest Theory. It incorporates the Cory (1999) contention that the Empathy is clearly a force in economic supply while the Ego plays a substantive role in demand. As stated in Lynne (2002, p. 584), Cory (1999) claims that we, in the economy

> unconsciously supply, as if by an invisible (empathetic) hand …involving "a mystical, unexplained dynamic … (Cory 1999, p. 92) that which the egoistic self wants, e.g., wheat and meat produced in a largely unconscious way to satisfy the material demand for food. Both society and the markets embedded in society have been "unconsciously and incrementally" (Cory 1999, p. 84) structured from the empathetic side. So, when the market clears, the tension between ego and empathy subsides. In the perfect market, then, the transaction costs are zero, which is to say the conflict is resolved in the reciprocal interplay of ego and empathy. Real world market transactions are a "mammalian legacy" (Cory 1999, p. 78), and with empathy driven trust, transactions costs will be low.

Metaeconomics also proposes that Empathy will keep transactions costs low; in fact, see an empirical test in Lynne, Shonkwiler, and Wilson (1991), which demonstrates transactions costs increasing at an increasing rate as Empathy-driven other (reflected in shared attitudes and norms)-interest diverges.

The Cory (1999) point that supply is heavily influenced by Empathy is well taken, in that a supplier must produce to the Market; similarly, demand is heavily influenced by Ego, in that hedonism as a part of egoism is a major driver in what is in demand. As stated in Lynne (2002, p. 585):

> Perhaps the ego wants organically grown wheat and meat, and the suppliers unconsciously provide wheat and meat using industrial processes with pesticides and hormones. The suppliers have to become aware … become conscious … with the need to empathize with the egoistic demand for organic product … and, then, only revert back to the again unconscious but new empathy path, producing organic products. The reoccurring consciousness of the empathetic side brings a continuous dynamic. Transaction costs rise as the tension builds; transaction costs decline as the market clears. It is through empathy, and reciprocity, that transaction costs are reduced. By leaving empathy out, we also fail to ask if all the children have enough wheat and meat [or, as Cory (1999, p. 91) asks it, "Do all the children have shoes?"

Empathy is essential in order to keep transactions low in the Market. Ironically, Ego has become ever more the only force in the Market, and in society in general, as indicated by rising narcissism (Piff 2015), and increasing tension in the Market. It is no small wonder why we see such chaos in the bad capitalism of the day, which has led to bad politics, too.

Arguably, the ideas from Cory (1999) are also consistent with framing and theory represented in Smith (1759/1790, 1776/1789), as characterized in Lynne (2002, p. 585):

> That is, Adam Smith also saw the potential complementarity, a kind of symbiotic balancing on a higher plane reflecting mutual limits, in his other book, *The Theory of Moral Sentiments.* He writes to us about "the third station" (and, thus, implicitly about "triality") which is Cory's empathic structure and its sympathetic programming, where the individual is "to go" (in an abstract sense) for contemplation and reflection, before making the substantive economic decision. Through such conditioning of the egoistic drive for self-interest, we emerge with a better decision. This is Smith's invisible hand. As E.L. Khalil (1990, p. 266) interprets Smith, we emerge not with a

> mixture of the two stations, but as a "distinct entity," beyond *both* self-interest (ego) and altruism (empathy). We achieve the true wealth of a nation only with such symbiotic and integrated balance, which is the take-home message from Cory, as well: "Our self-interest, whether expressed as local, state, national, or regional interests, must be tempered with empathy for all others who share the planet with us ... " (Cory 1999, p. 113) lest we fail to manage inherent scarcity, and fall victim to our individual self-expansion (Cory 1999, p. 62). The entire ecological system, all living creatures ... the plants, animals, and all humans ... are part of the other-interest.

So, Cory (1999) also finds the new Neoinstitutional Economics, as represented in North (1990) and Williamson (1975), as well as the Public Choice School of Economics (Buchanan and Tullock 1967), and Rational Choice Sociology (see Coleman 1987), as problematic. Again, from Lynne (2002, p. 586):

> the new institutional economics represented in North and Williamson; the public choice of Buchanan and Tullock; and rational choice sociology represented in Coleman, missing the point: All ignore empathy, which ironically is what institutions are largely about. While Cory does not mention it explicitly, it is the case that the old institutional economics following in the lines of both Commons and Veblen also misses the point, but in the other direction: It is so heavily focused in the empathetic realm that the necessary abstraction to represent the reality of self-interest, which has to be an abstraction in that it does not exist without empathy, fails to emerge as a substantive part of their analytical engine. Yet, the Commons' and Veblen lines both see the need to make the unconscious, conscious ... and actively design institutions, which is also a theme in Cory (1999, p. 84). The new institutional economics does contribute, as Cory argues it, by focusing attention on the individual, on the individual brain, as in methodological individualism. It also contributes by highlighting utility maximization within organizations involving opportunism, "self-seeking with guile," which then focuses attention on the reality that organizations largely exist to facilitate empathy. Such organizations serve "to order or regulate reciprocity" (Cory 1999, p. 67) for survival of the organization (and the individual) by placing opportunistic behavior in view as deviant behavior (Cory 1999, p. 87). The new institutional economics also highlights bounded rationality, that the neocortex, the rational part of the brain, has limits in acquiring and processing information. In the Cory model, bounded rationality also means we now see a kind of mutually limitative process at work, with ego limiting empathy and empathy limiting ego. We move to a higher plane, improving

our predictive powers on the "aggregated basis of probability" (Cory 1999, p. 43), with higher probability the measure of our success.

Cory focuses on statistical probabilities about the balance in Ego&Empathy, and Self&Other-interest, recognizing that (Lynne 2002, p. 586):

> Sometimes ego takes over: Some are wired and conditioned more toward self-preservation (Cory 1999, p. 42). Others are wired and conditioned more toward affection: These sub-groups can especially go awry if the mutual affection focuses on very bad things, perhaps even leading to killing the opposition that holds some other affection. Hope springs eternal, however, that rationality and balance will overcome, built upon "generalized moral stages" and shared moral development Cory 1999, p. 43). Given that even Adam Smith's confidence in the invisible hand construct waned over time (Cory 1999, p. 92), however, it is time to move on, to focus on the "invisible hand of brain structure" (replacing it with the) "intentional hand" (Cory 1999, p. 94) to build empathetic institutions, including the market.... Perhaps unfortunately, and that which leads to the real challenge for science, this empathetic part is largely in the unconscious, in the background and implicit in our seemingly only self-interested action, although virtually always operant and affecting the outcomes.

The need to build in the intentional hand, the Visible Hand, and that the Invisible Hand is a myth, is also a theme in Samuels, Johnson, and Perry (2011). We need an alternative Metaeconomics that includes role of an intentional, Visible Hand in tempering and conditioning the outcomes from the more primal Self-interest. And, like Tomer (2017), Metaeconomics sees the Visible Hand as a humanistic hand.

The first organized attempt by a group of scientists (1) to work in the spirit of consilience relating to the core ideas in Maclean (1990) as elaborated and connected to social and economic science by Cory (1999), and (2) to propositions coming more out of philosophy, economic and social science at about the same time as represented in Lynne (1995, 1999), led to a special session at a joint SABE/IARP conference in 2004. Cory and I had agreed that we needed a way for characterizing and representing the new theory, which we had both come to from quite different paths. He had come by route of neuroscience and biology; I had come by route of philosophy and social science.

We decided to call it Dual Motive Theory and explored what it was and could be at that conference (see Cory 2006a,b; Levine 2006; Lynne 2006; and Wilson 2006). An Ego-based Self-interest motive and an Empathy-based Other-interest was proposed, with the motives reconciled and balanced in the rational part of the brain, with a Visible Hand at work to accomplish the balancing. We proposed a parsimonious model to represent the evolving triune brain. We started with the sovereign consumer and retained the Enlightenment view that it is the person who is to count. It is the person with rights, freedom, and liberty who is the well-spring of action. We also proposed a theory consistent with methodological individualism: We focused on the person.

Also, as an aside: It was my suggestion in the early-2000s that we label it Dual Motive Theory. A few years later, while working in my own research program with several students and others, by the time of Sautter et al. (2011), we started to use the convention of referring to it as Dual Interest Theory, instead. We changed the name in that it potentially made for better communication with other economists. The idea of an interest is more commonly used in economics. Cory (2018) continued referring to it as Dual Motive Theory. To reconcile the two, it works to think of the interests as being reflected in the motives.

Thermodynamic and Spaceship Earth Reality

Neoclassical Economics is built on a Newtonian base, wherein everything could be reversed and started over, so there is no need to consider limits. Spaceship Earth is like a giant billiard table with cause and effect, and, the balls can always be re-racked and started over. Every person, every entity is independent of every other entity; interdependence is at best a minor, not important condition. The Market, composed as it is of independent people, with plentiful freedom and liberty, unbounded, to choose will always find the way. Any *Tragedy of the Commons* (as characterized by Hardin 1968) is presumed impossible, because the Market will adjust accordingly. Tragedy with social costs is a myth, according to the Libertarian Economics frame (see Cheung 1978), a close relative of Neoclassical Economics.

In rather dramatic contrast, Neoinstitutional Economics, as well as Metaeconomics, builds upon a foundation of thermodynamics (see Zimmermann 1933/1951; he was an institutional economist). Everything, every Traveler, is embedded within the Spaceship Earth System, which has limits, and, as a result, things are often if not always irreversible. As a result, Government is viewed as playing a key role in tempering the excesses of the Market. The role is especially in doing and funding basic research relating to pollution and energy, searching for what it means to be sustainable. Science-based knowledge can then be used to do things like set carbon emission limits, fishing limits, and water withdrawal limits, to list a few. The Government is seen as playing a key role in at least nudging if not picking the throughput rate and path, in order to avoid the Tragedy.

Metaeconomics recognizes 1st and 2nd Laws of Thermodynamics, the conservation law, and the entropy law. There are thermodynamic limits to Spaceship Earth. The 1st Law highlights, the limits to absorb and process residuals and pollutants. Spaceship earth can only handle so much waste, so there is pervasive interdependence, and large social costs. Every production process is joint with every natural process. Only Empathy can resolve it.

The other thermodynamic limit is the fact of ultimately reaching a state of maximum entropy, as 2nd Law highlights. The Sun ultimately burns out (the fusion reactor runs out of matter on which it runs), which also points to another kind of pervasive interdependence; massive social costs are the natural order of things, also pointing to the need to operate with Empathy.

So, the Metaeconomics key is Empathy, a point also made by Brown et al. (2019). Empathy is essential to making the way through time, recognizing we face limited absorption of wastes and eventual extinction of the Sun, and, perhaps, the extinction of every living organism traveling on the Spaceship at the time. Empathy is the key to making it a happier journey.

References

Ainslie, George. 1986. Beyond Microeconomics: Conflict among Interests in a Multiple Self as Determinant of Value, Chap. 6. In *The Multiple Self*, ed. John Elster, 133–176. New York: Cambridge University Press.

Altman, M. 2012. *Behavioral Economics for Dummies*. Mississauga: John Wiley and Sons, Kindle ed.

Angyal, Andras. 1941. *Foundation for a Science of Personality*. New York: The Commonwealth Fund.

———. 1965. *Neurosis and Treatment: A Holistic Theory*. New York: The Viking Press.
Berne, E. 1961. *Transactional Analysis in Psychotherapy*. New York: Grove Press.
Brown, K., W.N. Adger, P. Devine-Wright, J.M. Anderies, S. Barr, F. Bousquet, C. Butler, L. Evans, N. Marshall, and T. Quinn. 2019. Empathy, Place and Identity Interactions for Sustainability. *Global Environmental Change* 56: 11–17.
Buber, Martin. 1923/1958. *I and Thou (Translated by R.G. Smith in 1958 from the German Version, ich and Du)*. New York: Charles Scribner's Sons.
Buchanan, James M., and Gordon Tullock. 1967. *The Calculus of Consent*. Ann Arbor: University of Michigan Press.
Cheung, S.N. 1978. *The Myth of Social Cost*. London: The Institute of Economic Affairs.
Coleman, J.S. 1987. Psychological Structure and Social Structure in Economic Models. In *Rational Choice: The Contrast between Economics and Psychology*, ed. M.W. Reder Hogart. Chicago: The University of Chicago Press.
Cory, G.A. 1999. *The Reciprocal Modular Brain in Economics and Politics*. New York: Kluwer Academic/Plenum publishers.
______. 2000. *Toward Consilience*. New York: Kluwer Academic/Plenum Publishers.
———. 2006a. The Dual Motive Theory. *Journal of Socio-Economics* 35 (4): 589–591.
———. 2006b. A Behavioral Model of the Dual Motive Approach to Behavioral Economics and Social Exchange. *Journal of Socio-Economics* 35 (4): 592–612.
———. 2018. *Delusions of Economics: And the Way Forward*. Behavioral Ecology Press. (see https://www.amazon.com/Delusions-Economics-Jr-Gerald-Cory/dp/0692946926/ref=sr_1_2?dchild=1&qid=1597358203&refinements=p_27%3AJr+Gerald+A+Cory&s=books&sr=1-2&text=Jr+Gerald+A+Cory)
Deneen, Patrick J. 2019a. A Defense of Conservatism That Veers toward Liberalism. Opinion. *Washington Post* (Washington, DC), June 21, Digital.
———. 2019b *Why Liberalism Failed*. Kindle ed. New Haven: Yale University Press.
DeWaal, F. 2009. *The Age of Empathy*. New York: Harmony Books.
Elster, J. 1979. *Ulysses and the Sirens: Studies in Rationality and Irrationality*. 1993 ed. New York: Cambridge University Press.
———., ed. 1986. *The Multiple Self*. New York: Cambridge University Press.
Etzioni, A. 1986. The Case for a Multiple Utility Conception. *Economics and Philosophy* 2: 159–183.
Frank, R.H. 2004. *What Price the Moral High Ground? Ethical Dilemmas in Competitive Environments*. Princeton: Princeton University Press.
Friedman, Milton, and Rose Friedman. 1980. *Free to Choose: A Personal Statement*. New York: A Harvest Book: Harcourt.
Fukuyama, Francis. 2006. *The End of History and the Last Man*. Kindle ed. New York: Free Press.

Goldberg, Jonah. 2018. *Suicide of the West: How the Rebirth of Tribalism, Populism, Nationalism, and Identity Politics Is Destroying American Democracy.* New York: Crown Publishing Group.

Hardin, G. 1968. The Tragedy of the Commons. *Science* 162 (3859): 1243–1248.

Hayes, W.M., and G.D. Lynne. 2004. Towards a Centerpiece for Ecological Economics. *Ecological Economics* 49 (3): 287–301.

———. 2013. The Evolution of Ego and Empathy: Progress in Forming the Centerpiece for Ecological Economic Theory. In *Building a Green Economy: Perspectives from Ecological Economics*, ed. Robert B. Richardson, 107–118. East Lansing: Michigan State University Press.

Hedges, Chris. 2018. *America: The Farewell Tour.* Kindle ed. Simon and Schuster.

Hibbing, John R., Kevin B. Smith, and John R. Alford. 2014. *Predisposed: Liberals, Conservatives, and the Biology of Political Differences.* New York: Routledge.

Hirschfeld, Mary L. 2018. *Aquinas and the Market: Toward a Humane Economy.* Cambridge, MA: Harvard University Press.

Khalil, E.L. 1990. Beyond Self-Interest and Altruism. *Economics and Philosophy* 6: 255–273.

Lester, David. 1987. A Systems Perspective of Personality. *Psychological Reports* 61: 603–622.

———. 1995. *Theories of Personality.* Washington, DC: Taylor and Francis.

Levine, D.S. 2006. Neural Modeling of the Dual Motive Theory of Economics. *Journal of Socio-Economics* 35 (4): 613–625.

Lutz, Mark A., and Kenneth Lux. 1988. *Humanistic Economics: The New Challenge.* New York: The Bootstrap Press.

Lynne, G.D. 1995. Modifying the Neoclassical Approach to Technology Adoption with Behavioral Science Models. *Journal of Agricultural and Applied Economics* 27 (1): 67–80.

———. 1999. Divided Self Models of the Socioeconomic Person: The Metaeconomics Approach. *Journal of Socio-Economics* 28 (3): 267–288.

———. Review of Cory, G.A. 2002. *The Reciprocal Modular Brain in Economics and Politics: Shaping the Rational and Moral Basis of Organization, Exchange and Choice.* New York: Kluwer Academic/Plenum Publishers, 1999. *Journal of Socio-Economics* 31 (5): 583–586.

———. 2006. Toward a Dual Motive Metaeconomic Theory. *Journal of Socio-Economics* 35: 634–651.

Lynne, G.D., J.S. Shonkwiler, and Michael E. Wilson. 1991. Water Permitting Behavior under the 1972 Florida Water Resources Act. *Land Economics* 67 (3): 340–351.

Lynne, G.D., N.V. Czap, H.J. Czap, and M.E. Burbach. 2016. Theoretical Foundation for Empathy Conservation: Toward Avoiding the Tragedy of the Commons. *Review of Behavioral Economics* 3: 245–279.

MacLean, P. 1990. *The Triune Brain in Evolution: Role in Paleocerebral Functions.* New York: Plenum.

MacLean, Nancy. 2017. *Democracy in Chains: The Deep History of the Radical Right's Stealth Plan for America.* New York: Penguin Books.

Marglin, Stephen A. 2008. *The Dismal Science: How Thinking Like an Economist Undermines Community.* Cambridge, MA: Harvard University Press.

Maslow, A.H. 1954. *Motivation and Personality.* New York: Harper and Row.

McCloskey, D.N. 2019. *Why Liberalism Works: How True Liberal Values Produce a Freer, More Equal, Prosperous World for All.* Kindle ed. New York: Yale University Press.

North, D. 1990. *Institutions, Institutional Change, and Economic Performance.* New York: Cambridge University Press.

Perrings, C. 1987. *Economy and Environment: A Theoretical Essay on the Interdependence of Economic and Environmental Systems.* Cambridge, MA: Cambridge University Press.

Piff, P.K. 2015. Wealth and the Inflated Self: Class, Entitlement and Narcissism. *Personality and Social Psychology Bulletin* 40 (1): 34–43.

Reiner, Anton. 1990. Review of Maclean, Paul D the Triune Brain in Evolution. Role in Paleocerebral Functions. New York: Plenum." Book Review. Science (October 12, 1990).

Roberts, Russ. 2014. *How Adam Smith Can Change Your Life: An Unexpected Guide to Human Nature and Happiness.* New York: Portfolio/Penguin.

Samuels, Warren J., Marianne F. Johnson, and William H. Perry. 2011. *Erasing the Invisible Hand: Essays on an Elusive and Misused Concept in Economics.* Kindle ed. New York: Cambridge University Press.

Sautter, J., N. Ovchinnikova, C. Kruse, and G. Lynne. 2011. Farmers Decisions Regarding Carbon Sequestration: A Metaeconomic View. *Society and Natural Resources* 24 (2): 133–147.

Singer, Tania. 2009. Understanding Others: Brain Mechanisms of Theory of Mind and Empathy. In *Neuroeconomics: Decision Making and the Brain*, ed. Paul W. Glimcher, Colin F. Camerer, Ernst Fehr, and Russell A. Poldrack. San Diego: Academic Press.

Smith, A. 1759/1790. *The Theory of Moral Sentiments.* Edited by D.D. and A.L. Macfie Raphael. Indianapolis: Liberty Fund.

———. 1776/1789. *An Inquiry Into the Nature and Causes of the Wealth of Nations.* Edited by E. Cannan. New York: Random House.

Smith, Vernon L., and Bart J. Wilson. 2019. *Humanomics: Moral Sentiments and the Wealth of Nations for the Twenty-First Century.* New York: Cambridge University Press.

Söllner, F. 1997. A Reexamination of the Role of Thermodynamics for Environmental Economics. *Ecological Economics* 22: 175–201.

Solomon, R.C. 2007. *True to Our Feelings: What Our Emotions Are Really Telling Us*. New York: Oxford University Press.

Stanley, Jason. 2018. *How Fascism Works: The Politics of Us and Them*. New York: Random House.

Stanovich, K.E. 2011. *Rationality and the Reflective Mind*. New York: Oxford University Press.

Stiglitz, Joseph E. 2019. *People, Power and Profits: Progressive Capitalism for an Age of Discontent*. New York: W. W. Norton and Company.

Thaler, R.H., and C.R. Sunstein. 2008. *Nudge: Improving Decisions About Health, Wealth, and Happiness*. New Haven: Yale University Press.

Tomer, John F. 2012. Brain Physiology, Egoistic and Empathic Motivation, and Brain Plasticity: Toward a More Human Economics. *World Economic Review* 1 (1): 76–90.

———. 2017. *Advanced Introduction to Behavioral Economics*. North Hampton: Elgar.

Walker, B., and D. Salt. 2006. *Resilience Thinking: Sustaining Ecosystems and People in a Changing World*. Washington, DC: Island Press.

Williamson, Oliver E. 1975. *Markets and Hierarchies: Analysis and Anti-Trust Implications. A Study in Economics of Internal Organization*. New York: Free Press.

Wilson, E.O. 1998. *Consilience: The Unity of Knowledge*. New York: Alfred A. Knopf.

Wilson, D.R. 2006. The Evolutionary Neuroscience of Human Reciprocal Sociality: A Basic Outline for Economists. *Journal of Socio-Economics* 35 (4): 626–633.

Zimmermann, E.W. 1933/1951. *World Resources and Industries*. New York: Harper and Brothers.

CHAPTER 2

Landscape of the Metaeconomics Framework and Dual Interest Theory

Smith (1776/1789) & Smith (1759/1790) were in effect separated, in what was to become Neoclassical Economics and Neoinstitutional Economics. In fact, by the late 1800s, the scope of Neoclassical Economics had already been narrowed such that it became primarily a "study of the wealth getting and wealth using activities of individuals operating in the private marketplace" (Gruchy 1972, p. 33). Etzioni (1988, p. 6) characterizes it as the Whig view, essentially the same as the Neoclassical view, seeing the person as under-socialized "because individuals are assumed to be effective actors, able to act independently and to be psychologically complete unto themselves. It is a view of the social order as resting on the marketplace." People are Econ. Neoclassical Economics came to be about a person as an Econ who was focused exclusively on the price *P* in the Market Forum. It was abstracted from, and otherwise ignored, the fact that a person is also a Human who expressed value *V* in Other Forums, and often $V \neq P$. The moral and ethical dimension is represented in that value *V*, which evolves within the person, but is influenced from the outside. Econ live within their own skin, "psychologically complete unto themselves," so outside value *V* influences (even though internalized within the Own-self, as Metaeconomics suggests) are relevant only in the sense of being mediated through the price *P*. Outside interventions are also disallowed, in order to assure an unencumbered, nonattenuated, free choice. Neoclassical Economics, as a result, has become a science of Greed, by highlighting and considering only the primal drive to Self-interest, with

G. D. Lynne, *Metaeconomics*, Palgrave Advances in Behavioral Economics, https://doi.org/10.1007/978-3-030-50601-8_2

the presumption it is an ethical Self-interest. The science of Greed is represented in both the Microeconomics Framework and Single Interest Theory.

The focus on the Greed of the Econ contrasts with classical political economy (for an overview, especially as it relates to the political economy of natural resources, see Lynne and Milon 1984). As Etzioni (1988, p. 7) says it, in what he refers to as the Tory view, we would call it the Neoinstitutional view: "Individuals are assumed to be born with unsavory predispositions and not at all inclined to live harmoniously with one another. They must be inoculated with values to develop their moral character, and authority is needed to keep the lid on social order." It is about a Human embedded within, and ascribing to, a moral and ethical community, so external value *V* influences the content of the internal value *V*. It focuses on the moral and ethical dimension of the Human, as well as recognizing the more primal Econ at work within the Human.

Gruchy (1972, p. 332) characterizes such a political economy as one which (1) recognized the inherent conflict resolving activity in the political process, which was needed to undergird an economy, (2) explored alternative institutional arrangements for reducing conflict to facilitate the functioning of the human economy, and (3) recognized a multiplicity of human objectives in addition to seeking improvements in wealth. As early political economists knew, human conflict arising from scarcity often requires more than Market solutions, and thus humans may benefit from analysis based on a paradigm more broadly conceived than just Market economics.

Contemporary institutional economics, which has evolved into what we now call Neoinstitutional Economics, and referred to as Other-interest economics herein, has the essential features of the old political economics (Gruchy 1972, p. 333). As noted, it is more akin with Smith (1759/1790). It also focuses on conflict resolution, on the institutionalizing process for reducing conflict to tolerable competition. It focuses on ensuring that multiple, moral and ethical, objectives can be expressed and achieved within the institutions, which represents the value *V*, the Other-interest. Price *P* coming out of the Market is influenced by the value *V*, but may not reflect it, exactly.

Markets evolve under a specific kind of institution that includes private ownership and management, decentralized management, and a high degree of competition. Such an institution may be one of several that might be considered in an Other-interest-based economic analysis. While perhaps not yet having as much impact as has had the Neoclassical

Economics/Self-interest framework, clearly the Neoinstitutional/Other-interest framework and perspectives should be considered as one possibility for guiding the needed political economic analysis. Ideally, the best from both frameworks would be integrated into one frame, as Metaeconomics is designed to do.

Economic Science Has Become Tribal

It seems tribes are now back in vogue, not only in the two Political Isles, but also in economic science. What is going on? The breakdown representing Adam Smith as only Smith (1776/1789) is due in part to the Public Choice School, especially as represented in Buchanan (1987); Buchanan and Tullock (1967). The extreme elements in the Public Choice School of Economics contend the Government can do essentially nothing right, so the liberal democracy has been chained, as MacLean (2017) makes clear. MacLean (2017) also makes the case that Buchanan was much in favor of segregation, among other things having little to do with a widely shared Other-interest. Segregation is a narrowly shared Other-interest, only with other segregationists. It denies a role for an Empathy-based moral community, widely shared. If MacLean (2017) has it right, then Buchanan was much about protecting the status quo, in what he might have referred to as the natural order, even a moral order (see Buchanan 1987). So, the Government can do no right, unless it supports the status quo, the natural order, the moral order of things, as if guided by an Invisible Hand that can do no wrong. In contrast, Metaeconomics sees a Visible Hand actively monitoring the content of the Invisible Hand, and, if it is producing bad outcomes, fix it with a new moral community (e.g., stop segregation) that works better for everyone.

Another extreme take, which also focuses only on Smith (1776/1789), has arisen out of the plan of Milton Friedman, as alluded to in our chat with the business seat mate on the airplane. Friedman was a major contributor to what would become the Chicago School of Economics, which still dominates the Neoclassical Economics way of thinking. The frame is all about Market-only, through maximizing Self-interest only, as the Market cannot do anything wrong (Burgin 2012). In extreme renditions of Friedman's "free to choose" framework, the Market needs to replace all manner of heretofore, since the start of the Enlightenment, domains of Government, for example, even privatizing and thus eliminating all public schools and public universities. The Market, and the business enterprises in it, can always, it is presumed largely without empirical test, do it better.

As Friedman (in Knight and Friedman 1969) would have it:

> "Social responsibility is a fundamentally subversive doctrine in a free society," and have said that in such a society, "there is one and only one social responsibility of business–to use its resources and engage in activities designed to increase its profits so long as it stays within the rules of the game, which is to say, engages in open and free competition without deception or fraud."

It is all about the Ego-based expression of Self-interest within each business, focused on maximizing profit. Yet, even Friedman implicitly recognizes an Empathy-based Other-interest at work in the background, as represented in "the rules of the game… without deception or fraud." Where does Friedman think it arises?

Marglin (2008) sees that framing economic questions using Microeconomics not only does not represent community, wherein the norms, values, beliefs, mores, and, more generally the moral dimension, the institutions, reside. It undermines community. It would follow that using Microeconomics to guide the formation of a Market could also undermine the moral dimension, which Friedman-like framing requires. It also precludes any role by Government in representing the larger community.

Things are not much better on the Neoinstitutional Economics side, for a quite opposite reason. While there is more explicit recognition of the Moral Dimension, there is sometimes a dim view taken of the role for the Market. It can lead to pushing for an ever more active, controlling role of the Government, even fully replacing the Market, for example, in Government-only provided public education. The view emerges in the works of contributors, such as Gruchy (1972), Hodgson (1988, 1999), Samuels (1969), and Schmid (1978). Yet, Neoinstitutional Economics is far more open to including a role for the Market than is Neoclassical Economics for seeing much if any role for the Government.

Let us pause a moment here, for reflection: The Neoclassical, public choice contention seems to be that everyone working in and through Government must be inherently bad, which is the only way that everything being done by Government could be bad? And, everyone working in and through the Market is inherently good, which is the only way that everything done in the Market could be good? Then, when we go to the Neoinstitutional Economics side, it is all reversed. Overall, it seems we might legitimately say: Empirical evidence, please.

Scope, Boundaries, and Methodology

The most striking difference between the Neoinstitutional Other-interest and the Neoclassical Self-interest framework is how each views theory (Table 2.1). The Other-interest economist is primarily a pragmatist, judging the efficacy of a concept on the goodness and desirability of the result. The Self-interest economist is primarily a positivist (Gruchy 1972, p. 126).

McCloskey (1985, p. 4) goes further and argues that the current faith of most economists (speaking about the Neoclassicals here), described by modernism, consists of "...scientism, behaviorism, operationalism, positive economics, and other quantifying enthusiasms of the 1930's." The universe is characterized by order and harmony (Gruchy 1972, p. 81), and thus there is the possibility of discovering a once and for all truth about the way the system operates. In the underlying Self-interest philosophy, theories tend to take on a life of their own, with few attempts to reject same. Economists seeing only self-interest as the driver of economic choice have a tendency toward dogmatic behavior and can be regularly found espousing the merits of their economic beliefs. It leads to claiming evidence (but with little actual empirical, science-based testing and little in the way of ethical reflection) supporting the move to the Market and leaving little to no role for Government. On what guides empirical testing when it does occur, the Self-interest economist has a belief in common methodology for all sciences.

The Other-interest economist behaves in a more holistic manner in theoretical development, using both historical and statistical means, being more empirical in the description of actual conditions (Gruchy 1972). Theories are more likely to be built on empirical reality and are modified as technology and institutions evolve. So, in the Other-interest view, there is thought to be different methodologies appropriate to each science, referred to as "holism" (Wilber and Harrison 1978, p. 64).

The Self-interest approach is formalistic, speculative, deduced from well specified premises, and internally consistent. The Self-interest economist uses primarily reductionist techniques to gain understanding. For example, the producer's contribution is evaluated by examining the demand and supply for the goods and the Market value of that activity, the

Table 2.1 Characterizing frameworks, theories, and methodologies in other-interest (Neoinstitutional) and self-interest (Neoclassical) economics

Other-interest (Neoinstitutional) economics	*Self-interest (Neoclassical) economics*
Scope, Boundaries, and Methodology	
Economists need to address problems as inseparable social science and natural/ physical science problems	Economists need to first separate out the other social science and natural/physical science problems in order to focus on the economic problems
Truth about reality for a firm requires a look at custom, habit, and the economic theology in the background	Truth about reality for a firm lies in the logic of the theory of the firm, which, in turn, arises from human reason
Standard assumptions about the firm if contradicted by empirical analysis makes the theory unrealistic, and thus it needs to be replaced or at least modified with some alternative	The performance of a theory of the firm needs to be judged by the precision, scope, and conformity with experience of the predictions it yields; thus, the realism of the assumptions is a non-issue
Simulation modeling is the best way for accurately depicting and improving understanding of actual economic behavior	Econometric (statistical) techniques and programming models are the best way to accurately depict and predict economic behavior
Empirical testing of theory would largely be done through participating in and observing what is going on, filling in ever more details, and expanding understanding of the overall system	Empirical testing of theory using statistical techniques has limited usefulness in that the data tends to be inadequate to the task of really testing the formal model
Economics needs to focus on understanding and explaining motivations and economic behavior	Economics needs to focus on predicting economic behavior
Economic analysis needs to understand the nature of beliefs, values, and what motivates the evolution of tastes and preferences	Economic analysis needs to be limited to working under an assumption of given and stable tastes and preferences
Biological and Physical System	
The global system needs to be modeled as a thermodynamically closed system and thus it is necessary to recognize the inherent *interdependence*, meaning social costs are pervasive, as between and among human and natural systems, often needing control and management by a Government entity, both currently and in looking at connections over time	The global system needs to be modeled as a thermodynamically open system and thus it is necessary to recognize the inherent *independence*, meaning social costs are an aberration, seldom if ever arising between and among human and natural systems, both currently and in looking at connections over time

(*continued*)

Table 2.1 (continued)

Other-interest (Neoinstitutional) economics	*Self-interest (Neoclassical) economics*
There is inherent natural resource and environmental resource scarcity no matter how much effort (labor, capital, management, technology, knowledge, etc.) is brought to bear	There is inherent natural resource and environmental resource abundance when sufficient effort (labor, capital, management, technology, knowledge, etc.) is brought to bear
Wastes and pollutants are natural products that have to be handled inside the economic and social system, and need to be a part of economic efficiency	Wastes and pollutants are best considered as external to the system, and need be internalized only if it leads to economic efficiency
There is natural, inherent conflict due to ecological and physical limits on environment and natural resources	There is natural, inherent harmony due to an abundance of resources reflected in the boundless creativity of the human mind
Property	
Private property is a fundamental right within a democratic system. Public property institutions (e.g., the public ownership of water) often are needed to achieve shared values represented in the shared Other-interest. At best, Markets and Market-like processes based on private property can play but a limited role	Private property is a fundamental right within a democratic system. As a result, public property institutions (e.g., the public ownership of water) need to be avoided in order to best serve the Self-interest. Public property institutions with Government decision forums need to be replaced with private property and Markets as the decision forums
Private property rights ideally will be attenuated (restricted) to temper and restrain the Self-interest in order to best serve the shared, public based Other-interest	Private property rights ideally will be non-attenuated (not restricted) in order to best serve the public (Other-) interest, which is defined in terms of the summation of the outcomes from serving the Self-interest
Property duties (responsibility) are a key feature of and on par with the property right	Property rights precede duties
Psychology: Motivations and Pursuits	
Lower level wants and needs are satisfied before higher level needs, for example, it is not possible to substitute self-esteem for food due to the goods being incommensurable, that is, pushpins and poetry, material goods and the moral dimension, are operant at different levels, not on the same plane, and thus not a subject of trade-offs measured in relative prices	No hierarchy of wants and needs exists, for example, self-esteem can be substituted for food due to the goods being commensurable, that is, pushpins and poetry, material goods, and the moral dimension, can be reconciled on the same plane and thus are subject to simple trade-offs measured in relative prices

(*continued*)

Table 2.1 (continued)

Other-interest (Neoinstitutional) economics	*Self-interest (Neoclassical) economics*
Producers may in fact maximize output for every level of input used in production, or minimize cost for every level of output, but such behavior represents an acquired trait	Producers just naturally maximize output for every level of input use, and minimize cost for every level of output, with such behavior representing inherent, genetic traits
There is natural, inherent conflict due to differences in beliefs and values, preferences	There is natural, inherent harmony due to similarity in beliefs and values, preferences
Utility is multi-dimensioned with people obtaining utility from action taken in the Self-interest and from action taken in the shared/public/Other-interest	Utility is single-dimensioned with people obtaining utility only from action taken in the Self-interest
People pursue mainly if not only a shared Other-interest	People pursue mainly if not only the Self-interest
People have very limited capacity to comprehend, and compute	People have essentially an unlimited capacity to comprehend and compute
Sociology: Interdependence and Social Cost	
A person's behavior can only be understood with respect to the claims from the family, peer group, community, and society and how the person chooses to respond to each group. The claims of others are mediated through the shared Other-interest, which might just be a proposed way of doing things, but it might also be coerced, as in controlling the person	A person's behavior can be explained with knowledge only of a person, a unique biography. The claims of others are all mediated through the Self-interest, with the person always being able to act, with complete liberty and freedom to choose
The moral community, or moral dimension, in a community needs to be first understood before it becomes scientifically feasible to understand the economic behavior of people	The moral order, a narrow version of the moral dimension notion, in a community, is outside the domain of economics, so there is no particular need to first understand it before one proceeds to analyze the economic behavior of people
Markets are inherently incapable, or at least inadequate to the task, of resolving the widespread externalities and social costs in an economy, as represented in pervasive Market-failure	Even in the unusual situation of an externality and related social cost, it can easily be solved by assigning private property rights and using the Market. Government involvement is not necessary nor desirable, due to pervasive Government failure

(*continued*)

Table 2.1 (continued)

Other-interest (Neoinstitutional) economics	*Self-interest (Neoclassical) economics*
The person is the best judge of own welfare, but most people consider the community in making decisions. The whole is more than the sum of the parts	The person is the best judge of own welfare, independent of community. The whole is the sum of the parts
The pursuit of Self-interest, if it exists at all, is conditioned by community standards, with the focus on shared Other-interest considerations	The pursuit of Self-interest is the same as the pursuit of the shared Other-interest, if the latter is acknowledged at all, and is achieved by the pursuit of Self-interest by a person
Discounting the future, that is, selecting and applying a discount rate in a decision affecting the future, is an unethical practice	Economic concern for generations yet unborn can be adequately addressed through discounting, and has little or nothing to do with ethics
A firm (e.g., farm, ranch, agribusiness, and environmental business) is an entity having rational and simultaneously emotional decision makers, who often pay attention to the claims of others (e.g., family, farm or environmental organization, and community) while seeking a satisfactory level of profit	A firm (e.g., farm, ranch, agribusiness, and environmental business) is an entity acting as if composed of one rational decision maker that maximizes profits. Emotion and the interest expressed toward or shared with others has little to do with rational choice
Consumers and producers often are lacking in requisite abilities, missing key pieces of information, so at best act in satisfactory ways	Consumers and producers weigh the benefits and costs of developing more ability and obtaining more information, and act optimally
Due to paying attention to thermodynamic reality, people are inherently interdependent, so, as noted earlier, social costs are widespread and a normal part of economic activity	Through abstracting from thermodynamic reality, people are inherently independent, so, as noted earlier, social costs are an aberration rather than common in the economy
The economic system is held together by a system of cohesive social, political, and economic forces not usually in equilibrium. Chaos with resilience is a better description of both the Market and of the Government, with resilience arising out interaction	Market equilibrating forces determine the cohesiveness of the social and economic system. The Market is either in equilibrium or tending toward equilibrium, and the Government needs to stay out of the way
The concept of utility lacks in moral content, so maximizing the sum of utilities of people has little meaning in that the moral dimension is not adequately considered	The concept of utility includes moral content. A person optimizes the relative amounts of goods purchased in the pursuit of moral satisfaction relative to other satisfactions

(*continued*)

Table 2.1 (continued)

Other-interest (Neoinstitutional) economics	*Self-interest (Neoclassical) economics*
Moving to a condition of Pareto optimality represents one of many possible criteria that could prove instrumental in improving the economy	Moving to a position of Pareto optimality represents the criterion proving to be instrumental in improving the economy
Achieving some level of social welfare can be understood in the sense of many people achieving the satisfaction from the utility of realizing some shared value(s) as well as their own individuated values	Achieving some level of social welfare can be understood as simply maximizing the sum of individuated utilities gained by each person, with shared values not a consideration
Data, Variables, and Parameters	
Current prices, and values calculated using prices, are best viewed as normative information about the status quo, and quite likely no longer defensible, mainly reflecting what has already occurred in the past, and thus are a poor indicator of what needs to take place in the future	Current prices can be taken as objective information about the direction people and society need to take for the future.
Data is purposive, changing in meaning and value content through time, so, for example, using historical price data to look forward is not particularly useful in choosing directions for the future, in that meaning and values embedded in the data are likely to be quite different, and perhaps unstable, in the future	Data tends to be stable through time in the sense of humans expressing invariant meaning and value through time, so, for example, using historical price data to look forward is quite useful in choosing directions for the future, in that meaning and values embedded in the data are likely to be quite similar, and stable, in the future
Valuation, Costs, and Prices	
An appropriate economic analyses recognizes the legitimacy of Market behavior and wealth maximizing behavior, but also needs to recognize that people with other belief and value systems than that which support the Market system need to have an impact on decisions, and sometimes they are best made in Government forums as represented in legislative, judicial, and executive (administrative) forums	An appropriate economic analysis recognizes that people naturally favor (have the belief and value systems favoring) activities leading to Market and wealth maximizing behavior. The role of legislative, judicial, and administrative forums needs to be minimized through educating people to values and the efficacy of the Market Forum only

(*continued*)

Table 2.1 (continued)

Other-interest (Neoinstitutional) economics	*Self-interest (Neoclassical) economics*
Markets can play some important role in expressing values associated with satisfying more basic needs. Other decision forums (legislative, executive branch of Government, judicial, private clubs and organizations) also play a role in valuing, in evolving value *V*, and are better suited to achieving the higher level wants, demands, and needs. Non-market (Priceless) values *V* influence prices *P*, where *V* not equal to *P*	Markets need to be used as the primary vehicle to express values and satisfy all manner of wants, demands and needs. Other decision forums (legislative, executive branch of Government, judicial, private clubs, and community organizations) need to be reduced, minimized in influence. Prices *P* are values *V*. Markets are the only source of value $V = P$
Cost has little to do with physical, material realty, for example, having instead to do with the disutility of producing some material like fertilizer to produce crops, or producing the crops themselves	Cost represents something observable and physical, for example, the dollar equivalent of materials in manufacturing fertilizer used by crops, and the dollar value of the crops themselves
The expression of value in executive, legislative, and judicial realms, that is, Government, is a legitimate determinant of appropriate resource allocation	The expression of value in a Market is the only legitimate determinant of appropriate resource allocation
Relationships and personal interactions among people substantially affect relative values and prices	Relationships and personal interactions among people have no influence on relative values and prices
Technology, Institutions, and Change	
Multiple motives (profits, natural curiosity, higher values and needs) drive technological change, which, in turn, drives institutional (laws, rules) change, in sequential order	The profit motive in the face of changing relative prices simultaneously drives both technological and institutional (laws, rules) change, not necessarily in any particular order
There is pervasive uncertainty, requiring producers and consumers to ban together and build institutions and organizations reflecting shared risk values to address it	There is really no uncertainty, rather, there is probability, and consumers and producers with varying risk preferences handle it in the Markets
Risk management is a problem producers and consumers need to work on together in community, with claims and the support of others a key part of managing risk	Risk management is something an individual producer and consumer does alone and the claims and support of others in community have little to do with it
Supply and demand are inseparable and interdependent forces	Supply and demand are separable and independent forces

(*continued*)

Table 2.1 (continued)

Other-interest (Neoinstitutional) economics	*Self-interest (Neoclassical) economics*
Institutional arrangements (laws, rules, regulations, custom) reflect shared values which necessarily evolve in social interaction, sometimes counter to what the person would choose, and judged on different criteria than used for choosing among consumer and producer goods	Institutional arrangements (laws, rules, regulations, and custom) are a matter of what a person chooses, and are judged on the same criteria as used for choosing among consumer and producer goods
Institutional arrangements are resolved on the plane of Value V not in the Market which operates on the plane of price *P* for material goods	Institutional arrangements are like any other material good, selected based on the relative price *P*
Government plays many essential roles beyond the provision for the public defense and security, and the definition and enforcement of private property rights. Government is needed, for example, in order to help people develop and express shared values and achieve shared aspirations beyond what can be accomplished in Markets	The only essential role for Government beyond that needed to provide for the public defense and security is to define and enforce private property rights in order to facilitate rigorous competition in Markets. Government needs to be minimized, and Markets encouraged to take on all manner of actions
Technological change is endogenous to the broader social system and driven by natural curiosity or bent to do things differently, more than anything else	Technology is endogenous to the economic system and driven by price ratio changes reflecting small shifts in relatively stable and invariant consumer preferences
Science and technology are cultural imperatives, the driving force in institutional change due to creating conflict. The Market is influenced and reacts	Science and technology are the result of Market forces, so Market changes induce both technological and institutional changes
The outcomes of the Market may have to be overridden with the latest scientific and social knowledge, often found in Government, going beyond the knowledge of contemporary Market participants. Knowledge is difficult to come by, requiring solid empirical inquiry, good science	The Market needs to be left alone, with outcomes based on whatever knowledge that is brought to it by the participants in that Market, scientific or otherwise, and, by definition, is presumed to be perfect knowledge. Knowledge evolving in Government is unproductive, while knowledge coming out of the Market, no matter if science based or not, is perfect knowledge

Source: Author's creation

price P it evolves. It is presumed to have nothing to do with the non-market, priceless value V coming out of community, culture and/or the Government representing the community.

The preference assumptions in Self-interest economics specify that "people's preferences are stable and consistent (Altman 2012, loc. 862); and, "how people form preferences doesn't matter (Altman 2012, loc 890)," and, "people have the same preferences" (Altman 2012, loc 904). Other-interest economics sees continual change and evolution, seeing the need to understand deeper beliefs, values and motivations at work, and how they change through time (Table 2.1). It sees considerable variation in preferences, especially as related to wide variation in shared Other-interests. Empirical testing in Behavioral Economics, and in Self&Other-interest economics, confirms it.

Every household is not the same; every firm, production entity is not the same. Variability is the norm, not sameness. Also, while Self-interest economics presumes the consumers and producers are always maximizing something, the empirical reality is more akin to satisficing, especially in the single domain of Self-interest only (see Altman 2012, loc 1925).

Self-interest economics also presumes (Table 2.1, and Altman 2012, loc 1056) "People are capable of acting on their own preferences." In contrast to Other-interest economics, there is no need to pay attention to the institutions (culture; law; rules; property rights; families; religious organizations; groups, like car clubs and bowling teams, as we seek ways to not bowl alone, Putnam 2001) in the background of choice by each person. Self-interest economics presumes institutions to facilitate personal liberty and freedom to choose are already in place, which may not describe reality (Altman 2012, loc 1072). The following quote from Douglass North (Altman 2012, loc 1080) suggests a serious flaw in Neoclassical Economics, "Not only that institutions (Note: reflecting the shared Other-interest) are designed to achieve efficient outcomes, but that they can be ignored in economic analysis because they play no independent role in economic performance." Self&Other-interest economics solves the problem by directing attention to the Other-interest, seeing the institutions representing that interest playing a key and interdependent role in economic performance.

Empirical research in Self-interest economics has been likened to extracting the Madonna from a log; the beauty of the formal, Self-interest only idea is in the data, somewhere: Just refine the econometric technique enough, and it will appear. As soon as the correct sign in an econometric analysis is achieved, one supporting the theory, there has been success; if the expected sign and significance is not found, the data or the statistical technique, the idea of Self-interest only, is flawed. As a result, numerous papers are never published because they are not supportive of the Self-interest only stories being weaved in the Neoclassical Economics journals.

Alternatively, the Other-interest analyst behaves more with a mind to finding the theory that does the most good for people so affected. Because of the approach, there is less in the way of dogmatic behavior, but it also causes Other-interest economics to appear atheoretical. The focus is on understanding and explaining actual economic processes and solving problems at hand, and on examining the interactions among people (Gruchy 1972, p. 287). It entails more of an emphasis toward the ongoing, actual social process. It focuses on collecting new data as needed.

Dugger (1979, p. 900) contends the Other-interest economists construct pattern models and Self-interest economists develop predictive models. The Other-interest model is sensitive to the actual institutional and cultural setting, and seeks first to understand, and then to explain behavior only in that context. The Self-interest model uses assumptions and logical arguments, to deduce predictions (Dugger 1979, p. 900), irrespective of the social context.

The Self-interest economist attempts to capture only the essence of the setting, while the Other-interest framework tends to be filled with the details of the process. Dugger notes: "Occam's razor, in neoclassical (i.e. Self-interest only focused) hands, is used to cut away all the messy details (which Neoinstitutional Economists crave, and Neoclassical Economists abhor)" (Dugger 1979, p. 902).

The Market is always preferred by the Self-interest analyst also because of the fundamental belief in harmony, and the Market brings harmony, within a setting of cultural determinism (Table 2.1). Markets are the only decision forum considered for human interaction because they work best in ensuring the tendency (believed to be pervasive, domineering) toward equilibrium. Gruchy (1972, p. 337) notes, "Economic reality is found in a static pattern of logical relationships," as opposed to the Other-interest belief in an inherent evolution of the system, sometimes heading toward an equilibrium, but often not doing so. The Self-interest world is characterized by order and rationality, and the best way to discover its nature is through the human reasoning process. As noted by Wilber and Harrison (1978, p. 63), in Self-interest economics, the "truth about reality lies in the logic of the theory."

The Other-interest economist believes that conflict is the fundamental feature of human interaction, within a dynamic cultural setting (Wilber and Harrison 1978, p. 72). As a result, process, referred to as the "life process" by Ayres (1944/1978), becomes more important than achieving equilibrium, and process oriented to finding common ground in a shared Other-interest. Bromley (1978, p. 45) sees the same conflict when he notes that Institutional Economics "focuses analytical attention on power relationships among economic agents through the concept of entitlements." Said entitlements take on form within narrowly defined sets of Other-interest. Power comes and is focused as a result of participation in the activities of a group. It is reflected in the shared Other-interest of the group, which may exclude others. Power is often hidden in the Invisible Hand, perhaps even meaning a background that has evolved without enough Empathy. It could be a bad Invisible Hand, like the Invisible Hand in the background of the US slave market, which operated for 400+ years, and then was brought back for another 100+ Jim Crow years. The Other-interest framework leads to an emphasis on the interrelations between power, knowledge, and psychology, addressing them in a Visible Hand, as "they relate to the making of economic policy" (Samuels 1969, p. 70).

Because of the dogmatism inherent in the Self-interest belief system, an image of economic efficiency is created and used to judge economic performance. The only occasional social cost and externality problems, for example, can be easily addressed by defining and otherwise enhancing private property rights and the operation of Markets. Self-interest framing presumes pervasive Government failure, which can be fixed only with the Self-interest-driven Market. Alternatively, the Other-interest belief system leads to an analytical boundary that encompasses other human activities, seeing widespread social costs arising out of inherent interdependence, that need to be addressed in a variety of Other Forums in Government. Other-interest framing points to pervasive Market-failure from presuming independence.

Biological and Physical System

The differences in the scope, boundaries, and methodology of Other-interest and Self-interest economics are related to the worldview taken in the biological and physical frame. Thermodynamic reality, 1st Law pointing to the limited capacity of the Spaceship Earth system to handle residuals and 2nd Law highlighting the inexorable move to a state of maximum entropy, is in the foundation of Other-interest economics. Both laws point to the inherent and pervasive interdependence of every Spaceship Earth Traveler with every other Traveler, which is the main reason that social costs are always present. In contrast, social costs are a myth, as argued in the close relative of Self-interest economics, in Libertarian Economics (again, see Cheung 1978).

Self-interest economics sees such matters, when they are considered at all, as just something to be addressed through the Market. The forces of the Market induce the technological advances that make the limits described in thermodynamics irrelevant. Such limits are just probabilistic and statistical: There is always some small probability that every bad can be reversed, so, no need to be concerned.

Social costs that do occur, at best only on occasion, can be eliminated through privatizing the commons. Or, if it is currently a public property, convert it to private property. It is the main solution in Coase (1960): Problem solved. With non-attenuated private property rights, interdependence and the associated social cost disappears, magically, through the workings of the Invisible Hand. Just tip the balance toward private property and all will be well.

It is also intriguing how Self-interest economics addresses knowledge (see Table 2.1). As Altman (2012, loc 979) points out, participants in the Market have "perfect knowledge … (pertaining to) Alternative opportunities that are relevant to the decisions (at hand) … how their decisions will affect the future (loc 967) … how they'll think and feel in the future." In fact, knowledge from any source other than the participants in the Market is suspect. Value *V*, from Other Forums as associated with Government knowledge, even if based in the best that science can produce, is especially suspect.

Property

Self-interest economics rests in a widespread existence of exclusive, non-attenuated private property rights (Table 2.1). So, common and public property are to be eliminated, Government is to be minimized. The key role of non-attenuated property rights to the Self-interest view has been highlighted by several (Bromley 1978; Randall 1978). And, while private property is fundamental, it is not often made explicit in the writings of

Self-interest economists. Have you ever seen mention of property in a basic Neoclassical Economics–based Microeconomics text?

Bromley (1978, p. 44, footnote 1) notes that Baumol and Oates (1975), while offering a classic, seminal piece in the Self-interest economics of environmental management, never once mention property. Neoclassical-based Microeconomics texts rarely mention the essential role of nonattenuated private property to the framework and theory they teach. Yet, intriguingly, as noted by Randall (1978, p. 13), concentrating on the exclusive, nonattenuated private property rights end is tantamount to focusing on an "empty set or nearly so."

Bromley (1978, p. 839) argues that a social system is composed of three major components, namely the natural environment, the property relations or structural component, and the superstructure involving the "belief system, values, art, religion, and science." In short, the latter is the superstructure of science&ethics. Self-interest economics, in contrast, sees the natural environment as a subset of the economy; sees only private property; and ignores the belief system, the art and ethics, and other things in the value *V* system.

In contrast, the structural and superstructure components are drawn out by the Other-interest view for detailed examination. Property relations are synonymous with institutions; Other-interest economics is, in a primary sense, property economics. The early focus on tenure relations by economists, especially the Land Economists, highlighted what was shared. And, Other-interest economics sees a key role for the Other Forums to bring the value *V* into affecting the Market. Bromley (1982, pp. 836–837) has also noted that "Efficiency is a fickle master" as a choice criterion for economists, because "property arrangements determine what is efficient" and prices (and the level of efficiency) are "simply an artifact of prevailing property arrangements, technical conditions, and the wealth position of buyers and sellers." Yes: The Other-interest reflects the property arrangements, which affect the Self-interest.

Psychology: Motivations and Pursuits

A major proposition in Self-interest economics is that incentives matter. Other-interest economists agree. It is just that the context within which the Self-interest reacts to incentives, that is, the shared Other-interest, matters, too. Other-interest economists generally reject the notion that the behavior of a person could best be explained from that person's unique biography (Averitt 1981, p. 1043), in that the shared Other-interest shapes that biography. There is also a rejection of "economic rationality" being only a matter of Self-interest. Also, saying that everything done by a person is rational means you cannot use rationality to explain what is going on (a proposition attributed to Albert Q. Hirschman by Swedberg 1990, p. 30).

Rather, the rational behavior of a person is the product of the institutions in which the person participates (the social norm in social psychology, see Fishbein and Ajzen 1975; Ajzen and Fishbein 1980, which is a close relative of the moral community notion in Other-interest economics). So, a person may not appear to be rational in the Self-interest sense, but indeed may be rational when the shared Other-interest is considered. Self-interest is reflected in the attitude part of the Fishbein version of the social psychology. The field of social psychology well understands the interplay in the interests (see Lynne and Rola 1988), as represented in the interplay of the Self-interest-based attitudes and the Other-interest-based social norm.

Dugger (1979, p. 904) suggests that the Self-interest view assumes a psychology of subjectivism or methodological individualism as the foundation. Only attitudes (reflecting Self-interest) within the person count. So, social norms (reflecting Other-interest) play no role, even though internalized within the person.

Intriguingly, the Self-interest economist believes that rules are on the same plane as preferences for "guns and butter." Rules are as much a part of the Self-interest only preference structure as daily consumption items. In the old pushpins and poetry puzzle, while pushpins have price P and poetry has value V on an incommensurable value plane, it is simply a non-issue to a Self-interest economist. Like guns and butter, pushpins and poetry are just a matter for simple tradeoff, with relative price P, the measure of the relative value V of both, so $V \equiv P$. Material goods (i.e., pushpins) and the moral dimension (i.e., poetry) can be subjected to simple tradeoffs, and exchanged at their relative prices in the Market Forum. The moral dimension vanishes from Self-interest only reasoning, as does the moral community, and the value V coming from the poetry forum is irrelevant.

Overall, as Tomer (2017, p. 122) points out, Neoclassical (Self-interest) Economics presumes "100 percent self-interest, 100 percent rationality, and 100 percent self-control." So, all economic choices are Self-interest only, commensurable, non-social. And, it is rational to pursue only

Self-interest: Buy pushpins in the Market Forum, ignore poetry in the Other Forums. And, the person never waivers in the discipline to make the choice, and as a result, the Market is presumed disciplined. As Altman (2012, loc 1036) notes, it is assumed "People have willpower," presumed internal to the Own-self. There is no influence from outside the person, nudges or controls. Other-interest economics is more akin to sociology, with the essence of the widely different frameworks captured well in the quip by Duesenberry (1960, p. 33): "Economics is all about how people make choices; sociology is all about how they don't have any choices to make." Self-interest economics sees only Robinson Crusoe on the Isle. Other-interest economics sees Crusoe and the new arrival Friday inextricably intertwined, as though no self, in either Crusoe or in Friday, is of any concern. Neither frames reflect empirical reality.

Another aspect relates to the ability to find and process the information needed to make good choices, and, how the capacity relates to heuristics. Self-interest economists presume that (Altman 2012, loc 1002) "People have unbounded computational capabilities," which has been found quite unrealistic, leading to behavioral economists like Herbert Simon to point instead to bounded rationality (Altman 2012, loc 1010). In fact, the reality of limited and bounded capabilities, extreme elements of the Self-interest economics group, as represented in the work of Milton Friedman, argue it does not even matter. Rather, it is about behaving "as if" they were doing all the complex computing on the way to maximizing profits, fully understanding that real firms do not "literally solve the simultaneous equations" (Friedman quoted in Altman 2012, loc 1020).

We are bound by quite limited capabilities. In the face of the difficulty, it is more realistic to point to how people use simple rules of thumb, things that work, the decision-making shortcuts described as heuristics (especially documented in the work of Kahneman 2003). A heuristic could well lead to a more rational, balanced choice in Self&Other than to assume it easy to make choices (Self-interest economics) or there are not choices for each person to make (Other-interest economics). As Kahneman (2003, p. 1450) points out, we operate on intuition most of the time: "...effortless thought is the norm" (Kahneman 2003, p. 1450). Intuition in the subconscious gives rise to thoughts coming "spontaneously to mind" (Kahneman 2003, p. 1450). Damasio (1999) also makes the convincing case that much of what goes on is driven by the subconscious, which may or may not have been tempered by conscious, rational thought at some other time. The Other-interest is often in the subconscious, often invisible unless irritated, stirred into visible consideration.

Sociology: Interdependence and Social Costs

Self-interest economics assumes all behavior can be explained with knowledge of the biography of the person, with preferences not influenced by others (Table 2.1; Altman 2012, loc 869). In contrast, Other-interest economics, and Behavioral Economics, points to how, like Altman (2012, loc 876) says it, "People typically make decisions in a social, historical, and institutional context and the context affects their decisions. Change context, and you may well change people's decisions."

In Other-interest economics, attention to freedom and liberty also recognizes the other essential kind of capital, which is ignored in NeoClassEcon, as represented in the social capital (see Cordes et al. 2003; Siles et al. 2000; Zhang and Lynne 2016). Just like Other-interest goes beyond Self-interest, the notion of social capital goes beyond the standard material and money capital of Self-interest economics. Social capital is represented in a shared Other-interest in being productive. It is essential to making true wealth, helped by working together, especially in cooperative ways. As Behavioral Economics makes clear, good social capital is essential to economic growth and development (Altman 2012, loc 6013), to Making wealth, especially of the material&moral kind.

The Other-interest economist will also likely be more interested in the way in which goods are produced, for example, in food production, being concerned with being environmentally sound, decent to the animals, and sustainable. While Self-interest economics sees only the wants of demand and supply that satisfies same, an Other-interest economist sees the context for both sides. Ultimate ends are the focus in Other-interest economic analysis, especially how the process of technological development and the resulting production influences the desires: Supply and demand are interdependent. The attention of the Other-interest economist is on identifying both the wants and ends; how did people come by the goals; how do the types of desires influence the manner in which issues are to be resolved; and what obstacles favor reaching the wants or ends (Gruchy 1972, p. 289).

Just maybe consumers would be willing to pay more for grain grown on a farm using conservation practices, or for chickens from farms with free-range chickens, if the Market would relay such information to them. What think? The Self-interest economist believes that the Market will, through the Invisible Hand, ensure that enough soil conservation activity is installed on the farms (e.g., see McConnell 1983). It says the Self-interest view takes wants and ends as given, out of the bounds of the analysis: Price *P* in the supermarket represents all value V.

It is fascinating how a Self-interest economist can believe it would occur, as there are few product labels telling consumers if soil and water conservation was in play in producing the product. What does the label on a sack of corn chips tell you about how the corn was raised? Or, on the chicken package, about the quality of the life of the chicken?

Data, Variables, and Parameters

The Self-interest economist is generally comfortable with the use of econometric techniques that rely on the use of historical data sets to calculate parameters. It is because of the view that equilibrium states exist, or nearly so, brought about by the harmony of interests. Also, everything is stable, harmonious, in equilibrium and if not, tending toward equilibrium, so, only changes at the margin are of concern. Other-interest economists, alternatively, view the set of cohesive social forces as being fundamental, that any stability that exists is because of the institutional arrangements (as represented in the shared Other-interest) being acceptable and useful. Equilibrium? No such thing. So, data has a different meaning.

The Self-interest view is that data holds the ultimate truths waiting to be discovered, much like the physicist who believes a certain mass always accelerates at the same rate. Thus, the economic system reacts to certain stimuli with a high degree of stability through time (Wilber and Harrison 1978, p. 67). The Other-interest view is quite different. All economic data is designed, value-laden data, and as such must be viewed as dynamic and purposive in nature (Gruchy 1972, pp. 288–289).

Producers and consumers create their own future, and thus the importance of understanding the value content of data is fundamental. Behaviorally, the Other-interest perspective requires examining longer time frames, from now until there no longer people, so the thermodynamic limits are reached, which is also the view in Self&Other-interest economics. As Atkinson (1983, p. 1060) notes, Other-interest economics "focuses on the social rules governing future exchange," while Self-interest economics focuses on "instantaneous exchange where the relationship between people ends with the exchange."

The Self-interest view is to rely heavily on a repeat of history, using "factual" data sets over past time periods to suggest future directions, usually in increments no longer than 100 years, by discounting practices (i.e., discount rates considerably larger than zero) that place a zero value on anything occurring beyond that time frame. The conceptual view is Newtonian in character, wherein effect follows cause. In the Other-interest perspective, the perspective is reversed, where cause is viewed as following effect (Atkinson 1983, p. 1061). As a result, the Other-interest economist is concerned with uncertainty, and with power relations (the rules) in the future. Because the focus is on the future, where everyone full well recognizes that rules are changing, the search for parameters is not especially meaningful.

It does not mean the Other-interest economist would not generally use econometric technique. On the contrary, the view would be that such parameter estimates are useful in explaining behavior over some short time frame (hours, days, weeks), and over a limited and well-defined cultural context. That is, values and beliefs are relegated to ceteris paribus, so they best be homogeneous across the sample. The Other-interest view, however, is that it is the process leading to rule changes that must be understood to really know how to interpret the results. The important time and cultural frames are uncompromisingly different in the two views.

Valuation, Costs, and Price

Other-interest economists are quite concerned about the direction society is taking. In fact, Ayres developed the instrumental theory of value, seeing instrumental value as a kind of value *V* on an Higher Plane than mere price *P*. Action has economic value if it contributes to life-enhancement (Petr 1984, p. 6; Tool 1986). Values *V* beyond the Market heavily influence the price *P* values, the latter being ceremonial in nature. Instrumental value *V* is real, prices *P* not necessarily so. The felicitous choice of an economic policy is unmistakable: Select policies that contribute to the life process. Price *P* not being real will not necessarily enhance the life process. For example, if the pesticide DDT is destroying a vital ecosystem, and causing hormonal cancers in the Human, even though inexpensive (price *P* is low), ban it. If tobacco is causing health problems, quit growing it, no matter what the price *P* is saying.

Technology, Institutions, and Change

Both technology and the institutional setting are usually relegated to *ceteris paribus* by the Self-interest economist. Wilber and Harrison (1978, p. 68) suggest the notion is used because of the Self-interest economist claiming an inability to experiment. So, because of believing one cannot experiment, and given the desire to emulate the approach of the physical scientist, where other things can more easily be held constant, the Self-interest economist simply assumes they are constant. Thus, technology and institutions are handled as a parameter and as a "constraint" on human activity; technology is often put into econometric equations as simply "t," a time trend.

In contrast, the Other-interest economist views change as continuous, and especially sees technological change as fundamental, a dynamic precursor to all cultural and social change, and thus it needs to be studied and understood. The inherent conflict driven by technological change, and subsequent institutional change, is a major theme in Other-interest economics (Gowdy 1984, p. 398).

So, Other-interest economics sees a key role for the wider community, and the Government representing it. It would especially support public-funded research to undergird technological development consistent supporting the life process. In contrast, Self-interest economics sees privately funded research for private purpose, defined as maximizing profit and the material utility it can buy, no matter whether it contributes to the life process or not.

References

Ajzen, I., and M. Fishbein. 1980. *Understanding Attitudes and Predicting Social Behavior*. Englewood Cliffs: Prentice-Hall.

Altman, M. 2012. *Behavioral Economics for Dummies*. Mississauga: John Wiley and Sons Canada/Kindle.

Atkinson, G.W. 1983. Political Economy: Public Choice or Collective Action? *Journal of Economic Issues* 17: 1057–1065.

Averitt, R.T. 1981. Review of Wendell Gordon's Book "Institutional Economics". *Journal of Economic Issues* 15: 1043–1046.

Ayres, Clarence E. 1944/1978. *The Theory of Economic Progress*. Kalamazoo: New Issues Press, Western Michigan University.

Baumol, W.J., and W.E. Oates. 1975. *The Theory of Environmental Policy*. Upper Saddle River: Prentice Hall.

Bromley, D.W. 1978. Property Rules, Liability Rules, and Environmental Economics. *Journal of Economic Issues* 12: 43–60.

———. 1982. Land and Water Problems: An Institutional Perspective. *American Journal of Agricultural Economics* 64: 834–844.

Buchanan, James M. 1987. The Constitution of Economic Policy. *American Economic Review* 77: 243–250.

Buchanan, James M., and Gordon Tullock. 1967. *The Calculus of Consent*. Ann Arbor: University of Michigan Press.

Burgin, Angus. 2012. *The Great Persuasion: Reinventing Free Markets Since the Depression*. Cambridge: Cambridge University Press.

Cheung, S.N. 1978. *The Myth of Social Cost*. London: The Institute of Economic Affairs.

Coase, Ronald H. 1960. The Problem of Social Cost. *The Journal of Law and Economics* III: 1–44.

Cordes, S., J. Allen, R. Bishop, G.D. Lynne, L. Robison, V.D. Ryan, and R. Shaeffer. 2003. Social Capital, Attachment Value and Rural Development: A Conceptual Framework and Application of Contingent Valuation. *American Journal of Agricultural Economics* 85 (5): 1201–1207.

Damasio, A. 1999. *The Feeling of What Happens: Body and Emotion in the Making of Consciousness*. New York: A Harvest Book, Harcourt, Inc.

Duesenberry, James. 1960. *Comment on "an Economic Analysis of Fertility"*. In Demographic and Economic Change in Developed Countries, ed. Universities-National Bureau Committee for Economic Research. Princeton, New Jersey: Princeton University Press.

Dugger, William M. 1979. Methodological Differences between Institutional and Neoclassical Economics. *Journal of Economic Issues* 13 (4): 899–909.

Etzioni, A. 1988. *The Moral Dimension: Toward a New Economics*. New York: Free Press.

Fishbein, M., and I. Ajzen. 1975. *Belief, Attitude, and Behavior*. Reading: Addison-Wesley Publishing Company.

Gowdy, John M. 1984. Marx and Resource Scarcity: An Institutionalist Approach. *Journal of Economic Issues* 18: 393–400.

Gruchy, Allan G. 1972. *Contemporary Economic Thought: The Contribution of Neoinstitutional Economics*. Clifton: Augustus M Kelley.

Hodgson, G.M. 1988. *Economics and Institutions: A Manifesto for a Modern Institutional Economics*. Philadelphia: University of Pennsylvania Press.

Hodgson, G. 1999. *Evolution and Economics: On Evolutionary Economics and the Evolution of Economics*. North Hampton: Edward Elgar.

Kahneman, D. 2003. Maps of Bounded Rationality: Psychology for Behavioral Economics. *American Economic Review* 93: 1449–1475.

Knight, Frank H., and Milton Friedman. 1969. *The Ethics of Competition and Other Essays*. New York: Books for Libraries.

Lynne, G.D., and J. Walter Milon, eds. 1984. *The Political Economy of Natural Resource and Environmental Use*, Southern Natural Resource Economics Committee. Vol. 20. 79th ed. Southern Rural Development Center.

Lynne, G.D., and L.R. Rola. 1988. Improving Attitude Behavior Prediction Models with Economic Variables. *Journal of Social Psychology* 128 (1): 19–28.

MacLean, Nancy. 2017. *Democracy in Chains: The Deep History of the Radical Right's Stealth Plan for America*. New York: Penguin Books.

Marglin, Stephen A. 2008. *The Dismal Science: How Thinking Like an Economist Undermines Community*. Cambridge, MA: Harvard University Press.

McCloskey, D.N. 1985. *The Applied Theory of Price*. 2nd ed. New York: Macmillan.

McConnell, Kenneth. 1983. An Economic Model of Conservation. *American Journal of Agricultural Economics* 65 (1): 83–89.

Petr, J.L. 1984. Fundamentals of an Institutionalist Perspective on Economic Policy. *Journal of Economic Issues* 18: 1–17.

Putnam, Robert D. 2001. *Bowling Alone*. New York City: Simon and Schuster, Inc.

Randall, A. 1978. Property Institutions and Economic Behavior. *Journal of Economic Issues* 12: 1–22.

Samuels, Warren J. 1969. On the Future of Institutional Economics. *Journal of Economic Issues* 3: 67–72.

Schmid, A.A. 1978. *Property, Power, and Will Public Choice: An Inquiry into Law and Economics*. New York: Praeger Special Studies.

Siles, M., L. Robison, B. Johnson, G. Lynne, and D. Beveridge. 2000. Farmland Exchanges: Selection of Trading Partners, Terms of Trade, and Social Capital. *Journal of the American Society of Farm Managers and Rural Appraisers* 63: 127–40.

Smith, A. 1759/1790. *The Theory of Moral Sentiments*. Edited by D.D. and A.L. Macfie Raphael. Indianapolis: Liberty Fund.

———. 1776/1789. *An Inquiry into the Nature and Causes of the Wealth of Nations*. Edited by E. Cannan. New York: Random House.

Swedberg, Richard. 1990. *Economics and Sociology: Redefining Their Boundaries, Conversations with Economists and Sociologists*. Princeton: Princeton University Press.

Tomer, John F. 2017. *Advanced Introduction to Behavioral Economics*. North Hampton: Elgar.

Tool, Marc R. 1986. *Essays in Social Value Theory: A Neo-Institutionalist Contribution*. Armonk: M. E. Sharp.

Wilber, C.K., and R.S. Harrison. 1978. The Methodological Basis of Institutional Economics: Pattern Modeling, Story-Telling, and Holism. *Journal of Economic Issues* 12: 61–89.

Zhang, Zhenu, and G. Lynne. 2016. Is Social Capital Motivated by Self-Interest Only? A Case Study on a Well-Developed U.S. Rural Community. *Universal Journal of Agricultural Research* 4 (1): 25–31.

CHAPTER 3

Drifting Isles and Re-integration on the Metaeconomics Continent

It seems quite clear that the original economics books written at the time of the Enlightenment saw there were two interests at work in bringing about wealth. Smith (1759/1790) is all about an Empathy-based, Sentiment-based Other (widely shared with others)-interest. Smith (1776/1789) is all about Ego-based Self-interest. Metaeconomics integrates Self-interest and Other-interest economics, pointing to the fact that real people likely have dual interest, not just a single, Self-interest nor just an Other-interest. Hayek (1948, p. 6) notes, "Individualism postulates or bases its arguments on the assumption of the existence of isolated or self-contained individuals, instead of starting from men whose whole nature and character is determined by the existence of society." Countering individualism, a person isolated from the community, Hayek is instead seeing two interests at work. As Solomon (2007, p. 71) proclaims, "We do not just have our own interests. We share interests with others. Empathy is neither altruistic nor self-interested. It rather exemplifies the implicit solidarity of nature we share interest with others." It is the sharing of interests that is the Other-interest Metaeconomics, which integrates with, and influences, the pursuit of Self-interest. But, we are getting ahead of ourselves.

Starting back at the time of Adam Smith, new sciences would eventually evolve to represent the two, alternative views of humans, as represented early-on in the two books by Adam Smith. The two views are represented by the Isle of the SocioLogic and the OthSocSci in Fig. 3.1

G. D. Lynne, *Metaeconomics*, Palgrave Advances in Behavioral Economics, https://doi.org/10.1007/978-3-030-50601-8_3

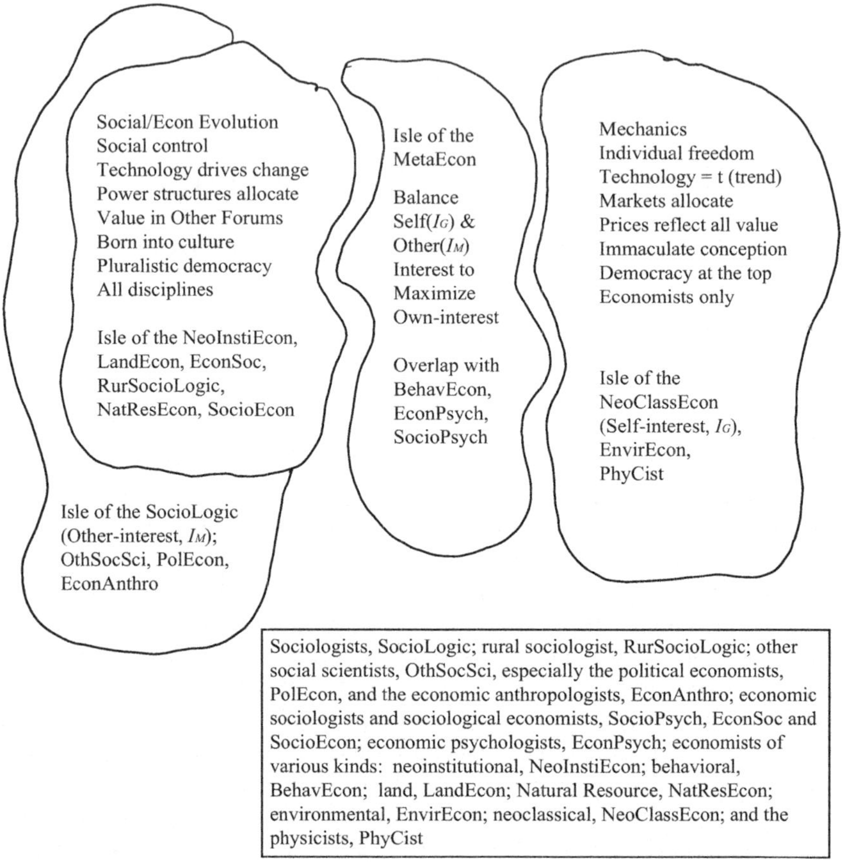

Fig. 3.1 Isles of economic frameworks and theories: Toward a metaeconomics continent. (Source: Author's creation)

(see the definitions of the acronyms therein), and their economic brethren, especially the NeoInstiEcon, SocioEcon, and the EconSocio. The Isle of the NeoClassEcon came to be the only allowed landscape for matters of economics. So, only the Self-interest landscape of Table 2.1, on the NeoClassEcon Isle, was to be considered: The NeoClassEcon demanded it be the only way with said domination still with us. And, the new Isle is that of the BehavEcon, the EconPsych, and the MetaEcon, where the

Hope lies. Perhaps someday there will be a re-integration into a Continent, if the InteGrator can get it done. Stay tuned.

The boundaries of what would become the NeoInstiEcon and the NeoClassEcon Isles were made abundantly clear in the *Methodenstreit* (Swedberg 1990, p. 10), in a particularly sharp confrontation at the meeting of the American Economic Association in 1894. The SocioLogic and what would become the OthSocSci, but especially the NeoInstiEcon, the EconSocio, and the SocioEcon, were told to stay away from economic questions, especially if they had not asked for the permission of what would become the NeoClassEcon. Ironic, indeed, in that the NeoClassEcon tout freedom, liberty, and being free-to-choose (Friedman, anyone). It was not to be: The NeoClassEcon narrowed the Other-interest to their own, and eliminated it for everyone else, as the consideration of community and ethics was for evermore removed from consideration. It seems the NeoClassEcon wanted to be a hard science, like that practiced by the PhyCists, in order to achieve a higher status in the universities of the day.

The event set in motion the development of separate departments for the SocioLogic and the NeoClassEcon. Actually, there were many others, like the PolEcon and the EconAntro, who never were to meet again, although there used to be a few RurSocioLogic in Departments of Agricultural NeoClassEcon. There were even a few LandEcon, and in more recent years, the NatResEcon were around. All of it is now ancient history, although a few NatResEcon hang-on, pretty much dominated by the NeoClassEcon-based EnvirEcon. Eventually, the NeoClassEcon would come to dominate, with only a few of the NeoInstiEcon tolerated. Occasionally one would be allowed at the table, given not too much is said, in some side office in the Department of the NeoClassEcon.

The separation was especially reinforced in the 1930s with the split in the territory between the rational and the supposed irrational, as delineated by Robbins of the NeoClassEcon and Parsons of the SocioLogic/NeoInstiEcon frame (Ingham 1996, p. 2). Mathematics also came to play in cementing in the separation: Karl Menger, a mathematician, also in the 1930s (Becchio 2009), wanted to mathematize economics (PhyCist envy, as it were), seeing it possible only if the moral dimension and ethics were left out of the formal model. It has been accomplished, especially in the purest version of it as represented in the Chicago School, the NeoClassEcon most "opposed to any ethical reflection whatever (McCloskey 2019, p. 93):" No ethics, please. By leaving the moral dimension and ethics out, the Isles have continually moved ever further apart with the result being "that our understanding of the modern world has been seriously impaired by the division of intellectual labour" (Ingham 1996, p. 244). Said understanding needs consideration of the ethics, and the community of shared interest within which it evolves, and, it is not irrational to do so. It is time to put some intellectual labor into putting the Isles back together, as the MetaEcon propose, and address true rationality.

Understanding of Economic Frames on Each Isle

As alluded to earlier, we can perhaps better understand what is on each Isle through seeing that the NeoInstiEcon, EconSoc, and the SocioEcon often co-exist with the SocioLogic. It is especially apparent in the rather eclectic subgroup of people, when you try to put them all under the same roof, as represented in the NeoInstiEcon (e.g., Bromley 2006), the EconSocio (e.g., Swedberg 1990), and the SocioEcon (e.g., Etzioni 1988). Also, some of said people will sometimes risk a meeting with a few of the NeoClassEcon who venture out, on the remaining bridges or ferries on foggy days when others cannot see. The more likely outcome, however, is meeting in the turbulent and shark infested waters in-between, which generally is not productive. Intriguingly, the NeoClassEcon have predicted, many times, the demise of the NeoInstiEcon, and, by association, the EconSocio and SocioEcon. Intriguingly, to the dismay of the NeoClassEcon, the NeoInstiEcon seem to have a certain resiliency, and ability, to stay out of the water, away from the sharks, and somehow manage to keep afloat. Intriguingly, keeping afloat has become much easier, now shored-up by the BehavEcon who are finding immense holes in the Isle of the NeoClassEcon Framework and Single Interest Theory. It is the NeoClassEcon that are sinking.

One of the more prominent members on the other main Isle, in fact, perhaps prematurely, went so far as to claim that the NeoInstiEcon are on the "threshold of a great transformation" (Samuels 1995, p. 570). He apparently saw some new Isle that it is not apparent to the NeoClassEcon. And, while he did not clarify where the Isle will be built, it is useful to consider how he sees it (following Samuels 1995, pp. 573–575): (1) emphasizing social and economic evolution with the need for an activist orientation (i.e., a Visible Hand) in order to affect that evolution, in contrast to the static, mechanical world operated by the Invisible Hand; (2) affirming the importance of social control in contrast to the Market as a system of individual freedom from control; (3) proposing technology as a major source of transformation in contrast to representing technology as simply a trend variable to handle the noise in equilibrium behavior; (4) seeing power structures as the ultimate determinant of resource allocation in contrast to a presumption of dispersed power in the markets; (5) focusing on the processes by which human values are ensconced in institutions, structures and individual behavior rather than on the relative prices of commodities; (6) seeing that culture molds people (and people mold culture) rather than presuming the immaculate formation of the consumers (and producers) tastes and preferences; (7) operating in pluralistic and democratic ways while paying attention to the values of the masses whether in the markets or not; (8) seeing problems in holistic terms, thus involving all the disciplines, and as such including much more than the Market for which the economist is the expert. Overall, the problem on the Isle of the NeoClassEcon is that the "pursuit of the mechanics of price determination trivializes what the economy is all about, and excludes considerations of social control and social change and all that they entail" (Samuels 1995, p. 575).

The MetaEcon also embrace the role of social control and social change, and people being part of institutions represented in the notion of the Other-interest brought to bear or not, dependent on the extent of Self-control. It is also about the Visible Hand, not the magical Invisible Hand, and about legitimate valuing processes beyond the Market, that is, value V may often serve to override price P in economic choice. The MetaEcon see the jointness of valuing processes, as in price&value, market-forums & Other Forums. Again, stay tuned.

Problems do still exist on the Isle of the SocioLogic and within the realm of the NeoInstiEcon, too, in that too much focus is perhaps put on the social control and social element. Again, after Duesenberry (1960), NeoClassEcon believe people are in command, making individual choices, each person choosing. The SocioLogic, and their close relatives represented in the NeoInstiEcon, see each person not having much choice. A less drastic view is that of Granovetter (1985): He proposes framing the economy as embedded in the social structure, and thus to consider looking at the persons economic actions as influenced by it, but not necessarily controlled by same. MetaEcon is more like the latter, seeing substantial individual freedom to choose, but seeing the possibility for nudging from the larger community, followed by control (generally involving Government) only if that fails.

The fundamental problem on the Isle of the SocioLogic is the lack of a common ground on which a common theory of human behavior rests. In fact, the SocioLogic (and the NeoInstiEcon in their midst) are generally atheoretical. And, until an alternative, at least equally as powerful a theory of individual economic behavior as that of the Econ held forth by the NeoClassEcon exists, it is unlikely that the Isle of the NeoClassEcon will lose its dominant influence. Metaeconomics sees the ever-evolving Isle of the MetaEcon, with Dual Interest Theory, the machinery at the core, reflecting dual interest at work in a human, as having the potential to be at least on par with the NeoClassEcon Single Interest Theory of the Econ. The NeoInstiEcon might consider adopting it into their own as a theory of the Human.

Residents of the Isles Are at Loggerheads in the Moral and Amoral Domain

While the Samuels (1995) list is quite helpful, it does not really get to the crux of the matter regarding why the Isles are separated. In fact, the defining line of the Isles is on the moral and amoral, and the ethical, division between the two Isles. We see the fundamental defining line between the Isles through Khalil (1998, p. 614) in his response to critiques of a paper he had written (see Khalil 1997) to suggest directions toward a truly unified social theory:

> In my essay I tried to locate exactly the origin of the disagreement between the moralist and the amoralist position and, consequently, the scope of economics. I argued that the bone of contention is not that the neo-classical paradigm does not recognize moral sentiments, which it clearly does. It is rather about how to model such sentiments. For the amoralist agenda, commitments are no different from ordinary tastes and, hence, both are smoothly substitutable at the margin. For the moralist position, commitments are some kind of pre-given precepts according to which human behavior must be judged. I suggested how to supersede, while retaining the positive elements of both positions. It is possible to avoid the implication of the moralist position—viz, moral norms are metaphysically given—without falling into the flat world of the amoralist view which cannot account for some empirical anomalies.

The crux of the matter lies in the chasm between the amoral tradition highlighted in the Khalil quote as exemplified in Robbins/Becker on the NeoClassEcon Isle. It is in contrast to the moral tradition, as highlighted in the Kahlil quote, represented in Durkheim/Etzioni (and Parsons) on the SocioLogic (and NeoInstiEcon) Isle. The MetaEcon, like Khalil (in the quote), proposes to supersede both traditions. It does so by proposing to account for the empirical anomalies by seeing Empathy as the starting point for forming the moral and ethical dimension, which goes beyond both the metaphysical origins and the amoral.

Nelson (1991) alludes to the issue is a somewhat different way, making the case that Self-interest, mainstream Neoclassical Economics is an economic theology, with the NeoClassEcon being the high priests. The NeoClassEcon, however, never tell the parishioners that a value system of a certain kind, a certain kind of moral and ethical dimension, a certain kind of moral community as it were, is in the underlayment of the economic preachments. In Metaeconomics terms, the NeoClassEcon hide, or at least do not make clear, just what is operating in the mythical Invisible Hand, and, that it is quite possible it is not inherently Good. In fact, the NeoClassEcon do not even acknowledge that the human has a moral and ethical dimension (at least do not make it conscious), who shares in an Other (moral and ethical, Empathy-driven, shared)-interest, which influences economic choice. The NeoClassEcon focus only on the material dimension represented in the Self-interest-driven part of the human.

Or, if we give the NeoClassEcon any due, which Khalil (in the quote) so does, the material and the moral "are smoothly substitutable at the margin," so we simply pay the price *P* for the moral as though it is like any other ordinary good? Where, exactly, in what Market, do I buy the moral good? Buy the ethics? Buy the other virtues? And, is the moral and ethical dimension actually commensurable with ordinary goods, in a simple tradeoff? Granted, with enough homework we might suppose we could gain some idea of the moral and ethical standards of the suppliers in the Market: Yet, it seems a bit much to leave it all to the Market Forum, alone? Empirical evidence, please.

As McCloskey (2006) describes it, all humans ascribe, Spaceship Earth wide, to the same virtues represented in prudence, temperance, courage, justice, faith, hope, and love. The NeoClassEcon see only one virtue, as represented in prudence-based Self-interest focused on maximizing profit and the utility it can purchase. Yet, the other virtues are hopefully resident in each person, too. In Metaeconomics terms, the other virtues rest in the

Other-interest. Intriguingly, as Hirschfeld (2018) convincingly argues, the NeoClassEcon focus on the prudence-based profit and the utility it can buy. Other virtues play no role in conditioning, giving context to that pursuit, especially temperance and courage/fortitude. Perhaps most importantly, justice as represented in doing the right-thing-to-do is never mentioned: No ethical reflection. So, as Hirschfeld makes clear, it is unlikely the profit and utility maximizer will achieve happiness, which needs something beyond the material. As Hirschfeld (2018, p. 106) also clarifies, "Fortitude and temperance are the virtues that respectively bring our aversions and desires into alignment with the judgments of reason." So, even efficiency, through reason, is not achievable without consideration of the other virtues. The Self-interest must be tempered by the Other-interest which holds said virtues.

In the Nelson (1991, see esp. pp. 20–21) story about NeoClassEcon as the new priests, we have the Roman tradition of reason and rationality on the Isle of the NeoClassEcon, We now see it is at best an amoral isle (due to ignoring the other virtues) in that the moral dimension is not revealed and debated (which can lead to a less than moral economy, a less humane economy, by not making the moral and ethical community explicit). We also have the protestant (read protest-ant) tradition of doing-the-right-thing in the moral sense, which is on the SocioLogic Isle (and within the NeoInstiEcon) where the one thing worth debating are the values *V*. As the SocioEcon like Etzioni contend, the institutions, emotions, social bonds, values, and a sense of morality (and ethics) are all key parts of economic decisions, all of which are Other-interest considerations. The problem is, we do not seem to be able to see that an element of truth rests on both Isles, that humans seek balance, which requires reasoned calculation and reasoned sentiment in seeking balance.

Activists and Interventionists: Objectivity Versus Subjectivity

As noted, around the turn into the twentieth century, economists (people who would evolve into the NeoClassEcon) distanced themselves from the SocioLogic and the NeoInstiEcon. The distancing (economic and social, like in a Pandemic) was due in part to the latter using more activist/interventionist approaches, in effect wanting to move away from the Invisible Hand framing to that of evolving a Visible Hand that worked better to solve real, contemporary economic problems. At the same time, the

NeoClassEcon became more closely associated with the physicists, the PhyCist, who were building a physical model consistent with Newtonian mechanics. The association ensured an ever-deeper chasm as between the NeoClassEcon and the SocioLogic/NeoInstiEcon, because of the latter being more closely associated with Darwinian evolutionary theory (and Thermodynamics) rather than Newtonian theory. It is the connection with evolution more generally and social/economic evolution specifically, that leads to the explicit activist orientation. It is deemed possible to affect the evolution of the economy, rather than just react to evolving conditions as in the Newtonian frame.

The fundamental problem is that people are more complex than that perhaps envisioned on either the Isle of the SocioLogic (and NeoInstiEcon) or that of the NeoClassEcon, as confirmed by the BehavEcon. In fact, people seem to be pursuing both a moral utility and a pleasure (more material) utility (Etzioni 1986), or perhaps a material and a symbolic utility (Khalil 1997). The Other-interest is represented in the former, and the Self-interest in the latter, with both utilities, though perhaps (but not necessarily) incommensurable, pursued in a joint, interdependent fashion. The two kinds of utility/interest play off against one another, in a dynamic fashion with feedback, although the Self-interest utility may be more fundamental, more primal. In fact, we would see the evolution of the preferences, and, over a long enough time, such evolution being related to the evolution of the brain itself. The MetaEcon propose a new theory of human behavior, seeing the material&moral, material&symbolic, and pleasure&moral, which also requires Self-control in order to achieve the best balance.

Isles Reforming onto an Isle of the MetaEcon

Etzioni (1988), from the Isle of the SocioLogic, seeing how the Isles had drifted apart, called for a reconsideration of the natural tension in the I&We, as represented in Self&Other-interest by the MetaEcon. He called for forming a new group called the SocioEcon, who are close relatives of the MetaEcon, bringing the Isles back together. The new Isle was to come out at the interstice, and re-integration, between modern-day sociology and economics.

The evolution to the frame of the SocioEcon was not to be, at least it has not emerged yet. It did point, as does Hodgson (1999), a well-known member of the NeoInstiEcon, to the need for a new theory of human agency. Such a theory needed to recognize the inherent conflicting tension, with the potential for mutual gain from both interests being accommodated, as Adam Smith also recognized.

The MetaEcon, working closely with the EconPsych, started out in collaboration with the SocioEcon, and eventually proposed such a theory, drawing heavily on the BehavEcon. Dual Interest Theory is seen as the core idea to help in slowing the drift of the Isles. Dual Interest Theory may even be the basis and guide for solidly reconnecting the Isles, in a new Continent. And, if not possible (we suppose there could be a crash, rather than a gentle reconnection), at least build some solid bridges with ends extending at the pace with the drift, if it cannot be stopped. It would help the courageous residing on the Isles to visit the other and see what best ideas might be imported, exported, and integrated. Metaeconomics encourages the new species, the InteGrator, the person who applies sociology to economics and economics to sociology, and, also, as in the realm of the EconPsych and BehavEcon, psychology to economics and economics to psychology.

Bringing the Moral and Ethical Dimension Back into Economics

We alluded to the Chicago School version of Neoclassical Economics as being opposed to ethical reflection. McCloskey (2019, p. 93) also suggests that "Harvard-School social engineering… is thoughtlessly attached to utilitarianism." Such social engineering is generally on the NeoInstiEcon Isle. The third possibility is the McCloskey (2019, p. 93) favored position "the humane liberalism… that Adam Smith and I espouse." Metaeconomics, too, is about a humane liberalism, made possible through bringing ethical reflection back into the framework and theory. Bring the moral sentiments back, please. It is also what Etzioni (1988) is about, writ large, in wanting to bring the moral dimension back into economics. It is done through bringing another kind of utility, another kind of interest into view: It is about introducing the moral and ethical reflection through Dual Interest Theory.

In Etzioni (1986, p. 159), with most of the material also represented in the 1988 book, Etzioni starts with the proposition that "neoclassical economists have made heroic efforts to accommodate within the confines of the concept of rational utility maximization the fact that individual behavior is significantly affected by moral considerations." The paper argues that mono-utility theory is too parsimonious, that we need to consider at least two irreducible utilities. As noted, he suggested one for pleasure and one for morality (and perhaps more utilities, but he cautions against the anarchy that could arise in a theory with too many).

Etzioni identifies three kinds of mono-utility commonly represented in standard Microeconomics with the analytical engine of single-interest, Self-interest only theory: (1) utility resulting from pleasure seeking, hedonic origins; (2) same hedonic origin, but now includes utility gained from knowing of the utility gains by others, commonly referred to as interdependent utility, and (3) utility as an attribute, resulting from, as a common denominator for, all quests for satisfaction. Etzioni ultimately rejects all three as insufficient to an all-encompassing theory. Metaeconomics rejects all three, too.

The interdependent utility concept, and the related, equally flawed, notion of other-regarding preferences needs special attention (for more detailed analysis, showing how Adam Smith would not have approved of interdependent utility and other-regarding preferences, see Lynne et al. 2016, esp. p. 246). It is pointed out how Self-sacrifice, Self-denial is incompatible with the concept (Etzioni 1986, p. 162), so it is not a useful concept for understanding a Human. And, in fact, normal people sacrifice all the time, by doing the right thing, doing what ought to be done, whether such acts give Ego-based hedonic pleasure or not.

In fact, the expansion of the self-interest/ pleasure utility to encompass other people's utility is just fundamentally flawed. As Etzioni (1986, p. 162) says: "Once a concept is defined so that it encompasses all incidents that are members of a given category (in the case at hand, the motives for all human activities), it ceases to enhance one's ability to explain … the concept ceases to differentiate …. To the degree that the 'theory' aims to shed light on motivation, it constitutes a conceptual failure, because the purpose of introducing concepts is to call attention to meaningful distinctions." If whatever one does is said to simply indicate pleasure coming from same, utility theory is nothing more than a tautology, which describes interdependent utility theory, and the related idea of other-regarding preferences.

It also challenges the MetaEcon and the BehavEcon more generally, to expand the utility model only if it will, as Etzioni (1986) notes, "call attention to meaningful distinctions." I also recall the argument, and I believe it is his, in another paper/book, that using the interdependent utility theory also precludes one from staying with the Invisible Hand concept, which undergirds NeoClassEcon thinking. The point is: Knowing how much utility someone else is gaining from some action is to make for a Visible Hand. Inconsistency.

In one sense, the MetaEcon preserve the Invisible Hand concept, that is, one does not have to know the utility gained by someone else before taking economic action, as in interdependent utility theory. It is the case in that both Self&Other-interest are internal to the person, and people are then still interdependent with others, but only through the shared Other-interest, which is internalized to each person. Metaeconomics also posits that the actual content of the Invisible Hand is represented in the Other (shared with others)-interest, which at some point was visible, perhaps made unconscious/made invisible for a time, as we run on automatic. So, what may be in effect invisible (not being mindful of it), may need to be made visible, that is, conscious, when shared interests are changing, especially when said interests are doing bad. It especially needs to be brought to the conscious, made visible, when the status quo is no longer working, as indicted by our becoming irritated (especially if experiencing outrage, for example, at slavery and segregation) into action. At that point, the invisible in the Other-interest is changed with the visible reconsideration of it.

Etzioni (1986, p. 180) concludes: "Attempts to accommodate moral behavior within the mono-utility theory model strain it." Both pleasure and morals motivate/ drive economic behavior, but they do not fit in the single-interest theory system. Etzioni (1986) was a major inspiration to the MetaEcon, leading to proposing at least two utilities. Later, it came to be two motives, and, then, eventually it was framed as having two interests. The MetaEcon now include the moral dimension highlighted by Etzioni as a another set of indifference curves, representing another kind of interest.

Khalil (1997 and 1998, as alluded to in the earlier quote), too, raises the same question in a somewhat different way, asking: "Do moral sentiments differ from ordinary tastes?" A good starting point is to say, "yes," and then subject the matter to empirical testing, which the MetaEcon have done. Based on empirical testing, the MetaEcon have found that ordinary (and, generally, material) tastes are represented in the Self-interest set of indifference curves and the moral (and ethical) sentiments are represented in the Other-interest set of indifference curves, and, that the two sets, like pushpins&poetry, could well be incommensurable. Both the material&moral, likely incommensurable, compose the Own-interest.

Metaeconomics as Objectively Analytical and Subjectively Activist

The MetaEcon see Metaeconomics as both objectively analytical and subjectively activist in that objectivity and subjectivity, fact and value, are now both recognized as legitimate realms for inquiry. It is recognized that all humans are endowed with both dimensions. On the analytical side, the MetaEcon point to the essential need to measure, and test empirically the extent to which both Self-interest and Other-interest are driving and served by some economic choice. The challenge here is in finding ways to measure the shared Other-interest reflecting the moral (and ethical) community. Also, much like the rest of the BehavEcon, the MetaEcon depend upon both statistical and substantive influence (i.e., science) on outcomes from the variables found significant.

On the subjectively activist part, the MetaEcon point to a substantively different, subjective value *V* theory, in contrast to, but also a supplement to, price *P* theory. The MetaEcon see the need to recognize balance between the complete freedom in the Market, which produces *P*, and perhaps significant Government nudging and control reflecting *V*. The value *V* reflects the nudging of the other virtues, especially temperance, on the evolution of *P*. If it does not work, when the person fails in Self-control, the control (rules, laws, judicial judgments reflecting *V*) may have to be imposed.

The MetaEcon points to perhaps adopting the BehavEcon notion of libertarian paternalism as characterized in Thaler and Sunstein (2008). Or, another possibility, use the humane liberalism frame from McCloskey (2019), which overlaps, greatly. So, MetaEcon put full attention to the freedom-of-choice, individual rights and liberty in a gentle (humane) nudge, or, maybe just some gentle (humane) persuasion, hopefully arising from within the Own-self. Restraining that choice (paternalism) would be applied sparingly, and only when Empathizing with the content of the moral and ethical community that works for everyone. Overall, too, and it is extremely important: Nudging whether sourced in the person and/or from outside, is based in Empathy not Ego. And, many empirical questions, here, the ultimate one being: What works best?

Attention gets focused on the choice architecture, wherein experts delineate an array of better choices, for example, in helping design the layout of food in a school cafeteria in order to influence what students choose (Altman 2012, loc 3605). Such architecture is another kind of framing, and, again, is reflected in the notion of the shared Other-interest as proposed by the MetaEcon. The NeoInstiEcon would say: Focus on the institution. Visibly work to give the context to the Self-interest choice. The MetaEcon Other-interest embeds the NeoInstiEcon institution.

References

Altman, M. 2012. *Behavioral Economics for Dummies*. Mississauga: John Wiley and Sons Canada/Kindle.

Becchio, Giandomenica. 2009. A Historical Note on the Original Meaning of Metaeconomics. *Intellectual Economics* 1 (5): 7–11.

Bromley, D.W. 2006. *Sufficient Reason: Volitional Pragmatism and the Meaning of Economic Institutions*. Princeton, New Jersey: Princeton University Press.

Duesenberry, James. 1960. Comment on "An Economic Analysis of Fertility." In *Demographic and Economic Change in Developed Countries*, edited by Universities-National Bureau Committee for Economic Research. Princeton, New Jersey: Princeton University Press.

Etzioni, A. 1986. The Case for a Multiple Utility Conception. *Economics and Philosophy* 2: 159–183.

———. 1988. *The Moral Dimension: Toward a New Economics*. New York: Free Press.

Granovetter, Mark. 1985. Economic Action and Social Structure: The Problem of Embeddedness. *American Journal of Sociology* 91: 481–510.

Hayek, F.A. 1948. *Individualism and Economic Order*. Chicago: The University of Chicago Press. (paperback edition 1980).

Hirschfeld, Mary L. 2018. *Aquinas and the Market: Toward a Humane Economy*. Cambridge, MA: Harvard University Press.

Hodgson, G.M. 1999. *Evolution and Economics: On Evolutionary Economics and the Evolution of Economics*. North Hampton: Edward Elgar.

Ingham, Geoffrey. 1996. Some Recent Changes in the Relationship Between Economics and Sociology. *Cambridge Journal of Economics* 20 (2): 243–275.

Khalil, E.L. 1997. Etzioni Versus Becker: Do Moral Sentiments Differ from Ordinary Tastes? *De Economist* 145: 491–520.

———. 1998. Interests and Commitments: Replies to Etzioni, Dolfsma, and Van Staveren. *De Economist* 146: 613–618.

Lynne, G.D., N.V. Czap, H.J. Czap, and M.E. Burbach. 2016. Theoretical Foundation for Empathy Conservation: Toward Avoiding the Tragedy of the Commons. *Review of Behavioral Economics* 3: 245–279.

McCloskey, D.N. 2006. *The Bourgeois Virtues: Ethics for an Age of Commerce.* Chicago: The University of Chicago Press.

———. 2019. *Why Liberalism Works: How True Liberal Values Produce a Freer, More Equal, Prosperous World for All.* Kindle ed. New York: Yale University Press.

Nelson, R.H. 1991. *Reaching for Heaven on Earth.* Savage: Rowman and Littlefield.

Samuels, Warren J. 1995. The Present State of Institutional Economics. *Cambridge Journal of Economics* 19 (4): 569–590.

Smith, A. 1759/1790. *The Theory of Moral Sentiments.* Edited by D.D. and A.L. Macfie Raphael. Indianapolis: Liberty Fund.

———. 1776/1789. *An Inquiry into the Nature and Causes of the Wealth of Nations.* Edited by E. Cannan. New York: Random House.

Solomon, R.C. 2007. *True to Our Feelings: What Our Emotions Are Really Telling Us.* New York: Oxford University Press.

Swedberg, Richard. 1990. *Economics and Sociology: Redefining Their Boundaries, Conversations with Economists and Sociologists.* Princeton: Princeton University Press.

Thaler, R.H., and C.R. Sunstein. 2008. *Nudge: Improving Decisions About Health, Wealth, and Happiness.* New Haven: Yale University Press.

CHAPTER 4

Formal Metaeconomics: Recycling Choices

See the Appendix for the formal character. The mathematical metaeconomics of demand related to the indifference between two goods in consumption arising because of nonallocable goods is developed in Appendix A. The mathematical metaeconomics of supply (and derived demand) associated with isoquants in production arising because of nonallocable inputs experienced by a producer (perhaps a rancher of sheep) is developed in Appendix B. And, if you find mathematics doesn't work for you, no problem: We use graphics to bring in our empirical testing related to recycling choices and to the notion of Empathy Conservation.

Do you recycle? We now turn to explaining why, or, why not, with the help of dual interest theory.

Subtlety of Jointness Arising Out of Nonallocable Inputs and Goods

Based on years of working to market Metaeconomics, as represented in efforts at explaining it to colleagues; publishing papers and book chapters; giving conference presentations; teaching classes; working with potential users of our analysis in Government agencies; and, in working to convince the Reviewers of this first ever Metaeconomics book, one thing has become clear: *Grasping the subtlety of jointness, interdependence, and nonseparability arising because of nonallocable inputs and goods is not easy.* Yet, nonallocable inputs and goods is the fundamental feature of interdependence

G. D. Lynne, *Metaeconomics*, Palgrave Advances in Behavioral Economics, https://doi.org/10.1007/978-3-030-50601-8_4

among people, as well as interdependence between people and the Spaceship Earth system, is all around us. It is in our daily experience. Maybe that is why we do not see it: We are embedded in it. It is invisible (that invisible hand, I guess). The subtlety is perhaps the reason why the original development by (Frisch 1965, Chapters. 14 and 15) did not go anywhere. We have looked in the literature; we contacted the Frisch Center in Norway. Few seem to have understood what Frisch was trying to say, and even fewer apparently realized the significance of it. We are interdependent, and overlapping isocurves is the way to represent it.

Instead, the rather peculiar notion of "jointness with allocable inputs" in production (and jointness in consumption never mentioned, at all) coming out of Neoclassical Microeconomics has come to dominate. It is peculiar because "jointness" in that framework ostensibly comes out of independence? It is the case even though there is no basis in empirical reality that allocable inputs (or goods) and, thus, independence, nonjoint in inputs and goods, and separability as presumed in NeoClassEcon renditions could somehow produce "jointness." Not logical.

As made clear later, in a Metaeconomics jointness on the production side (see Chap. 8, and, also see Appendix B), a rancher cannot have complete control, and allocate hay and grain between wool and mutton, as described in the original example in Frisch (1965). Also, in the conservation problem, a farmer cannot completely allocate water and fertilizer between corn and wildlife production in the same field. It is the fact of little control, that is, nonallocable inputs, that leads to jointness and interdependence. It is the fact of "we Travel on the Spaceship together" that leads to jointness and interdependence. It is the fact that our Brains evolved with two tendencies, the Ego&Empathy, which cannot be separated, which leads to jointness and interdependence. So, we have two, nonseparable interests: Both inputs and goods are often nonallocable.

True jointness arises in cases where the outcomes from input or good allocation cannot be controlled completely by human intervention and control. We might speculate it is why the notion has not gained traction in Neoclassical Economics, which presumes the person, as an Econ not a Human, is always completely independent, always in control. And, then, for the occasional times when that is not the case, an "externality adjustment" is used to patch a flawed framework and theory. Also, it is presumed that if the Econ is not now in complete control, the Econ will soon be so in control. The Market with only the Econ represented in it will solve every problem. Pretty optimistic, and clearly not realistic? How does the

Market, alone, do with pandemics? With overuse of the Spaceship Earth capacity to handle excessive Greed-driven releases of carbon dioxide?

The notion of complete independence, freedom, and liberty to choose is also a kind of magical part of Enlightenment framing in general, so the implications of seeing the subtlety have much larger implications. Enlightenment framing misses the fact that we more often are interdependent rather than independent, joint in nonseparable Market&Government. So, in some ways, the presumption of independence is more about a kind of philosophy rather than reality. It needs, instead, to be based in facts about the true nature of production and consumption systems, and behavior relating thereto. There are in fact, often, nonallocable inputs and nonallocable goods, for individual producers and consumers, at the micro scale. We explore the implications of nonallocable inputs and goods at a more macro scale, later in the book, in the notion of saving capitalism.

So, it is also perhaps time to re-write the Microeconomics books, at least bring in some reference to the possibility of nonallocable inputs and goods. At least one-chapter please (Frisch had two). Said books typically start with a single indifference curve showing a single interest outcome. Microeconomics is about a consumer who is independent of every other consumer. Then, when isoquants are introduced later in the typical Microeconomics book, it is presumed all inputs are allocable. It means the producers of goods are also independent of every other producer, every consumer, and every system on Spaceship Earth? Metaeconomics says: Not. Rather, systems are interdependent.

Metaeconomics Story Starts with a Dual Set of Interests

The intriguing question, then, is how to begin the story, but now in a Metaeconomics book, or in a Dual Interest Theory chapter or two (perhaps someday) of a standard Microeconomics book. The new story needs to take the student closer to the nature of the real Spaceship, and real relationship with other Travelers on it. There is also the matter of jointness in Market&Government. Also, it would be nice if we could use a rather simple, parsimonious way of representing the new understanding of reality, as in the single indifference curve and single isoquant of an introductory Microeconomics book. Some variant on the isocurve models of Neoclassical Economics could work well.

Metaeconomics Suggests the Empirical Questions to Ask About Recycling

We illustrate the nonallocable goods case first, using the real-world case of recycling. The nonallocable inputs case is illustrated in the Empathy Conservation section of Chap. 8. Both representations have been empirically tested. The indifference ideas in the area of recycling behavior have been tested in Kalinowski, Lynne, and Johnson (2006); Shrestha and Lynne (2011); and Shrestha (2014). The overlapping indifference curves of Fig. 4.1 demonstrate nonallocable goods.

Figure 4.1 looks much like it would in a Microeconomics book. As noted, typically such a book starts with the set of indifference curves I_G, which are presumed to come out of the egoistic-hedonistic tendency, and

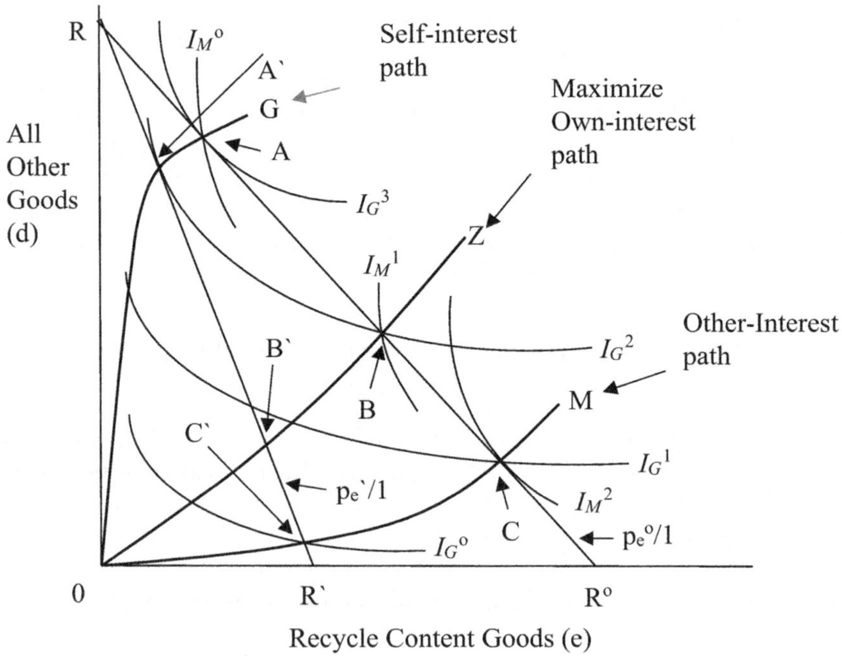

Fig. 4.1 Self-(I_G) & other (I_M)-interest indifference curves for joint and nonallocable goods: Recycle content goods (e) and all other goods (d). (Source: Author's creation)

represents the Ego-based Self-interest. Budget or income line RR^o shows various combinations of all other goods d and recycle content goods e when the price of e is p_e^o. The consumer, the person, works at maximizing Self-interest, and moves to A when the price is p_e^o. If the price of e increases to $p_e^{'}$, the new budget line is RR', with the person now maximizing Self-interest at point A'. Each person is independent of every other person, as the Market magically, invisibly evolves the price P that makes everyone (supposedly) happy.

Microeconomics teaches (and preaches) that the Self-interest path 0G is the only path, as one gains the most payoff from the limited budget, limited income, moving up and down the path as prices decrease and increase. So far, so good: It is just standard Microeconomics. It is all about (and the more the better, excessive is best) Greed on Self-interest path 0G. A consumer, every person, driven by the primal egoistic-hedonistic-greed tendency, reptilian-core at work, stays on the Self-interest path. It is the Econ at work.

Here is the kicker: Metaeconomics adds the possibility that a human also has an inherent capacity for empathy-sympathy (and, yes, even compassion) not only for own-self, but it is something we share with others. Maybe it is not so magical, invisible, after all. Yet, just like the Self-interest, it is still internalized to the Own-self, so, we represent empathy-sympathy in the set of indifference curves I_M, and refer to the set as the Empathy-based Other-interest. A person having mainly an Other-interest orientation moves along the Other-interest path 0M, going to point C when the price is p_e^o and C when the price increases to $p_e^{'}$. And, to emphasize: It is sympathy-with, as in an internalized sharing, within the Other-interest, all within the Own-self. It does not have anything directly to do with the other, per se. It is not interdependent utility. It has nothing to do with other-regarding preferences. It is about utility within the Own-self, which is the only utility one can ever know how to consider in any accurate and useful way.

Metaeconomics, then, is all about maximizing the joint Self&Other-interest represented in maximizing the Own-interest on the happiness path 0Z, which also means the emergence of some degree of compassion. And, a good economy, a good capitalism needs it. It is about being happy, not unhappy in an excessive Greed-driven pursuit of Self-interest only.

So, the first thing to be noticed is, especially as it relates to being happy: Altruism has a new meaning. Moving from A to B means some sacrifice represented in less payoff in Self-interest: We move from I_G^3 to I_G^2. Moving from C to B means some sacrifice in less payoff in Other-interest: We move from I_M^2 to I_M^1 . So, altruism, sacrifice, in each domain of interest is essential to maximizing Own-interest at point B. Altruism is inherent to maximizing Own-interest: One must sacrifice in order to maximize Own-interest. It does not please a NeoClassEcon. And, it makes one happy to sacrifice a bit. Ironic.

It explains a lot of things, resolves a lot of paradoxes, like why would a person go into a burning building to save a stranger, or, a soldier dive onto a hand grenade to save the platoon? Well, Self-interest is reduced, and even goes to 0 when the soldier or the rescuer dies. The Other-interest, however, increases dramatically, as in a hero funeral, or other respect for the act. It is easily explained with Dual Interest Theory, which embeds sacrifice. It is rational to sacrifice. The whole story makes even more sense in the context of the selfish&selfless analysis of excessive Greed: Stay tuned.

But that is only part of the story: Metaeconomics also claims that a human feels tension in the dual interest, and works to reconcile it, which is the only way to be happy. And, no, path 0Z is not the path of the Wizard of OZ, albeit the Wizard did help in the end. The help related to the Other-interest: It represented the other-virtues in the Lion wanting courage; the Tin man finding a heart, and the Strawman finding a brain to help find balance in his life. The Wizard was also helped by the elimination of the Wicked Witches of Self-interest who were in control. Dorothy and Friends eventually emerged on happiness path 0Z, because of being able to act on their shared Other-interest: Dorothy, Lion, Tinman, Strawmen and all the residents of OZ joined in celebration on path 0Z. It also took a great deal of Self-discipline, Self-control effort, each in their Own-way, to find path 0Z, the path of Market-discipline.

Metaeconomics also claims it takes a great deal of Self-discipline, or, another way to say it, Self-control, to be happy, to bring the shared Other-interest into a position of influence. Self-control takes the information from the Other-interest path 0M and uses it to temper condition and perhaps even bound the more primal tendency to being only on the Self-interest path. The other virtues need to be present in order to operate on the happy, and with virtues at work, also now a humane path 0Z.

So, what does empirical reality suggest? Well, testing over the past three to four decades points to such a joint, interdependent, nonseparable dual interest at work. It has been found especially descriptive in recycling, as we now consider. Recycling involves Self-control and Self-discipline to work out and balance the tension and conflict within the dual interest through time. Also, buying recycled content goods, and recycling in general, involves buying two goods with payoffs that cannot be allocated (internally, by the mind working with the brain) between the two interests. They are nonallocable: The mind cannot separate out the payoffs in the two domains of interest embedded, biologically, in the brain. They are joint in the dual interest. The payoffs occur jointly. Make sense? Fits your experience?

Relating Fig. 4.1 back to the metaphor of the Isles, the NeoClassEcon see only the Self-interest path. The NeoInstiEcon see mainly the Other-interest path, which represents the "institutions, emotions, social bonds, values, and a sense of morality" in the case pertaining to recycling. The Other-interest set and path (and there may be many, in that we share interests with many different groups, clubs to political parties to families, many institutions). Each set can also perhaps be considered a kind of identity, as in identifying with others who recycle, a recycle identity.

We now have the essence of Metaeconomics, on the consumption and demand side, pertaining to how a person looks at buying recycle goods or not, as represented Fig. 4.1. An important aside: The two fields of (joint) interest (or, again, utility, if we choose to measure outcomes in utils, as a Utilitarian might propose) can be incommensurable, following Etzioni (1986). Or the interests could be commensurable, with the matter an empirical question. The two sets of indifference curves can also be thought of as one being in the material dimension of Self-interest and one in the moral dimension of Other-interest. Another way to think about it, in an old paradox and debate in economics and philosophy about commensurability and incommensurability: One is in the arena of the Pushpins (the Self-interest) and the other in the arena of the poetry (the Other-interest).

We also see the possibility over time of not only inherent tension and conflict between the interests, but also of one set influencing the other set, especially the Other-interest influencing the more primal Self-interest. How? Well, again, through that Self-control, through an active will. So, we recycle (or not) because our friends do, in a shared Other-interest. But it takes Self-control, the will, the discipline to do it.

There is also the larger community, and perhaps the Government representing the community in a widely shared Other-interest in recycling, at work here. So, if the Other-interest is not expressed, that is, insufficient Self-control, perhaps failing to temper Self-interest at all, then the

Other-interest could be nudged. A community, generally through a Government agency or department, might run an advertising campaigns like the famous "Don't Mess with Texas" campaign. It substantively reduced littering by tough (Don't Mess with Us), young men in Texas (see Kalinowski, Lynne, and Johnson 2006). Also, if said nudging fails, mandates could be put in place. Government could mandate recycling. Libertarians would not be happy, or would they? Recall happiness needs a bit of sacrifice.

Intriguingly, once a recycle identity, whether nudged or mandated, is established, the person could find happiness on the Own-self path 0Z. It occurred with the young men in the Texas campaign. Also, with a recycle identity in place, it is thought that the person is now being unconsciously guided by the Invisible Hand. Recycling will occur without thinking about it. So, the magic of the Invisible Hand once again, but only after the Visible Hand has made consideration of recycling a conscious choice. And, how is it made conscious? Well, it is nudged. Or, if nudging does not work, conscious consideration is whacked into the Visible by the Big Stick of Government.

Need Another Analytical Device

We also need another analytical device to better understand the mix of satisfactory (satisficing) and optimal conditions along the alternative paths and demand curves, and the main way ethics enter the choice. It helps make even more sense of the notion of how the Invisible Hand actually starts out as a Visible Hand, which the MetaEcon see coming from a Higher Plane of Value. Said plane represents another part of the moral and ethical dimension, pertaining to the balance in Self&Other-interest. We get to the Higher Plane of value analytical machinery by first moving along a budget line RR^0 of Fig. 4.1 and tracing the relationship between the dual interests into Fig. 4.2. Notice how it is in the Self-interest to also increase the Other-interest in RA (higher valued I_G and I_M curves as we move from R to A) and in the Other-interest to increase the Self-interest in R^0C (both isocurves become higher valued in the move), in both Figs. 4.1 and 4.2. So, it is irrational to stay within either the RA or R^0C regions.

Metaeconomics gives new meaning to the "100 percent rational" proposition offered by the NeoClassEcon. Every choice between and including points A to C is rational. And, a Self-interest only choice suggested by a NeoClassEcon, which is the vertical axis in Fig. 4.1, is irrational, as one is operating in a zone RA. And, how does it become rational to

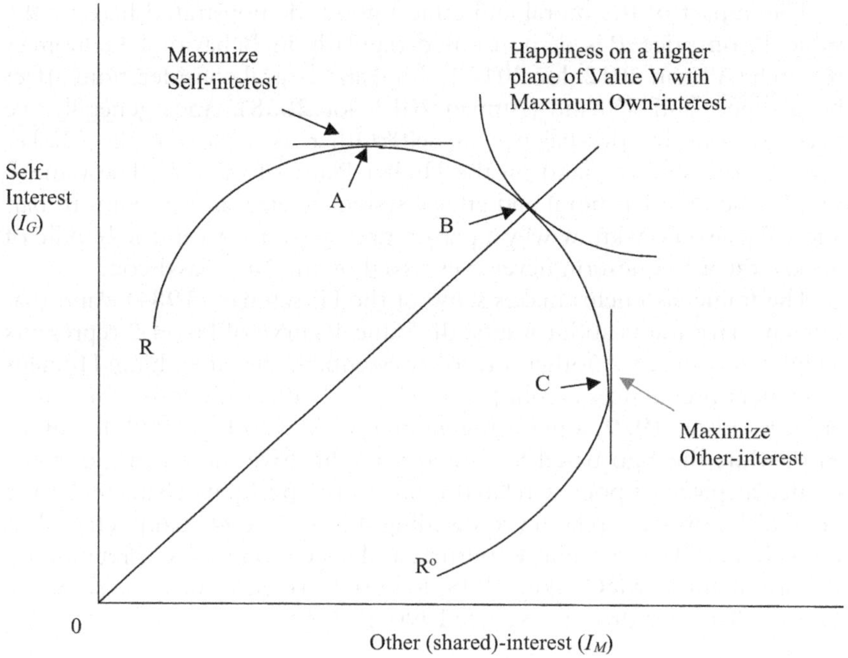

Fig. 4.2 Dual interest frontier representing balance in the joint pursuit of self- (I_G) & other (I_M)-interest in recycle content of goods (Fig. 4.1) or in conservation products (Fig. 8.1). (Source: Author's creation)

operate in A to C, bounded by the Self-interest path 0G and the Other-interest path 0M? The MetaEcon, like do the NeoInstiEcon, see rational choice arises out of a tempering and conditioning from the Value *V* in Fig. 4.2 working to influence choice in Fig. 4.1.

That is, while there are price *P* effects in the Markets for the two kinds of goods, the recycle content good *e* could also become a "moral good" of sorts. The moral dimension of the good would arise in people doing the right thing, coming out of the value *V* (going beyond mere price) indicated at point *B* in Fig. 4.2. The value *V* is a kind of indifference curve, in its own right, on the Higher Plane of value. The tangency at point B in Fig. 4.2, a Visible Hand at work, would affect what would eventually appear as the Invisible Hand affecting the relative price of good *e* relative to good *d* at some *B* in Fig. 4.1.

The impact of the moral and ethical good, demonstrated here by the value *V*, on price *P* is demonstrated regularly in Behavioral Economics research (Altman 2012, loc 2047): Moral and ethical considerations affect both supply and demand (Altman 2012, loc 2058). And, generally, we need to consider the balance in Self&Other as a part of the Market through the Visible Hand on the Higher Plane of value *V*. The value *V* reflects the broader moral and ethical system at play, as it pertains to balance. We also now know why a person prefers some mix in the bundle of goods, the why question never even asked by the NeoClassEcon.

The frame also helps makes sense of the Hirschman (1984) claim that humans have wants about wants; the value *V* curve of Fig. 4.2 represents a higher level want. Another way to say essentially the same thing: Humans have meta-preferences at a higher level, which affect the lower-level preferences (Elster 1979, a point highlighted in McCloskey 1998, loc 603). Also, while the Ego-based Self-interest might drive the reading of some particular piece of poetry, related more to the pushpins character of the poetry, the override relating to deciding if it is good or bad poetry arises on a Higher Plane of value *V* (putting a Metaeconomics interpretation on the argument in McCloskey 1998, loc 608). To help make sense of the Higher Plane, we draw on Khalil (1990, p. 266):

> Egoistic theorists … (assume) that humans can never rise above their (self) interest – humanist theorists (assume) that humans are essentially martyrs. Smith takes a different view … (that the individual) could examine the competing claims… impartially… (that the result) is not the mixture of the two (but rather) a distinct entity.

The distinct entity emerges on path 0Z, and the person arrives at point B in both Figs. 4.1 and 4.2. Metaeconomics gives analytical content to the distinct entity proposition from Khalil (1990) as arising in the joint expression of Self&Other-interest.

One can also think of a kind of resilience (after Walker and Salt 2006; Perrings 1987) with the rational zone bounded by paths 0G and 0 M and can also posit there could well be switching and vacillation within that zone, the bounded rationality zone. The zone is a kind of attractor. Also, peace (another kind of attractor) emerges among and between people when each carry similar elements in their shared Other-interest, again, resolved on the Higher Plane of value *V* in Fig. 4.2.

It is also now possible to address the paradox of price distortion. Said distortion can, ironically, and often does, lead to good outcomes, in contrast to what the NeoClassEcon claim. That is, it is often argued by the NeoClassEcon that anytime the price *P* emerging in a Market Forum (in Fig. 4.1) is influenced by *V* coming from Other Forums (in Fig. 4.2), as represented in the Administrative, Legislative and Judicial Forums in Government, it is, now, an inherently distorted price *P* . Said distorted price *P* is an inherently bad outcome. Maybe. Metaeconomics suggests, instead, that it is an empirical issue, that it could now actually be a better price *P*. It could, instead, be a doing-the-right-thing-price *P*, a *P* reflecting justice, as in a "Just *P*." Justice, a just price *P*, occurs because of being influenced by the Higher Plane of value *V* brought in to temper the economic choice.

So, Government being involved in recycling causes distortion in the price of recycle content good *e*? Probably not. Arguably, it is the price *P* from the Market that is distorted, not accurately reflecting the community value *V*.

Bottomline: Metaeconomics does not see inherent distortion from the Government. Rather it sees Other Forums operating in a community, a widely representative community (mainly made possible through Government), as often being quite legitimate. It is legitimate to influence, condition, and perhaps even bound the Market Forum. And, it goes in the other direction, too: Metaeconomics also sees the Market as legitimately influencing the community and the Government, that is, *P* also influences *V*. And, the distortion vanishes on the efficient path 0Z.

NeoClassEcon and MetaEcon Arriving at the Same Point

The only way the NeoClassEcon and MetaEcon could arrive at the same point in an analysis is if the Self-interest and Other-interest are one and the same thing, which is to say the Other-interest I_M set lies identically on top of the Self-interest I_G set of indifference curves. If so, there is only one, what seems to be a Self-interest only, albeit both interests are still there (Frisch 1965, identifies such a case in production, Fig. 14b.3, p. 273). It would also explain why Smith (1776/1789) is misrepresented: It is because Smith (1759/1790) is being ignored, as the complete overlap is not likely (albeit an empirical question) to be the case. It would be an unusual case in that most of the time people feel conflicted as between how to balance Self&Other-interest. Now, it is possible the tension has dissipated: Overlapping sets could be possible, perhaps arising from resolving the tension at some other point in time, and now identifying as a recycler. So, now, the Invisible Hand is recycling! Another way to think about it is suggested in the Hodgson (1999, p. 139) quote of La Rochefoucauld: "Virtues are swallowed up by self-interest as rivers are lost in the sea."

The virtues in the shared Other-interest can get swallowed into the Self-interest, which changes the character of the Self-interest. It is the only way that pursuing the Self-interest by itself can also be virtuous. It is the only way one could claim that Self-interest economics includes the moral and ethical dimension. Metaeconomics clarifies, however, that it also cannot just be presumed it is present in choice driven by Self-interest. Indeed, a Market composed of Self-interest-driven persons can do very bad things, presumed goodness of the Invisible Hand notwithstanding. Empirical questions.

Now, with some due credit, the NeoClassEcon may be partly right, if one is focused only on the narrow shared Other-interest of the immediate family, the household (generally presumed run by a male, as the feminist and humanist economists make clear) as the NeoClassEcon say it. With a narrow group in mind, the overlap of Other-interest with Self-interest could more easily occur. It would also explain why the larger, widely shared Other-interest represented in a Government who is to represent everyone's interest would be downplayed by the NeoClassEcon: You have heard the call, right? Minimize Government. So, implicitly, the NeoClassEcon would be giving license to only a very narrow shared Other-interest. There is no community, beyond the immediate family, the household.

To help understand it at a more personal level: Recall the conversation with my wife, for readers that are married, or, spend substantive time with any other significant other, you can perhaps identify here. Most relationships are characterized by each "I" (Self) having somewhat different interests than the shared "We" (an "Other" on common ground between the two in the relationship), with tension and conflict quite common. Why? Well, each person is faced with the need to balance the Ego and Empathy, the Self and Other driving the two interests. So, while the two people share the Other-interest I_M set, each person has their own Self-interest I_G set, with neither one lying identically on top of the shared I_M set. Yet, it is possible that a totally conflict free relationship can emerge, especially over time, with both sets moving to lie ever more identically on top of each other, perhaps describing the "soulmate." Make sense? And, if either or both are out of balance, especially with two egoists not willing to do a bit of Self-sacrifice: Divorce.

Self-Control Becomes a Key Variable

Another mistake arises in presuming unlimited Self-control. Metaeconomics, instead, points to Self-control as a kind of variable, and intertwined with Self&Other-interest. That is, the Self-interest, as noted, is likely more primal, and generally needs to be tempered, with Self-control and Self-discipline onto path 0Z, as influenced by the Other-interest. If the Self-control languishes, the movement is toward the Ego-driven Self-interest, so one will move toward or stay at *A*. In contrast, if Self-control is present, it is more likely the moral community of recycling would nudge some recycling, in the extreme moving the person to toward *C*. If the Self-control, instead, works at balance, recognizing both interests at work, the result will be a more satisfactory mix at intermediate point *B*. With Self-control, we satisfice in each domain of interest: We maximize the Own-interest in a disciplined market, not the Self-interest.

Point *B* type choices also give new meaning to the NeoClassEcon contention of 100 percent Self-control. We might now say, yes, that is possible, but the reason for it is to achieve peace of mind, and happiness, rather than to maximize Self-interest. Findings in Kalinowski, Lynne, and Johnson (2006) confirm that people who recycle operate more on path 0Z, and are happy with their choice, at locations like point *B*. Also, it is not unreasonable to expect that some at some point were internally conflicted, and perhaps even vacillated between paths 0G and 0M over time. It is quite rational to move around within that region. In addition, we now have a better way to make sense of a failure: Market-failure results when most are on path 0G. Government-failure results when most are on path 0M. Success without failure means the best balance of Market&Government, which emerges on path 0Z, which depends on Market&Government discipline.

It is now also possible to make economic sense of such claims as "unethical behavior, above the law." The law, reflecting the moral community, represents widely shared ethical behavior. It is Empathy-based. The law, whether of constitutional, legislative origins, or, especially the Common Law origins, represents what is on path OM. So, unethical behavior, operating above the law in extreme expressions of Self-interest only behaviors, is at best on path 0G, but more likely is on the vertical axis. Being above the law also means the *V* in Fig. 4.2 reflects a move to even the extreme point *R* where ironically Self-interest is even less: Violating the law can cause a loss in the overall payoff in both domains of interest.

Other-Interest Frames the Demand for Goods

To add precision to our thinking about the character of the demand for a recycle content good (e), we can consider the equation, using the form of Eq. (A.10) in Appendix A:

$$q_e^D = q_e^D\left(\kappa_e p_e, \kappa_d p_d, I_G, I_M, y\right)$$

For the reader not attuned to thinking in mathematical terms, it is just saying that the quantity of the recycle content good consumers purchase is affected by the consumer income y; price of the recycle content good p_e, the price of all other goods p_d, and, intriguingly, in contrast to a NeoClassEcon, Microeconomics rendition of demand, the outcome represented in achieving different levels of Self-interest I_G and Other-interest I_M, and balance in same on the Higher Plane of value *V*. The κ multipliers on the prices, too, bring the value *V* into play, bring ethics into play. Also, notice that both interests now have to be measurable and measured; the arguments for interest (or, for utility in Utilitarian NeoClassEcon thinking) represented in I_G and I_M do not "drop out" of the demand curve, as in the NeoClassEcon Microeconomics. The Interests or Utilities must be quantified, as Kahneman, Wakker, and Sarin (1997) argue, in the notion of "Back to Bentham."

More directly, by ignoring balance in the interests, and with only Ego playing a role, the standard Microeconomics-based demand curve only has prices and income:

$$q_e = q_e\left(p_e, p_d, y\right)$$

So, the NeoClassEcon, when they do any empirical analysis to test theory, which is not often, include variables that presume only Ego-based Self-interest, which at best gives a representation of an Amoral Demand. The moral dimension is hidden in the parameters. In addition, the NeoClassEcon presumes full Self-control, a completely self-disciplined person. So, again (sorry, but it is an important point) the person is like a Robinson Crusoe on the Isle only needing to be concerned with Self-interest, as not even Friday is about. It represents the demand of an isolated Econ, not a Human. And, as a MetaEcon would say, the extent to which we are a Human or an Econ is an empirical question that can be objectively asked and answered, with all evidence pointing to the Human.

There has been considerable research in Behavioral Economics about how the framing of the choice space has a profound influence on the choice. It has been found, for example, that the default option, like for donating organs, or joining into a retirement program at work, is generally the one chosen (Altman 2012, loc 3553). It is easily understood as a matter of what shared Other-interest is in the plan, for example, the shared Other-interest in opting into a recycle program on some path 0M in Fig. 4.1 could lead to some limited recycling on path 0Z, but the path would more likely be path 0G. If path 0 M was instead an opt-out path, that is, everyone was automatically put into a recycling program, we would likely find many people staying on path 0M (not opting out). We would likely find many more on path 0Z than on path 0G, as compared to the opt-in plan.

Focusing Only on Self-Interest as an Error in Rational Choice

It seems focusing only on Self-interest raises all manner of issues not only for the person but for all people. As Boorstein (2020) says it, in an overall concern for how to offset the tendency:

> Defined as the ability to notice suffering (in ourselves and others) and then the desire to take action to alleviate it, "compassion" has become the buzzword for an angry nation. It is increasingly being held up by neuroscientists, corporations, business schools and psychologists as a concrete, powerful health strategy—and a successful business model.

So, noticing (mindfulness) is the first step on the way to compassion, as in mindfulness→ empathy→ sympathy→ compassion, and thus being influenced by path 0M. It is only with attention to path 0M can we address the anger, with said path representing a health strategy. A successful business would operate on path 0Z, not path 0G, and certainly not the vertical axis, the angry axis. Anger needs to be tempered with empathy-sympathy driven compassion.

Actually, the essential need to temper Self-interest is documented in science, based in the Stanovich (2011, p. 99) finding that maximizing Self-interest only is a kind of error in rational thinking (leading to resentment, anger, among other things). As pointed to in the review of Stanovich by Lynne (2011, p. 35):

> The main reason this may be the case is the failure to engage in the modeling of the minds of others via simulation (i.e. a failure to empathize; see esp. Stanovich 2011, pp. 91–93), and, then, possibly restraining the self-interest. These are "mindware problems" especially in the arena of "contaminated mindware" wherein the "self" encourages only egocentric processing. The act of modeling of the minds of others (i.e. empathize) could work to temper and restrain this ego-only processing as reflected in self-interest only driven motives and choices (for a very similar argument, as reflected in metaeconomics ... and dual interest theory, see Sheeder and Lynne 2011; Czap et al. 2012). Stanovich notes this may have served a substantive role in evolution at an earlier time, but no longer works with modern social and psychological (and, economic) requirements, related to such matters as "fairness, rule-following despite context, even-handedness, sanctioning nepotism, unbiasedness, universalism, inclusiveness, contractually mandated equal treatment, and discouragement of familial, racial, and religious discrimination" (Stanovich 2011 p. 103).

The Stanovich list, starting with fairness and ending with discrimination, are all dimensions of the shared Other-interest, which potentially holds the compassion. So, consistent with the Stanovich claim, if the Other-interest is not considered, Self-interest only leads to all manner of error as represented in distortion (including anger) in the economic and community system. And, a NeoClassEcon sees any expression of the shared Other-interest as a distortion to the Market. Who has it more right? In that the error is represented in not seeing the rational path 0Z, it is likely that Metaeconomics guided testing will confirm the Stanovich contention: It is an error in the rational mind, an error in rational choice, to operate on the Self-interest path 0G.

Empirical Testing of the Recycle Question: Person as Econ or Human?

The first test is described in Kalinowski, Lynne, and Johnson (2006). In a nutshell, the research was focused on (1) explaining what drives a person to recycle or not, both now and five years from now, and (2) explaining what drives an individual to be willing to pay more for a recycle content good, looking both at the willingness to pay more, and, also, how much more. The results are displayed in Table 4.1. The behavior variable was measured to represent the Self-interest tendency, and the Jointness variable used to measure the tendency to move to path 0Z kinds of choices, as influenced by the shared Other-interest in environmental improvement through recycling. Strong support was found for Metaeconomics: Statistically significant and substantive in size coefficients were found for all the variables suggested by it.

The jointness variable is especially intriguing here, in that it points to people tempering their Self-interest, leading to doing more recycling (first two columns in Table 4.1), and being willing to pay more for goods with recycle content (last two columns in Table 4.1). Using Microeconomics would have led to including only the behavior and income variables; clearly the essence of the real drivers in recycling would have been missed, which is the Empathy-based Other-interest in enhancing environmental quality through recycling. So, again, Humans recycle, not Econs.

Recycling Is Rational

In general, unless an Other-interest favoring recycling is evolved, there will be massive Market failure to recycle, in that there is little payoff in the domain of Self-interest from recycling: So, a NeoClassEcon would conclude it is not rational to recycle. What think? A lot of us do it: Are we all irrational? In fact, the NeoClassEcon have a long list about what it means to be rational, and all participants in Markets are presumed to have the characteristics (after Altman 2012, loc 1089); "materially selfish, maximizing his or her material wealth; focuses very much on himself or herself in making decisions; maximizes profits and productivity; is a prodigious and rational calculator; is forward looking; has stable and consistent wants and desires or preferences; has willpower." Other-interest economics, and Behavioral Economics–based empirical science, puts all the presumptions in question: science&ethics at work.

Table 4.1 Orientation in joint interests toward recycling, Nebraska, 2002

Item	*Recycle now*	*Recycling in five years*	*Pay more for products made with recycled materials*	
Cumulative				
Model type	Logit	Logit	Logit	Tobit
Behavior	(0 = no; 1 = yes)	(1–5 scale)[a]	(0 = no; 1 = yes)	(0 = no; X = percent)[b]
Constant	0.1252[ns]	0.7865[c]	−1.7039[c]	−0.9903[c]
Jointness	0.0255[c]	0.0211[c]	0.0310[c]	0.0157[c]
Orientation squared	−0.0593[c]	−0.0534[c]	−0.0386[c]	−0.0180[d]
Income	0.0442[e]	0.0239[e]	0.0342[e]	0.0175[d]
Group[f]	1.245[d]	0.7059[d]	0.8863[g]	0.5077[g]
X group	−0.0490[c]	−0.2038[e]	−0.0376[e]	−0.0200[e]
Predict	80.1%[h]	13.0%[i]	64.0%[h]	45.1%/45.7%[j]
Observations				
At 0	105	–	267	267
At 1, or X	437	535	260	225
Total	542	535	527	492

Source: Kalinowski, Lynne, and Johnson (2006, Table 2.1, p. 346)

[a]Scale was 1/5 = very unlikely; 2/5 = unlikely; 3/5 = possible; 4/5 = likely; 1 = very likely. A small value of 0.05 was subtracted from each to give p, and then the logit transformation of $z = \ln[p/(1-p)]$ was applied, with the z being the dependent variable in the multiple regression

[b]Percent means like 12.5 percent more. The question asked how much more one would pay for a $5.00 product; an answer of $0.50–0.74 more is 12.5 percent more

[c]$p < 0.01$

[d]$p < 0.05$

[e]$p < 0.02$

[f]Income Group, defined as 0 for <$45,000 and 1 for > or = $45,000

[g]$p < 0.10$

[h]Percentage of right predictions

[i]R-square between observed and predicted

[j]Predicted probability of the dependent being greater than zero/actual observed frequency

[k]Probability goes from 0.15 to 0.95, so there are no "limit" observations

How does the list translate into the recycle good question, as represented in Figs. 4.1 and 4.2? First, materially selfish, maximizing only material wealth is on path 0G: Little to no recycling here. Why is that being rational?

Second, focusing on Self-interest contributes to ignoring path 0M, the path of shared Other-interest that is concerned about 1st Law reality, that is, that one cannot destroy matter or energy, so waste accumulates; again, little to no recycling. It does not seem to be rational to ignore accumulation of waste, plastic jugs in whale bellies as a case in point?

Third, maximizes profits and productivity: Figures 4.1 and 4.2 are for a consumer, but we can refer to Fig. 8.1, where the choice would put the producer on path 0G. Such a choice means little to no conservation, so little to no recycling.

Fourth, is a prodigious and rational calculator, which again is along path 0G, with little to no recycling or conservation behavior, albeit would seem quite rational to temper Self-interest to ensure long-term survival. It is quite rational to consider the shared Other-interest represented on path 0M, but Self-interest economics ignores the community. It ignores the moral community, and anything that reflects sharing with, or being influenced by, other Travelers on the Spaceship Earth. Now we are getting somewhere, about our true rationality: Metaeconomics rationality in the region between and including the paths 0G and 0M is a kind of attractor, like noted earlier. Also, intense calculation in the moral and ethical dimension is not a requirement in order to stay reasonably rational: Just do the right thing, and at least do a bit of recycling.

Fifth, is forward looking: Well, a Self-interest only styled rationality is not looking too far forward if recycling and conservation are not on the near horizon.

Sixth, has stable and consistent wants and desires or preferences: It is an intriguing feature, as Fig. 4.1 suggests the opposite, in that a person could move around, vacillate between paths 0G and 0M. It is quite rational to have unstable and inconsistent wants and desires, it being quite rational with unstable preferences, in effect, satisficing, to stay within the ellipse.

Seventh, has absolute, total willpower (how much do you have?): It takes willpower, that is, Self-control, to act on the shared Other-interest to recycle and conserve Spaceship Earth resources. There is little in the way of willpower involved in running on automatic, on the primal, excessive Greed, Self-interest path 0G. We also now see why we "rationally" head down the path predicted by Hardin (1968): The path of tragedy is path 0G, close to, if not the vertical axis, because Econs move to tragedy with Self-interest only.

Recall that even studying NeoClassEcon (it happened to me) reinforces and perhaps even creates Econs (I became one, for a while, lasting through passing my qualifying exams, and, then, later, when I had to adopt the frame of an Econ in order to be promoted in a NeoClassEcon dominated Department at the University). It is to say: People who choose to study Neoclassical Economics may not be any more Selfish than anyone else before they choose the field, but they become ever more Selfish the longer they study it (again, sorry to point back, but see Frank 2004; for a review, see Lynne 2008); students under the influence of the NeoClassEcon become the Econ, seemingly denying the fact they are really Human. I recall one such colleague, who was an exacting Econ at work, and, walking with him, one could observe an amazing transformation to a Human the moment he exited the University occupied by the NeoClassEcon. Multiple-selves displayed: Intriguing, indeed.

The Humans in the recycle good survey did not choose path 0G: Instead, they were choosing path 0Z. Humans buying a mix of not recycle and recycle content goods would be considered "unconventional," "not smart," "not rational" in the frame of Microeconomics. Buying on path 0Z reflects an error, a bias, an inaccurate heuristic. In contrast, Metaeconomics suggests it is a smart, rational behavior, a good and humane heuristic, a truly Rational Mind at work, on path 0Z. It certainly is not irrational. As Altman (2012, loc 1139) says it, "Behavioral and institutional assumptions matter big time and … conventional (Self-interest only) economics gets it wrong, also big time."

Metaeconomics Posits Switching and Re-balancing in Recycling Choices

The empirical findings also highlight the fact that traditional framing represented in Microeconomics suggest that when we go to the store we would always purchase mainly goods without recycle content staying on path 0G; as is now clear, there is no recognized payoff from doing the right thing as represented in the Other-interest domain. Ever done the wrong thing? I have. Metaeconomics could also admit the right thing might not prevail. We might switch. After feeling guilty about not paying more attention to the shared Other-interest in recycling during some shopping trip, one may instead buy mainly goods with recycle content *e* on the next trip. We might even over-react on path 0M. Over time,

Metaeconomics would suggest that the tension is eventually settled, satisficing across the conflicted tendencies, along the path 0Z.

In fact, the context represented in the Other-interest may also change over time, or even from store to store: Perhaps the store we are shopping in appeals to many who belong to the Sierra Club, acquaintances of ours, who favor recycle content goods *e*, which then may affect our purchase in that context. And, if one is committed to and feeling part of that particular Sierra Club, we may buy at point *C*, such that we can have good dinner conversation with our Sierra club friends. On some other day, or at some other time or place, we may still respond to that Other-interest, but less so, choosing a different point *B*. It is all quite rational, even though not appearing so to the NeoClassEcon, who would say that one always, unequivocally, in stable preferences, will always choose *A*, with minimal recycling, as it does not pay. So, to a NeoClassEcon, recycling, and an array of Other-interest related choices like organ donation, blood donation, and, again, the dramatic behaviors, like running into a burning building to save a stranger or a soldier diving onto a live grenade to save the platoon, are all irrational. Yet, real people regularly do such things: Are they all irrational? Or, the story goes, in the flawed attempt to save Self-interest only rationality, the instant the soldier blows Own-self to pieces the Self-interest is maximized. Really?

Dynamic Interdependence as Joint Interests Evolve in Recycling Choices

The interplay within a dual interest also leads to the potential for a kind of dynamic interdependence in preferences. It is the case because we are truly interdependent one with the other, with prices *P* carrying a shared moral and ethical element in the value *V*, the notion of the moral dimension in Etzioni (1988). The *V* influences *P*, in a dynamic way. At the same time, the relative prices *P* of the goods have, over time, an influence on the character of the moral dimension *V* coming from the Empathy with the environment, and, thus, also the Empathy with others with whom we share the environment, share Spaceship Earth. So, it is not nonsense to do rational calculations in the moral dimension, and, as a result, choose to recycle. It is also now clear that an overemphasis on the arithmetic and the calculation along the Self-interest path 0G leaves out much that is important.

The emotions, the feelings, the affective (sometimes put into form through Government, for example, through the US Environmental Protection Agency reflecting the value *V*, nudging as long as it works, and mandating, regulating, and controlling when it does not) all condition and influence the recycling we do. Value *V* also influences the economic efficiency as between the right amounts and prices *P* of good *d* and good *e* that are sold in the Markets. So, we decide that efficiency has an affective, Empathy-based moral dimension while the moral has an efficiency dimension: The dichotomy has been fused. The Isles of Fig. 3.1 are now fused.

Metaeconomics for Most Every Case, Microeconomics for Some

Ok, so, are you convinced? A dual interest arises in virtually every consumption good? So, a person buys a cell phone: Self-interest in having a phone to deal with day-to-day issues like calling the car dealer for an oil change but also serving the Other-interest on Instagram with friends. Well, how about buying steak at the grocery story: Clearly a Self-interest in the protein it provides, but it also plays a role in serving the Other-interest in having a barbeque in the back yard with good friends. Yet, maybe the single interest of Microeconomics works for something very personal, like a toothbrush. Even here, while the Self-interest in keeping away decay and having healthy gums dominates, there is also a shared Other-interest in good breath around your friends. Lower dental bills for the family are also part of the shared Other-interest. It is all in the framing, and, then, the empirical evidence one searches for, and, does or does not find. A MetaEcon sees shared Other-interest, and, thus, the real possibility of jointness and interdependence in virtually every good.

The approach is: Posit Self-interest only, in effect setting the null to make Microeconomics the default. Look for Other-interest. If one finds it in a robust empirical test, including both (1) statistical significance and, most importantly, (2) the extent to which it matters, in absolute quantitative magnitude (looking for large coefficients, relatively speaking), suggest a dual interest is at work. If not, nothing is lost: Still have the Microeconomics intact. Empirical questions.

Kinds of Metaeconomics

As has now been said perhaps too many times: Metaeconomics refers to a situation of nonallocable inputs and/or goods, leading to jointness, non-separability, and interdependence within demand and supply, as well as between demand and supply. It also refers to the interplay of price *P* emerging in the Market Forum and the value *V* emerging in Other Forums. The Other Forums are in the community in general, and in the (if good) Government who represents it. It especially works to bring the moral and ethical dimension back into the formal structure. Doing so leads to a dual interest theory. It is a formal, mathematical, and graphics-based analytical engine of Metaeconomics, which puts the moral and ethical front and center. So, it is also empirical, focused especially on science-based measurement of economic phenomenon. It is about science&ethics, integrated.

Yet, there are other versions of Metaeconomics out there (Google it: The version herein does show, but it is not the only one; Google "Metaeconomics Empathy" and you will find the one in this Book: Empathy distinguishes it from the rest), none of which has the formal structure developed here. So, I regress a bit, to clarify how the formal and mathematical Metaeconomics relates to other uses of the term through time.

As Buracas (2016, p. 16) points out, the term Metaeconomics has been used to refer to the methodology of economics; to describe a system of higher logical order for economic research; to frame the study of the philosophical or moral foundations of sustainable economics; and to describe a meta-system approach to organizational decisions. It is also sometimes used to market consultancy services, focusing on more integrative kinds of approaches especially on broader Spaceship Earth issues, with several firms "providing advisory and consultancy services in environmental policy analysis (asset valuation, resource efficiency, climate change mitigation, structural adjustment…)."

Both Becchio (2009) and Buracas (2004, 2016) claim the notion of Metaeconomics goes back to Karl Menger, a mathematician in Vienna in the 1930s. Becchio (2009, p.7) points to how Menger was a supporter of the "Hilbertian program on economic theory," which Menger referred to as applying a kind of Metaeconomics, which followed the "philosophical framework of… the neoclassical approach." Sorry to bring it up again, but the aim was to free economics from ethics, and thus from logical mistakes, by applying a "metamathematical model" to economic theory (Becchio 2009, p. 7). It also meant freeing economics of all consideration of the shared Other-interest, as ethics arise therein. In effect, it freed it from all the other social sciences, and philosophy (Adam Smith would not be happy), which are all more attuned to moral and ethical considerations. Menger perhaps did it just on practical grounds: He believed one could not bring the soft notion of ethics, the moral dimension, into mathematical representations. The MetaEcon disagree.

It actually started quite some time before Menger: There was a particularly sharp confrontation between what were to become the modern day NeoClassEcon, NeoInstiEcon, and SocioEcon, at the meeting of the American Economic Association in 1894. Again (sorry, as alluded to earlier, but it is really important): It was declared: "Sociologists have no right to stake off for themselves a portion of social science without the consent of the economists" (Swedberg 1990, p. 10). It was driven in part, perhaps mainly, by what we might call Physics-Envy: Academic physicists had more status at the universities of the day, because of being considered a hard science. The group that would evolve into the NeoClassEcon did not want to be associated with the imprecision, messiness of social science and ethics, and wanted to create a mathematical science on par with physics. Menger, in 1934, is simply reinforcing, working to refine, and helping to justify the path started by what would become the NeoClassEcon in that 1894 meeting. NeoClassEcon is still on the path: science&ethics have been separated, into science (to the extent NeoClassEcon is being tested, and that is Not Much) and ethics, with the latter set off to the side.

As demonstrated in Figs. 4.1 and 4.2 (and in the Appendix), we have used the term Metaeconomics in quite a different way, in part to mean the essence of economics, the Meta meaning self-referential (Merriam-Webster), as originally conceived, at least going back to Smith (1759/1790, 1776/1789). The essence of economics is the moral and ethical dimension, as moral philosopher Adam Smith well understood.

Parkinson has also proposed, under the banner of Metaeconomics, but he favors Metanomics, "for a paradigm shift in the substance, rather than the form of economics, a move which will, paradoxically, take economics back to its origin in the field of moral philosophy" (https://www.metaeconomics.co.uk/metaeconomics.html). We generally agree, but in contrast to Parkinson, we believe the moral and ethical dimension can also be represented in mathematical characterizations, as demonstrated in the Appendix. Also, in contrast to Parkinson, Metaeconomics does not reflect paradigm shift. Instead, Metaeconomics builds on what has gone before, represented in literally thousands of journal papers and books represented in both Neoclassical and Neoinstitutional Economics. Metaeconomics works to take the best ideas from same, including the precise mathematical versions of it.

Rather than working toward a paradigm shift, we do an integration, in some ways a re-integration, especially including the empirical findings in behavioral science, as we work to represent the moral and ethical dimension in modern economics, as Smith (1776/1789) & Smith (1759/1790) originally intended. We also propose to build Metaeconomics on an empirical, scientific base of how the human brain and mind work, rather than on ideology about how it might work.

We have also used Metaeconomics at times in a critical manner. As one reviewer of the book claimed, we sound critical of Neoclassical Economics. It is true that the MetaEcon have been critical, because the NeoClassEcon leave out consideration of the shared Other-interest, the moral and ethical side of the economy. The term Meta is often "used with the name of a discipline to designate a new but related discipline designed to deal critically with the original one" (Merriam-Webster). It is true: The MetaEcon have especially been critical of the Neoclassical-based Microeconomics. The MetaEcon critique, however, has always been consistent with the Leijonhufvud (2004) contention: "Instead of looking for an alternative to replace it, we should try to imagine an economic theory to transcend its limitations...." Metaeconomics is not designed to replace Neoclassical and/or Neoinstitutional Economics, but rather to "transcend... limitations" to "go beyond, transform it (Merriam-Webster)," through an integration of the best ideas from the older traditions. It does so by drawing on the empirical reality of Behavioral Economics (and the many other newer behavioral and neurosciences).

Intriguingly, there is also substantive overlap with the sustainability economics literature, which we have made clear in Hayes and Lynne (2004, 2013). As Buracas (2016) notes, a similar notion, meta-economics, is used in Schumacher (1973), which also sees thermodynamic limits and the role of the moral dimension in achieving sustainability. Like Schumacher's meta-economics, Metaeconomics works to draw the best from a variety of disciplines into the integration, which is essential to finding a more sustainable path, very much in the spirit of Consilience (Wilson 1998). We also see how Metaeconomics could be used to guide all manner of consulting and advice from real world firms: A consulting firm (e.g., Meta Economics Consulting Group, Economic Intelligence Consulting 2019; Metaeconomics Asesores S.L. 2019) that saw the inherent need for bringing the moral and ethical dimension back into the way Market&Government (and, both can easily go off-track when Ego-based Self-interest takes over) operates could be extremely helpful (and likely quite profitable) in helping build a truly sustainable, good capitalism. It is especially essential if the firm deals with environmental and natural resources, that is, Spaceship Earth issues. Environmental framing sees Empathy as essential (again, see Brown et al. 2019).

Criticisms of Metaeconomics and Response

The main criticism is framed by the long-term conversation and debate about single versus multiple utility frameworks, in that the Dual Interest Theory of Metaeconomics might be considered consistent with dual utility. Neoclassical Economics, with Utilitarian philosophy in the background, has historically argued there is only one utility, in that even if other utilities exist, each would be mediated into a simple, one-dimensional utility (Brennan 1989, 1993). Proposals like that of Etzioni (1986) calling for recognizing at least two utilities are rejected. So, by focusing all attention on the pleasure utility, and that everything a human ever does is about pleasure, the moral utility is viewed as redundant if not irrelevant: People simply mediate everything into the utils of pleasure. Egoism-hedonism, perhaps even narcissism, anyone? The Khalil (1990, 1997, 1998) contention of material and symbolic utility would also be denied. Humanistic Economics, such as represented in Lutz (1993), also gains no traction. In contrast, behavioral economists like Tomer (2017, esp. p. 145) argue that Dual Motive/Dual Interest Theory, seeing dual utility, too, could be an important component of a Humanistic Economics, which is needed to supplement if not replace the Neoclassical Economics.

Arguably, the NeoClassEcon frame on single utility may also, then, explain why InstiEcon is deemed largely redundant. The concern for the moral dimension is simply mediated into the pleasure utility, so why do we need the NeoInstiEcon? Ego-based, hedonistic-driven choices are at work: It is all about pleasure, and not about the moral. We might imagine it is possible for the other virtues to be embedded in, identical with, the Self-interest: Invisible Hand, again.

If so, the virtues related to doing-the-right thing could influence the Self-interest, in theory, making it inherently Good. Then, again, maybe not. Metaeconomics would suggest the matter is empirical. And, keeping both Self-interest (pleasure) and shared Other-interest (moral) in sight is essential in order to make sense of what is ongoing in both consumption and production processes, to better ensure the choices are moral and ethical. It is about the Visible Hand. It is about looking especially to the moral and ethical dimension in the Visible Hand, and not leaving it entirely to an Invisible Hand that may or may not result in a virtuous Self-interest.

Power of the Formalized Mathematical Metaeconomics

Like Microeconomics, one can do Metaeconomics using more formal models, as represented in the mathematical metaeconomics in the Appendix. In fact, that formal modeling has influenced and guided the nature of the empirical testing of Metaeconomics going back to the mid–1990s. Why would one want to do so? Well, it potentially contributes to the precision already represented in carefully selected (yes, paying attention to their roots, origins, too) words and phrases, and helps immensely in subjecting propositions to empirical test. It helps in building scientific substance to both the framework and the theory. It is entirely plausible that at some time in the future, the impressive structure and rigor of Microeconomics will also emerge in Metaeconomics: The core, the starting point, is in the Appendix.

References

Altman, M. 2012. *Behavioral Economics for Dummies.* Kindle ed. Mississauga: John Wiley and Sons Canada, Ltd.

Becchio, Giandomenica. 2009. A Historical Note on the Original Meaning of Metaeconomics. *Intellectual Economics* 1 (5): 7–11.

Boorstein, Michelle. 2020. In an Angry America, a New Solution Emerges: Compassion. Religion, *Washington Post* (Washington, DC), January 30. Digital.

Brennan, Timothy J. 1989. A Methodological Assessment of Multiple Utility Frameworks. *Economics and Philosophy* 5 (2): 189–208.

———. 1993. The Futility of Multiple Utility. *Economics and Philosophy* 9 (1): 155–164.

Brown, K., W.N. Adger, P. Devine-Wright, J.M. Anderies, S. Barr, F. Bousquet, C. Butler, L. Evans, N. Marshall, and T. Quinn. 2019. Empathy, Place and Identity Interactions for Sustainability. *Global Environmental Change* 56: 11–17.

Buracas, Antanas. 2004. On Paradigm of Metaeconomics: Essence and Sense. *Management of Organizations: Systematic Research* 54: 1–12.

———. 2016. On Metaeconomics Consensus in Global Management. *Research in Economics and Management* 1 (1): 15–22.

Czap, N.V., H.J. Czap, M. Khachaturyan, G.D. Lynne, and M.E. Burbach. 2012. Walking in the Shoes of Others: Experimental Testing of Dual Interest and Empathy in Environmental Choice. *Journal of Socio-Economics* 41 (5): 642–653.

Economic Intelligence Consulting. 2019. http://www.metaeconomics.org/

Elster, J. 1979. *Ulysses and the Sirens: Studies in Rationality and Irrationality*. 1993rd ed. New York: Cambridge University Press.

Etzioni, A. 1986. The Case for a Multiple Utility Conception. *Economics and Philosophy* 2: 159–183.

———. 1988. *The Moral Dimension: Toward a New Economics*. New York: Free Press.

Frank, R.H. 2004. *What Price the Moral High Ground? Ethical Dilemmas in Competitive Environments*. Princeton: Princeton University Press.

Frisch, Ragnar. 1965. *Theory of Production*. Chicago: Rand McNally and Company.

Hardin, G. 1968. The Tragedy of the Commons. *Science* 162 (3859): 1243–1248.

Hayes, W.M., and G.D. Lynne. 2004. Towards a Centerpiece for Ecological Economics. *Ecological Economics* 49 (3): 287–301.

———. 2013. The Evolution of Ego and Empathy: Progress in Forming the Centerpiece for Ecological Economic Theory. In *Building a Green Economy: Perspectives from Ecological Economics*, ed. Robert B. Richardson, 107–118. East Lansing: Michigan State University Press.

Hirschman, Albert. 1984. Against Parsimony: Three Easy Ways of Complicating Some Categories of Economic Discourse. *American Economic Review* 74 (May): 89–96.

Hodgson, G. 1999. *Evolution and Economics: On Evolutionary Economics and the Evolution of Economics*. North Hampton: Edward Elgar.

Kahneman, D., P. Wakker, and R. Sarin. 1997. Back to Bentham? Explorations in Experienced Utility. *Quarterly Journal of Economics* 112: 375–405.

Kalinowski, C.M., G.D. Lynne, and B. Johnson. 2006. Recycling as a Reflection of Balanced Self-Interest: A Test of the Metaeconomics Approach. *Environment and Behavior* 38 (3): 333–355.

Khalil, E.L. 1990. Beyond Self-Interest and Altruism. *Economics and Philosophy* 6 (October): 255–273.

———. 1997. Etzioni Versus Becker: Do Moral Sentiments Differ from Ordinary Tastes? *De Economist* 145: 491–520.

———. 1998. Interests and Commitments: Replies to Etzioni, Dolfsma, and Van Staveren. *De Economist* 146: 613–618.

Leijonhufvud, A. 2004. The Trento Summer School: Adaptive Economic Dynamics. In *Economics Lab: An Intensive Course in Experimental Economics*, ed. Daniel Friedman and Alessandra Cassar, 5–11. New York: Routledge.

Lutz, Mark A. 1993. The Utility of Multiple Utility: A Comment on Brennan. *Economics and Philosophy* 9 (1): 145–154.

Lynne, G. D. Review of Frank, R.H. 2004. What Price the Moral High Ground? Ethical Dilemmas in Competitive Environments (203 pp). Princeton: Princeton University Press. In *Journal of Socio-Economics* 37 (2008): 1287–1291

Lynne, G.D. 2011. Review of Stanovich, K.E. Rationality and the Reflective Mind. New York: Oxford University Press. *Journal of Behavioral and Experimental Economics* 53 (2014): 34–35.

McCloskey, D. N. 1998. *The Rhetoric of Economics (Rhetoric of the Human Sciences)* (Second Ed. (Kindle)). Madison: University of Wisconsin Press.

Metanomics. https://www.metaeconomics.co.uk/metaeconomics.html. Accessed 23 Mar 2020.

Perrings, C. 1987. *Economy and Environment: A Theoretical Essay on the Interdependence of Economic and Environmental Systems.* Cambridge, MA: Cambridge University Press.

Schumacher, E.F. 1973. *Small Is Beautiful: A Study of Economics as If People Mattered.* London: Blond and Briggs.

Sheeder, R.J., and G.D. Lynne. 2011. Empathy Conditioned Conservation: Walking in the Shoes of Others as a Conservation Farmer. *Land Economics* 87 (3): 433–452.

Shrestha, Prabhakar. 2014. Comparative Study of Understanding Recycling Behavior of University Students. Doctor of Philosophy, University of Nebraska-Lincoln.

Shrestha, P., and Lynne, G. D. 2011. Sustainable Practices Like Recycling: Could Colleges and Universities Be Role Models? August 17. Department of Agricultural Economics, University of Nebraska-Lincoln, Lincoln.

Smith, A. 1759/1790. *The Theory of Moral Sentiments*, ed. D.D. and A.L. Macfie Raphael. Indianapolis: Liberty Fund, Inc.

———. 1776/1789. *An Inquiry into the Nature and Causes of the Wealth of Nations*, ed. E. Cannan. New York: Random House.

Stanovich, K.E. 2011. *Rationality and the Reflective Mind.* New York: Oxford University Press.

Swedberg, Richard. 1990. *Economics and Sociology: Redefining Their Boundaries, Conversations with Economists and Sociologists.* Princeton: Princeton University Press.

Tomer, John F. 2017. *Advanced Introduction to Behavioral Economics.* North Hampton: Elgar.

Walker, B., and D. Salt. 2006. *Resilience Thinking: Sustaining Ecosystems and People in a Changing World.* Washington, DC: Island Press.

Wilson, E.O. 1998. *Consilience: The Unity of Knowledge.* New York: Alfred A. Knopf.

CHAPTER 5

Metaeconomics as Behavioral Economics and the Focus on Happiness

As is now clear, Metaeconomics draws heavily upon Behavioral Economics. We have already alluded to many of the connections in examining and comparing the two kinds of economics in Table 2.1, drawing especially on Altman (2012). We now turn to relating Metaeconomics to Behavioral Economics at a broader scale, drawing on Tomer (2017a). Neoclassical Economics uses Microeconomics (and, as Tomer 2017a, pp. 102–103 argues, New Classical Macroeconomics), and Neoinstitutional Economics is largely atheoretical, that is, no standard framework or theory used in the field. We show here how Behavioral Economics more specifically relates to, and could use, the Dual Interest Theory from Metaeconomics.

Metaeconomics is also a close relative of Buddhist Economics, by seeing jointness and interdependence among all persons, and, between each person and nature, the Spaceship Earth System: As Brown (2017, p. 2) says it: "In Buddhist economics, people are interdependent with one another and with Nature, so each person's well-being is measured by how well everyone and the environment are functioning with the goal of minimizing suffering for people and the planet." So, like Metaeconomics, Buddhist Economics is also about bringing empathy, and, then, through sympathy, potentially bringing compassion into affecting economic choice, as all are essential to addressing the interdependence. And, all people are interdependent with each other, and with other Travelers on the Spaceship Earth. Both frames are about the essential role of finding balance in order to achieve happiness. Also, see Tomer (2017b), where

G. D. Lynne, *Metaeconomics*, Palgrave Advances in Behavioral Economics, https://doi.org/10.1007/978-3-030-50601-8_5

Buddhist Economics framing, especially in seeing the role for empathy and compassion essential for addressing interdependence, is viewed as playing a key role in avoiding the tragedy of the commons.

Tomer (2017a) delineates the main strands of Behavioral Economics as follows *(relationship to Metaeconomics in italics):*

1. Herbert Simon and Bounded Rationality: "... investigating the degree to which decision-making is rational and self-interested... replace the motivational assumptions of NC economics *(Neoclassical Economics)* with more accurate assumptions... humans have to learn how to make decisions in the real world by employing simplifications, finding new data, adjusting aspirations, developing improved decision-making processes, resolving uncertainty ... find ways to decide and act that are sufficient, not optimal... focused... on individual decision-making... conception of individual decision making involved a significant role for social influences on the individual in and outside organizations" (Tomer 2017a, pp. 13–14).

Bounded rationality is given substantive meaning as the area in Fig. 4.1: Rationality is bounded by an orientation to Self-interest only on path 0G and an orientation to Other-interest only on path 0M. As made clear in Fig. 4.2, it is irrational to be outside the bounded region, such as in area RA or R°C. It is also clear that there are many satisfactory (satisficing) points within the rational region, and a best choice at point B, albeit no simple way to find it. Lots of uncertainty, here. Also, the choice is the result of social influence, represented in the Other (shared with others)-interest on path 0M; yet, we keep the notion that it is still about individualism, individual choice, individual decision making, but a choice with a joint outcome in the dual interest. Choices cannot be separated out, made independent, but rather are interdependent between the Self&Other-interest.

2. George Katona: "... emphasized psychology... interested in understanding consumer behavior and the behavior of the macroeconomy... emphasis on empirical observation of behavior... use of surveys, often involving interviews, to learn about attitudes, aspirations, expectations, optimism/pessimism, social learning/cognition, habituation, and stereotypes... interdisciplinary" (Tomer 2017a, pp. 14–15).

Metaeconomics grew out of tests using data from surveys and focus groups, interviews regarding what motivated soil and water conservation decisions by farmers, and recycling behavior of consumers. The first paper published, as we started down the path of what would become Metaeconomics was based on a farmer survey, pertaining to Attitudes and Farmer Conservation Behavior (Lynne, Shonkwiler, and Rola, 1988): The survey data used to estimate the econometric model resulting in demonstrating that only 15–20 percent of the variation in conservation decisions was explained by Neoclassical Economics. Also, the attitude measurements came from approaches developed in Social Psychology, making the approach quite empirical and interdisciplinary, and showed how the methods for gaging attitudes was a way to in effect measure utility, or, at least a proxy for it. The path from a low- to a higher-level theory of Metaeconomics was paved by surveys, interviews, focus groups, and, eventually, data collected in an experimental and behavioral laboratory setting. The latter also included more than just "captured" university students, inviting participation from the general public in the experiments. Metaeconomics is a reality-based, science-based economics.

3. Harvey Leibenstein and X-Efficiency (XE) Theory: "... develop a conceptual framework for understanding why less than optimal internal efficiency (X-inefficiency) is the usual state of affairs in firms... questioning the rationality assumption, particularly the idea that people maximize... variables in XE theory are generally quantitative ones, and the theory is in principle testable... generally use graphs to depict the essential theoretical relationships... present... novel behavioral ideas in a language familiar to neoclassical economists... has an interdisciplinary element but it is not fully integrated with social science disciplines like psychology and sociology...focuses very much on the individual, an individual who is self-interested, but generally not fully rational...(rather is) constrained by commitments, social obligations, conventions, identifications, and attitudes about cooperation...(individual has) achievement need, contaminating emotion, and motivation/enthusiasm affected by the degree of bureaucracy" (Tomer 2017a, pp. 15–16).

X-Efficiency is about a production process, within a firm, like examined in Fig. 8.1. Importantly, the sufficient, satisfactory point B is interior to the possibility frontier on which only Self-interest path 0G products would arise; the internal efficiency of the firm is, thus, constrained and otherwise affected by matters outside the firm. Said matters are represented in the Other-interest in commitments, social obligations, conventions, identifications, and the felt need to cooperate with others to achieve the shared interests. As Altman (2012, loc 615) points out, even such things as whether the workers feel they are being treated fairly in their compensation packages, or working conditions (things included in the shared Other-interest) also affect both X-efficiency and efficiency relative to wages. And, while bureaucracy has not heretofore been considered in Metaeconomics, clearly it could be so considered, as bureaucracy pertains to perhaps a burdensome Other-interest that pulls the firm too far from the Self-interest path 0G, with too much of a bureaucratic orientation on path 0M. Yet, Metaeconomics also allows for the possibility of maximization as associated with least cost use of inputs, which occurs at point B on path 0Z, but now X-efficiency involves balance in the two outcomes, the two interests, and a bit of sacrifice in each domain of interest.

4. Psychological Economics: "… focuses…on the cognitive functioning of the human mind and why people are prone to make predictable errors in their judgments and decision-making… focuses on smaller decisions and on less complex situations in order to isolate specific types of human cognitive bias… empirical research often takes place in laboratory settings…(findings of) unrealistic optimism…strong tendency to go along with the status quo or default option…systematic departure from the economically rational decision-making behavior…the core of Neoclassical Economic assumptions of self-interest, rationality, and self-control (will power) are challenged… (yet, the overall approach is) to modify one or two assumptions (in Neoclassical Economic) theory in the direction of greater psychological realism…documenting how human behavior typically violates the patterns of behavior predicted by Neoclassical Economics' subjective expected utility model… full range of empirical methods of Neoclassical Economics as well as laboratory and field experimentation, use of field data, computer simulation, surveys, and even brain scans…much less individualistic…recognize that behavior may not be self-interested or strictly rational… recognize important social influences on individual decision making" (Tomer 2017a, pp. 16–18).

As noted, Metaeconomics grew out of using a full range of empirical methods, especially using field data and surveys, with econometric analysis of said real data showing failure in Neoclassical Economics propositions, the kind leading in some cases to massive Market-failure. Using said propositions contributes to a Tragedy of the Commons scale of failure, as in not dealing with downstream water quality effects from using chemicals in agricultural fields, or not addressing the capacity of the atmosphere to hold greenhouse gases. Continued findings of failure to bring about conservation behavior were found after progressing to collecting data in controlled laboratory settings. Not only do the core assumptions simply not hold, the theory predicts badly. In reality, people pursue Dual Interest, not just Self-interest; they satisfice in each domain of interest, rather than maximize exclusively in either domain, which is deemed not rational in Neoclassical Economics; and Self-control is the key to understanding how the Other-interest tempers, influences (or not) the Self-interest. Admittedly, the testing of Metaeconomics has focused on relatively small, micro decisions, like whether to use drip irrigation to save water or to apply minimum tillage to save soil, or to recycle or to purchase a recycle content consumer good. Metaeconomics-based testing needs to be taken to the larger context, to macroeconomic type questions.

5. Richard Nelson, Sidney Winter, and Evolutionary Theory: "...borrows the evolutionary idea from biology, especially Darwin's notion of natural selection involving differential rates of survival ... focus on firms' regular, predictable behavioral patterns ... routines ... analogous to genes in that the better ones are selected due to the survival and prospering forms containing these (genes) ... compatible with the hypothesis of an industry lifecycle ... many applications to and implications for understanding technological change processes ... while human behavior frequently conforms to regular patterns or routines, humans generally do not behave in a maximizing way...very compatible with concepts in the field of organizational behavior... strongly interdisciplinary...modern organizational theory, business strategy, business history, and cognitive psychology" (Tomer 2017a, pp. 19–20).

The current version of Metaeconomics is short on evolutionary dynamics; it relies on comparative statics much like Neoclassical Microeconomics. Yet, it does suggest a potential dynamic within the dual interest. It would be especially powerful in helping examine the interaction among contentious firms. Metaeconomics suggests the nature of that interaction evolves out of the evolution of the Other (shared with other firms)-interest. An evolutionary moral and ethical community shared by the firms would ebb and flow, perhaps crash and reaffirm itself (again, consistent with notions in resilience theory, see Walker and Salt 2006*) through time. Theories in organizational behavior, and ways to measure the key variables, would help in giving empirical content to the Other-interest at work in an industry. Also, Metaeconomics is interdisciplinary, even with Evolutionary Biology, e.g. crossing over with the strand in seeing the importance of Darwinian ideas about the organism&ecosystem, survival of the fittest individual fittest group, as a key to understanding firm industry, Self&Other-interest. It is likely, albeit an empirical question, that both the fittest individual and the fittest group both need balance in the Self&Other-interest. Metaeconomics also draws heavily upon cognitive psychology, especially in the notion of the interplay of Child&Parent, Me&We Ich&Du, Self&Other, all representing the Ego&Empathy balance in the brain and mind, with the Adult bringing the Self-control, seeing the jointness and seeking the balance.*

Tomer (2017a, p. 21) also distinguishes the "old Behavioral Economics (BE)" and the "new BE." He sees everything other than some more recent applications of Psychological Economics as of the "old" variety. A MetaEcon would add the behavioral parts of Neoinstitutional Economics, too, as part of the "old" framing. So, what is the "new Behavioral Economics?"

Tomer sees new Behavioral Economics as that tightly tied to Neoclassical Economics, involving mainly empirical attention to base assumptions, like examining utility or profit maximization. There is, within the new Behavioral Economics, an insistence, too, on the Self-interest as the only driver of choice. Metaeconomics would also suggest adding to the list of new Behavioral Economics the work of such prominent experimental economists as Vernon Smith (see his Nobel Lecture, Smith 2003, to understand the point). His paper "The Two Faces of Adam Smith" (Smith 1998), by seeing only Self-interest, misses the point that Adam Smith really saw two interests at work: Adam Smith did not have two faces. The contention vanishes when framed in Metaeconomics. So, joining with Tomer (2017a), Metaeconomics is also more firmly connected with old than with the new Behavioral Economics.

Kahneman (2011) is also helpful, here, in thinking about the old Behavioral Economics. Applying the two systems he identifies, the affective, emotional undergirding of both the Self-interest path 0G and Other-interest path 0M arises out of System 1, the "fast thinking" part of the brain. We just react, and do things. The cognitive, "slow thinking" system

2 part (again, Kahneman 2011) then resolves the path 0G and path 0M on path 0Z, being thoughtful about that resolution.

Stanovich (2011) takes it further, breaking the slow thinking system 2 down into the algorithmic mind (the one that does the mathematics in the Appendix) and the rational mind (the one that actually does the resolution, and, with sufficient Self-control, picks some point B on the happiness path 0Z). In a nutshell, using the child–adult–parent frame, which is perhaps more intuitive: The algorithmic mind part of the adult works at intelligent consideration (Intelligence Quotient/IQ), and the rational mind part of the adult works at being the controller and balancer (Rational Quotient/RQ), with the goal of integrating across the Child&Parent, which parallels the Self&Other tendencies. The adaptive child gives into the critical parent. The free child works best with the nurturing parent, bringing about things like innovation in agriculture (see Lynne 2002). So, there are several subselves at work.

In other easy terms, in the Ego-based domain of Self-interest, we find the adaptive and free child; in the Empathy-based domain of Other-interest, we find the critical parent and the nurturing parent; in the adult section, we find the algorithmic mind and the rational mind, the latter being the controller, manager, and balancer, the one (hopefully, if rational) making a good decision. It means at least six sub-selves. Again, important reminder here: Research has shown that most people see several sub-selves, so, another way to think of our experience as a human has to engage in *Managing Your Mind* (Butler and Hope 2007), the manager (and, eventually, the controller-within) dealing with "the committee of subselves" (Lester 1987). In Metaeconomics terms, the rational mind/manager (engaging self-control), working with all parts of the mind, finds the solution within the rational zone.

Adam Smith as Both Behavioral and Metaeconomist

We can now see how Adam Smith is really a behavioral economist, and, likely would find Metaeconomics a useful way to integrate the array of ideas he proposed, and, especially bringing in *The Theory of Moral Sentiments*, the Empathy part. The Other-interest path 0M also brings the Invisible Hand into play, which sometimes must be made a Visible Hand, in order to achieve happiness.

Roberts (2014) makes it clear that Smith (1759/1790) understood what peace and contentment was all about: "To be content, you need to be loved and be lovely." So, one could not Be Lovely when operating in Self-interest only. In fact, on the Self-interest path 0G, one can only Be Loved, admired and respected for what you have accomplished, especially as measured in money wealth. Being more specific, and it takes us to what happiness was all about, Smith (1759/1790) said (quotations cited in Roberts 2014, p. 40):

> What so great happiness as to be beloved, and to know that we deserve to be beloved? What so great misery as to be hated, and know we deserve to be hated?

Happiness came from jointly pursuing both, and, thus, avoiding being hated, which was essential to both peace and happiness. As the title of the Roberts (2014) book would have it, *How Adam Smith Can Change Your Life: An Unexpected Guide to Human Nature and Happiness*, the guide is to temper the Self-interest with doing the right thing, the moral and ethical thing. And, with enough Self-discipline and Self-control, and influenced by the Higher Plane of value *V* used to balance the dual interest, the person moves to peace, contentment, and happiness on a humane path 0Z.

Eventually, through each person pursuing happiness path 0Z, the entire system could be at peace, and happy. With said conditions for each person, it would mean the entire capitalism-based economy could demonstrate a good capitalism. How? Well, there would have to be a substantial overlap in the Empathy-based Other-interest among all people on the Spaceship.

As an aside, and focused on the matter of peace, specifically: Wight (2002) argues that Smith (1776/1789) was purposely published in 1776 in protest to the American Revolution, a protest to war of all kinds, always between the tribes, in that he favored Peace not War. Smith saw wide-spread trade on Spaceship Earth (we would call it globalization, now) facilitated through tempering Self-interest with Empathy—the Sentiments—could ensure peace. The Impartial Spectator so engaged would give good trade, an Empathy-conditioned trade, a peaceful trade. Peace, happiness, and good trade arose from the expression of the sentiments on both sides of the trade. Also, over time peace would be sustained: There would be a convergence in the shared Other-interest among the trading partners.

People who stir tribalism and nationalism, and rattle swords, really need to go back to both Smith (1759/1790) and Smith (1776/1789) books, and, do some serious empirical questioning of tribalistic and nationalistic frames. Such questioning would likely show, empirically, that both tribalism and nationalism are untenable positions, at least not if the goal is peace and happiness. Smith would likely support globalism, but Empathy, the sentiments, must be at work. Said Empathy would point to not stealing intellectual property rights or manipulating currency values to distort the terms of trade. Trade and tariff wars among nations would vanish, too, with Empathy (shared Other-interest) working to temper Ego (Self-interest) on all sides of the trade.

Metaeconomics Is About Seeking Happiness, Not Only Wealth

Happiness, as Adam Smith understood, is a far more complex concept than the notion of a linear relationship between more happiness arising out of more income and wealth (Altman 2012, loc 6838). The level and distribution of the public goods represented in access to health care, education and public safety matters, and higher income and wealth does not necessarily offset low amounts of the goods. Happiness also requires "strong relationships, a good sex life, a good job, good health, a sense of community, and good governance" (Altman 2012, loc 6889), which are all part of the shared Other-interest. To achieve happiness, people need more than just higher income and wealth, in contrast to what the NeoClassEcon claim. The goods in the shared Other-interest, many of them being non-market goods, are also essential. The content of the Other-interest becomes a focus in Metaeconomics due to the key role it plays in tempering the Self-interest. Said tempering, in turn, is essential in order to achieve peace, happiness, and efficiency for each person and for the larger Market&Government system.

Happiness Is Found on a Continuum

Metaeconomics points to continuums in the content of the Other-interest from extreme Left through Progressive and Conservative to the extreme right (Table 5.1). Said continuums also recognize the possibility and reality of progressives on the right, and conservatives on the left, especially in the middle-ground. Metaeconomics suggests that in order to address and hopefully find happiness (and peace) and efficiency we need to avoid the

Table 5.1 Content within the shared other-interest on the continuum from left and progressive to conservative and right

Left and Progressive	*Conservative and Right*
Public property	Common property
Public property	Private property
Communism	Capitalism
Extreme equality	Extreme inequality
Resentment	Performance
Pure socialism	Pure capitalism
Liberal democracy	Fascism
Liberal democracy	Totalitarianism
Socialism	Fascism
Communism	Fascism
Social democracy capitalism	Liberal democracy capitalism
Democratic socialism	Democratic capitalism
Wilsonian	Madisonian
Humane economy	Ego economy
Empathy economy	Ego economy
Left political Isle	Right political isle
Competent government	Incompetent government
Community	Economy
Community solidarity	Individual freedom
Individual choice	Hierarchical community
Communitarian capitalism	Libertarian capitalism
Communitarian capitalism	Neoliberal capitalism
Moral community	Moral order
Moral community	Amoral
Law	Natural rights
Government precedes rights	Rights precede government
Peace through understanding	Peace through natural rights
Peace through empathy	War through ego
Deep state	Anarchy
Administrative state	Anarchy
Administrative state	Neoliberal
Progressive	Status quo
Evolving rights	Natural rights
Majority rule	Natural rights
Constitution	Bill of Rights
Progressive Constitution	Conservative Constitution
Nurture	Nature
Malleable	Fixed
Society	Economy
Globalization	Nationalism

(*continued*)

Table 5.1 (continued)

Left and Progressive	*Conservative and Right*
United nations government	National government
Culture	Economy
Community	Economy
Institutional economics	Classical economics
Control	Liberty
Control	Freedom
Majority choice	Individual choice
Designed order	Spontaneous order
Visible hand	Invisible hand
Majority	Minority
Heteronomy	Autonomy
Homonomy	Autonomy
Interdependent	Independent
Joint with nature	Master over nature
Limits (Thermodynamics)	No limits (Newtonian)
Paternalist	Libertarian
Leftish liberal statist	Rightish liberal statist
Strict parent	Adapted child
Nurturing parent	Free Child
Be lovely	Be loved
Other virtues	Prudence
Market failure	Government failure
We	Me
Unity	I
Lesbian, gay, bisexual, transgender	Heterosexual
Family	Individual
Thou	I
Liberal	Neo-liberal
Cosmopolitan	Nationalist
Barbarism	Civilization
Oppressed	Oppressor
Coercion	Liberty
Harvard school social engineering	Chicago school libertarianism
Neoinstitutional economics	Neoclassical economics
Government	Market

Source: Author's creation

extremes. Metaeconomics points to the integration in Conservative&Progressive (sorry for the use of all the "&" notation, pointing to jointness, and all the "pointing" with capitalization, but it is important) across the continuums as generally giving the best outcome. Also, the task of finding the best integration, the best balance, generally requires making the Invisible Hand a Visible Hand, at least until the problem is fixed. Once the new best integration, balance is selected, it can once again be relegated to the Invisible Hand. A new status quo can then go into play, but always subject to a mindful, conscious re-consideration when it no longer is giving good outcomes.

An important aside, here: MetaEcon can see the potential critique about making things visible, especially by the believers in the spontaneous order of things (after Hayek 1948, p. 16), all left to the unconscious, the Invisible Hand. The Hayek styled concern is that making the Invisible Hand into a Visible Hand seems to imply a kind of top down planner taking control, and losing the spontaneity of the economy.

On the contrary, the MetaEcon sees full well the key role of spontaneity, allowing for the unforeseeable, and how no one can see everything (and certainly not a few central planners). The problem with leaving it all to spontaneity and the Invisible Hand is that it can and often does lead to bad outcomes, to bad capitalism. Spontaneity has to be good, not rooted in bad, unethical context (e.g., in slavery, or in people trapped on the lower rung of the income and wealth ladder). Spontaneity needs to be framed as coming out of the empathy-sympathy, the fellow-feeling, the shared Other-interest with moral and ethical content.

So, as you peruse the list in Table 5.1, think in terms of the content of path 0M in Fig. 4.1 (as well as in Figs. 7.1 and 8.1), and what would evolve on the humane and liberal, happy and efficient path 0Z. Self-interest is what it is, for every person, on some path 0G: It is in the core of every Human (and the only thing in an Econ), and primal. The economic choice, then, is largely determined by which Other-interest is at work. Dependent upon where one lands on the continuums in Table 5.1, the payoff in the domains of joint Self&Other-interest on path 0Z (again, see Fig. 4.1) is quite different. Also, to emphasize, the point chosen on each continuum is driven by the choice in the value *V* space of Fig. 4.2 (and Fig. 7.2), which then drives the price *P* space in Fig. 4.1 (and Figs. 7.1 and 8.1).

It is also understood that the continuums are nuanced. For example, on the pure socialism to pure capitalism spectrum, we find democratic socialism and social democracy toward the Left end, but not all the way. The social democracy brand is demonstrated in the Nordic countries, in the idea of Viking Economics (see Lakey 2016). Said economics is focused on building a good capitalism, one with a more optimal level of inequality, and the elimination of poverty within a well-educated and healthy, and, thus, happy population. In fact, it is likely somewhere to the right of middle on the continuum, with substantive freedom for each person to innovate and freely choose.

Points more toward the Right end are equally nuanced, with all manner of casino capitalism; money manager and stock price maximizing capitalism; shareholder capitalism; crony capitalism; and, on the extreme Right, even authoritarian capitalism in fascism. Things are no better on the extreme left with authoritarian capitalism in communism. All are versions of bad capitalism, producing a lot of unhappiness.

Also, of special importance in Metaeconomics: What is the liberal to neoliberal continuum? And, essentially the same question: What is the Leftish Liberal Statism to Rightish Liberal Statism continuum? We need to know, in order to understand more exactly the content of the Enlightenment idea about a liberal and humane democracy-based good capitalism. McCloskey (2019, loc 250) explains: Statism is about lots of outside control over the person. Using the Angyal (1965) characterization, it is about heteronomy over the person, controlling the person from the outside.

McCloskey (2019, loc 96) argues against statism in any form. Modern liberalism is instead a "humane true liberalism .... Do unto others as you would have them do unto you." Sounds like Metaeconomics. It is about an Empathy-tempered and -conditioned expression of the Ego. McCloskey is in effect, in Metaeconomic terms, seeing the key role of Empathy, due to it producing an ethic, in making for a modern humane liberalism. Both the statism of heavy-handed Government control, which is Leftish, and of heavy-handed community control fostered through Government (e.g., Fascist Religion and Fascist Politics come to mind), which is Rightish, need to be avoided. Avoid heteronomy in any form if at all possible, the possibility considered through the moral and ethical dimension.

In Metaeconomics, modern liberalism, a truly humane liberalism, is represented in an autonomous (Self-interest) person. Said autonomous person freely considers homonomous (Other-interest) influence, integrates and internalizes it, as Adam Smith suggested would happen at the Station of the Impartial Spectator. Autonomy&Homonomy is about seeking balance in Ego&Empathy, Self&Other, Market&Government. And, heteronomy is used only in extreme situations, like in eliminating slavery in the first place, and then passing the Civil Rights Act of 1964 and Voting Rights Act of 1965 to dampen the effects of 100 years of Jim Crow? Perhaps putting caps on how much carbon dioxide is released, recognizing the inherent limits in how much greenhouse gas can be processed in the atmosphere and ecosystem of Spaceship Earth? Empirical questions.

References

Altman, M. 2012. *Behavioral Economics for Dummies.* Mississauga: John Wiley and Sons Canada, Kindle.

Angyal, Andras. 1965. *Neurosis and Treatment: A Holistic Theory.* New York: The Viking Press.

Brown, Clair. 2017. *Buddhist Economics: An Enlightened Approach to the Dismal Science.* New York: Bloomsbury Press.

Butler, G., and T. Hope. 2007. *Managing Your Mind: The Mental Fitness Guide.* New York: Oxford University Press.

Hayek, F.A. 1948. *Individualism and Economic Order.* Chicago: The University of Chicago Press (Paperback Edition 1980).

Kahneman, D. 2011. *Thinking Fast and Slow.* New York: Farrar, Straus and Giroux.

Lakey, George. 2016. *Viking Economics: How the Scandinavians Got It Right – And How We Can, Too.* Kindle ed. Brooklyn/New York: Melville House Publishing, 2017.

Lester, David. 1987. A Systems Perspective of Personality. *Psychological Reports* 61: 603–622.

Lynne, G.D. 2002. Agricultural Industrialization: A Metaeconomics Look at the Metaphors by Which We Live. *Review of Agricultural Economics* 24 (2): 410–427.

Lynne, G.D., J.S. Shonkwiler, and L.R. Rola. 1988. Attitudes and Farmer Conservation Behavior. *American Journal of Agricultural Economics* 70 (1): 12–19.

McCloskey, D.N. 2019. *Why Liberalism Works: How True Liberal Values Produce a Freer, More Equal, Prosperous World for All.* Kindle ed. New York: Yale University Press.

Roberts, Russ. 2014. *How Adam Smith Can Change Your Life: An Unexpected Guide to Human Nature and Happiness.* New York: Portfolio/Penguin.

Smith, A. 1759/1790. *The Theory of Moral Sentiments.* Ed. D.D. Raphael and A.L. Macfie. Indianapolis: Liberty Fund.

———. 1776/1789. *An Inquiry into the Nature and Causes of the Wealth of Nations*. Ed. E. Cannan. New York: Random House.

Smith, V.L. 1998. The Two Faces of Adam Smith. *Southern Economic Journal* 65 (1): 1–19.

———. 2003. Constructivist and Ecological Rationality in Economics. *American Economic Review* 93: 465–508.

Stanovich, K.E. 2011. *Rationality and the Reflective Mind*. New York: Oxford University Press.

Tomer, John F. 2017a. *Advanced Introduction to Behavioral Economics*. North Hampton: Elgar.

———. 2017b. Why Buddhist Economics Is Needed: Overcoming Large Scale Biophysical and Socio-Economic Dysfunctions. *Real-World Economics Review* (82): 143–158.

Walker, B., and D. Salt. 2006. *Resilience Thinking: Sustaining Ecosystems and People in a Changing World*. Washington, DC: Island Press.

Wight, J.B. 2002. *Saving Adam Smith: A Tale of Wealth, Transformation, and Virtue*. Upper Saddle River: Prentice Hall PTR.

CHAPTER 6

Elections Policy: Voting Is Not Only About Self-Interest

Metaeconomics is focused primarily on the political economy, that is, on how the Government interacts with and provides the context for the Market, and how the Market also interacts with and influences the Government. So, it is especially intriguing to look at how we select who will represent us, and work for us, in the political part of the political economy.

Paradox of Voting

The paradox is: It is not in a person's Self-interest to vote but it is in a person's interest as part of a democracy to vote. Yet, many do so vote, even though the payoff in the domain of Self-interest is often negative. That is, the time and effort to learn about the candidates; being engaged in the political conversation in a meaningful way; and, even the simple cost of taking the time traveling to, and casting a ballot at an often crowded voting place, can be costly. When all added together, said cost far exceeds the specific benefit a person might experience from voting.

The payoff in something like a general election for president, or even in state and national elections for the House or the Senate, is especially characterized by the reality of low specific payoff to the person as voter. The NeoClassEcon, who is focused on Self-interest only, must conclude that voting is irrational. Similarly, a NeoInstiEcon could see no reason to expect that anyone would choose not to vote. There is presumed enough

G. D. Lynne, *Metaeconomics*, Palgrave Advances in Behavioral Economics, https://doi.org/10.1007/978-3-030-50601-8_6

shared payoff, shared Other-interest, in the outcomes from voting, such that everyone would rationally vote.

Yet, it is true that many do vote, while some do not ever vote, and some vacillate in their voting patterns. What is going on?

Using Metaeconomics, it is easily explained, once it is recognized, first, that voting mainly gives payoff in the domain of the shared Other-interest, and, second, voting requires sacrifice in the Self-interest, and it is rational to so sacrifice. Such sacrifice in Self-interest comes with gains in the Other-interest. Said gains pertain to outcomes associated with participating in a viable, liberal democratic system, and, especially so if one's political party, "the tribe one prefers," a brand of shared Other-interest, is put into power.

Seeing dual interest causes the voting paradox to vanish: The payoff is from pursuing mainly the Other-interest while sacrificing a bit of Self-interest at some point *B* on the balanced (happy to vote) path 0Z. Notice, too, that there is also a bit of sacrifice in Other-interest at that same point, as one does not always get exactly what one wants in a candidate. Every point on path 0Z reflects a bit of sacrifice in both domains of interest, a feature of the rational choice to vote.

Metaeconomics can also explain the lack of turnout on election day. We can now surmise that the main reason is that the people who do not vote do not see a clear connection to the shared Other-interest in the outcome. Regarding the two dominant political parties on the Right and Left Isles, a person who does not have a real tight connection to either party may not vote. We might also surmise that at least some non-voting people, even if identifying with a particular tribe/party, believe that their interest will not be served by the politicians currently on the ballot, that is, feeling disenfranchised or otherwise distanced from the Other-interest being represented by any candidate.

It might be especially the case for extreme individualists, for example, people who share an Other-interest perhaps with an anarchic type survivalist group, to not much care who is in power, so, they, too, would not vote. People may feel no need for any general community, society, or political support. Neither their Self-interest nor their shared Other-interest with which they identify is served by participating.

Gerrymandering also now makes easy sense: It is about splitting up blocs of shared Other-interest that could bring the candidate into power. The narrower Other-interest works to "bust-up" the power of the larger Other-interest. So, for example, historically, in many southern states it worked to keep the shared Other-interest of the former slaves from bringing anyone into power that might support and otherwise help their shared Other-interest in economic opportunity. Gerrymandering is all about the narrow view of what the Other-interest needs to be. And, it is not associated with building a moral and ethical community of voters, one that potentially works for everyone.

Metaeconomics also, then, points to voting for politicians that would seek to find balance in Self&Other-interest, with the Other-interest of everyone recognized, no matter their political tribe. An elected politician needs to be about building a moral and ethical community that serves every Traveler on the Spaceship. It is especially true for people in the Administrative Branch of Government, who are especially charged to represent everyone, not only a few select tribes. The US president, especially, is not to simply satisfy narrow partisan, ideological, and tribal interests.

Also, it is not all good. While it is quite rational from the Self-interest perspective to not put much time and effort into understanding the issues and how the politicians they choose will address them, it can be a huge problem at the Other-interest level. As Will (2019, loc 3531) points out that while "choosing to remain ignorant—to not invest the time and effort necessary to become knowledgeable—is rational individual behavior, it can and often does have destructive collective outcomes." Voting with a narrow Other-interest, not bothering to become thoroughly informed about the issues, or voting with coalitions of other narrow Other-interest configurations, again with many in the groups not being well-informed, can indeed be destructive. A truly humane, liberal democracy-based capitalism needs to find and operate on good common ground across all interests.

Recent Election: Presidential Election and the Tribes

A candidate for the 2016 presidential election, at one point referred to supporters of the other candidate as "deplorables." No doubt there perhaps were some deplorables, but also arguably there were also some in that candidate's camp. Using Metaeconomics, we can now make sense of what is meant by a deplorable: It is someone who is part of a shared Other-interest of a different ilk, and, likely one with a quite different ethical and moral system than that found in the group finding the other group deplorable. So, for example, white supremacists and white nationalists within their narrow Other-interest would be deemed deplorable by people seeing good and bad in all races, no matter their color. On the other side, the shared Other-interest of a white supremacist group would probably lead to suggesting people with the shared Other-interest in not seeing color and race as any kind of issue, as deplorable. As Kling (2019) makes clear, we see mainly expressions of tribal anger, rather than any Empathy with the other tribe, an unwillingness to even consider the possibility of common ground, searching for a shared Other-interest with that tribe.

A kind of tribal analysis, seeing narrow shared Other-interest within a tribe at work, helps make sense of the misogyny, homophobia, and gunphobia (the list is long, each representing a narrow type of shared Other-interest). It also explains how a tribe identifying with a specific Other-interest can easily be in conflict with a tribe having a different Other-interest. The conflict is over the content of the Other-interest, with little overlap between and among the tribes.

Metaeconomics would point to the need to work at nudging each tribe into practicing Empathy in every direction, that is, asking that each group project themselves into the situation of the other group and asking themselves, while in that situation, "how would I wish to be treated." A truly civil and humane society is one that finds a way to bring the "&" (the jointness, interdependence, one-with-the-other) in the gap between the person&government, the person&people, on the way to building a moral community, an ethical system, in the Market&Government, a truly joint political economy. Metaeconomics would hope for the outcome that all would temper their views, coming onto common ground, into sympathy with an overall shared cause, one that is cognizant and sympathetic to both minority and majority views. Empathy would suggest seeing human nature as it is, with every Traveler on Spaceship Earth being a potential contributor, in their own way, and, thus, resolving the conflict that comes from each seeing the other as deplorables. Empirical reality, anyone? Ethics, anyone?

Enlightened political leaders that formed the US government in 1776, and especially in forming the Constitution in 1787, had in mind that the Government, especially the Administrative branch, would work to represent all the shared Other-interests at work in the diverse population of the country. In fact, an enlightened (humane) president would not only practice Empathy but would also encourage everyone to Empathize, to nudge everyone to walk-in-the-shoes of each other. Such a president would work to forge new ground on which all could stand together as part a Truly

Great United States of America. As Metaeconomics would suggest, unlike a king who can and generally will select whose narrow Other-interest shared within a select group will count (only the narrow tribe who supports the king), a president is to appeal to everyone to get on board with the common, shared-by-all, Other-interest of the country at large. Any president (or any person in any other branch of Government) that fails to help build a widely shared Other-interest is not doing the job in a manner consistent with the original (humane and liberal) intent of the enlightenment.

Recent Appointees to the Supreme Court

The clash of Other-interest can be especially apparent in appointments to the US Supreme Court, as in some appointments in 2019, as played out on the media. Other-interest groups who oppose abortion, and people who buy into the notion that "boys will be boys," were especially prominent. The latter group was served by denigrating a protestor to the nominee, going to the level of mocking and bullying.

On the other side, the main shared Other-interest opposing the appointee saw value in supporting women's rights, dealing especially with sexual aggression on the part of males. The shared Other-interest was also about maintaining a woman's right to choose an abortion, which the appointee seemed on the side of retracting, and perhaps eliminating, once appointed. It is clear the balance in Self&Other-interest puts more emphasis on the Self-interest of females, empathizing and joining in sympathy with people who have had such experiences.

The recent appointment process is not a good example of how shared Other-interest in the higher court of the country is supposed to work. By long tradition, coming out of English Common Law, the Supreme Court is to represent the shared Other-interest of the commons. The Supreme Court is to represent all people, not narrow partisan-interest. The Supreme Court is charged with ensuring the application of both Common (especially Common, as it broadly reflects what people will go along with, as reflected in their Ethical System) and Legislative Law, as well as administrative rules. The Supreme Court is to be balanced, with actions consistent with a widely shared ethical system and moral community, of all the people. As Metaeconomics suggests, the Supreme Court is to be wise, becoming so after empathizing with everyone affected by some law or rule, walking in their shoes as real people. It is about past, present, and future people, focused on arriving at a position consistent with not only precedent but what might work best for the future.

Mid-Term Congressional Elections

Mid-term elections for US Congressional House and Senate seats are often quite revealing as to whether the people see the most recently elected Administration as representing their shared Other-interest. As highlighted about voting, it is all about electing someone to represent one's shared Other-interest, and not so much about achieving Self-interest outcomes per se. The 2018 mid-terms are a case in point.

Intriguingly, some substantive shifts occurred when the Democrats regained control in the US House of Representatives. It reflected a kind of repudiation of the shared Other-interest represented in populism, nationalism, tribalism and identity politics that emerged in the recent years leading up to the 2018 mid-terms. It had put lots of extreme Right Isle politicians and a populist, tribal president into power. Or, was it really a repudiation? Did the switch to Democrats actually, instead, simply reflect a shift to some other, also narrow, shared Other-interest at work, for example, concerns about inequality and women's rights, sexual freedom, income inequality, and taxes on the wealthy, to list a few?

There has also been no shortage of populism, in recent years, among the Democrats, especially as related to equity and equality; inequality of wealth and income; and tax-the-rich issues. The concern over extreme concentration of power and wealth in the top 1 percent is a continuing theme: The shared Other-interest is to temper and restrain the perceived (and, it is an empirical question) Self-interest and Greed at the top. It is manifested in the notion that the wealthy need to take a greater monetary responsibility for the costs of such things as roads, air traffic control, dams and reservoirs, internet services, medical care, public health, public education and other things from which they benefit in their business endeavors.

It seems, instead, at least it is the contention which needs empirical examination, that wealthy are especially adept at not paying the price of Government through paying ever smaller shares of their income and wealth in taxes. That is, there has been substantive Market-failure to pay a fair share, so use Government to rectify it. The shared Other-interest points to progressive taxation plans, reflecting a major tribal instinct of the Democrats in general. The shared Other-interest is also over greater opportunity to climb the wealth ladder, to get beyond the lower rungs.

There are also some substantive differences on women's rights, with Democrats, and progressives more generally, being supportive of such shared Other-interest as represented in the Me Too movement. Support for gay and lesbian rights, another kind of shared Other-interest, is also more likely to be found in tribal instincts and shared interests on the Democrat's side.

So, in many ways, the 2018 mid-term election outcome just shifted attention from one set of narrow shared Other-interest frames on the Republican side, which includes mainly Conservatives, with a sprinkling of Libertarians, to a different set of narrow, shared Other interest frames on the Democrat side, which includes mainly Progressives. The thing to watch, as Metaeconomics suggests, is if the new mix of Other-interest in Congress can be somehow resolved into a common set of shared Other-interest for Republicans&Democrats, Conservatives&Progressives, and, thus, for the people of the US. Metaeconomics suggests it will require substantial and visible efforts to empathize. Working to common ground across the narrow shared Other-interests leads to gains for all, moving away from tribal, partisan framing onto the sum-being-greater-than-the-sum-of-the-parts path 0Z? Empirical question.

Government Bureaucrats, Staff, and Employees

If we are to believe Buchanan and the Public Choice School of Economics contention, then every Government employee, staff member, bureaucrat, and, the politicians who influence them, needs to be screened. It would be a screening, we might surmise, during the interviewing and hiring process, and during the election process for the politician, and the appointment process for the political appointee. It would be a screening about the degree to which the person will always act only in Ego-based Self-interest, which Buchanan and the Public Choice economists claim is the only thing that a person in Government does. Their solution? Well, Ego-based Self-interest dominates, it is the only nature, so, the solution is to greatly reduce, if not eliminate, Government.

The solution suggested by Metaeconomics would likely be quite different (empirical question): It would suggest that Government employees, politicians, and appointees, everyone involved in the Government, really need a substantive capacity for Empathy in order to work in the shared Other-interest with the population, people they serve and help, in the Market and elsewhere. Every person in Government needs to be careful to not just be about maximizing their own Ego-based Self-interest. If a screening was to be done, it could then be productively used to nudge balance in Ego&Empathy in Government, and not be about eliminating Government.

The notion that people in Government only operate in their Ego-based Self-interest is largely without empirical, scientific basis. The opposite may be true, pointing to the reasonable expectation that many if not most employed or otherwise involved in the Government likely have a greater capacity for Empathy. Most seeking to be in the Government would likely see the essential need to work with the Empathy-based Other-interest tendency. In contrast, people in the Market would likely be more oriented to the Ego-based Self-interest. Empirical questions.

Another suggestion that needs empirical test: People in Markets would also be the most likely to work at using Government to obtain special strongholds on Market outcomes, for example, in keeping competitors out of Markets with monopoly type controls; encouraging the Government to help them with rent-seeking (taking and keeping) actions; obtaining and maintaining Government subsidies while at the same time avoiding taxes; and, many other Self-interest only efforts. Empirical questions.

Metaeconomics would suggest that it is likely the balance in Self& Other-interest is far more toward the Self-interest in the Market than in the Government, but, again, it is an empirical question that needs scientific attention. Perhaps it is the reason we see Market-oriented thinkers like in the Public Choice School and the Chicago School claiming that the Government is also only focused on Self-interest, by projecting their own personal tendencies on the Government? Again, it is an empirical question.

Metaeconomics would suggest that people in Government be reminded (and trained, in the case of employees and staff) to work at finding ways to act in the Empathy-based and shared Other-interest with people in the Market, but also to consider the Other-interest of people not able to be part of the Market. The Other Forums of Government do not use the same currency: Other Forums do not require money to have influence. The Other Forum, after all, is mainly what Government is to be about, representing the Other-interest in such things as equal opportunity; fair trade; viable and robust competition, not cronyism; safe food and drugs; fair access to housing; high and sustained environmental quality; safety net programs, shifting to low-carbon production systems; and many other "shared Other-interest" things, shared by all Travelers on Spaceship Earth.

Happiness Associated with the Outcomes

As made clear using Metaeconomics, people elected and appointed to political positions represent an Other-interest, or more generally a coalition of Other-interest groups that find some candidate at least somewhat close to what they want as a group, faction, or tribe. So, what are the main features of the Other-interest on both sides of the Isle? We draw on Will (2019) to help make sense of what is at issue, the "sensibilities" on both sides of the Political Isle, as summarized in Table 6.1. Metaeconomics also clarifies that while liberty and freedom as associated with Ego-based Self-interest is primal no matter on which Isle one resides, the virtues as associated with Empathy-based Other-interest must temper that Self-interest in order to achieve happiness in both Isles, and across Isles, as well.

In addition to Will (2019), Kling (2019) is helpful in understanding what each Isle is trying to say. A three-axes model (already entered as continuums in Chap. 5) is suggested (Kling 2019, p. 22):

1. Libertarian (Both Left and Right Isle): Coercion…Liberty
2. Conservative (Right Isle): Barbarism…Civilization
3. Progressive (Left Isle): Oppressed…Oppressor
   And, in the latest axes leading up to the 2016 election, with Kling (2019) not providing a name for it, although he alludes to a rough characterization as Populist-Nationalist, I will just call it:
4. Resentment: Cosmopolitan…Nationalist

The Resentment is against what is perceived as the Cosmopolitan Elite, the person who is open minded to an array of cultures, races, sexual preferences, seeing essential role of science, just simply more willing to being open to and engaging with every Traveler anywhere on the Spaceship. Also, considerable Resentment has built due to the extreme inequality in wealth and income. People feel left behind, as the yachts and expensive sports cars pull away.

Within Resentment, the Cosmopolitan is viewed as mainly on the Left, but also is seen to reside on the Right, especially as represented in the super-wealthy (and, the Left has said people, too). The Nationalist is mainly on the Right, with a few on the Left: On the latter, a not insignificant number in the Left-center voted the anti-cosmopolitan line in 2016. And, as Kling (2019, p. 89) states, the Resentment (again, my name for it) continuum is "tribalism stripped to its essence." It is about Draining the

Table 6.1 Characteristics of self-interest, other-interest and control for the progressive left aisle and the conservative right aisle

	Progressive left aisle			*Conservative right aisle*		
Location in Will (2019)	*Self-interest*	*Other-interest*	*Control*	*Self-interest*	*Other-interest*	*Control*
90,153, 161,190, 210,263, 299,345, 399,401, 410,435, 498,870, 945,975, 994,1025, 1064,1083, 1102,1184, 1193,1279, 1346,1450, 1488,1510, 1627,1757, 1805,1831, 1861,1928, 1949,2152, 2219,2415, 2930,2960, 3006,3253, 3407,3503, 3680,3711, 8123,8608, 8779,8896	Rent seeking; Government must do for the individual; Conscious; Evolving human nature; Human nature molded by social context; Government can deliver happiness; Government uses science of public administration and political science; Human nature is malleable; Humans born with a blank slate; Move toward human perfection; Individual socially constructed; Eugenic evolution; People and individualism arise out of social and political achievement, and the result of Government; Visible Hand directing the social machine; Civil servants act only on shared Other-	Wilsonian malleable human nature; Scientific Government; Evolving rights philosophy; William James pragmatism; Balance toward Government; Designed order; Expansive Government; Evolving views on moral questions; Evolve culture; Government sometimes must dominate; Managed inequality; Virtuous Government; Government bestows rights; Humans need Government to represent the sociable; Rights come from law; Do for people what cannot, do not, or should not do; No natural rights to bar Government doing; Pragmatism; National	Collective will; Collective rights; Majority rule; Bound in nature; Interdependent with others and nature; Non-partisan experts; Rehabilitate criminals; Limitless plasticity of humans; Politics drives progress; Administrative branch with more power to ensure progress; Regulate against rent-seekers; Leave politics behind in an age of science-based administration; administrative law; More administrative staff; Supreme Court support majority rule; Rehabilitate criminals; Constitution represents change; Interstate Commerce regulated by Legislative Branch;	Rent seeking; Government not do to the individual; Unconscious; Fixed human nature; Human nature invariant to social context; Happiness arises in people; Government does not need science of public administration and political science; Human nature cannot be molded; Humans born predisposed to a nature; Cannot change imperfect humans; Individual self-constructed; Survival of fittest; People and individualism are natural, pre-political and the cause of Government; Invisible hand directing the social machine; Civil servants act only in self-interest; Well-being	Madisonian fixed human nature; Non-science Government; Fixed natural rights philosophy; Jeremy Bentham utilitarianism; Balance toward Market; Spontaneous order; Limited Government; Fixed knowledge on moral questions; Given culture; Government mediates and ameliorates; Natural inequality; Lack of virtue in Government; Government secures rights; Humans naturally sociable not needing Government; Rights come from nature; People do, without Government; Natural rights bar Government doing; Utilitarianism; Individualist and	Individual will; Individual rights; Minority rule; Free in nature; Independent of others and nature; Partisan experience; Penalize criminals; Limited plasticity of humans; People drive progress; Administrative Branch with less power to influence progress; Factions naturally become rent-seekers; Politics necessary to deal with nature of human nature, e.g., inherent factious behavior; legislative law; More congressional staff; Supreme Court support minorities; Punish criminals; Constitution prevents change; Reduce/ eliminate Legislative

interest; Well-being without explicit attention to virtue and character; Boundless presidential responsibility to help the social good; President is to inflame passion and give it new objects to feed upon; Individual rights represented in majority rule; Government can improve character; Individualism, self-restraint, and self-reliance are enhanced by Government	consciousness and collective undertakings; Government as wise school marm; Government replaces role of civil society; Social harmony molded to override disunity and conflict across factions; History unfolding in progress as humans change; Factions become harmonized across the spectrum, pursuing a broadly based shared interest; Administrative branch drives Government; Government morally responsible for making things good; Government as com-passionate; We the People (Group, Community); Majority rule to create rights constructed by the Constitution	Federal Government over State, Local; Administrative, Legislative and Judicial to represent the majority; Activist judge creates rights; Government attending to what the majorities want; Competent Government strengthening culture; Find Government solutions to problems	with implicit attention to virtue and character; Boundless presidential responsibility to serving people; President is to moderate, restrain, deflate passionate wants; Individual rights binding majority rule; Government corrupts character; Individualism, self-restraint, and self-reliance are subverted by Government	provincial democracy; People wiser than the Government (school marm); Civil society mediates between the individual and Government; Inherent disunity and conflict caused by factions needs to be respected while limiting toll on public welfare; History repeats without progress due to unchanging nature of human nature; Factions of like-minded people pursue narrow shared interests; Legislative branch drives Government; People morally responsible for making things good; People as compassion-ate; We the People (People); Natural rights of people affirmed by the Declaration of Independence	regulation of Interstate Commerce; State and local choices, reduce/no Federal Government; Only House of Representatives to represent the majority, other branches to represent minorities; Engaged judge defends rights; Government attending to what the factions want; Incompetent Government fraying culture; Find Government causes of problem

Source: Author's creation, drawing primarily from materials in Will (2019)

Swamp, within which the elites from the Libertarian, Conservative, and Progressive persuasions are claimed to be mired. Also, Kling (2019, p. 89) makes clear the Resentment has little in the way of a coherent tradition. Yet, it seemingly is a close relative with older themes in populism, with a bit of Fascism mixed in.

Globalization (which a Cosmopolitan sees as normal) is a main focus of the Resentment, apparently wishing to go back to a time when the tribes did battle (rather than participate in Empathy-based, the sentiments at work, peaceful global trade) for everything, we might surmise. World Wars, again, perhaps. It goes back to our proto-reptilian core, the Ego supported in a narrowly focused tribe, without any hope for bringing Empathy, the neo-mammalian ability, into dampening said reptilian tendencies. It is about the Ego of a narrowly defined Tribe, and in support of only a very narrow circle for which any Empathy is possible in that Tribe.

So, to help the communication, keep the Four in mind as you peruse and consider Table 6.1. The table displays the traditional way of thinking by the Conservatives on the Right, the traditions of the Progressives on the Left. And, because it lacks in tradition, the Resentment in effect is about rejecting much if not most of what is in Table 6.1. And, also keep in mind that Metaeconomics suggests seeking productive integrations using ideas and the language of all four, dependent upon the problem one is trying to solve. Pragmatism.

The striking differences in Table 6.1 suggest the main Left and Right Political Isles, much as on the Isles of the NeoInstiEcon and NeoClassEcon, see quite different Travelers on the Spaceship. While both admit that there may be rent seeking (i.e., Self-interest is primal) on both Isles (people on the lower rungs of the income and wealth ladder taking money from Government programs, and people on the upper rungs taking money through cronyism and Government power), beyond that, it is as though there are two to three different species of people, which Kling (2019) is also, in effect, alluding too.

And, intriguingly, it may be genetic. As Hibbing, Smith, and Alford (2014) have documented, some travelers are genetically, biologically predisposed to being Conservative and some are predisposed to being Progressive, and others are predisposed to being an Independent. We might expect Libertarians distributed across all types. Most importantly, the genetic disposition means the main types cannot be persuaded, cannot be changed. Only the Independents (and perhaps the Libertarians) can be persuaded to lean Left or Right, and do in fact lean different ways as persuaded by the data and evidence. And, then, there are also the populists (and the Fascists), who come and go as the conditions change.

It follows that, as Darwinian evolution might suggest, a high degree of specialization in subgroups and thus diversity across political tribes of Humans is essential to successful evolution for the population writ large? Perhaps evolution needs both Progressives and Conservatives in some proportion, along with all the Independents in-between, with the ideal proportions likely an empirical question to be assessed for each case in point? And, how many Libertarians do you need? Indeed, it just may be that rather than thinking about Progressive versus Conservative as separable and independent, we perhaps need instead to see Conservative&Progressive, with the Independents helping bring about the "&" represented in the essential need to see the interdependence and jointness in the alternative ways of thinking? And, the Libertarians? Well, one finds them in both ends of the spectrum, on both Isles, depending on the issue. Metaeconomics sees the potential for synergistic and symbiotic outcomes of a positive kind drawing on good ideas from both Isles, and especially in the jointness (again, that "&") made possible with Empathy.

It is also intriguing how the economic science represented in NeoInstiEcon is consistent with and supports some of the main contentions in the Progressive Isle while NeoClassEcon is consistent with and supports some of main contentions in the Conservative Isle. It suggests there is, indeed, some scientific basis in fact on both sides. It also suggests that Metaeconomics as an alternative, empirical and thus reality-based economic science could potentially be most productively (in contrast to either Neoclassical or Neoinstitutional Economics by themselves) used to find the best balance in Conservative&Progressive ideas to make Market&Government work better. It also suggests why the Dual Interest Theory seems to withstand and thrive on empirical testing, in that it parallels the Conservative&Progressive, with its orientation to Self&Other, being representative of real political economic choice.

Metaeconomics to Explain Behavior on Both Political Isles and in the Interstice

Intriguingly, though, in contrast to the Will (2019) claim that it is the Progressives that favor using Government, while the Conservatives favor using the Market, both use various balances of Market&Government to serve their Other-interest. Yet, there is substantive variance in the content of the shared Other-interest, even though having Market and Government elements within each. As Deneen (2019a, b) points out, many Conservatives have lost faith in the Market. Faith has been lost in what they see as Self-interest only in the Market. The social agenda, and often a religious agenda, the shared Other-interest is not being satisfied by the Market. For example, Deneen (2019a), in a critique of Will (2019), points to how in the case of some states working "to pass legislation protecting religious liberty, restricting transgender normalization or banning abortion, powerful corporations have used threats of economic ruination to attack and even overturn duly enacted legislation friendly to social conservatives."

So, what is going on here is that the Other-interest as viewed by the "powerful corporations" differs from the Other-interest, the social agenda, of the social conservatives. Deneen (2019b) wants a Conservative Government to temper and condition the Progressive Market, which reflects a different view of what is in the shared Other-interest. It seems to be a kind of Rightish Liberal Statism at work? Empirical question. Presumably Deneen would, then, not want the Government involved in tempering the expression by a Conservative Market, which would be a kind of Leftish Liberal Statism, but would want the Government involved in bringing about Rightish Statism to affect a Progressive Market?

Intriguingly, the perspective that Conservatives might use Government to mold their brand of Other-interest, bring it into influence is simply not acknowledged by some Conservatives, for example, in the study of Will (2019) as characterized in Table 6.1; it is only the Progressives that (wrongly) use Government to influence the conditions of expressing Self-interest. Yet Conservatives, just like Progressives, do use Government regularly, for example, in reducing and/or banning abortion rights: Rightish Liberal Statism? On the Market side, it was Progressives that drove the formation of sulfur emissions Markets, through bringing science into setting the terms for trade, that is, determined the capacity, the cap: Leftish Liberal Statism?

Ironically, the trade&cap outcome, with sulfur allowances traded in the Market, and Government setting the cap, is an illustration of a truly humane liberalism, in a good balance in Market&Government. Similarly, the Affordable Care Act was also attempt at that balance: It set mandates on everyone having to buy health insurance, and then used the Market to find the efficiency in the health insurance Markets. Extreme elements on the Right pulled the mandates: Why? It stopped the possibility for an effective and efficient Market, which can only arise in cases with good balance in market&mandate, the latter usually from the Government.

Trade-Offs and Symbiosis Within and Between the Political Isles

Analysis using the value *V* curves on the Higher Plane illustrated in Fig. 4.2 can also be helpful in making sense of the degree to which Progressives and Conservatives lack common ground, as illustrated in Table 6.1, and what finding common ground would tend to produce. In particular, if Progressives from the Left Isle win the elections, then we would expect such value *V* curves to get ever further apart (illustrated later, in Fig. 7.2) for the Progressives as we move up path 0Z with equal expenditures for inputs (as we will see later in Fig. 8.1) or in consumption of two products (as in Fig. 4.1). The complementarity of Self&Other-interest among Progressives would lead to an increasing at an increasing rate pattern of value *V* outcomes on the Higher Plane, value *V* greater than price *P* measured outcomes in the Markets. Alternatively, if Conservatives win the elections, similar outcomes will arise, but now for the Conservatives, with the payoff from their balance in Self&Other-interest also leading to a kind of symbiotic, sum-greater-than-the-sum-of-the-parts outcomes.

So, what happens to Conservatives (their Happiness, measured on the Higher Plane) when Progressives win the election? To think about it, consider an individual characterized by the descriptors in the Conservative Self-interest trying to express Self-interest when the shared Other-interest is coming out of the Progressive Other-interest column. Also, control would be coming out of the Progressive control column, too. So, what would become of the Happiness of the Conservatives? Well, ironically, Conservatives will likely become happier, as they would be nudged, or if it fails, perhaps regulated, away from the Greed path 0G toward the Happiness path 0Z. It is quite possible Conservatives would be happier with a Progressive Government in place. Intriguingly, a Progressive could be substantively happier, too, on the other side of the vote. If Conservatives win, the Progressives will now be nudged away from path 0M toward the Happiness path 0Z. So, ironically, it is quite possible that both Progressives and Conservatives could be happier if the other Isle is elected, if the balance in power is not shifted too far in either direction. Independents, and Centrist Politicians, please.

As a case in point, it appears Happiness in the outcome of the 2020 election would draw main notions from both the Right and Left Isle. As noted in Willer and Voelkel (2019), citing Ellis and Stimson (2012):

> national polling data by Professors Ellis and Stimson suggests… that the most effective candidate … would combine the most popular feature of the Democratic Party, progressive economic policies, with the most popular feature of the Republican Party: the invocation of conservative ideology and values like patriotism, family and the "American dream."

Metaeconomics suggests (again, always an empirical question) that such a move to jointness often does work best, as in Conservative&Progressive. Why? Well, because Humans have both Ego&Empathy and Self&Other-interest at work. If the reality of the need for balance disappoints, well, we have just been built, evolved in said way.

Irritation Leads to Policy Change: Metaeconomics Can Help Make the Change

As Bromley (2006, for reviews, see Lynne 2007, 2009) makes clear, the main force driving change in policy, and in changing institutions (culture, custom, law, regulations, represented in the Other-interest) in general, is irritation. And, when it becomes extreme, outrage. That is, there is a natural, human tendency to go along with the current situation as long it works reasonably well, as in the adage "if it ain't broke, don't fix it." It is only when it gets broken, or broken enough, that we get irritated, and thus are stirred to act. Banning slavery and getting rid of Jim Crow laws, anyone? Dealing with the over-use and abuse of the Spaceship Earth atmosphere and ecosystem to handle excess greenhouse gases, anyone?

One of Bromley's empirical examples is that of the tobacco industry, who for years covered up the evidence regarding the damage caused by cigarette smoke, both to the smoker and people around the smoker. The science was there. The ethics were not. It was time to integrate into science&ethics, and act on that integration. And, experiential evidence was all around us, as we all knew people who became ill, and died, from smoking. People were irritated into action to change the moral community, the ethical system, surrounding smoking, that is, changing to a non-smoking community. It also entailed asking Government to become more involved in regulating the tobacco industry, including requiring such things as health warnings on cigarette packs. The notion of subsidizing tobacco farmers also came into question, as policy and the institution, the shared Other-interest, gradually changed. Intriguingly, the nicotine addiction problem did not go away with the change in the Other-interest about tobacco. Now we see irritation (literally, in the users' lungs), and growing outrage, over vaping. Perhaps vaping will eventually go the way of tobacco.

Overall, the political economy is about dealing with irritation and outrage, sometimes stirred by the politicians themselves, in all manner of policy matters, from health care to immigration to carbon emissions, all of which might productively be alleviated with Metaeconomics. As Metaeconomics makes clear, the task is to evolve a new, shared Other-interest, finding common ground. It is about finding a fact, reality-based common ground. It is about finding a new shared Other-interest that works across the various factions on the way to peace on the balanced, happy path 0Z.

References

Bromley, D.W. 2006. *Sufficient Reason: Volitional Pragmatism and the Meaning of Economic Institutions.* Princeton: Princeton University Press.

Deneen, Patrick J. 2019a. A Defense of Conservatism That Veers Toward Liberalism. Opinion, *Washington Post*, Washington, DC, June 21, Digital.

———. 2019b. *Why Liberalism Failed.* Kindle ed. New Haven: Yale University Press.

Ellis, C., and J. Stimson. 2012. *Ideology in America.* Cambridge, MA: Cambridge University Press.

Hibbing, John R., Kevin B. Smith, and John R. Alford. 2014. *Predisposed: Liberals, Conservatives and the Biology of Political Differences.* New York: Routledge.

Kling, Arnold. 2019. *The Three Languages of Politics: Talking Across the Political Divides.* 3rd ed. Washington, DC: Cato Institute.

Lynne, G.D. 2007. Review of Bromley, D.W. Sufficient Reason: Volitional Pragmatism and the Meaning of Economic Institutions. Princeton: Princeton University Press, 2006, 244 Pp. *American Journal of Agricultural Economics 89* (4): 1120–22.

———. 2009. Review of Bromley, D.W. Sufficient Reason: Volitional Pragmatism and the Meaning of Economic Institutions. Princeton: Princeton University Press, 2006, 244 Pp. *Journal of Natural Resources Policy Research 1* (1): 118–20.

Will, George F. 2019. *The Conservative Sensibility.* Kindle ed. New York: Hachette Books.

Willer, Robb, and Jan Voelkel. 2019. Progressive Policies Meet Conservative Values. News Release, December 1.

CHAPTER 7

Financial Policy: Tempering Greed

The economic actions leading up to the 2008 financial crisis and continuing economic challenges reflect anything but a humane economy. Wealth is being concentrated beyond any reasonable assessment of genuine needs. Exchange in trade, typified by the irrational "bubble" in real estate prices right before the 2008 crash, gave prices *P* serving extreme Greed rather than justice reflected in value *V*. Again, and it is important: Moral and ethical considerations are represented in the shared Other-interest and in value *V* determining how the Self&Other-interest are to be balanced. All such reality, especially becoming real prior to the 2008 crisis, has focused attention on the need for capitalism to be rebalanced, with a special focus on tempering the excessive Greed that was a major driver in the crisis, and continues as a major force.

As an article in an issue of Newsweek at that time, with the cover page *The Capitalist Manifesto,* proclaimed (Zakaria 2009, p. 41): "Greed is Good (To a Point)." Seemingly, Greed not tempered by virtue, focusing only on money, prices, profits and markets, insensitive to the humane side of the economy, is not Good. The immediate task became one of finding the new Point, which really says it was time to search for a new ethic, and bring a new moral community, into banking and finance. It also became apparent that the longer-term task was to develop an alternative economic framework and business paradigm, which will keep the search for the Point an active element in a changing, truly resilient, and moral, financial and economic system. The new paradigm needs to facilitate the explicit,

G. D. Lynne, *Metaeconomics*, Palgrave Advances in Behavioral Economics, https://doi.org/10.1007/978-3-030-50601-8_7

continuing evolution of ways to temper, condition, and, if necessary, restrain, Greed. It is about tempering the selfish with the selfless, as depicted in Fig. 7.1, which helps us make Metaeconomic sense of the matter of excessive Greed.

A well-known columnist, who also often is consistent with the NeoClassEcon way of thinking (compare the Self-interest column in Table 2.1 and the Conservative Columns in Table 6.1) proclaimed (Will 2009):

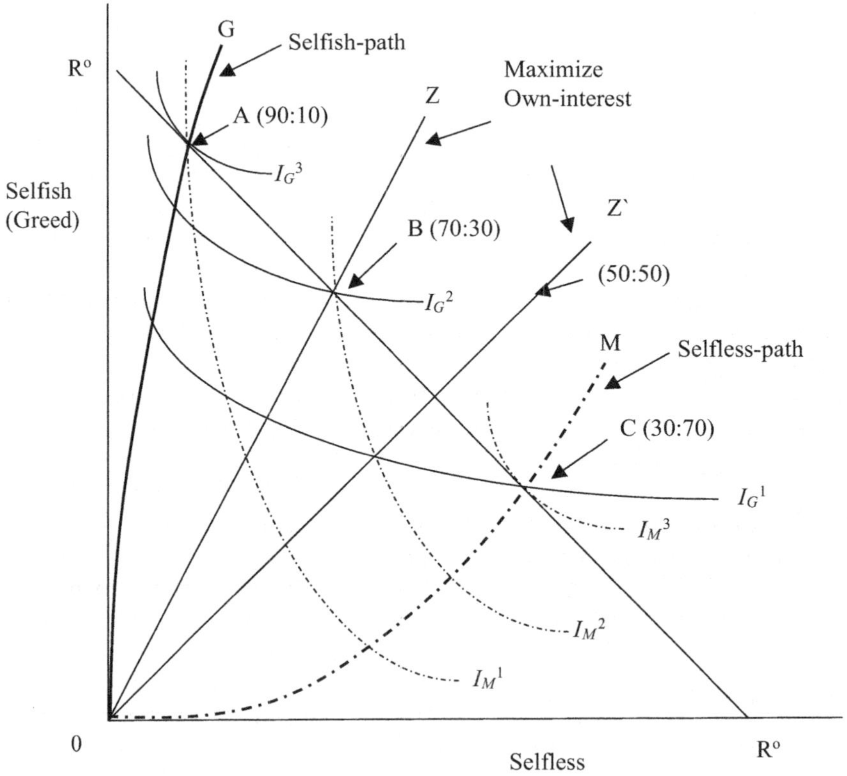

Fig. 7.1 Selfish (I_G) & selfless (I_M)-interest indifference curves for the allocation of a resource R, given the tendency to be jointly selfish&selfless while maximizing own-interest. (Source: Author's creation)

> Greed is worse than a moral defect; it is a cause of foolish pricing. That is why markets know it when they see it. And when markets are allowed to operate, Greed generates its own punishment.

It would be better, at least more "restful" as he puts it (referring to the turmoil around the 2008 crash, and subsequent debate about the role of Government relative to the excessive Greed which contributed in substantive ways to that crash), "to give moral reasoning a rest and give economic reasoning a chance." And, Metaeconomics, based as it is in empirical reality, might also put to question that Greed generates its own punishment. Maybe.

The perspective leaves it all to magic, to the Invisible Hand to do to the punishing. The Invisible Hand somehow just magically does the new moral reasoning, evolves the new ethic, and solves the problem of Greed in the Market. Metaeconomics suggests, that by the time Market sees it, if the Market ever sees it at all, it can easily be too late, as in the 2008 crash. Metaeconomics points to the need for a Visible Hand, at minimum as a supplement to the Invisible Hand (if there even is such a thing, which is highly questionable, as Samuels, Johnson, and Perry 2011, convincingly argue).

The book by *Financial Times* journalist Tett (2009, p. x) points to how an entire financial and banking system too heavily influenced by Greed, and other related human weaknesses, went awry:

> The story of the great credit boom and bust is not a saga that can be neatly blamed on a few Greedy or evil people. It is a story of how an entire financial system went wrong as a result of flawed incentives within banks and investment funds as well as the ratings agencies; warped regulatory structures; and a lack of oversight. It is a tale best understood through the observation of human foibles…

Yet, it is the flawed incentives that facilitated the Greed: It is still about excessive Greed. And, while excessive Greed as a main foible combined with a lack of oversight played a substantive role, Tett also makes it clear that a great deal of good has evolved out of the events leading to the 2008 (and ongoing) crisis. Empirical evidence suggests there is an interplay and jointness of the Greed and the Good, and, real possibilities through better balance in Market&Government. Like my grandmother always used to say, "There is nothing so bad that it isn't good for something."

To understand and frame the matter of excessive Greed, we need to first clarify that "the Market" is neither more nor less than a (generally large) number of people interacting through buying and selling in the exchange of some good or service, or, in production, some input. It is nothing more nor less than a Forum for Humans (not just Econs), buying and selling items they hold as private property. Also, if each person in the Market is moral and ethical, the Market could also, then, seemingly be moral and ethical, if the shared Other-interest has that content. So, if each person is tempering their own more primal tendency to Greed, then the Market, too, will express and represent less Greed. How is it tempered? Metaeconomics makes it clear that it may not be the Market that tempers Greed, in that Self-control is always a challenge; if Self-control is lacking, then the community of shared Other-interest perhaps needs to be brought forward in doing so.

People may perhaps even wish to ask for help in tempering their own Greed tendencies: Again, using the fun, profound and insightful story of the Sirens and the ship captain, "bind me to the mast" (Elster 1979), which essentially is about being more Selfless and less Selfish (as depicted in Fig. 7.1 on path 0Z). The Selfless role is played by a Good Government, and, in the process of Empathizing, asking "how would I wish to be treated," with the way we treat each other often evolved and made explicit in that Government. Seemingly, the banking and financial industry need to be bound to the mast.

As Blinder (2014, pp. 27–28) would have it, the kinds of events leading up to the crisis are the following, the "malevolent seven" as he refers to them:

> 1. inflated asset prices, especially of houses (the housing bubble) but also of certain securities (the bond bubble); 2. excessive leverage (heavy borrowing) throughout the financial system and the economy; 3. lax financial regulation, both in terms of what the law left unregulated and how poorly the various regulators performed their duties; 4. disgraceful banking practices in subprime and other mortgage lending; 5. the crazy-quilt of unregulated securities and derivatives that were built on these bad mortgages; 6. the abysmal performance of the statistical rating agencies, which helped the crazy-quilt get stitched together; and 7. the perverse compensation systems in many financial institutions that created powerful incentives to go for broke.

We now turn to making sense of it all with Metaeconomics. Overall, the malevolent seven came from largely unrestrained selfishness, a kind of "free-for-all" in Markets without bounds on the more primal Selfish tendency to excessive Greed. What do we mean by Greed, and, especially, excessive Greed, in economic terms? It is not even an issue in Microeconomics, which is a science of Greed, due to having extracted the Ethics; in contrast, Metaeconomics brings some (common) sense to it.

Making Sense of Economic Greed

Greed is all about the balance in being selfish&selfless, something that perhaps has not had enough attention in economics (see Kirman and Teschl 2010, for how Empathy has at best played a limited role in economic thinking). Figure 7.1 helps make sense of it all. A person can choose to be more selfish (Greed) oriented along path 0G, and giving into excessive Greed, as did the bankers and Wall Street traders leading up to 2008, even operate on the vertical axis. The person can be more selfless, first empathizing, resulting in joining in sympathy with others, perhaps even having compassion, along the selfless path 0M. Being extremely selfless is to operate near or even on the horizontal axis. Yet, the overlapping isocurves suggest most people are jointly, nonseparable selfish&selfless at the same time: We cannot separate the two tendencies into simple, separable, accounts in the brain. Also, any joint choice within and on the paths is rational: Areas outside the selfish path 0G and the selfless path 0 M (especially the extreme paths represented by the axes) are generally considered irrational, but still may be chosen (again, bankers and Wall Street traders on the vertical axis, the soldier and the hand grenade on the horizontal axis).

Also, the selfless path, and the shared Other-interest, likely rests mainly in the subconscious (represented as dash-dot in Fig. 7.1), the Invisible Hand of the NeoClassEcon. The lines are brought into the conscious, and solidified, through the Visible Hand of the NeoInstiEcon, and perhaps then once again relegated to the dots of the Invisible Hand, but now with new direction. Being Selfless tends to be more in the background, "invisible" to each person in their daily activities. Recall the story about the Christmas Scrooge: It took the Ghosts to bring Scrooge to more reasonable senses.

So, to what extent did the bankers and Wall Street traders bring the other virtues represented along path 0M—temperance, courage/

fortitude, justice, faith, hope and love/charity—into play? What role did the other virtues play in banking and Wall Street choices? The other virtues, as McCloskey (2006) makes clear, historically played a substantive role in truly an able and successful (good) business and industry, also a main point in Hirschfeld (2018, p. 138). Answer: It seems not much of a role, at all.

Various sharing paths are labeled: 90:10 (the "tithing" path); 70:30 (common income tax rates at the margin); 50:50 (often found to be favored experimental economic laboratory tests: See Camerer, Loewenstein, and Perry 2005; Ledyard 1995); 30:70 (close to Warren Buffet's allocation of his estate between heirs and the Gate's Foundation, actually around 15:85); and, finally, Mother Theresa (and others who devote themselves more totally to the poor, the environment, a mission-oriented common, shared cause) probably at something like 10:90 (not illustrated), or, in the extreme, the horizontal axis. It is also now easy to explain why a person would choose the 70:30 (70 for me, 30 for someone else) rather than the 90:10, which is a mystery in the experimental testing by the NeoClassEcon (see Smith and Wilson 2019, p. 39, 49), requiring inserting an other-regarding patch like an inequity aversion or social preference or perceptions of other intentions into the max U function. Metaeconomics makes it clear that it has nothing to do with other-regarding, and simply has to do with the sentiments, the empathy-sympathy with $I_M^2 > I_M^1$. The payoff is greater in the domain of shared other-interest at B than at A: It is just the right-thing-to-do. And, like Smith and Wilson (2019, p. 42) point out, the max U, maximize self-interest only theory is even more silent when a person selects a 30:70 point like C, or even the horizontal axis: Again, the soldier on the grenade, anyone?

Also, which path is chosen is heavily influenced by the emotions, which, in turn, are related to the underlying virtues. Like Camerer, Loewenstein, and Prelec (2005, p. 18) say it, "cognition by itself cannot produce action; to influence behavior, the cognitive system must operate via the affective." And, the emotions, or the "affects" as it were, have two dimensions: The actions coming out of feelings represented in hunger, desire, anger, and all part of the hedonistic, Egoistic domain of emotion as represented on selfish path 0G are likely more primal. The actions coming out of the moral and ethical dimension on selfless path 0M are perhaps more heavily dependent on being stirred to become mindful, become aware of same, and, perhaps less influential (and, thus, the dash-dot lines in Fig. 7.1).

Not paying deeper attention to the affects resulted in Scrooge being almost on the vertical axis (he does share a bit with Bob Cratchit, a few crumbs, a bit of trickle-down wealth) before the visits by the Ghosts of Christmas, who nudge him onto something closer to a path 0Z. Regulators nudging bankers, we might say. It also allows the possibility that the two tendencies, the two interests, are inherently (perhaps even biologically, as suggested in triune brain formulations, especially) evolved and "wired" into the brain circuitry within each of us. Selfish path 0G represents the survival of the fittest organism and the selfless path 0M represents the survival of the fittest group, an assessment with which Darwin would probably agree, with balance between organism&ecosystem on path 0Z: It seems that in 2008 we had lost balance, clearly not on path 0Z, between banker&people.

With selfishness being more primal, we can easily stray to the selfish path 0G. It occurred even to some extent within the Tribe named as J.P. Morgan, wherein many knew it and valued a more tempered and restrained peaceful, happiness path 0Z (Tett 2009, e.g., see pp. 151, 211, 212, 245, 246, 249). It is to say, the "Markets do not see it until they (explicitly) know it," and, even if they know it, the Market may stray from it. Selfless path 0M considerations must be made conscious in order to affect choices before the trade.

And, what exactly will the Markets not see? Figure 7.2 makes it clear. Recall we derive the possibility frontiers of Fig. 7.2 by moving along a path R^oR^o in Fig. 7.1. A Market will likely fail to explicitly recognize the potential for synergy arising in a tempered, conditioned, and balanced Market. The Dual Interest frontiers expand at an increasing rate, as resources in the economy are increased at a constant pace. The expanding frontiers illustrate the potential for a kind of synergy arising out of good balance in selfish&selfless, as represented generally in Market&Government (both must be Good). Selfish&Selfless interact to produce a kind of sum-greater-than-the-sum-of-the-parts outcome: The economy does well. It is stable. Everyone has reasonable shares in the bounty of Market&Government.

We also now gain new understanding of the pushpins poetry conundrum applied to the financial markets and in the banks: There are non-money (poetry) things going on in the arena of finance and banking (pushpins). Again, they do not have to be commensurable on the same $V \equiv P$ plane as presumed in Neoclassical Economics; instead, value V can arise out of a higher, balanced selfish&selfless-interest plane, which can

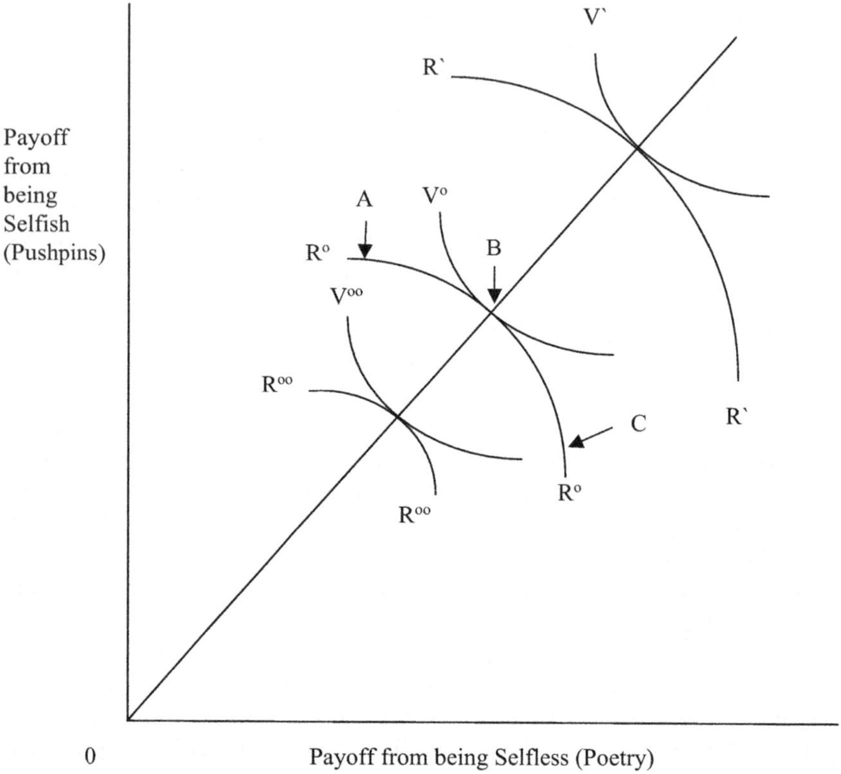

Fig. 7.2 Synergy on the selfish&selfless-interest path 0Z, going beyond greed to happiness and maximizing own-interest on a higher plane of value *V*. (Source: Author's creation)

drive and otherwise influence the price *P* coming out of the Market, with the two values jointly determined, so price *P* also influences value *V*. The Market, when not tempered and bounded, misses the value *V*.

Making Sense of "Fools Gold"

With the analytical system of Figs. 7.1 and 7.2 in mind, we can now explore specifically how Metaeconomics helps us make more sense of what happened on the way to the financial and economic melt-down of 2008 described in Tett (2009) and Blinder (2014). We move to suggesting ways that Metaeconomics can help in avoiding such crashes in the future. Tett (2009) is especially insightful through using the results of in-depth and extensive interviews with the major players in various banking and other financial firms, as well as regulators, some of whom tried to temper the over expressions of Greed. Tett (2009) also draws on published articles in the *Financial Times* (for whom she worked as a financial reporter), and from study reports produced by a variety of firms and other entities, including several financial industry analysts. The rich array of empirical observation and anecdotes provide an informal empirical test of the power of Metaeconomics.

Both a Metaeconomics analysis and Tett (2009) offer a counter to the view still held by many in the financial sector that "excessive pay did not cause the crisis" (Robert Profusek, Dow Jones, on MSNBC financial news channel, June 10, 2009). Metaeconomics clearly points to the need to at least ask the empirical question regarding the role of excessive Greed, excessive pay, as well as expected casino returns from risky instruments. There was also excessive Greed powering extreme exuberance in the housing Market (Blinder 2014, p. 29), that eventually proved to be built on smoke and mirrors. The exuberance was especially present and spread in the derivatives markets built on questionable lending practices and unsustainable housing mortgages (many of the so called "NINJA loans—granted to people with no income, no jobs, and no assets," Blinder 2014, p. 69).

We start at the end of the Tett (2009, p. 254) book, in the Epilogue, with the conclusion, that we need (think poetry, here, relating to the culture):

> a wider rethinking of the culture of finance. For too many years, bankers have treated 'credit' as merely an isolated game of numbers. The roots of the word, though, come from the Latin *credere*, meaning 'to believe.' It is a concept centered on wider social relations, which financiers forget at their peril. For if there is one element, above all, that is now needed to restore sanity to banking, it is that policymakers, bankers, and politicians must adopt a more *holistic* vision of finance. In essence, what is needed is a return to the seemingly dull virtues of prudence, moderation, balance, and common sense.

Metaeconomics supports the holistic vision and points to the same need for balance in due consideration of all the virtues, which acknowledges a role for culture (poetry), especially in the tempering of prudence-only (selfish) choices (pushpins). Culture and its role in tempering behavior is represented in the empathy leading to sympathy-driven selfless choice. The focus shifts from a complete emphasis on the strong version of prudence and what it can buy (resulting in "max U" as McCloskey 2006, characterizes it), to the balanced, tempered version of prudence called for by Tett (2009).

Tett (2009) focuses our attention on J.P. Morgan, which came to be JP Morgan Chase with several negative consequences from their acquisition. The actual namesake, J.P. Morgan, in testifying in 1933 to a hostile US Congress fueled by populist concerns of excessive Greed on Wall Street in the 1920s, which led to the crash of 1929 (the crashes, fueled by excessive Greed, are not new), noted they were a "first class business.... (run) in a first-class way (Tett 2009, p. 15)." J.P. Morgan saw "first class" to include reasonable compensation structures, commitment to doing the right thing by their customers and the larger society, as well as commitment and loyalty (on Selfless path 0 M, shared with customers and the shareholders) within the Tribe of J.P. Morgan employees. The commitment and loyalty were especially apparent on the derivative swap teams that came to dominate.

In more recent versions of Wall Street, especially in the 1990s, commitment and loyalty have been deemed rather "quaint," being replaced by a Greed-based aggressiveness in trading guided by "kill or be killed" (Tett 2009, p. 15). The acquisition of J.P. Morgan, resulting in JP Morgan Chase, tore down most of the tempering structures, albeit many of the organizing guides in years past still have some force: Tett argues that JP Morgan Chase has not taken the selfish path of excessive Greed, which came to dominate in so many other firms. Yet, the merger with Chase shifted the company to a less reasonable, not so happy path 0Z, much closer to the selfish path 0G (and the vertical axis) than in the old J.P. Morgan company.

We can now go back to the beginning of the story, and relate it to make more economic sense of it. First, Metaeconomics points to the substantive role played by the moral and ethical dimension, what is overall a good thing to do, represented in the domain of selflessness I_M. The story, as Tett (2009) tells it, starts with the J.P. Morgan Tribe seeing early-on how derivatives could do a great deal of good in the financial Markets. Derivatives served to spread the risk. Everyone could carry a bit of the risk, and, together, everyone would become better off, perhaps even experiencing the synergy between the selfish&selfless on some lower risk, happier path 0Z.

The way it would work was quite simple (albeit the instruments themselves later became quite complex; see Blinder 2014, p. 72). For example, in the case of the credit default swap (CDS) derivative, the first one was arranged by J.P. Morgan involved Exxon, as related to the problem with the Valdez oil tanker spill. After being threatened with a $5B fine, Exxon asked for a $4.8B credit line. J.P. Morgan wanted to provide it by their loyalty (think I_M) to an old customer, Exxon (Tett 2009, p. 47), even though there was little money to be made from so doing: Here we see the need for self-sacrifice in selfish I_G driven by the commitment represented in selfless I_M. It was realized that a CDS could not only keep J.P. Morgan closer to the selfless path 0M (keep their loyalty, commitment, feeding the sense of community with their clients) but could also free-up funds to help move toward selfish path 0G. It was found that the European Bank for Reconstruction and Development (Bank) might be willing, for a fee, to carry the risk of default by Exxon. The bank needed to increase its income flow; J.P. Morgan wanted to free-up capital to lend to other entities.

So, providing the credit line to Exxon raised their reserve capital requirements as well as pushed on credit limits imposed on the part of J.P. Morgan (Tett 2009, p. 46). A deal was struck, with J.P. Morgan paying the bank to cover the risk of default, which the bank was happy to accept, because the risk of Exxon defaulting is exceedingly small. J.P. Morgan had found a way, through trading in CDS instruments to maintain loyalty with less self-sacrifice. It meant now being able to make interest income on at least part of the $4.8B credit line more than enough to cover the fee payment, moving toward Selfish path 0G. As Tett (2009, p. 48) tells it, such trading in CDS fed the dream to free-up reserve cash: "credit derivatives would allow J.P. Morgan—and in due course all other banks, too—to exquisitely fine-tune risk burdens, releasing banks from age-old constraints and freeing up vast amounts of capital, turbocharging not only banking but the economy as a whole." It means lending could be greatly leveraged, way beyond reasonable limits (Blinder 2014, p. 47).

It supercharged taking rather than making wealth. It was going to be possible while still retaining the tradition in J.P. Morgan of loyalty, relationships, and commitment to the loan customer. The problem became: Not all banks and their traders had such well-defined loyalty and "doing-the-right-thing" paths 0M as did J.P. Morgan, keeping the company tempered and bounded on happy (for everyone) path 0Z. As Tett (2009) shows, not having a sense for the need to embrace selfless path 0M resulted in Market-failure to temper and bound the Greed, now even more easily expressed by using derivatives without Market-discipline.

The CDS derivatives became one of just many types of derivatives. By the time of the crash in 2008 derivatives were represented in currency, interest, and, the one that broke the bank, the collateralized debt obligations (CDO) of asset-backed securities (ABS), especially the CDO squared (CDOs of CDOs) and CDO cubed (CDOs of CDOs of CDOs) versions, the ultimate in encouraging speculation and Greed. The rating agencies also contributed, with many of the instruments obtaining grades way beyond any reality as to their real risks (Blinder 2014, p. 79). The high ratings exacerbated a kind of "bandwagon" effect, which is commonly found in Behavioral Economics research of financial markets (see Altman 2012, loc 2013): Many were getting on the bandwagon with little understanding of the instrument itself.

The CDOs associated with subprime mortgages became especially problematic because of the higher interest rates to which the mortgages were supposed to move (and, thus, produce ever higher payoffs to the investors), and the substantive default rates that emerged as interest rates increased: Such mortgages were viewed like "gold dust" (Tett 2009, p. 95) to selfish, Greed-driven, returns-hungry investors. Clearly the instruments were effective in taking wealth. The result was runaway bank lending and massive accumulation of private debt. And, it was all smoke and mirrors, a house of cards.

We might ask: Where were the regulators? Where was good government, a Government that keeps a liberal and humane democracy-based capitalism operant? Where was the selfless path 0M influence? Why didn't Government step in to at least slow down and temper the obvious taking of wealth (with little to no making but a lot of taking of wealth) that the derivatives facilitated?

Tett (2009) documents several attempts by the regulators to temper the frenzy, which evolved in the various derivatives markets. As Tett (2009, p. 25) argues, finance in many ways is like a public utility, and "the question government regulators must wrestle with is to what degree private financiers should be allowed to seek a profit (the Selfish-interest) and to what degree they must be required to ensure that money flows safely [the Selfless-interest]." When Self-control fails, it becomes the task of regulators, through the Government, to influence the movement toward the better balance on some happier path 0Z.

Tett (2009, pp. 25–26) points to how the Glass-Steagall Act, tracing back to the Great (and excessive Greed-based) Depression of the 1930s, which separated commercial and investment banking, did just that. The act also imposed reserve limits. An international agreement, the Basil Accord of 1988, set reserve requirements of 8 percent of the value of assets for all banks, worldwide. The kinds of rules tempered traditional loans, debt obligations, better ensuring path 0Z outcomes. By the 1990s, the regulators realized they perhaps needed some way to also temper the derivatives, in that derivatives in effect gave the banks the ability to move beyond the limits. The derivatives extended their debt obligations, as risk was supposedly "sold-off" from their portfolios (Tett 2009, p. 26).

Another problem was that one of the main regulators, the Federal Reserve, was headed by Alan Greenspan, who had been for years a true believer in the Ayn Rand contention that unfettered selfishness, only Self-interest at work, will regulate itself. Ayn Rand claimed (without empirical test, by the way) that Self-control and Self-discipline would prevail and that, in fact, it was immoral to ever consider bringing any kind of influence to bear on expressions of Self-interest. Vertical axis, please. As Greenspan admitted later, he was "shocked" by the lack of Self-discipline in the financial industry (Blinder 2014, p. 57), which is really about ignoring the moral and ethical dimension that is needed to temper financial transactions: The Market was not disciplined.

Tett (2009, p. 27) documents how the Commodity Futures Trading Commission (CFTC) was the first to try extending regulations to the derivatives, introducing a more selfless path 0M that would temper the selfish path 0G. Intense lobbying by the International Swaps and Derivatives Association (ISDA), which was dominated by Self-interest only, the Selfish Market is somehow good, prevailed. The CFTC backed off (Tett 2009, p. 27). CFTC tried again in the late-1990s; their admonishments were again quashed (Tett 2009, p. 75). Concerns were expressed along the way by people in positions of influence, including Jerry Corrigan, president of the New York Federal Reserve (Tett 2009, pp. 23–24).

The forces keeping the regulators at bay were immense, including Alan Greenspan (Ayn Rand and Milton Friedman, combined), Federal Reserve Chairman. It spoke against any kind of direct regulation of the derivatives Markets (Tett 2009, p. 39). So, we moved even beyond the Selfish path 0G. It was even unswayed by rather trenchant, public commentary like calling derivatives "financial hydrogen bombs, built on personal computers by twenty-six-year-olds with MBAs" (Felix Rohtyn, "legendary Wall Street figure" as referred to and quoted by Tett 2009, p. 31). Perhaps they were terrible two-year-old MBAs, operating very close if not on the vertical axis, without bounds?

Tett (2009, p. 31) also notes the influence of the Austrian School of Economics, a close relative of the NeoClassEcon, as represented in Hayek. It was brought into the mix by a Mark Brickell, a member of the derivatives swap team at J.P. Morgan, who saw any kind of regulation, akin to the Buchanan/Public Choice School, and to Hayek, as stifling innovation. No need for a tempering selfless path 0M in the Self-interest only, Selfish only frame: We simply free-up the selfish path 0G, and move out of the way of the "innovation." The cause of the Self-interest only, selfish only economics was also served by the trust in the NeoClassEcon development of mathematics and mathematical models devoid of the moral and ethical dimension. Such mathematical models and computing power were used to find trading opportunities (Tett 2009, p. 74). Ethics, anyone?

The Gaussian copula model is a case in point: It served to help in estimating the degree of dependency among variables, looking internal, within the CDOs (Tett 2009, p. 102). In effect, all the judgment of risk was now turned into a nice, precise, number. Long-Term Capital Management, created in 1994 and framed by Self-interest economics-based academics and traders, also used mathematical, computer-based models: It "imploded" in 1998 (Tett 2009, p. 74). The problem is: The "certainty" of the Microeconomics-based mathematical models (again, "made more certain" by ignoring the moral and ethical dimension) means the triggers are the same in every instrument. In effect, the math models take any influence from the selfless path 0M, out of the system. Microeconomics-based mathematical models abstract from, so they in effect leave out: Empathy, sympathy, sentiments, compassion, moral community, ethics, institutions (except private property), and community. Math models based in mathematical microeconomics, ignore the shared Other-interest.

A bit of history here: Smith (1759/1790) would likely have argued, if there had been a Wall Street in his day, for seeking a richer, peaceful Own-interest on some path 0Z. Smith (1776/1789) was all about efficiency, yes, but also about peace-of-mind. The "war-like" conditions that evolved in the 2008 financial and economic crisis, and in our now tribal political system more generally, would have greatly disturbed Adam Smith. It makes for bad capitalism, with the only way to save capitalism being to move to the peaceful, happiness path 0Z. And, even more importantly,

Adam Smith was about building a humane Market, a humane capitalism, conditioned by the sentiments, which came out of Empathy.

The "good, ethical lot (Tett 2009, p. 110, quoting a Jamie Dimon, who was brought into the new JP Morgan Chase by the merger with Bank One)" from the old J.P. Morgan, were also disturbed by what happened. Blythe Masters, one of the original swap team members at the old J.P. Morgan, "was livid … at how bankers had perverted her derivatives dream (Tett 2009, p. 249)." Masters also noted (quoted in Tett 2009, p. 251), in commenting on the Microeconomics models that were being used to drive the derivative trading "…were right in a sense, but the problem is that they did not give enough emphasis to all the human issues, the regulatory structures, and things like that …. The idea was that such happenings were just noise in the models but that is just dead-arsed wrong. We don't live in that kind of world of perfect economic models." Masters, too, saw the shared Other-interest in the background. Greenspan also spoke of "irrational exuberance" (Altman 2012, loc 6207), another feature of the irrationality represented in excessive Greed on selfish path 0G.

Even J.P. Morgan Chase, however, did not keep selfless path 0M adequately in mind, as confirmed by their strong financial position even after most of the crisis had subsided, as proclaimed in a July 16, 2009 article "J. P. Morgan's Profits Soar…" (Rieker and Benn 2009). Yet, with due credit, J.P. Morgan Chase did continue to fight for a more tempered path 0Z for derivatives trading, albeit they did not support going to Government, the proposal at the time to create a special derivatives exchange, for help (Sidel 2009).

What Greenspan and many others missed (not including J.P. Morgan) is: The Self-interest only, NeoClassEcon child (drawing on Berne 1961) often goes beyond reality, living in an imaginary world, on (and perhaps even above) selfish path 0G. The child works at delineating, perhaps even isolating and hiding, it's world from the Other-interest, more selfless path 0M coming out of the (NeoInstiEcon) parent. Don't forget: The terribles-2s prior to when a child gains in Self-control, can have bad outcomes: If not tempered by a parent, and the self-controller who integrates and balances, things can get out of hand. Self-interest economics, the Neoclassical Microeconomics-based mathematical models, essentially are models of the terrible two-year-old, with a presumption of complete Self-control on the way to maximizing Self-interest only.

On a more positive note, the child also, however, by child-like innovation in the Market, expands the world for the parent (sometimes too restrictive, as represented in the Government), making things better: Derivatives trading has helped the economy. The parent (the Government), if operating with restraint, perhaps a kind of "tough love" approach, operating from path 0M positions, provides for ways to "reel-in" and "rationally bound" (as well as perhaps encourage) the child (the Market), material for use by the controller within own-self. Taking derivatives Markets to the extremes represented in "CDO-squared" and "CDO-cubed" derivative products are cases in point, fueled heavily by the "shadow banking system" who were developing and selling the derivatives (Blinder 2014, p. 60): Innovative, in a child-like sense, but perhaps a bit too much, as noted, such products shifted path 0G toward the vertical axis. The derivatives were sold as leading to efficiency, that is, ostensibly (as an irrationally exuberant Child would describe it) "transferring risk efficiently around the system" (Tim Frost, J.P. Morgan, quoted by Tett 2009, p. 86).

Tett (2009, p. 252), drawing on a background in social anthropology, a close relative of the SocPsych and NeoInstiEcon, says it well (think poetry within the shared Other-interest I_M):

> the finance world's lack of interest in wider social matters cuts to the very heart of what has gone wrong. What social anthropology teaches its adherents is that nothing in society ever exists in a vacuum or in isolation. Holistic analysis that tries to link different parts of a social structure is crucial, be that in respect to wedding rituals or trading floors. Anthropology also instills a sense of skepticism about the official rhetoric. In most societies, elites try to maintain their power not simply by garnering wealth, but also by dominating the mainstream ideologies, in terms of both what is said and what is not discussed. Social "silences" serve to maintain power structures, in ways that participants often barely understand themselves let alone plan.

Tett goes on to call not only for more holistic analysis, but also in involving the social sciences in breaking the "social silence" about the practices in the world of finance and banking. Tett calls for debate, now that we have been irritated into thinking about it all. Metaeconomics, too, sees the role of irritation in stirring the needed for debate in rational ways. It sees the potential for a truly rational choice emerging in the region between selfish path 0G and selfless path 0M on the way to a truly sustainable, rational, stable, peaceful, and happy path 0Z. Metaeconomics gives a framework and a theory to help break the silence, and resolve any crisis in Market&Government.

Cronyism in the Financial Industry

It seems the most important lesson beyond the need to temper the Greed Capitalism, Casino Capitalism that characterized the 2008 crisis has yet to be learned. A significant amount of crony capitalism was also around, as revealed in how the banks and government interacted: The interaction was a long way from good capitalism, with an ethical base to join banks&government in good balance.

First, what is crony capitalism? Munger and Villarreal-Dias (2019) characterize it as a situation where Self-interest, Greed for power-driven Government joins into cronyism with Self-interest, Greed-driven, generally large, corporations and enterprises. The result is Self-interest-driven mutual gain at the expense of the shared Other-interest with taxpayers and consumers (Hodgson 2019). It is accomplished by using a variety of "political instruments" including "subsidies, tariffs, import quotas, exclusive production privileges such as licenses, antitrust laws, and compulsory cartelization designs" (Munger and Villarreal-Diaz 2019, citing Labeit 2009). The 2008 crisis led to using a number of political instruments including massive bailouts of the large banks, who had lots of Government friends, former bank and Wall Street leaders, and politicians, who were in sympathy with said large banks, as "in too big to fail." Intriguingly, politicians were claiming the moral and ethical community was all about the need to bail out the banks, who, in fact, probably should not have received any taxpayer money because the actual, low level (not) moral and ethical community that was operating. Metaeconomics points to the need to go find out, empirically.

Ethical Standards for Corporate Executives and Government Bureaucrats

Metaeconomics clarifies it is about the ethics, the moral content of the Other-interest at work in influencing Corporate Executives within their own business environment, as well as in interacting with politicians, bureaucrats, and Government staff who also need to operate on high ethical standards within Government. Regarding the corporate executives, Sorkin (2019) points to an idea put forth by a Jamie Gamble, former partner at the law firm Simpson, Thacher and Bartlett, a lawyer with wide and deep experience with many large US corporations. Gamble concluded that most if not all US corporate executives "are legally obligated to act like sociopaths… (characterizing corporate America as a) complex network of horribles… The corporate entity is obligated to care only about itself and to define what is good as what makes it more money… Pretty close to a textbook case of antisocial personality disorder. And corporate persons are the most powerful people in our world." Perhaps much the same could be said about many in Government, too?

What is the solution? Sorkin (2019) points to the Jamie Gamble suggestion for new governance rules, in that corporations in the Market (and, we might add, in the Government):

> should "adopt a binding set of ethical rules, approved by stockholders and addressing the key ethical dimensions of corporate life" including:
>
> - Their "relationships with employees."
> - Their "relationships with the communities in which they produce and sell."
> - Their "relationships with customers."
> - Their "effects on the environment."
> - And their "effects on future generations."

Seemingly a similar set of guidelines might also be approved by voters, as regards the Government. All said domains of Other-interest are somewhat separable, but all overlapping. Sorkin (2019) goes on to point out, that Gamble sees that once the rules are in place "any shareholder could sue the board of directors for violating the ethical rules —just as any shareholder can today sue the board of directors for violating the maximize rule." It seems voters, too, should have similar recourse in the Government.

In Metaeconomic terms, we develop new governance rules defining the Empathy-based selfless path 0 M in Fig. 7.1. It puts in place an influence (homonomy) on corporate executives (Metaeconomics suggests we add Government officials and politicians) to stop focusing strictly and exclusively on the Ego-driven Selfish path 0G (autonomy). In fact, any shareholder (add the voter) now has the right to sue, otherwise force and control (heteronomy) movement toward the selfless path 0M. We encourage and require (if necessary) the tempered, conditioned selfish&selfless

path 0Z. Perhaps it is the 70:30 path in Fig. 7.1, albeit the best path for happiness is an empirical question.

On said path, there are also likely to be less payoffs in the domain of rent-seeking associated with Government awards of special privilege, as in the massive bank bailouts in 2008–2009. As Blinder (2014, p. 81), characterizes it: "Specifically, many financial companies' compensation plans created perverse incentives for key employees to take excessive risks with OPM—other people's money. Which is just what they did." Seems we bailed out bankers on the vertical axis of extreme Greed.

Intriguingly, many financial executives even felt justified, entitled, after crashing their industry, to take bonus payments from bailout money paid by the taxpayers. Such entitlement reflects a personality syndrome regularly observed in the extremely wealthy. It is not uncommon to find the extremely wealthy believing they are entitled to the wealth even though any reasonable assessment of what they actually contributed to making it suggests otherwise (Ryan 2019, p. 176). Ironically, it is also common for many on the lower rungs of the wealth ladder to also feel entitled. Perhaps the sense of entitlement at both ends is why the middle-class has become so irritated, and resentful? Empirical question.

And, for the one who had to deal with the 2008 crisis, the *Audacity of Hope* book by Obama (2006) referred to the kind of Empathy represented here in the selfless path, a strong version of the Golden Rule. It is not simply sympathy or charity, but rather something far more demanding "a call to stand in somebody else's shoes and see through their eyes (Obama 2006, p. 66)," arising out of the Virtue of Hope. He saw that the inadequate expression of Empathy has led to the fundamental economic, financial, and political turmoil. Perhaps the bankers and Wall Street traders could have done some walking in the shoes of others (after Obama 2009)? Perhaps the result would have been some tempering of the excessive Greed demonstrated by said financial industry leaders who took massive amounts of bail-out money and even demanded bonuses to reward bad decisions. Empathy, anyone?

Rational Market Myth: Failure to See the Role of the Shared Other-Interest

From *The Economist* (June 11, 2009), in a review of Fox (2009), "The Myth of the Rational Market:"

> THE financial crisis that has engulfed the world in the past two years is not just, or perhaps even mainly, a tale of Greed run riot; it is the result of an idea that failed. That idea, which over the past four decades became the dominant belief among those generally regarded as the savviest participants in the financial system, was that the market is rational and efficient. So much for that .... The only disappointment about "The Myth of the Rational Market" is that it does not say more about how the ideas that shape financial markets will change in response to this catastrophic intellectual failure.

The review missed the more fundamental point as to why the market is not rational and efficient: The failed idea is that people in the Markets need only pursue Self-interest to be efficient. The intellectual failure is to acknowledge there is a role for the Empathy leading to ethics-based Other-interest (the sentiments, Adam Smith said), giving the context to the Market, and to see the payoffs from balance in the dual interest. In fact, a rational market is only possible with said balance. And, as noted in Tett (2009, p. 251), quoting one of the former J.P. Morgan team members who helped develop the derivatives: "Now it is clear we need a new paradigm. But we haven't found it yet, and frankly I don't know where we will." Metaeconomics could serve well as that new paradigm due to introducing the shared Other-interest reflecting the Adam Smith sentiments, which are essential to Market discipline and rationality. And, the new Humanomics, too, points to the key role of the sentiments in what makes for a rational and efficient Market.

Making Further Sense of the Rational Market

Nobel Laureate Vernon Smith has spent a career devoted to testing propositions about the Market, as to the rationality of it, how it evolves price, how it clears or not. Also, he has been a pioneer and leader in using the experimental economics laboratory for said exploration and testing, much like we have done in testing Metaeconomics propositions. And, while historically the experimental results by Vernon Smith and colleagues, as well as many others doing experimental economics, supported the rationality of the Market, more recent findings suggest it may not be as rational as the earlier research seemed to suggest. Reason? Perhaps a rational market rests on the foundation of the moral sentiments, as Adam Smith (1759/1790) suggested?

So, laboratory testing was redesigned, in search for the possible role of the sentiments, the empathy-sympathy of Metaeconomics. Findings resulted in Smith (2012), Smith and Wilson (2019) proposing a Humanomics, to deal with the personal and social side of economic choice. The claim is that the NeoClassEcon—with the exclusive focus on "max U," the self-interest only, the Econ—by not considering the sentiments are missing a key feature of the Market, the social context for the Market. Not seeing the context for the Market (the NeoInstiEcon would say, not seeing the underlying institution) is to not seeing the Human side of the Market. In Metaeconomics, not seeing the role of the empathy-sympathy, the sentiments-based institution representing a Human, is like not seeing what is in the foundation of a good capitalism. And, said good capitalism runs on Own-interest, to include the Other (shared social)-interest, not just Self-interest: Like Smith and Wilson (2019, pp. 2–3) remind us, Adam Smith "speaks not of self-interest but of one's 'own interest,' which includes prudence but is always mediated by what 'other men can go along with.'" What other men can go along with is in the institution, the shared other-interest, in the sentiments arising out of empathy-sympathy. And, Adam Smith referred to self-interest as being selfish, as is depicted on path 0G in Fig. 7.1, which does not serve a good capitalism.

It is essentially the same claim that has been made in Metaeconomics as first proposed in Lynne (1999, 2002), with the empirical testing documented in Lynne et al. (2016). A number of laboratory experiments have also been conducted, for example, see Czap et al. (2018; for a quick overview of the results, as well as a brief summary of the progression in Metaeconomics over the 1999–2020 period, see the Empathy Conservation section in Chap. 12). The two-decade long effort, which intriguingly parallels the effort in Humanomics, is represented in the current version of Metaeconomics. It sees the Empathy-based Other-interest, the social (writ large, represented in the Empathy with other Spaceship Earth Travelers) on path 0M and the Ego-based economic (prudent) self on path 0G. The person seeks balance in the Self&Other while maximizing Own-interest on path 0Z, a path that others can go along with.

Like Smith (2012, p. 3) says it, Humanomics sees that a truly rational Market must be sensitive to the "conduct, and its propriety and fitness with the rules of fair play… (and the person's) capacity for self-command in controlling what others might see as excesses of self-love." Metaeconomics sees the matter of excess self-love manifesting in excessive Greed, and is tempered through the shared other-interest and the Self-control, producing the social capital (Smith and Wilson 2019, p. 10, see this kind of capital, too) to bring it to bear.

Humanomics and Metaeconomics Both See the Key Role of the Sentiments

We now examine the extent of the overlap of Humanomics and Metaeconomics through looking at main points from Adam Smith's two books that have been used by Vernon Smith and Bart Wilson to build Humanomics, and how they also underlay Metaeconomics. Lynne (2016, pp. 245–250) examines several other points from Adam Smith's two books, especially as related to seeing self-interest as primal, but making the case that Adam Smith's sentiments are best thought of as being represented in shared other-interest. The resulting dual interest notion is that a person seeks to maximize the balanced Self&Other-interest within an own-interest.

Humanomics also alludes to Adam Smith's pointing to own-interest, but still focuses (see Smith and Wilson 2019, in Table 10.1, p. 147) on self-interest, with each person's Impartial Spectator imagining the self in the role of the other in judging intent and probable responses, leading to rule-following behavior. In effect, the rule-following works to temper the self-interest. Metaeconomics sees self-interest as more primal, while such imagining is seen as a key part of forming the shared other-interest, which once determined can lead to a kind of rule-following while maximizing the own-interest, also working to temper the self-interest. There is much common ground in the overlap.

In terms of the specific overlap, a good starting point is to consider how Adam Smith thought about the benefits of trade, especially the beneficence, a good and ethical trade. As Smith (2012, p. 5) makes clear, in quoting Smith (1759/1790, p. 78):

> Beneficence is always free, it cannot be extorted by force, the mere want of it exposes to no punishment …. It may disappoint of the good which might be reasonably expected, and upon that account it may justly excite dislike and disapprobation: it cannot, however, provoke any resentment which mankind will go along with.

So, Humanomics highlighting the two forces at work as represented in beneficence and others going along with it suggests a specific overlap. Metaeconomics clarifies the two forces are a Self-interest and Other (shared with others, but still internal to the person, so, not other-regarding)-interest, a dual interest represented in the own-interest.

Beneficence the Ornament, and Justice the Foundation, of a Market Society

More overlap is suggested in the jointness of beneficence&justice. Metaeconomics, due to recognizing dual interest, sees that a Market can only facilitate beneficence (a close relative of benefits) if it is not unjust. Humanomics sees the same thing: Smith and Wilson (2019, p. 201) help here, with the quote from Smith (1759/1790, Second.II.III, pp. 124–124):

> Nature (read the Spaceship Earth System) has fitted the human species to live, to subsist, in society only. All of us require one another's assistance. Society flourishes where that mutual support is provided in the reciprocity of gratitude and friendship bound together in good offices of affection and esteem.

Notice how this also means the economy is embedded within both the community and the larger Spaceship. Adam Smith also noted the tendency for all people, embedded therein, to want to barter and trade (globalization, anyone?). So, as the Adam Smith story goes, there is then the real possibility of beneficence from the interaction: People potentially can benefit from trade, with both trying to do good. But, it is not without issues; there is still the matter of justice.

Smith and Wilson (2019, p. 201) continue, quoting Smith (1759/1790, Second.II.III, pp. 124–125) some more, noting that no society can

> subsist among those who are at all times ready to hurt and injure one another. The moment that injury begins, the moment that mutual resentment and animosity take place, all the bands of it are broke asunder, and … dissipated and scattered abroad by the violence and opposition of their discordant affections.

The hurt, the injury, the injustice must be tempered, bounded, and reduced as much as possible, albeit perhaps never totally eliminated, before a Market can trade with beneficence. Smith and Wilson (2019, p. 202) in giving more content to Humanomics continue to quote Smith (1759/1790, Second.II.III, pp. 1245–125), referring to the fact that while nature (read the Spaceship Earth System)

> exhorts mankind to acts of beneficence ... she has not thought it necessary to guard and enforce the practice of it by the terrors of merited punishment in case it should be neglected. It is the ornament which embellishes, not the foundation which supports the building, and ... was ... sufficient to recommend, but by no means necessary to impose. Justice, on the contrary, is the main pillar that upholds the whole structure.

So, there it is: Humanomics sees beneficence (reflecting prudence) in the barter and trade is the ornament, and justice (to include all the other virtues, too) is the pillar in the foundation. Metaeconomics sees that the ornament originates on the self-interest path 0G (prudence) and the foundation is represented on the shared other-interest (other virtues, including justice) path 0M, referring here to Figs. 4.1, 7.1, and 8.1. Clear overlap.

Market Trade and Moral Sentiments

So, now bringing in Smith (1776/1789), it all comes together, as in Metaeconomics. In Humanomics, as Smith and Wilson (2019, p. 206) say it, Smith (1776/1789) made it clear, "All ... trades are an exchange of gifts in the beneficence sense, that each has to give in order to receive." Market trade runs on beneficence. Yet, from Smith (1759/1790), said trade must not be unjust: In Metaeconomic terms, an Empathy-based other-interest, ethics (and empirical, science)-based fellow-feeling, must temper it. And, both parts are essential. It is recognized in Humanomics, too, in the Smith and Wilson (2019, p. 206) quote of Smith (1776/1789, pp. 26, 687):

> Give me that which I want, and you shall have this which you want, is the meaning of every such offer; and it is in this manner that we obtain from one another the far greater part of those good offices which we stand in need of... (and) Every man, as long as he does not violate the laws of justice, is left perfectly free to pursue his own interest his own way, and to bring both

> his industry and capital into competition with those of any other man, or order of men

Humanomics clearly sees the play of the Self-interest-driven trade in the Market Forum (give me that which I want, and you shall have this which you want), and what Metaeconomics clarifies as the role of shared Other-interest, especially in justice, and (which Metaeconomics sees) coming out of the Other Forums. The quote is describing the essence of a humane liberalism (and democracy)-based capitalism. In Metaeconomic terms, as long as the other virtues-laden path 0M, as the pillar, ensures no injury, harm, and injustice, then trade is potentially beneficent, in effect, beneficial to everyone. It is about a person's conduct, about doing good things (e.g., don't sell smoke-and-mirrors based CDOs). A mutually beneficial trade arises as long as each person moves away from the (tarnished, unjust) ornaments only path 0G and moves to a tempered path 0Z, with each person pursuing the own-interest. The own-interest balances the beneficence&justice.

So, back to the matter of the Myth of the Rational Market, and needing a Humanomics (representing a "mature rule-following socialized person") and Metaeconomics (representing an "empathy based other-interest, ethics-based fellow-feeling person") understanding to make sense of it: The excessive Greed (the tendency to excessive self-love, the tarnished ornament) needs to be, and, in a good and truly efficient Market is, tempered. Being on path 0Z ensures a moral and ethical, a rational Market efficiency—and everyone is happier, with no more 2008 Greed-driven crashes. The myth of efficiency is converted to real efficiency through ethics, the sentiments, as Adam Smith would have it, which came out of "thinking, feeling, and knowing" (Smith and Wilson 2019, p. 32).

We might legitimately ask just what were the sentiments of the bankers and other money managers, and cronies in government, that caused the 2008 crash, and, then gave away a lot of tax-payer money to repair the damage coming out of unethical conduct? With the moral (and ethical) sentiments being the "gravity of the social universe (Smith and Wilson 2019, p. 46)," that universe encompassing Market&Government, what pull of gravity led to crashing the economy? Putting attention on path 0Z, then, also raises the potential for actually moving to a humane liberalism-based capitalism, which—as both Metaeconomics and McCloskey (2019) make clear, Adam Smith fully understood, and Humanomics helps in bringing back to modern attention—has to be built on the pillar of ethics.

References

Altman, M. 2012. *Behavioral Economics for Dummies*. Kindle ed. Mississauga: John Wiley and Sons Canada, Ltd.

Berne, E. 1961. *Transactional Analysis in Psychotherapy*. New York: Grove Press.

Blinder, Alan S. 2014. *After the Music Stopped: The Financial Crisis, the Response, and the Work Ahead*. Kindle ed. New York: Penguin.

Camerer, C., G. Loewenstein, and D. Prelec. 2005. Neuroeconomics: How Neuroscience Can Inform Economics. *Journal of Economic Literature* 43: 9–64.

Czap, N.V., H.J. Czap, M. Khachaturyan, M.E. Burbach, and G.D. Lynne. 2018. Experiments on Empathy Conservation: Implications for Environmental Policy. *Journal of Behavioral Economics for Policy* 2 (2): 71–77.

Elster, J. 1979. *Ulysses and the Sirens: Studies in Rationality and Irrationality*. 1993rd ed. New York: Cambridge University Press.

Fox, J. 2009. *The Myth of Rational Markets: A History of Risk, Reward, and Delusion on Wall Street*. New York: HarperCollins.

Hirschfeld, Mary L. 2018. *Aquinas and the Market: Toward a Humane Economy*. Cambridge, MA: Harvard University Press.

Hodgson, G.M. 2019. Capitalism, Cronyism, and Democracy. *Independent Review: A Journal of Political Economy* 23 (3): 345–356.

Kirman, Alan, and Miriam Teschl. 2010. Selfish or Selfless? The Role of Empathy in Economics. *Philosophical Transactions of the Royal Society* 365: 303–317.

Labeit, Michael. 2009. Explaining the Difference between Capitalism and Corporatism to Michael Moore. *Economic Policy Journal*. http://www.economicpolicyjournal.com/2009/11/explaining-difference-between.html

Ledyard, John O. 1995. Public Goods: A Survey of Experimental Research. In *The Handbook of Experimental Economics*, ed. J.H. Kagel and A.E. Roth, 111–181. Princeton: Princeton University Press.

Lynne, G.D. 1999. Divided Self Models of the Socioeconomic Person: The Metaeconomics Approach. *Journal of Socio-Economics* 28 (3): 267–288.

———. 2002. Agricultural Industrialization: A Metaeconomics Look at the Metaphors by Which We Live. *Review of Agricultural Economics* 24 (2): 410–427.

Lynne, G.D., N.V. Czap, H.J. Czap, and M.E. Burbach. 2016. Theoretical Foundation for Empathy Conservation: Toward Avoiding the Tragedy of the Commons. *Review of Behavioral Economics* 3: 245–279.

McCloskey, D.N. 2006. *The Bourgeois Virtues: Ethics for an Age of Commerce*. Chicago: The University of Chicago Press.

———. 2019. *Why Liberalism Works: How True Liberal Values Produce a Freer, More Equal, Prosperous World for All*. New York: Yale University Press, Kindle Edition.

Munger, Michael C., and Mario Villarreal-Diaz. 2019. The Road to Crony Capitalism. *Independent Review: A Journal of Political Economy* 23 (3): 331–344.

Obama, B. 2006. *The Audacity of Hope: Thoughts on Reclaiming the American Dream*. New York: Three Rivers Press.

———. 2009. Obama's Speech in Cairo. *The Wall Street Journal*, June 4.

Rieker, M., and Benn, K. G. 2009. J.P. Morgan's Profit Sours 36%. *The Wall Street Journal*, July 16.

Ryan, Christopher. 2019. *Civilized to Death: The Price of Progress*. New York: Simon and Schuster.

Samuels, Warren J., Marianne F. Johnson, and William H. Perry. 2011. *Erasing the Invisible Hand: Essays on an Elusive and Misused Concept in Economics*. Kindle ed. New York: Cambridge University Press.

Sidel, R. 2009. With Fresh Verve, J. P. Morgan Fights Proposed Limits. *The Wall Street Journal*, July 15, Business.

Smith, A.. 1759/1790. *The Theory of Moral Sentiments*, ed. D.D. Raphael and A.L. Macfie Raphael. Indianapolis, Liberty Fund, Inc.

———. 1776/1789. *An Inquiry into the Nature and Causes of the Wealth of Nations*, ed. E. Cannan. New York: Random House.

Smith, V.L. 2012. Adam Smith on Humanomic Behavior. *Journal of Behavioral Finance and Economics* 2: 1–20.

Smith, Vernon L., and Bart J. Wilson. 2019. *Humanomics: Moral Sentiments and the Wealth of Nations for the Twenty-First Century*. New York: Cambridge University Press.

Sorkin, A.R. 2019. Ex-Corporate Lawyer's Idea: Rein in 'Sociopaths' in the Boardroom. *New York Times* (New York), July 28, Digital, Business and Policy.

Tett, G. 2009. *Fools Gold: How the Bold Dream at J.P. Morgan Was Corrupted by Wall Street Greed and Unleashed a Catastrophe*. New York: Free Press.

Will, George F. 2009. Greed's Saving Graces. Columns, *The Washington Post*, May 17.

Zakaria, F. 2009. The Capitalist Manifesto: Greed Is Good (to a Point). *Newsweek* 22 (June): 41–45.

CHAPTER 8

Food Policy: Stability, Sustainability, and Safety

Everyone needs to eat, and eat well, as it is essential to the process of slowing down the pace to and time of our death, the point of maximum entropy for each person. As a result, it is perhaps the best example of the need to seek one's Self-interest. It also puts us in the position, however, to more easily Empathize, walk-in-the-shoes of someone who may not have enough food, or the best kind of food, and help in forming a shared Other-interest, too. As a result, we might choose to support, with our tax money, some kind of a Government program like the US Food and Drug Administration to ensure food safety; the US Department of Agriculture (as well as fund public research, teaching and extension services, associated with the public US Land Grant Universities), to help keep the supermarkets full, through a strong scientific base for food production; and, the US Natural Resource Conservation Service to help sustain soil, water, and other Spaceship Earth Systems working in the background of the food production and supply system, to list a few.

The shared Other-interest in food might also result in seeing the need to provide background support for the profitability of agricultural producers, to ensure that food supplies are forthcoming and stable over time. It is in our shared Other-interest with the farmers to ensure a viable, stable agricultural production system. There has been a long history in the US, starting especially in the 1930s, about the extent to which Government is to be involved in the agricultural Market system, reflecting the shared Other-interest in food. We now explore several of the different kinds of

G. D. Lynne, *Metaeconomics*, Palgrave Advances in Behavioral Economics, https://doi.org/10.1007/978-3-030-50601-8_8

shared Other-interest; it becomes clear that food production is about far more than just the Self-interest represented in the payoff from producing and eating it.

Stability: Subsidizing Crop Insurance

One of the key programs is federal crop insurance. Calamities in growing crops generally are hard to predict, involving such things as drought, floods, crop pests and disease, windstorms, and other natural disasters. As a result, it is virtually impossible for private insurance companies to survive, because of the generally wide-spread disaster when it does occur: While said companies could offer insurance, the premiums would have to be so high that few farmers could buy it. Yet, it is especially desirable from the consumer perspective to ensure the survival and continuance of the agricultural production sector through such events. The result has been a heavily subsidized federal crop insurance program, with farmers still buying the insurance from private companies. As Metaeconomics would suggest, it is about finding a balance in private&public-insurance by which we achieve stability in the food supply.

Stability in food supply is also ensured by the sharing of costs for research and development about food production and nutritional needs, which is also a matter of the shared Other-interest. It is a major reason that, historically, there was substantial federal and state commitment to providing funding of food-related research in the US Land Grant University of each State. Said budgets have been cut back drastically. One wonders what the politicians (and the constituents who vote for them) who cut public research budgets for food research are thinking? Metaeconomics analysis would likely show there is a clear Other (shared broadly across the entire set of Travelers)-interest inherent in the public research related to food. Metaeconomics would likely suggest it is impossible to justify the rationale of the politicians and their supporters who oppose public-funded research. Metaeconomics would also likely suggest that a Market-only approach, that is, private sector research, only, would be inadequate to the task of providing an adequate and stable supply of food. Empirical questions.

Also, it seems to have been missed that the empirical reality is: Most of the agricultural scientists are educated and trained in public universities, in the US Land Grant Universities, so just, who exactly, is going to do the research in the private universities and private companies when the budgets of the public universities are cut? Empirical questions, with the Metaeconomic answers likely to be that there needs to be good balance in private&public-research and education.

Sustainability, Through Empathy Conservation

A close relative of stability pertains to that of ensuring a long-term, sustainable capability to produce food. It is about being a virtuous farm, ensuring "the goods and services… are of value to the community… and the resources … are used wisely" while seeking and providing reasonable profits consistent with sustaining the farm financially (Hirschfeld 2018, p. 137). Farming needs to be done in such a way as to not mine soil and not to pollute or otherwise waste the water. Historically, said sustainability has been helped by Government efforts to bring about soil and water conservation, going back to the 1930s. The 1930s were a time in which there was widespread drought, with huge soil loss, in the infamous dust belt area of the US. It was also a time of severe poverty in the agricultural production sector caused not only by extremely bad weather conditions but also by inadequate Market prices, reflecting a great deal of bad capitalism at work.

The situation had evolved into inordinate power in the banking industry that provided capital to farmers; monopolized food transportation (mainly railroads in that time), food processing and manufacturing; and, considerable concentrated power in the larger grocery stores. There was massive Market-failure to address both long-term sustainability and the short-term reality that farmers were nearly destitute.

So, there was a growing, felt need to use Government to move a larger share of the wealth to the farming sector, to do something about the poverty, as well as ensure sustainability of the food system. A shared Other-interest evolved in keeping producers operating within a truly Sustainable Spaceship Earth system, such that a continuous supply of food would find its way into the stores.

Yet, there was inadequate agreement in the US Congress, and US Administrative branch, and perhaps in society in general, about the extent to which agricultural producers should be subsidized. It was considered "socialism" to provide Government payments to (even if destitute) agricultural producers. So, to get around the stigma associated with the "socialism" framing, it was decided to make direct conservation payments to farmers for taking care of soil and water systems, and the agricultural land in general. By paying farmers to do a better job of managing soil and water, and farmland in general, it would ensure a stable food supply in years to come. Buying soil and water conservation also meant it could be framed as in effect buying a Good in the Market without handing out money in the Government/Socialism frame.

The shared Other-interest changed content. That content reflected a new moral and ethical community, one that saw it legitimate to make conservation payments to farmers from general tax revenues. The new shared Other-interest also, reflecting said shift in value *V*, in effect asked everyone to join in paying the price *P* of a more sustainable food supply. A new balance in Market&Government emerged regarding soil and water conservation.

Early Intrigue with Drivers in Farmer Soil and Water Conservation

As might be imagined, the fact that Government had been involved in buying soil and water conservation effort by farmers going back to the 1930s had led to a substantial research literature by the late-1980s on what motivated adoption. We set out to contribute to that literature.

Our first study applied the framework of the NeoClassEcon, as represented in Production Microeconomics. To our dismay, the best we could do was to explain 15–20 percent of the variation in conservation choices (Lynne, Shonkwiler, and Rola 1988). Something substantial was clearly missing in Neoclassical-based Microeconomics, which turned out to be the exclusive focus on Self-interest. Neoinstitutional Economics did not work, either, even though the emphasis on what we eventually came to call the Other-interest was found as a major force. The problem was that the NeoInstiEcon had no way of connecting the Other-interest to the Self-interest being expressed by farmers: There was no coherent, integrating theory.

The empirical and theoretical shortfall of both Neoclassical and Neoinstitutional Economics became especially apparent in homogeneous farming communities. In said communities, essentially the same seed, chemical and machinery technologies were available to all the farmers, who were all similarly educated to the best farming practices, and who were all farming similar quality land. Profit opportunities through the Market were in effect identical for everyone, and Government prices paid for conservation were the same. Self-interest-based maximizing profit (and utility) should have led to the same mix and level of conservation practices.

Instead, the earliest Metaeconomics-based look, which is what we eventually called it, at reality showed tremendous variability in the behavior of real farmers. So, what was going on? It did become clear that it had something to with the shared Other-interest at work in said communities, as suggested by Neoinstitutional Economics. Somehow the community (again, what we eventually call the shared Other-interest) was conditioning the Self-interest, albeit Neoclassical Economics did not address it, and had no way to address the linkage if it did.

In the first study we did (Lynne, Shonkwiler, and Rola 1988), it became obvious that Conservation attitudes varied widely within otherwise homogeneous farming communities, again, including even the attitudes toward Self-interest only profit (and the utility it could buy). Profit seeking was a driver, but the degree to which it was being pursued was found to be highly variable. Not every farmer, indeed, just a very small percentage, were profit maximizers as presumed in Neoclassical Microeconomics. It had become clear, in what would be called Metaeconomics, it was not the only driver at work. One also could not think in terms of farmers choosing conservation "as though they were profit maximizers," a common approach in Neoclassical Economics, obviating the need to go find out what farmers are really doing. In addition, it was found that Conservation Norms, a close relative of what Metaeconomics eventually represented as the shared Other-interest, again, the community, also played a substantive role but also did not explain much of the variation by itself.

A breakthrough of sorts came in the Lockeretz (1990) paper. A review of the conservation literature to that date showed clearly that the theoretical framing being used to understand farmer choices in soil (and water) conservation was rather ad hoc. And, the answer to the question in his title "What Have We Learned About Who Conserves Soil?" (and, highly related to it, the water) was simply "Not much." In fact, regarding the lack of a coherent theoretical framework, the NeoClassEcon conservation researcher would often insert sociological kinds of variables, without theoretical justification. Why? Well, we can only surmise it was because of the frustration arising in the reality that Microeconomics did such a poor job at explaining conservation choices. So, why did they, the Microeconomists, persist in using what looked to be a flawed theory at explaining what is really going on?

Similarly, the SocioLogic and NeoInstiEcon would sometimes allude to the power of price in the Market, and profit seeking, in enhancing their favored framing. Yet, they generally would not insert said variables into their largely Other-interest frames. We showed in Lynne and Rola (1988) that doing so, inserting Microeconomics suggested variables into the widely used, in SocioPsych framing, the Theory of Planned Behavior, gave substantive improvement.

It started to become clear that a framework and theory was needed that integrated the best notions from both the NeoClassEcon and NeoInstiEcon Isles (recall Table 2.1). And, it worked: In a nutshell, we finally figured it out. Integration across the frames and theories was not only needed, but shown to be possible. The entire story of how it was done, in substantial detail, is in Lynne et al. (2016). The following is a brief overview of it.

Early Testing Led to Proposing the Overlapping Isocurves of Conservation

The first breakthrough came in the early-1990s, arising out of the jointness framework from Frisch (1965). Lynne (1995) proposed for the first time (as far as could be found, based upon an extensive research of the economics literature, albeit Ainslee 1986, had alluded to the possibility) overlapping isocurves as in Fig. 8.1. It was first proposed in Lynne (1995, p. 75) that farmers pursue I-utility as represented in the Self-interest-oriented possibility I_G set of isocurves, and, at the same time, pursue We-utility as represented in the I_M set of isocurves. Notice too how the proposal identifies the impossibility of separating the two payoffs, with I-utility and We-utility occurring at every place in the space, such as at points *A*, *B*, and *C*. It also became clear that efficiency took on a new meaning, now defined in the area bounded by path 0G and path 0M.

Empirical testing of the proposition rested on arguably the most empirical science of such things, as represented in social psychology, as practiced by the SocioPsych. It was clearly demonstrated in the Lynne (1995) paper that including measures of both I-Utility (attitudes) and We-Utility (norms) in the model improved the capacity to explain variation in farmer soil and water conservation behavior. Interaction terms would also be shown to be needed, as represented in attitudes&norms, a precursor to Self&Other-interest framing. Utility in both domains was viewed as cardinal, so utility had to be measured, or at least some proxy found for it. It was demonstrated that the level of utility, in both domains, jointly drove

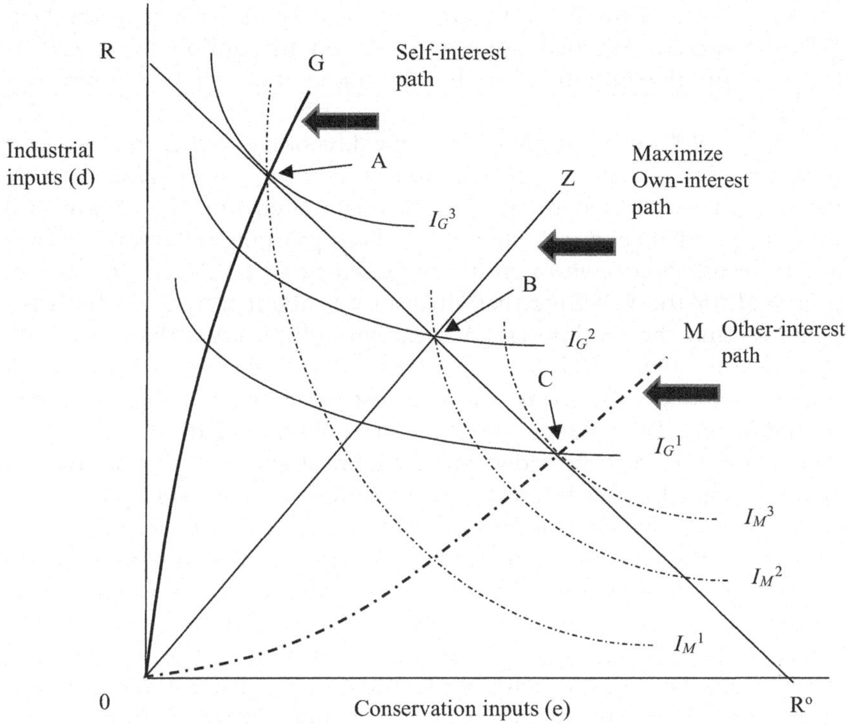

Fig. 8.1 Industrial inputs (d) joint (nonallocable) with conservation inputs (e) to produce a market product in the self-interest (I_G) and a non-market environmental production in the other-interest (I_M). (Source: Author's creation)

the amount of drip irrigation technology installed in Florida strawberry fields.

Lynne et al. (1995), Lynne and Casey (1998), Casey and Lynne (1999) continued to apply and refine the methods developed by the SocioPsych to measure utility, focusing on expected utility. The methods developed by the SocioPsych were adopted (see especially Lynne et al. 1995) to measure attitude as a proxy for the expected utility related to Self-interest, and for measuring the Social Norm as a proxy for the expected utility related to Other-interest. The effort also started to consider the role of Self-control, as an influence on economic choice (Lynne et al. 2016, p. 263). It also started to become clear that conservation choice involved balance in the

I&We-utility, and by the end of this set of research, balance in the Self-&Public-interest. We had not yet developed the notion of an Other-interest, but the notion of an Interest rather than that of utility was emerging.

Lynne (1999) took another step in the direction of Other-interest, now speaking of the balance in I&We-interest. Also, it was in Lynne (1999) that the phrase Metaeconomics was first associated with the idea of dual interest, and that economic choice was about pursuing the balance. It was about maximizing Own-interest, composed of that balance. It was also proposed for the first time that altruism was about sacrifice in both the I-interest and the We-interest. A breakthrough idea was that one could maximize the Own-interest while sacrificing in both domains. Indeed, it was clarified that maximizing Own-interest inherently meant sacrificing in both domains. The paradox of self-sacrifice only vanished.

Siles et al. (2000) provided more empirical evidence that something akin to a shared Other-interest, described therein as Social Capital, was a major influence in farmland markets. It was not just in conservation. The price *P* of farmland was influenced by the shared value *V* represented in the community surrounding that Market trade, the Social Capital influencing the Private (farmland) Capital. Cordes et al. (2003) also showed the key role of Social Capital in rural community resilience and development, again the norm, which is represented in the shared Other-interest. It was also demonstrated in Zhang and Lynne (2016). Cutforth et al. (2001) further confirmed the role of social norms in influencing the diversity of crops and livestock on farms. Said norms represent another way to think of both social capital and the shared Other-interest. By the time of Lynne (2002), the notion of a shared others-interest (notice the "s") was starting to move toward what would eventually be the shared Other-interest.

It was now recognized there were likely many of said kinds of Other-interest, perhaps in overlapping sets, influencing the Self-interest. It also came to be realized, after considering Nelson (1991), that the NeoClassEcon claim that only Self-interest was at work in economic choice was only weakly supported in empirical science. Self-interest only is instead primarily a theological and ideological claim (Lynne et al. 2016, p. 264). Among those of us who became the MetaEcon, we started to ask our NeoClassEcon brethren to "show me." Show the MetaEcon, with solid empirical testing, that only Self-interest is the driver in a real Human. Generally, the request could not be satisfied, as testing is not generally part of the NeoClassEcon claim, at least not in the arena of soil and water conservation, and other research on sustaining Spaceship Earth Systems.

While the relationship with Ego and Empathy had already been suggested, going back to Cory (1999) and Lynne (1999), the proposition was more fully developed as the Ego'N'Empathy idea in Hayes and Lynne (2004). It suggested the new framework and theory about I&We, Self&Other, and, more fundamentally, about an integrated Ego&Empathy, be placed at the core of the emerging field of Ecological Economics. The latter sees inherent interdependence, in that the economy is seen as embedded within the Spaceship Earth System (Gowdy 1984; Daly and Farley 2011; Hayes and Lynne 2013; Lynne et al. 2016, p. 264).

It had it come to be realized that Metaeconomics could now be formalized. Mathematical Consumption Metaeconomics was developed in Lynne (2006a; essence of it in Appendix A herein). Mathematical Production Metaeconomics was developed in Lynne (2006b; essence of it in Appendix B herein). A couple of major conclusions came out of that effort. First, the formal derivations in Lynne (2006a) demonstrated that it is essential to abandon the NeoClassEcon contention that utility is ordinal; utility has to be viewed as cardinal, and has to be measured, in that it does not just "drop out" of the mathematical formulations. Second, the formal derivations in Lynne (2006b) demonstrated that the NeoClassEcon contention that all production was independent of every other kind of production had to be abandoned: Production, by being embedded in the Spaceship Earth System, always had an Other-interest component. We are all Travelers on the same Spaceship, a system governed by 1st and 2nd Law of Thermodynamics. Perhaps most importantly, Metaeconomics had matured enough to give a way to consider Self&Other-interest choice in a specific way, through the concise language of mathematics.

Also, by 2008 or so, Metaeconomics had been moved away from the other-interest as being a kind of Empathy-altruism phenomenon. Sautter et al. (2011) made it clear that Metaeconomics posited an Ego-based Self-interest and an Empathy-based Other-interest (Lynne et al. 2016, p. 264). The influence of Other-interest in farmer choices of environmental technologies (e.g., an anaerobic digester) was also confirmed in a couple of other tests at about the same time, by Chouinard et al. (2008) and Bishop, Shumway, and Wandschneider (2010).

The next major breakthroughs came in Sheeder and Lynne (2011). It came out of the realization of the strong connection between empathy, compassion, and ethics, after Solomon (2007), and how to bring the insight into the Dual Interest Theory. It led to the idea of staging: Mindfulness on the part of the farmer of possible downstream (both physically and temporally) effects, leading to Empathy, to "walking-in-the-shoes of the downstream entity." The next step would involve sympathy, arising from asking "how would I wish to be treated if in that situation." Finally, there would be the possibility of compassion, leading to action to do more soil and water conservation onsite, on the farm. The pieces of the puzzle converged: Empathy sympathy (which gave rise to ethics shared widely) compassion, and, then, tempering of the Self-interest.

Also, while the idea had been proposed in Sautter et al. (2011), it had also become clear that Self-interest was likely a more primal driver. The Other-interest was now viewed as more about nudging the Self-interest (in the Market), or, bounding and otherwise regulating and restraining (with Government) when nudging failed (Lynne et al. 2016, p. 266).

So, where did it all lead? Specifically, referring to Fig. 8.1, similar to Figure 1 in Sheeder and Lynne (2011, p. 437): Metaeconomics suggests that while producing more marketable agricultural product (e.g., field corn) at point *A* gives more profit, it also produces much less of the environmental product (e.g., wildlife), as represented at level I_M^1. In fact, if the Other-interest were maximized, level I_M^3 would be achieved, but with much less corn represented in I_G^1. The best, rational point is *B* with corn at I_G^2 and wildlife at I_M^2 : It is the point of maximum Own-interest, with sacrifice in both domains of Interest. We might say the farmer has to "give a little" in both domains in order to "gain a lot" overall: It is efficiency at work.

Another breakthrough in Sheeder and Lynne (2011) was the recognition of a Higher Plane of interests represented in the value *V* (see Lynne et al. 2016, p. 266), the wants about wants, and the meta-references idea. The relationship between the dual interests is represented in the space of a Production Possibilities Frontier, and the Higher Plane of value *V*. Using Fig. 4.2 for the purpose, think of it now as representing produced outputs rather than consumed goods. We move along RR^0 in Fig. 8.1 to produce the Possibilities Frontier in Fig. 4.2, but now think of the Self-interest axis I_G representing the product (field corn) grown for profit while the Other-interest axis I_M represents, again, some environmental possibility like more wildlife, or enhanced atmospheric (e.g., lower carbon) quality. Again, maximizing profit suggests Point *A* outcomes; maximizing environmental quality, shared with others, serving the shared Other-interest, is represented at Point *C*. Experience will generally suggest that neither is best:

The best place to be is where we sacrifice a bit in both domains, with the outcome more sustainable through time, as represented at the maximum payoff of the joint interest at point *B*.

Notice, too, how the Higher Plane of Value *V* represented at point *B* in Fig. 4.2 now influences the ultimate choice at point *B* in Fig. 8.1. Selecting point *B* in Fig. 4.2 says the higher environment value *V* (more wildlife produced, in general, more biodiversity) also influences the price *P* of the product (field corn), that is, $V \rightarrow P$, and, $P \rightarrow V$, and, possibly not commensurable. The *V* can easily be priceless.

So, looking back, the intriguing empirical question over the years of the research program was one about were all the farmers landed in the spectrum. It might reasonably be expected that some would likely be found at *A*, others at *B*, and still others at *C*, dependent upon the influence of the Other-interest on their economic choice. The choice would also be influenced by higher values *V*, such as doing the right thing by having a few more wildlife in the corn fields, which could serve to override the influence of the price *P* of corn from the Market. As expected, we found huge, substantive, lots of variability in actual conservation choices. Such findings also led to asking, too, if we wanted to nudge farmers, with Government policy and programs, to move toward path 0M, point *B* choices, what would be the best way to accomplish it?

Clearly it would not work to apply a "one size fits all approach." The answer depended on the starting point of the farmer being nudged, with quite different programs needed if at point *A* or *B* or *C*. And, as always, it was about finding the best balance in Market&Government.

Experimental Laboratory Tests Continue to Confirm Dual Interest

In order to further confirm whether Metaeconomics worked better or not, it was decided to also do testing under controlled settings. We developed the Experimental and Behavioral Economics Laboratory at the University of Nebraska-Lincoln.

Findings under controlled, laboratory conditions include the following, examining a wide array of conservation and sustainability related behaviors, not just soil and water conservation:

1. In a carbon offsets trading experiment, participants could sell carbon offsets to an environmental organization, who would retire the offset, in effect reducing the carbon load on the atmosphere. Or, they could sell the offset on the market, which maintains the current level of carbon load, except to the extent that people selling the offset would not normally be able to do so unless they first reduced their own contribution to the load. Strong support was found for Metaeconomics on three fronts (Ovchinnikova et al. 2009, pp. 227–228):

   First, subjects in the experiments demonstrated overall tendencies to seek balance within their Own-interest as between the egoistic–hedonistic pursuit of material gains and the empathy–sympathy based pursuit of shared Other-interest as reflected in providing an environmental good. Second, subjects were willing to sacrifice more in one domain or the other as they oriented and reoriented their interests in going through the various phases of each experiment, giving new meaning to the notion of altruism, as metaeconomics proposes. Third, by stirring their thought processes in the priming and the psychological questioning, we stirred rational consideration and reconsideration, moving choice out of the domain of only intuition-based habitual behavior, within which the pursuit of Self-interest is likely more primal, as the play of the experiment evolved. By stirring thought, this Self-interest is tempered and conditioned by the consideration of shared Other-interest, leading to a truly rational choice.
2. Follow-up experiments (Czap and Czap 2010, 2011) added the option to donate the offsets to the environmental organization, who then retired same; the experiments gave additional support:

   (a) 10 percent took the option of donating options, even when prices that could be received for selling the offsets were increased: "the participants consider donations as something that they 'ought to do' regardless of the income that they are getting from other (selling) activities" (Czap and Czap 2010, p. 2038), suggesting pecuniary and non-pecuniary domains of interest are not subject to a simple trade-off.
   (b) Changing the prices for offsets did influence the selling choices as between the environmental organization and the offsets Market, suggesting that Self-interest also conditions and otherwise influ-

ences the Other-interest, if both are in the pecuniary domain (both have Prices).

(c) Decisions to join in the shared Other-interest, environmental cause were stirred by people who first start moving more offsets to an environmental organization (Czap and Czap 2011); Other (shared with others)-interest can be nudged by people already in the cause.

3. Czap, Czap, and Bonakdarian (2010) measured the level of Empathy, and probed into the matter of contributing to the provision of public goods, finding:

   (a) The degree of Empathy is the important driving force behind the shared Other-interest in a common cause.
   (b) Locus of control and past contributions (i.e., habit, represented in longer standing shared Other-interest) are among the most important determinants of current behavior.
   (c) More empathetic people are more likely to engage in a new Other-interest, to "join the cause" of providing a public good.
   (d) People will contribute more in the Other-interest when it reflects a true public (i.e., nonexcludable) good than an excludable public good, suggesting they are more likely to join in sympathy with goods they cannot freely opt out of being affected by the outcomes; having less freedom to affect outcomes results in more voluntary engagement in the shared Other-interest of the common, truly public good, suggesting another dimension of control and Self-control, with control a main focus of Metaeconomics.

4. A series of downstream water pollution experiments were conducted, relating to upstream soil and water conservation efforts, keeping soils from eroding (and, related thereto, keeping chemicals and fertilizer from entering downstream waters), with substantial support for Metaeconomics as follows:

   (a) A one-unit change in Empathy (as measured on the Likert scale) leads to an increase in conservation effort by 3.3–9.5 percent depending on the model, which is quite substantial (Czap et al. 2012a).
   (b) Empathy framing works in nudging people toward more environmentally friendly behavior; an Empathy frame caused upstream farmers to allocate on average 47 percent of their land toward conservation, while in the Self-interest frame only 19.6 percent.

Metaeconomics would propose that Empathy tempers Self-interest, which is confirmed by the finding.

(c) Farmers on the river who also drew water from the river for drinking purposes gave strong evidence for the balancing of Self&Other that Metaeconomics predicts is essential. Such farmers (experimental participants in the role) did the balancing to a substantial degree, no matter which framing was used: They allocated 45 percent and 39.2 percent of their land for conservation in the Empathy and Self-interest treatments, respectively. The group, as designed in the experiment, had to "walk-in-the-shoes-of-others" and they indeed chose to give up a significant share of their potential profit even when nudged to look for their Self-interest.

(d) Emotional feedback was examined in Czap et al. (2013b) via players being able to send smiley ☺ and frowney ☹ emoticons to other players. Several findings support Metaeconomics, and especially the finding that the expression of the frowneys by the downstream water users was quite effective in moving the upstream farmers toward giving up some of their profits in favor of the downstream users. Passing on the negative emotions resulting in evoking Empathy in upstream farmers and stirred the Other-interest in better quality water for everyone.

(e) Follow-up studies compared the effectiveness of inducing conservation by imposing a fine for non-compliance (Czap et al. 2012b, Czap et al. 2014) and the assignment of property rights to the downstream water user (Czap et al. 2013a, 2018b). In both approaches, participants chose levels of conservation close to the shared optimal level, with inducing Empathy working better for achieving more equal profit distributions than imposing a fine (Czap et al. 2012b). Intriguingly, as Metaeconomics predicts, imposing monetary fines was found to be counterproductive: Fines lowered conservation levels, while not affecting sharing. In contrast, Empathy nudging increased sharing behavior but did not significantly affect conservation (Czap et al. 2014). Assigning the property rights to the downstream water users led to more sharing (Czap et al. 2013a, 2018b). Overall, Metaeconomics suggests that Empathy nudging would be more effective than fines, that is, encouraging people to temper their Self-interest, rather than to punish (fine) them for not doing so.

(f) Continuing the conservation behavior testing, Czap et al. (2015, 2016) examined four alternative conservation policy designs: financial incentives through a crop insurance subsidy given regardless of conservation nudging; crop insurance subsidy associated with and used to directly nudge conservation; and, Empathy nudging with each of the subsidy cases. Intriguingly, as Metaeconomics would predict: "only the combination of increased pecuniary incentives (appealing to the egoistic-hedonistic self-interest) AND nudging for empathy (appealing to other (shared ethic)-interest) is effective in achieving more balanced, more rational decisions, providing financial/environmental gains to upstream farmer as well as downstream water user" (Czap et al. 2016). Other Behavioral Economics studies have given similar outcomes: Financial incentives matter, but money isn't everything (Altman 2012, loc 1731), as the Other-interest framing and influencing the pursuit of Self-interest makes clear.

(g) Czap et al. (2015) also found that no matter the current level of conservation, financial incentives focused on the Ego-based Self-interest are far more powerful and effective in inducing more conservation when combined with Empathy nudging.

(h) Gender also makes a substantive difference, in contrast to NeoClassEcon contentions that male and female preferences are essentially identical (Altman 2012, loc 5113). In general, the differences arise in the Other-interest, with Empathy playing a larger role in females than in males (Czap et al. 2014; Czap et al. 2018a).

Bottomline: The empirical testing going back to the late 1980s suggests the missing variable in the conservation research literature, and the reason, again, sorry, Lockeretz (1990) said "no, we do not know why farmers conserve soil (or water):" The reason is in not seeing Empathy. As we have perhaps indicated too many times, but it is extremely important: It has also been emphasized in Brown et al. (2019), as relating to all manner of environmental and sustainability issues. So, overall (also, see Reimer et al. 2014; and for overall implications for conservation policy, see Czap et al. 2018c):

1. The notion of "Empathy Conservation," as part of good capitalism, has emerged, that is, the empirical evidence on what drives conservation choices historically had missed the role of empathy-sympathy, the

resulting compassion that leads to action. The focus is on tempering Self-interest, especially the excessive Greed associated with moving to a state of a Tragedy. Another way to say the same thing: Historically, researchers had missed the role of the moral and ethical dimension (both arising out of Empathy) in producing a shared Other-interest in conserving resources, and avoiding the Tragedy driven by excessive Greed.

2. The empirical testing also provides substantial support for Metaeconomics and little support for Microeconomics, except for a rather small proportion of the population. That is, Microeconomics represents the people who operate on Self-interest only, which at most is likely about 15–20 percent of the farming population, or, overall, on average every farmer operating more strictly in the Self-interest frame only 15–20 percent of the time, albeit the question also needs more empirical assessment. Specifically, point *A* (or, perhaps even point R) is the only choice possible under a Neoclassical Microeconomics analysis, and it occurs only 15–20 percent of the time. Testing continues.

Specific Conservation Programs

Metaeconomics makes it clear that one size does not fit all. Also, Metaeconomics helps makes sense of why various approaches that have been used work, or do not work.

Importantly, if Self-interest is left to its own, while listening to the Neoclassical Microeconomics claims that it is only about the money, we arrive at point *A* in Fig. 8.1 with lots of corn but little to no wildlife and other environmental products. Clearly it would not be efficient, in that when asked, both farmers and consumers would likely support having some wildlife traveling along with us on the Spaceship? Also, most farmers and consumers would like value *V* keeping carbon emissions within the limits of what the Spaceship can hold and process? So, what do?

Neoclassical Microeconomics pointing as it always does, implicitly, to pure capitalism (everything privately owned) would call for creating private property in the wildlife (and/or the capacity of the atmosphere to process carbon), with said owners then negotiating with the farmer. The owners of wildlife would pay the farmer the price *P* for having wildlife in the fields. We would see a price *P* evolving for both grain and wildlife, which theoretically could result in the efficient choice at point *B* in

Figs. 8.1 and 4.2. It is theoretically possible that the slope of the value *V* in Fig. 4.2 could be the relative price of wildlife and corn: Theoretically. The problem is, how would you establish private property in wildlife that would be allowed to freely wonder through corn fields? Minor issue, we might suppose, for a NeoClassEcon.

The fact is, Microeconomics by seeing only a single interest at work, does not even have the I_M set of wildlife production curves in the analytical lens. It is about corn, not wildlife. So, Microeconomics does not deal with the reality that most farmers and consumers are Human, and may indeed have Empathy with wildlife (and with other systems on the Spaceship), all generally ignored by the Econ. As one farmer asked, during a focus group styled research meeting, oriented to designing a questionnaire: "So, you are trying to figure out what turns my crank?" Answer: Yes. And, the Metaeconomics testing shows that it is about what turns the crank of a Human, not just the Econ.

Seeing farmers and consumers as Human, Metaeconomics might point, empirically, to offering some Government programs and not just use the Market. Metaeconomics is not ideologically bound to not including Government in a good mix with the Market. Metaeconomics would see it as efficient to offer payments to farmers (reflecting the value *V* reflected in the shared Other-interest between farmers and everyone else), to provide for some wildlife habitat on their farms with point *B* outcomes.

More specifically, given enough political attention to the problem (and the willingness to pay the price/taxes by hunters and bird watchers to produce the money for the farmer payment), the Government could in effect reflect the value *V* of wildlife relative to the price *P* of corn. With payments reflecting shared value *V*, the farmer might shift a bit toward path 0M, perhaps moving to path 0Z, and arriving at point B. In fact, if the payment for wildlife habitat is high enough, overall profits coming from the price&value-payments could be identical at both points A and B.

Another scenario also suggested as an empirical question by Metaeconomics would have the Government require, mandate wildlife production, without any financial compensation, at point *B* or perhaps even at the extreme point *C*. Profit would be considerably less, with hunters and bird watchers having a "free ride" while the farmer pays all the cost. Farmers would likely not be pleased, either, as liberty and freedom have been sacrificed for wildlife production. Metaeconomics encourages freedom and liberty, free to choose within context, in a liberal and humane democracy-based capitalism-based outcome at point *B*.

Notice, too, that in the Metaeconomics styled analyses and policy, wildlife and other Spaceship Earth Systems are retained as a public property, with the Government reflecting the value *V* of that property. Private property is respected in the farmer using the land to produce corn. Public property is respected by asking both farmers and consumers to pay a bit more in taxes, now reflecting the value *V* coming out of the Other Forum of Government.

The reality since the 1930s, here in the US, has put farmers and consumers into all three Metaeconomic frames. Government has been operating to represent the overall shared Other-interest along path 0M and using tax dollars/prices to in effect pay for more wildlife, funneled through the US Farm Service Agency, to bring about point *B* outcomes. We have also explored mandates/controls, as in conservation compliance to receive crop subsidy payments. Government, through the US Natural Resource and Conservation Service and the US Cooperative Extension Service, has also engaged in nudging farmers through technical support and educational programming to become conservation farmers.

Microeconomics approaches simply do not work: In fact, turning it too much into a "money game" tends to cause farmers to want even more money. Farmers move away from any semblance of a path 0M within: The Econ stops empathizing with wildlife. Metaeconomics-based Empathy Conservation does work, as already confirmed by historically, reasonably good balance in Market&Government in the conservation arena of agriculture. To make it even better, add more Empathy.

Safety: GMO and Coronavirus

The fact that the Coronavirus likely is a crossover from the lower animals into the human animal led to wild speculation in some quarters about crossover genes, orchestrated in a laboratory, as in a Genetically Modified Organism (GMO). Conspiracy theory, anyone? It appears to have no basis in scientific reality (Conrow 2020). Another matter also came to the fore: The Wet Markets in China may have contributed to transmission of the virus, SARS-CoV-2, from animals to humans. So, as a result, some have called for said markets to be immediately shut down (recall Kling 2019, and Conservative barbarism), completely, while others welcomed (recall Kling 2019, and Libertarian liberty, as well as, ironically, Progressive stopping of the oppressors) the reopening (Fickling 2020). Metaeconomics helps clarify.

Clearly a Shared Other-Interest in Food Safety

On the matter of food safety, Metaeconomics suggests that Empathy already plays a substantive role in bringing Government into influencing the safety of food supplies in the Market. Examples include the US Food and Drug Administration to assure safety and the US Department of Agriculture to monitor and recommend nutrition needs for the population. Both food safety and nutrition respond to the notion that "walking in their shoes, I would want a safe and nutritious food supply" for not only myself but for everyone else. A safe and higher quality, nutritious diet ensures longer lived people, a more productive population. So, while it is in the Ego-based Self-interest to eat whatever one wishes, it is in the Empathy-based shared Other-interest to eat safe food and follow dietary guidelines developed by Government agencies. It would be beneficial if everyone helped pay the price *P* to support agencies, which have a value *V*. It is the case that one wants the shared Other-interest to temper and otherwise restrain food producers from providing less than safe food products that are not sufficiently nutritious to ensure long lived, sustainable populations.

A specific case in point, regarding food safety, revolves around the matter of food produced using products coming from a GMO, for example, a tomato with a fish gene in it, that makes the tomato more cold hardy (plants less likely to freeze and be killed in a cold snap). Another example: A corn plant resistant to corn borers, or another corn plant that will not be killed when sprayed with an herbicide while the weeds working to out compete the plant for fertilizer and water will be stopped. Groups having joined in sympathy with the contention that GMOs are somehow not safe have also joined in the shared Other-interest in reducing the amount of GMO foods produced and sold. Suppliers have responded, with many food products labeled, and, indeed, marketed to people with the shared Other-interest, as "non-GMO." Intriguingly, there is essentially no scientific evidence linking GMOs to any kind of health issue, so what is going on?

Microeconomics can only see "irrational" behavior, in that GMO food prices *P* are generally lower, since yields, the amount produced, can be increased significantly with GMO plants and animals. Metaeconomics, in contrast, can easily explain what is going on, and, also, suggest ways to address and arrive at a resolution of the GMO question.

Through recognizing there is an Other-interest to be considered here, a moral dimension, alternative moral community, as it were, Metaeconomics suggests at least two considerations. First, if people avoiding GMOs are concerned with health issues, it appears to be completely unfounded, based on the science, so, an educational program showing the scientific facts could change views on GMOs in substantive ways. Second, if Other-interest is about Empathizing with the natural system, then the conversation could be focused here. It could be pointed out that the Spaceship Earth, ecosystem has always, within itself, changed the gene pool, as plants and animals have crossed, and otherwise inter-bred, over thousands, perhaps millions of years. The process of creating a GMO is in many ways a process of mimicking the natural system, which has been all about gene manipulation since the beginning.

The kind of shared Other-interest in not having humans directly change the gene pool can now be better understood. For example, a concern might be that the pace of change is too fast, so we might ask if the natural system will be able to adequately adjust as the GMO-based genes are released into it? Back to the fish gene in the tomato: To what extent is moving genes between plants and animals an issue for the sustainability and resilience of the natural system? Importantly, while Microeconomics can only proclaim consumers are irrational, Metaeconomics can help in framing what is at issue, and suggest that no concern for the shared Other-interest is what is irrational.

Chinese Wet Markets

The Wet Market issue is far too complex to address in a short paragraph here. Yet, Metaeconomics could perhaps be helpful by focusing attention on both ethics and empirical reality, and the need for balance in Market&Government. In particular, the shared Other-interest in better ensuring a virus is not moved from the animal into the human (as animal, too) system is clear. Regulations on just what is food for a human (perhaps keeping certain animal species out of the human food chain) are probably needed. Also, hygiene in food markets needs standards, for example, the fact that wild animal cages are right next to vegetable stands in some Chinese Wet Markets likely needs attention. Also, animals are often slaughtered on site, causing challenges in managing virus contamination. A free-for-all-wet-market, without the shared Other-interest giving context, tempering Self-interest, does not work: Extremes do not work, balance does. Many empirical questions here, to find out just what is going on.

References

Ainslee, George. 1986. Chap. 6: Beyond Microeconomics: Conflict among Interests in a Multiple Self as Determinant of Value. In *The Multiple Self*, ed. John Elster, 133–176. New York: Cambridge University Press.

Altman, M. 2012. *Behavioral Economics for Dummies*. Kindle ed. Mississauga: John Wiley and Sons Canada, Ltd.

Bishop, C.P., C.R. Shumway, and P.R. Wandschneider. 2010. Agent Heterogeneity in Adoption of Anaerobic Digestion Technology: Integrating Economic, Diffusion, and Behavioral Innovation Theories. *Land Economics* 86 (3): 585–608.

Brown, K., W.N. Adger, P. Devine-Wright, J.M. Anderies, S. Barr, F. Bousquet, C. Butler, L. Evans, N. Marshall, and T. Quinn. 2019. Empathy, Place and Identity Interactions for Sustainability. *Global Environmental Change* 56: 11–17.

Casey, F., and G.D. Lynne. 1999. Adoption of Water Conserving Technologies in Agriculture: The Role of Expected Profits and the Public Interest. In *Flexible Incentives for the Adoption of Environmental Technologies in Agriculture*, ed. F. Casey, A. Schmitz, A.S. Swinton, and D. Zilberman, 229–247. Norwell: Kluwer Academic Publishers.

Chouinard, H.H., T. Paterson, P.R. Wandschneider, and A.M. Ohler. 2008. Will Farmers Trade Profits for Stewardship? Heterogeneous Motivations for Farm Practice Selection. *Land Economics* 84 (1): 66–82.

Conrow, J. 2020. "Covid Crisis Captivates Conspiracy Theorists." https://geneticliteracyproject.org/2020/03/31/covid-crisis-captivates-conspiracy-theorists/?utm_source=TrendMD&utm_medium=cpc&utm_campaign=Ancestry_%2526_Evolution_TrendMD_0.

Cordes, S., J. Allen, R. Bishop, G.D. Lynne, L. Robison, V.D. Ryan, and R. Shaeffer. 2003. Social Capital, Attachment Value and Rural Development: A Conceptual Framework and Application of Contingent Valuation. *American Journal of Agricultural Economics* 85 (5): 1201–1207.

Cory, G.A. 1999. *The Reciprocal Modular Brain in Economics and Politics*. New York: Kluwer Academic/Plenum publishers.

Cutforth, L.B., C.A. Francis, G.D. Lynne, D.A. Mortensen, and K.M. Eskridge. 2001. Factors Affecting Farmers' Diversity Approach. *American Journal of Alternative Agriculture* 16 (4): 168–176.

Czap, N.V., and H.J. Czap. 2010. An Experimental Investigation of Revealed Environmental Concern. *Ecological Economics* 69 (10): 2033–2041.

Czap, H.J., and N.V. Czap. 2011. Donating-Selling Tradeoffs and the Influence of Leaders in the Environmental Goods Game. *Journal of Socio-Economics* 40 (6): 743–752.

Czap, H.J., N.V. Czap, and E. Bonakdarian. 2010. Walk the Talk? The Effect of Voting and Excludability in Public Goods Experiments. *Economic Research International.* https://doi.org/10.1155/2010/768546.

Czap, N.V., H.J. Czap, M. Khachaturyan, G.D. Lynne, and M.E. Burbach. 2012a. Walking in the Shoes of Others: Experimental Testing of Dual Interest and Empathy in Environmental Choice. *Journal of Socio-Economics* 41 (5): 642–653.

Czap, N.V., H.J. Czap, G.D. Lynne, and M.E. Burbach. 2012b. *Inducing Empathy or Imposing a Fine? Finding Solutions to the Downstream Water Pollution Problem.* Lincoln: University of Nebraska-Lincoln.

Czap, H.J., N. Czap, G. Lynne, and M. Burbach. 2013a. *Who Should Own the Property Rights? Revisiting the Downstream Water Pollution Problem.* Lincoln: University of Nebraska-Lincoln.

Czap, N.V., H.J. Czap, M. Khachaturyan, M.E. Burbach, and G.D. Lynne. 2013b. Smiley or Frowney: The Effect of Emotions and Empathy Framing in the Downstream Water Pollution Game. *International Journal of Economics and Finance* 5 (3): 9–23.

Czap, N.V., H.J. Czap, M.E. Burbach, and G.D. Lynne. 2014. Gender in Environmental Context: An Effect of Property Rights, Fines, and Empathy Nudging. *International Journal of Economics and Finance* 6 (7): 11–23.

Czap, N.V., H.J. Czap, G.D. Lynne, and M.E. Burbach. 2015. Walk in My Shoes: Nudging for Empathy Conservation. *Ecological Economics* 118: 147–158.

Czap, N.V., H.J. Czap, M. Khachaturyan, and M.E. Burbach. 2018a. Comparing Female and Male Response to Financial Incentives and Empathy Nudging in an Environmental Context. *Review of Behavioral Economics* 5: 61–84.

Czap, H.J., N.V. Czap, M.E. Burbach, and G.D. Lynne. 2018b. Does Might Make Right? An Experiment on Assigning Property Rights. *Ecological Economics* 150: 229–240.

Czap, N.V., H.J. Czap, M. Khachaturyan, M.E. Burbach, and G.D. Lynne. 2018c. Experiments on Empathy Conservation: Implications for Environmental Policy. *Journal of Behavioral Economics for Policy* 2 (2): 71–77.

Czap, H.J., N.V. Czap, M.E. Burbach, and G.D. Lynne. 2016. Farm Bill 2014: An Experimental Investigation of Conservation Compliance. *Journal of Sustainable Development* 9 (3): 23–38.

Daly, Herman E., and Joshua Farley. 2011. *Ecological Economics: Principles and Applications.* 2nd ed. Washington, DC: Island Press.

Fickling, D. 2020. "China Is Reopening Its Wet Markets. That's Good." Bloomberg L.P., accessed April 6, https://www.bloomberg.com/opinion/articles/2020-04-04/coronavirus-closing-china-s-wet-markets-isn-t-a-solution.

Frisch, Ragnar. 1965. *Theory of Production.* Chicago: Rand McNally and Company.

Gowdy, John M. 1984. Marx and Resource Scarcity: An Institutionalist Approach. *Journal of Economic Issues* 18 (June): 393–400.

Hayes, W.M., and G.D. Lynne. 2004. Towards a Centerpiece for Ecological Economics. *Ecological Economics* 49 (3): 287–301.

———. 2013. The Evolution of Ego and Empathy: Progress in Forming the Centerpiece for Ecological Economic Theory. In *Building a Green Economy: Perspectives from Ecological Economics*, ed. Robert B. Richardson, 107–118. East Lansing: Michigan State University Press.

Hirschfeld, Mary L. 2018. *Aquinas and the Market: Toward a Humane Economy*. Cambridge, MA: Harvard University Press.

Kling, Arnold. August, 2019. *The Three Languages of Politics: Talking across the Political Divides*. 3rd ed. Cato Institute: Washington, DC.

Lockeretz, W. 1990. What Have We Learned About Who Conserves Soil? *Journal of Soil and Water Conservation* 45 (5): 517–532.

Lynne, G.D. 1995. Modifying the Neoclassical Approach to Technology Adoption with Behavioral Science Models. *Journal of Agricultural and Applied Economics* 27 (1): 67–80.

———. 1999. Divided Self Models of the Socioeconomic Person: The Metaeconomics Approach. *Journal of Socio-Economics* 28 (3): 267–288.

———. 2002. Agricultural Industrialization: A Metaeconomics Look at the Metaphors by Which We Live. *Review of Agricultural Economics* 24 (2): 410–427.

———. 2006a. Chap. 6: On the Economics of Subselves: Toward a Metaeconomics. In *Handbook of Contemporary Behavioral Economics*, ed. M. Altman, 99–122. New York: M.E. Sharpe.

———. 2006b. Toward a Dual Motive Metaeconomic Theory. *Journal of Socio-Economics* 35: 634–651.

Lynne, G.D., and C.F. Casey. 1998. Regulatory Control of Technology Adoption by Individuals Pursuing Multiple Utility. *Journal of Socio-Economics* 27 (6): 701–719.

Lynne, G.D., and L.R. Rola. 1988. Improving Attitude Behavior Prediction Models with Economic Variables. *Journal of Social Psychology* 128 (1): 19–28.

Lynne, G.D., J.S. Shonkwiler, and L.R. Rola. 1988. Attitudes and Farmer Conservation Behavior. *American Journal of Agricultural Economics* 70 (1): 12–19.

Lynne, G.D., C.F. Casey, A. Hodges, and M. Rahmani. 1995. Conservation Technology Adoption Decisions and the Theory of Planned Behavior. *Journal of Economic Psychology* 16: 581–598.

Lynne, G.D., N.V. Czap, H.J. Czap, and M.E. Burbach. 2016. Theoretical Foundation for Empathy Conservation: Toward Avoiding the Tragedy of the Commons. *Review of Behavioral Economics* 3: 245–279.

Nelson, R.H. 1991. *Reaching for Heaven on Earth*. Savage: Rowman and Littlefield.

Ovchinnikova, N., H. Czap, G.D. Lynne, and C. Larimer. 2009. "I Don't Want to Be Selling My Soul:" Two Experiments in Environmental Economics. *Journal of Socio-Economics* 38 (2): 221–229.

Reimer, A., A. Thompson, L.S. Prokopy, J.G. Arbuckle, K. Genskow, D.J. Jackson-Smith, G. Lynne, L. McCann, L. Wright Morton, and P. Nowak. 2014. People, Place, Behavior, and Context: A Research Agenda for Expanding Our Understanding of What Motivates Farmers Conservation Behaviors. *Journal of Soil and Water Conservation* 69 (2): 57A–61A.

Sautter, J., N. Ovchinnikova, C. Kruse, and G. Lynne. 2011. Farmers Decisions Regarding Carbon Sequestration: A Metaeconomic View. *Society and Natural Resources* 24 (2): 133–147.

Sheeder, R.J., and G.D. Lynne. 2011. Empathy Conditioned Conservation: Walking in the Shoes of Others as a Conservation Farmer. *Land Economics* 87 (3): 433–452.

Siles, M., L. Robison, B. Johnson, G. Lynne, and D. Beveridge. 2000. Farmland Exchanges: Selection of Trading Partners, Terms of Trade, and Social Capital. *Journal of the American Society of Farm Managers and Rural Appraisers*: 127–140.

Solomon, R.C. 2007. *True to Our Feelings: What Our Emotions Are Really Telling Us*. New York: Oxford University Press.

Zhang, Zhenu, and G. Lynne. 2016. Is Social Capital Motivated by Self-Interest Only? A Case Study on a Well-Developed U.S. Rural Community. *Universal Journal of Agricultural Research* 4 (1): 25–31.

CHAPTER 9

Health Policy: Universal Pre-existing Conditions

Next to food policy, perhaps no domestic policy issue has raised the ire of more people than that related to the healthcare system. The US Affordable Care Act, which was based in and otherwise formulated with a heavy orientation towards the shared Other-interest in health, has been rejected outright by many who see the healthcare system is only to facilitate maximizing one's own Self-interest. The latter perspective is easily understood, as there is perhaps nothing more in one's own Self-interest then taking care of one's health. So, it would be easily expected that many people would consider mainly their own Self-interest, selfishly guarding their money to provide that care, and not willing to be selfless about something so essential.

People focused on Self-interest want to personalize their health care, and seek the best doctors and facilities that would help serve their own health goals. It will also mean they probably would not much care to pay for anybody else's healthcare. So, any move to a universal healthcare kind of policy and program, which recognizes that we are in effect "all in it together," that is, there is a shared Other-interest at work, will be resisted.

Pre-Existing Conditions

First, we need to understand, based in thermodynamic reality, that at birth, every living creature is at the low(est)-entropy point, and that at death we move to a state of maximum entropy. Second, the primal drive of Self-interest is about availing our Own-self of energy (food as carbon;

G. D. Lynne, *Metaeconomics*, Palgrave Advances in Behavioral Economics, https://doi.org/10.1007/978-3-030-50601-8_9

carbon fuels; as well as other sources), and being healthy enough to use it effectively, to slow the pace to the inevitable point of maximum entropy. Third, every living creature has a pre-existing condition, something will eventually bring everyone to the point of maximum (death) entropy. Pre-existing conditions are just thermodynamic reality, and everyone has same, so, deal with it accordingly.

Trade&Mandate in the Insurance Markets

The matter of how to balance Market&Government was directly addressed in the original version of the US Affordable Care Act. Due to everyone having pre-existing conditions, and in need of health care at some point, a Government mandate to purchase insurance to address the costs was put in place. Everyone had to purchase private health insurance when they turned 18, with the option of waiting until they were 26 if the parents were willing to keep paying the family premium. The Market was then turned lose to find the best way to insure everyone. Using Metaeconomics, the Affordable Care Act moved the system toward path 0Z (Figs. 4.1, 7.1, and 8.1), although not nudged, but mandated.

The Mandate came from Progressives using science to make the point that everyone has pre-existing conditions: Entropy is at work in everyone, we all eventually die, everyone will face medical challenges, and bills: So, mandate. The trade came from Conservative principles, the insurance would be provided through the private sector, the Market. And, with Medicare still in place, it meant that a trade&mandate, private&public-system had been put into place.

Some of the younger buyers did not like the mandate to buy insurance, nor the tax/fine if they did not. Said individuals wanted out. Also, if the pre-existing condition had not yet emerged, they could gamble that Self-interest would serve them best. Empirically, it just shifts the costs, creating social costs outside of themselves, as eventually someone must pay that cost on the path to maximum entropy. And, without insurance, said people often end up on government assistance, more social cost. The tax provision would offset it a bit, in that it produced federal revenue to cover unplanned medical costs. As a result of said complaints, the system was dismantled, the mandate was removed: The insurance Market quit working efficiently, relying as did on everyone was in the risk pool, keeping costs down for everyone. While trade&mandate, Market&Government works, the Right Isle, who generally favors the Market, removed the mandate, and, ironically, undid the Market.

Vaccinations

The movement to not have one's children, or Own-self, vaccinated can now be understood as arising out of a narrowly shared Other-interest held by a few people that have come to believe that vaccines can lead to diseases and conditions like autism. Metaeconomics points out, however, that the approach ignores the shared Other-interest in keeping the overall population safe from such things as measles, mumps, whooping cough, some cancers, polio, and, perhaps COVID-19, someday, among other things. The choice to not be vaccinated is questionable, as the scientific and experiential evidence suggest extremely low risk and high payoff both to the person and the larger community. In fact, not being vaccinated generates substantive social costs, the costs shifted to others. Ethics, anyone?

Doctor–Patient Relationship

Topol (2019) makes the convincing case that healthcare could be vastly improved with more Empathy. Costs would be reduced, and happiness would be increased, because of better outcomes for the patient and provider. The proposition is easily explained with Metaeconomics.

Using Fig. 8.1, consider input *d* as all the complex tests, drugs, and other medical interventions relating to the patient, while input *e* involves the time and patience, and other efforts related to the doctor walking-in-the-shoes-of-the-patient, trying to find out what the patient is really experiencing not only with the condition but also with the treatment process. Lots of tests, high use of drugs, sometimes not really customizing treatment to the patient (impossible in 5-minute office visits, where the patient waits 60-minutes to spend 5-minutes with the doctor who passes through the examination room on the way to another patient) might serve the Self-interest in mere survival on the Ego-only (largely the doctor's Ego) path 0G. At the same time, too much Empathy, paying too much attention to the relationship and not enough to medications, tests, and other treatments may produce better feelings but less survival on path 0M. The best outcome, however, throttling back a bit on the expensive tests, drugs, and perhaps putting more time into helping the patient heal self, including patient influence on testing and drugs, as well as more empathy going in every direction, could put the process on a more humane and happier path 0Z.

Coronavirus Pandemic

There is perhaps no better example to demonstrate the tension between the Self&Other-interest, the selfish&selfless (again, see Figs. 7.1 and 7.2), as related to the coronavirus pandemic. It has resulted in the spreading of the SARS-CoV-2, and causing the COVID-19 disease in millions of people on the Spaceship. It points to how the more primal Ego drives one onto the selfish path represented in Self-interest. The selfless path represented in Other-interest is also at work: On the good side of it, Empathy drives helping others. On the dark side of it, the easily transmitted virus is being shared, too.

Figures 7.1 and 7.2 can be used to organize the questions, and, perhaps, help make sense of it. To establish boundaries, a person who is quite selfish, operating with excessive Greed, tends to take (buy way beyond reason) and hoard essentials. Everything from beans to toilet paper, as demonstrated in the early-2020 crisis, was emptied from the shelves. Additionally, there were runs on gun shops, to buy and hoard both guns and ammunition. Afraid of the excessive Greed by others, we might guess, or, use the guns to be even more excessive, to take from others? It is all about losing Self-control, and not being influenced by the shared Other-interest in everyone having some toilet paper and food (and, we must surmise, some guns and ammunition). Excessive Greed also drove several US senators who sold vulnerable stock and purchased stock in medical supply companies, after an early (the public was not yet informed) intelligence agency briefing indicated the pandemic was on the way. Excessive Ego-based Greed also drove politicians who did not want the bad news to adversely affect the economy. Metaeconomics would suggest that better balance with Empathy would have predictably focused more attention on the Human side of the pandemic with less on the Econ side of it.

Similar framing is represented in the outcry from another small group in the US along the lines of the infamous Patrick Henry call for: "Give me Liberty, or give me Death!" in response to Government mandates for social distancing, for sequestering, and for shut down of business enterprise. And, that might be all good and fine if it is a science, fact-based position. One can reasonably expect that Patrick Henry had some empirical basis (some facts, some science) that the protest directed at the English Monarchy could, indeed, be productive. Also, it had an ethical foundation, too, as in liberty is good, if so based. It is not as clear that a protest directed at a deadly virus, without the science and fact-basis (as in minimal to no testing of workers) for finding out the level of risk in not social distancing, and going back to work too soon, is rational, and likely not ethical. Also, it seems, as in the myth of social cost stance, to be with almost total disregard for the shared Other-interest in not exposing others to the disease. All of this is at best path 0G, and, in some cases, extreme vertical axis choice: It seems said liberty can well lead to death, being it is not based in science&ethics. It is about a kind of blind attempt at maximizing Self-interest at point A (or anywhere in the irrational zone R^oA, including the vertical axis) in Fig. 7.1, which could well put the protestor at the origin, at 0 = death. Maximizing Self-interest without regard to a widely shared Other-interest is not usually the best choice.

At the other extreme, first response and health care workers who give it all to helping others, sharing in the Other-interest in managing the virus and the illness, could well land on the horizontal axis, dying from the selfless act. Without enough help from the shared Other-interest side, as in not providing sufficient numbers of N95 masks and other protective gear for said workers, several did pay that price. Many ended on the horizontal axis.

Choosing in either R^oA or R^oC, including the vertical or horizontal axis, is not a rational choice. It is not rational for either a person or the larger community, the Market or the Government. The rational choice involves balance in person&community, Self&Other-interest, Market&Government, on some path 0Z. Granted, there could be wide-variation in which path was chosen. Some would find it rational to be more oriented to a path 0Z closer to the Self-interest on path 0G, working to avoid the virus if possible, yet at least being a bit sensitive to the situation of others. And, science-based facts would be used to decide, like in lots of testing, and, perhaps, tracing. Others would find it rational to operate closer to path 0M, such as social distancing to keep grandma and grandma from being exposed: For that case, think of balancing the interests with the value *V* of grandma and grandpa, which might lead to a point B choice in Fig. 7.1 due to choosing point B in Fig. 7.2, as in grandma and grandpa are perhaps not priceless, but nevertheless are valuable.

Fisher, Sellers, and Wilson (2020) raise the question, regarding how to interact with others during the corona pandemic "is that being selfless to offer help or is it being selfish because I need to do something like that to get up in the morning?" Metaeconomics clarifies it is both. We need to be selfish (need work, money, equipment, time) to Be Loved, and selfless to

Be Lovely (so can get up in the morning). Payoff arises in both domains for every choice. Also, is it strictly a price *P* ratio, Be Loved driven matter (like the relative prices of toilet paper to food prices, in a Figs. 4.1, 7.1, or 8.1), as Neoclassical Microeconomics has to say? No, it also involves value *V* (the grandma and grandpa case), which must be addressed (as Neoinstitutional Economics makes clear) in order to Be Lovely.

Before we look at the Metaeconomic balance, consider the two extremes: First, path 0G is the Market doing it pretty much without Government. So, private firms step forward to manufacture the test kits and do the testing. Private firms also produce the protective masks, clothing and the ventilators. The private nurses, doctors, and private hospitals handle every case. Private insurance companies pay the claims, and only people with money to buy insurance make claims. The patients who have enough money do well; the patients without money, do not do so well, literally. The price *P* of toilet paper and beans would rise rapidly, rationing through the price. Value *V* has no influence. Right Isle, anyone (see Table 6.1)?

Second, on the other path 0M, we might find a quite different pattern, with heavy involvement by the community, especially as represented in Government. It might mandate social distancing, and only essential workers. It might use the most socialist styled (Government owned) organization the US has, namely the military, to provide field hospitals and hospital ships. It might command private companies to produce protective gear and ventilators. It might get involved in rationing the gear and equipment among the hospitals, especially the public ones, but also monitor and distribute to the private hospitals, assuming there are any. It might press the State-owned national guard units into doing coronavirus-related testing (for both how the virus spreads, and how the disease is evolving) as well as ensuring grocery shelves of all the privately owned stores have at least some food. It might put a lockdown on all non-essential travel. It might provide trillions in payments to workers now stopped from working, especially people who are independent contractors like Uber drivers and beauticians. It might shore up Medicare and Medicaid programs to help the elderly and the poor, which are often the same people, and perhaps even consider a single payer system for everyone. It might first nudge the Market to produce N95 personal protective masks, and, if that fails, it might evoke the Defense Production Act and require the Market to produce the equipment. It might do wide and deep testing, and perhaps nudge if not mandate tracing. It might rely on data and science, as well as science&ethics, to manage the pandemic. Left Isle, anyone (see Table 6.1)?

Neither extreme works. Being sequestered alone on the NeoClassEcon Isle does not produce enough economic activity. Being in a petri-dish for spreading the virus in a community such as a congested sporting event, shopping mall, meat packing line, nursing home, or prison with no choice, as on the NeoInstiEcon Isle, spreads the disease. So, in seeing it more from the MetaEcon Isle, how do we think about balancing the actions on the happier, humane, and efficient path 0Z? Path 0Z is about economic&public-health, jointly pursued.

Well, in some cases, it is quite simple: Limit (Government sets caps) the amount of toilet paper and beans a person can buy and evolve the Market price (trade) for each. Limit (Government) the number of workers on the meat packing line, give them protective gear, and, only then, with adequate attention to the shared Other-interest in safety, put the Market to work to produce the meat product. Finding path 0Z also would mean doing substantive testing and tracing in order to obtain the data needed for a science-based management on the meat line, as well as all other aspects of dealing with the pandemic. The Government would mandate testing (the cap) and the Market would do it (the trade). The Government would bring the science and data; the Market would implement based on that science and data. The Market would do the food production and keep the distribution systems running, and producing the protective gear and ventilators (unless the nudge from Government to produce said items fails): Trade. The Government would mandate the wearing of the protective gear in the food processing, distribution, and grocery stores. So, trade&cap, cap&trade. And, perhaps most importantly: Pour lots of Government money into both private&public-research, to fund the science needed to develop the vaccines, the medicines, while the Market makes and distributes same (while paying the Government back, through paying the price/taxes, for the research costs).

Now, could path 0Z also be found by the Market alone? Theoretically, sure. A distillery shifting from the profit path to producing hand sanitizers, and to giving away the product, is approaching a path 0Z choice. Markets could produce all the personal protective gear with reasonable profits. A CEO acting as a Chief Empathy Officer (Bersin 2020) would operate on path 0Z.

So, how did the US do, overall? How did it compare with actions in other areas on the Spaceship? The analysis is not yet in, but it will probably show substantive Market-failure and Government-failure. One case in point: China produced over one-half of the Spaceship Earth masks prior to the Corona outbreak, with several US factories involved in production in China (Bradsher and Alderman 2020). Problem is, China nationalized all the personal protective equipment manufacturers early in the outbreak of COVID-19, and hoarded the masks (Sutter, Schwarzenberg, and Sutherland 2020, p. 11). It seems Ego-based Self-interest was also the main force in China, both in the Market and the Government, just like it will likely be proven to be the case in the US: Empathy, anyone? It represents a clear failure on the part of Government to put in place a shared Other-interest between China and the US that banned hoarding.

So, in contrast to the standard story on the Right (see Table 6.1), the Market instead did a lot of bad, for example, moved virtually all N95 mask manufacturing capacity to China. The Government which can do good, especially in public health, was stopped from doing so with substantive failures, mainly driven by the Right, in not funding the public health system after the 2008 financial crisis. The Government had invested little in masks and other protective equipment. It seems, too, that perhaps "deep state" and "administrative state" conspiracy theories had a bad effect: Pandemic response team resources were cut heavily (Sun 2018). In addition, significant numbers of scientific experts were removed, otherwise discounted, by the Government. One can make Government fail by not respecting what it is good at doing, such as in helping with key actions needed in a pandemic, for example, using data-based (lots of sampling through testing) science for nudging social distancing and controlling it when it does not come forward from the nudge.

Most important lesson from Metaeconomics: Do the empirical work. Stay with the facts. Pay deep attention to the science. Encourage expert assessments and interactions. Do not squelch the scientific input. Look for balance in Ego&Empathy, Market&Government, with attention to the shared Other-interest playing a key role. And, overall, do what works.

References

Bersin, J. 2020. What the Coronavirus Teaches Us About Leadership: A Lot. *Business Trends/Leadership Development*. joshbersin.com/2020/03/ceo-the-chief-empathy-officer/. Accessed 28 Mar 2020.

Bradsher, K., and L. Alderman. 2020. The World Needs Masks. China Makes Them, but Has Been Hoarding Them. *New York Times* (New York), March 13/April 2 2020.

Fisher, M.F., S. Sellers, and S. Wilson. 2020. Stay Home, or, Carry On? *Washington Post*, March 21, 2020, Digital.

Sun, L. H. 2018. Top White House Official in Charge of Pandemic Response Exits Abruptly. *Washington Post*, May 10, 2018.

Sutter, K.M., A.M. Schwarzenberg, and M.D. Sutherland. 2020. *Covid-19: China Medical Supply Chains and Broader Trade Issues.* Congressional Research Service: Washington, DC.

Topol, Eric. 2019. *Deep Medicine: How Artificial Intelligence Can Make Healthcare Human Again.* New York: Hachette Book Group, Inc.

CHAPTER 10

Family Policy: Failed Liberalism and Lost Sensibilities

Deneen (2019a, b, p. 178, 188) claims that liberalism is leading to dysfunctional, disintegrating families. He lays blame to Progressive Government on the Left for the social libertarianism in the sexual and familial domain and Conservative Government on the Right for the economic libertarianism in the Markets. Will (2019, loc 318) also points to the disintegration of families as one of the most destructive social problems: It is the fault of Progressive Government, by having built a sense of entitlement on the lower end of the income and wealth ladder. Metaeconomics sees little in the way of merit in any of the claims, especially not in the implication that moving more to the Right with Conservative sensibilities and/or with Rightish Liberal Statism, or to the Left with Leftish Liberal Statism, is going to fix it. Metaeconomics points in quite different directions. So, how do we make sense of the claims? What is the solution?

Unity Candle: I&We, Self&Other Joint in a Family

To make sense of the fundamental issue, recall the conversation with my wife about the unity candle. The couple is often presented with the symbolic opportunity to think about unity, through jointly lighting a unity candle, using each person's candles.

G. D. Lynne, *Metaeconomics*, Palgrave Advances in Behavioral Economics, https://doi.org/10.1007/978-3-030-50601-8_10

And, what exactly is the driver in the unity candle? Well, other than the energy to make it work, it is about the moral and ethical dimension of it. Metaphorically, it is the wax (ethic) holding the wick (energy) which is fundamental. It is the ethic that forms the Other (shared, integrated within)-interest in a marriage and the family. Empathy is the solution, as it leads to the ethic.

The nature of a well-functioning marriage and family also helps us understand the controversy over same-sex marriages, and/or other kinds of sexual relations, as it relates to a family. While clearly it is in the Self-interest for people to seek the kind of sexual partners they prefer, there is also a clear shared Other-interest with the larger community within which the family is embedded. And, as a result, it is the social and especially religious institution (the shared we, shared Other, shared community of interest) over which the controversy arises. And, again, Empathy resolves it.

Lesbian, Gay, Bisexual, and Transgender (LGBT) Rights

Deneen (2019b) argues the Self-interest only, autonomous individual (liberal, plentiful liberty and freedom) unbounded by the shared Other-interest represented in "manners and morals" leads to a Market-like approach in sexual practice involving unbounded, not tempered buyers and sellers. Specifically (Deneen 2019b, loc 1111):

> ...(while) "progressive" liberals declaim the expansive state as the ultimate protector of individual liberty, they insist that it must be limited when it comes to enforcement of "manners and morals," preferring the open marketplace of individual "buyers and sellers," especially in matters of sexual practice and infinitely fluid sexual identity. (Deneen 2019b, loc 1111)

Deneen, in effect, deplores the Governments role in supporting the expression of Self-interest by sexual practice other than the heterosexual variety, deploring then a kind of Leftish Liberal Statism that supports the person's right to choose. Yet, at the same time, he seems to implicitly support a kind of Rightish Liberal Statism that wants to give inordinate control to some other outside controlling element, like perhaps some religious framing.

The latter controlling element is also reflected in the headline: "Will the nation's third-largest church split up over LGBT debate? Leaders try to reach an answer" (Zauzmer and Bailey 2019). The analysis points to a schism in the United Methodist Church, with a split into two groups, in effect between the Leftish Liberal Statists who want to ensure the right to choose sexual expression and the Rightish Liberal Statists who want it stopped. Both might involve outside intervention: By the Government on the Left or by a sub-group of the Methodist Church on the Right. Heteronomy at work.

Metaeconomics easily explains what is going on here, while pointing to the possibility for a humane (empathy tempered, ethics based) and liberal position, on some path 0Z. Metaeconomics points to developing a widely shared Other-interest in the matter, an ethics about the freedom to choose. Metaeconomics focuses on a more encompassing Other-interest.

Metaeconomics suggests that the group supporting the LGBT shared Other-interest is apparently drawing on the Christian, new testament (grace by faith) part of the Bible. Christ practiced empathy and then joining in sympathy-compassion for anyone and everyone, including a person in a LGBT frame. Metaeconomics suggests that people on the other side apparently are connecting, instead, to the kind of shared Other-interest coming out of the old testament Bible, where it proclaims "Thou shalt not" (law) have such behaviors.

Overall, then, a preview here: Metaeconomics sees the potential play, in a commonly shared Other-interest, across the entire body of the Methodist Church, to resolve the matter. It is about integration and balance in grace&command (as in saved by grace, but, also, there are the 10-commandments), person&church, which it appears the Methodists cannot do. Bringing Self-interest and Other-interest together, and avoiding the split on the schism, would require finding common ground in the Other (shared among all Methodists)-interest, again, a kind of humane liberalism at work on path 0Z.

Back to the story: Delegates to a Methodist Conference voted on February 26, 2019, to not allow local churches to decide on LGBT policies, including not allowing the joining in unity (marriage being one way to do it) of any two people with an LGBT orientation with another. The African church delegates were especially adamant, a Reverend Jerry Kulah of Liberia claiming (The Associated Press 2019): "We can't do anything but to support the Traditional Plan – it is the biblical plan (i.e. read, the old testament traditional plan against anything other than heterosexuality, not the plan of empathy-sympathy-compassion-grace from the new testament) … the church in Africa would cease to exist (if they go outside the traditional plan)."

The Metaeconomics question becomes: Is there a way to evolve a shared Other-interest, a shared moral community, perhaps drawing on the science of sexuality to help form that new moral and ethical community? The science points to the empirical reality that humans are, genetically with respect to sexuality, on a continuum. So, perhaps it is not a sin to be born somewhere on that continuum, with only the heterosexual devoid of sin? Empirical questions.

In order to adequately consider what LGBT church policy should be, one needs to project one's self into the situation of the person with a different sexual preference. Ask yourself: "how would I wish to be treated if I had that preference," having been born that way? After working through the act of Empathy, one would expect that most people would generally arrive at a more reasonable kind of policy position, perhaps joining in sympathy with, and compassion for, other sexual preferences than one's own?

Notably, Neoclassical Microeconomics would point only to the Self-interest for deciding on the nature of Methodist policy, with the Invisible Hand of Other-interest buried in the status quo. So, the matter could never be resolved, as the divergent Self-interest lacks any common ground: The schism would be efficient, as each independent unit can now maximize Self-interest. On the other side, in the Other-interest only perspective, as in Neoinstitutional Economics, some religions do ban certain kinds of arrangements between partners. An Other-interest only frame results in such things as denying marriage except between heterosexuals. The best Neoinstitutional Economics can say is: It is irritating, so make it visible, and hope for the best. In contrast, Metaeconomics points to stirring mindfulness and the Empathy it produces, as the basis for a LGBT policy. Take it out of the Invisible (Neoclassical Economics), make it Visible (Neoinstitutional Economics) and, then, fix it with science and Empathy-based (new) ethics (Metaeconomics).

The LGBT issue is also about discrimination, with substantive negative impacts on the economy. All kinds of discrimination, whether based on sexual preferences, gender or race, or any other grounds, adversely affect the economy. Discrimination reduces both efficiency and productivity, and slows the growth of an economy, as documented in empirical research in Behavioral Economics (Altman 2012, loc 3828). Metaeconomics easily explains how: Discrimination causes the person not being able to operate on their best and efficient path 0Z, because a perverse path 0M of discrimination is pushing them off course. Path 0Z is the best in that it represents a humane and liberal (a person's right, decided by that person) path. It is the Metaeconomics efficient path.

It seems the Methodist church, by not seeing the fundamental need to form a shared Other-interest based in the virtues, the ethics widely shared, is actually contributing to the family disintegration pointed to in Deneen (2019a, b) and Will (2019). Ego causes the problem; Empathy solves it, in balance.

More on Family Disintegration

Family disintegration is attributed to a failed social liberalism by Deneen (2019a, b) and to not paying enough attention to conservative (including economic liberalism) sensibilities by Will (2019). Will (2019, loc. 318) goes on to say: "No one understands what opaque tangle of factors has caused it, which is one reason no one knows what public policies might ameliorate it." Yet, Will (2019, loc. 5588) as a Conservative goes on to blame the Progressives as in "ominous developments have coincided with Great Society policies: For every adult man ages twenty to sixty-four who is between jobs and looking for work, more than three are neither working nor seeking work, a trend that began with the Great Society." Will (2019, loc. 7736) claims

> the nation's mood is tinged with sadness stemming from well-founded fear that America's new, post– Great Society government is subverting America's old character. This government's agenda is a menu of temptations intended to change the nation's social norms by making Americans comfortable with dependency. And with the degradation of democracy by the practice of financing dependency by piling up public debt that forces unconsenting future generations to finance current consumption.

Maybe. It is true that we are seeing a massive failure in the economics of the family on the lower rungs of the income and wealth ladder (recall the original meaning of economics, Oikonomia, was household management), as Will is documenting. It is also true, however, that Rightish Liberal Statism and Conservative approaches have also contributed to dependence at the top, as represented in the financing of rampant cronyism (recall the bank bailouts, and recent massive tax cuts for the wealthy), taking and keeping wealth, rather than making it. Entitlement at the top is also leading to piling up public debt: Pay taxes, please. So, is that the fault of the Progressives, too? Both kinds of dependency-based entitlement clearly contribute to disintegration of the family at all levels. And, seemingly there are just as many Progressive sensibilities as there are Conservative sensibilities, made clear by reviewing the contents on the Left and Right of Table 6.1. So, what is really going on?

Metaeconomics can easily make sense of it, especially with the help of McCloskey (2019). It is fundamentally about the ethics, the virtues underlying and conditioning the choices for the family. It is about a humane liberalism, as represented in the I&We of the person&unity-candle in a family, writ large to include all families. As McCloskey (2019, p. 93) says it, "a humane liberal doesn't hesitate to face up to the ethical questions necessary to economics, and in a serious way." The unity candle is the metaphor for facing up to the ethical questions in the family, and, then, a good and humane economics of the family. A MetaEcon faces the ethical questions: Metaeconomics is about carefully selecting the sensibilities from both the Left and the Right (again, see all the sensibilities in Table 6.1, as well as Table 2.1), to form an ethical system that works.

So, taking each claim in turn. Deneen (2019a, b) is concerned first about democratic socialism, as if it is the cause of family disintegration. Well, first, how are families in the Nordic countries, with their Viking Economics, the social democracy version of democratic socialism, doing? Lakey (2017) makes it clear: Quite well. Second, maybe McCloskey (2019) has it about right, and Metaeconomics points in the same direction:

> If the progressives and conservatives stopped to think it through, I am confident that they would speedily repent, and cease interfering in the lives of free adults who are not committing force or fraud. Surely. Humane liberalism combines free markets with free identity. It's the adult way, avoiding crushing people from above.

It seems the statement very much characterizes the Nordic economies and families. In fact, it appears there is plentiful freedom to choose and little in the way of crushing people from above. Rather, it is all about joining in for shared cause, investing in the Human as a resource, and, building a widely shared Other-interest? Empirical question.

Deneen (2019a, b) seems to favor a kind of Rightish Liberal Statism regarding LGBT rights. We might suppose the solution is a sanctioning by some religious board, composed we might guess, of sexual preference and activity controllers. In contrast, a truly humane liberalism, would liberate sexual minorities (after McCloskey 2019, p. 267), which seems to have little to do with Left or Right, Progressive or Conservative. It just has to do with humane and liberal sensibilities, and there are some on both Right and Left (again, Table 6.1, please)? Empirical question.

Moving on, Deneen (2019a, b) is concerned with the Right in the support of "economic libertarianism and market forces on national solidarity and social stability." Stiglitz (2019, p. 21) also points out that "…liberalization and globalization brought wealth to a few but stagnation, insecurity, and instability to the rest." Why?

Metaeconomics makes it clear: It was the lack of Empathy. It was the lack of an Empathy-based ethics to develop a shared Other-interest that worked for everyone, better ensuring the payoff from globalization was widely shared. It meant helping families find perhaps even higher paying jobs, in effect sharing in the largesse from moving the factories elsewhere. It meant working toward a humane liberal economy, Empathy-driven ethics in the structure and content of it, widely accessible to all. It meant using more cooperative structures, wherein selling the factory and/or moving it elsewhere also meant some capital gain, return on capital for everyone. The fact that the opportunity for gain is not just for a few is what a liberal and humane, democracy-based capitalism is all about. So, yes, the kind of Statism, in the case mainly of the Rightish style, did not work.

And, finally, on the Will (2019) claim that somehow the old character of the US has been lost, so, we should go back to the Conservative sensibility about it? Well, maybe. It seems the old character, embedded in the Invisible Hand holding said sensibilities, had some serious flaws. In fact, said flaws needed to be fixed in the Visible Hand of the Civil Rights Act of 1964 and other 1960s' era legislation. As McCloskey (2019, p. 84) says, Government sometimes does good deeds, as in "the passing of liberal laws to make people free, as in the Civil Rights Acts of 1866 and of 1964." Another rare and good deed was the Voting Rights Act of 1965, and, at least some good came out of the Great Society efforts of Progressive Government started about that time, not all bad as Will (2019) claims.

Good deeds, rare or otherwise, are about freeing (through Empathy) people to choose a tempered path 0Z. Empathy-based deeds are too rare. Ego is primal. A humane and liberal capitalism needs balance in Ego&Empathy as Metaeconomics makes clear. The Deneen (2019a, b) and Will (2019) claims can only be resolved with an Empathy-based ethics, the kind described by McCloskey (2019), and in the core of Metaeconomics.

Families Can Barely Find $400: Ethics Would Help

The title of the Akerlof and Shiller (2015) book points the direction: *Phishing for Phools: The Economics of Manipulation and Deception*. The book uses the well-known tune about "How much is that doggie in the window..." to point to how, in a free to choose, free no-holds-barred (bad) capitalism, we are constantly stirred to buy, buy, and buy some more, whether it is good for us (and for capitalism in general) or not. Families are disintegrating on the financial side because of unethical business behavior, who really are the Phools, and not just the people they Phool.

As Metaeconomics suggests, the Milton Friedman call for "free to choose" misses the point by not seeing the need to temper and condition the Market, working to do the right (moral, ethical) thing. Phishing for Phools is not part of a truly moral community, an ethical system that would work best across all people. The Phishing perhaps even suggests the need for Government nudging and controls, if it is not Self-controlled by people who are Phishing. It is seemingly about walking (and talking) softly and carrying a big stick, and using the stick when necessary, if self-control fails, and nudging does not work, to restrain both Phishing and Phooling? It helps both the Phools and people who would Phish? Empirical questions.

As Akerlof and Shiller (2015) explain, Phishing is "about getting people to do things that are in the interest of the phisherman, but not in the interest of the target ... a phool is someone who, for whatever reason, is successfully phished." Phishing, too, is about stirring that more primal, hedonistic, egoistic tendency. Phishers often work from a less than ethical, less than moral community frame. As Akerlof and Shiller (2015) point out, the Phool tends to buy things not really needed (again, whether you really need a doggie or not, everyone is stirred to ask "How much is that doggie in the window..."). The result is not even having $400 left, to buy the important things, like a reasonable retirement, or health care, needed for a person's longer-term Other-interest. People lack Self-control, as is well understood in Metaeconomics.

For the economics trained reader, but anyone can follow along (and learn some economics in the process), we can use Fig. 4.1 to help make specific sense of the contentions. One reason the "don't even have $400" is an issue related to longer-term savings for retirement. Think of good *e* as a bundle of retirement content goods *e*, the bundle of goods bought with more consideration for the shared Other-interest. That is, pay attention to a moral and ethical community, which suggests perhaps living a more modest life style; reasonable saving levels, including perhaps buying of mutual funds, bonds, and real estate; wishing to reduce the burden on the family, on the younger taxpayers, by saving more money; and, most of all, not acting on what the Phishers are pushing. In turn, think of Good *d* as composed mainly of (but not necessarily exclusively) the kind of goods the Phishers stir the Phools to buy, things you just "have to have." The Phishers stir the need for that boat; cruise in the Caribbean; fancier clothing, houses, and automobiles. "Infomercials" come to mind, as well as hour after hour, commercials that appeal to base instincts like being macho, sexy, a fast and daring driver, "cool," among others. Social media, too, with advertisement paying the costs, is evermore the place for the Phishers and their Self-interest only framing, pushing good (or is it bad) *d*. And, too, the worst of the worst, the spammers and scammers: Ethics, anyone? The best retirement plan emerges on path 0Z, with balance, and, needing lots of Self-control.

References

Akerlof, George A., and Robert J. Shiller. 2015. *Phishing for Phools: The Economics of Manipulation and Deception*. Princeton: Princeton University Press.

Altman, M. 2012. *Behavioral Economics for Dummies*. Kindle ed. Mississauga: John Wiley and Sons Canada, Ltd.

Deneen, Patrick J. 2019a. A Defense of Conservatism That Veers toward Liberalism. Opinion, *Washington Post* (Washington, DC), June 21. Digital.

———. 2019b. *Why Liberalism Failed*. Kindle ed. New Haven: Yale University Press.

Lakey, George. 2017. *Viking Economics: How the Scandinavians Got It Right – And How We Can, Too*. Kindle ed, 2016. Brooklyn, New York: Melville House Publishing.

McCloskey, D.N. 2019. *Why Liberalism Works: How True Liberal Values Produce a Freer, More Equal, Prosperous World for All*. Kindle ed. New York: Yale University Press.

Press, The Associated. 2019. United Methodist Delegates Defeat Bid to Ease LGBT Bans. *New York Times* (New York), February 26.

Stiglitz, Joseph E. People. 2019. *Power and Profits: Progressive Capitalism for an Age of Discontent*. New York: W. W. Norton and Company.

Will, George F. 2019. *The Conservative Sensibility*. Kindle ed. New York: Hachette Books.

Zauzmer, Julie, and Sarah Pulliam Bailey. 2019. Will the Nation's Third-Largest Church Split up over LGBT Debate? Leaders Try to Reach an Answer. *Washington Post*, February 22.

CHAPTER 11

Education Policy: Need for Science and Ethics

Locke, Rousseau, and Smith (as well as other Enlightenment thinkers), and the founders of the US as reflected in the Declaration of Independence, the Bill of Rights, and the Constitution, all saw the essential need for a well-educated population. The population needed to be able to find, learn, use, and otherwise deal with and apply the facts. It is the only way to avoid becoming a simpleton, living with a simple folktale. A person who does so easily becomes a victim of totalitarianism, fascism, communism, socialism, and the other "badisms," including various types of bad capitalism. The ability to understand and use facts, and integrate the same with ethics, is essential to building a humane and liberal-based democracy into the foundation of good capitalism: science&ethics education, please. Education rests in science and the liberal (humane) arts: again, science&ethics. Education ensures it is a reality-based system as well as a moral system; a moral community; an ethical system. Education is about paying attention to the content of the Invisible Hand and fixing it with the Visible Hand when it is the ethical, humane and fact-based thing to do. Education is about nudging, encouraging a better set of norms (Altman 2012, loc 3946), norms reflecting facts and ethics. By being empirical&ethical, education is also, then, in the foundation of Metaeconomics.

At the time the US was founded, it was deemed especially important to use the facts, in order to move away from the notion of the divine right of a select few (i.e., and, unethical they were) to be the political leaders

G. D. Lynne, *Metaeconomics*, Palgrave Advances in Behavioral Economics, https://doi.org/10.1007/978-3-030-50601-8_11

and cronies. There were really no facts and ethics underlying the rule by a monarchy and the religious figures and favored business enterprises embedded in the rampant cronyism of previous times. It was only through such things as the emergence of Common Law, which came to also subject the monarchy and other political and religious leaders to the law, that made for progress. It also, then, became possible to legitimately question religious leaders relying on old books that had little in the line of empirical testing (and, as a result, also unethical) to support the contentions. Fake news becomes an oxymoron, as an educated public doing their homework can easily spot what is fake, and only fact-based, ethics-based news survives.

Fascism is especially a problem. Stanley (2018) warns that it is exactly what Fascism works to do, as represented in Fascist Politics. The danger of an uneducated and/or idereducated populous cannot be emphasized enough, as it is easy to be fooled by Fascists, who replace reality with propaganda. As Hedges (2018, p. 15):

> When reality is replaced by the whims of opinion and expediency, what is true one day often becomes false the next. Consistency is discarded. Complexity, nuance, depth, and profundity are replaced with the simpleton's belief in threats and force. ... Totalitarianism (and the close relative in Fascism) ... is at its core the desire for a simple folktale. Once this folktale replaces reality, morality and ethics are abolished.

It is also the case in Fascist Religion, too (see Hedges 2007). Education works to ensure people can deal with the complexity, the nuance, and the depth. Education is all about ensuring there are few to no simpleton frames, which is essential to ensure the moral and ethical dimension can evolve.

A Fascist diverts attention from the facts coming out of solid investigative reporting in the competent news services. It is also the Fascist frame to debunk, otherwise discredit science-based facts coming out of research from universities. Fascists seek to push people into not trusting any source of information other than what is produced by the propaganda arm of the Fascists, pushing a simple but dangerous folklore. Metaeconomics suggests essential interaction between private&public-education and research to counter it, bringing the complexity to light.

References

Altman, M. 2012. *Behavioral economics for dummies*. Kindle ed. Mississauga: John Wiley and Sons Canada, Ltd.

Hedges, Chris. 2007. *American Fascists: The Christian Right and the War on America*. New York: Free Press.

———. 2018. *America: The Farewell Tour*. Kindle ed. Simon and Schuster.

Stanley, Jason. 2018. *How Fascism Works: The Politics of Us and Them*. New York: Random House.

CHAPTER 12

Natural Resource Policy: Avoiding the Tragedy of the Commons

As alluded to perhaps too many times, we are all Travelers, together, on Spaceship Earth. Importantly, the way we travel together matters a great deal, suggested in the main point of Hardin (1968), that unbridled Self-interest will more likely than not lead to the *Tragedy of the Commons*. Intriguingly, the recommended solution is to privatize the commons, or, if it is already public property, convert it to private property. The solution comes out of the NeoClassEcon in Microeconomics, as famously subscribed to by Friedman and Buchanan, the overlap in the Chicago and Public Choice School of Economics, and is especially touted from the Libertarian Economics frame (e.g., see Anderson and Leal 2001).

The plan is to build a "free" Market, eliminating Government "intervention" and "distortion." Any time a value *V* is brought into influence the price *P*, it is considered a distortion. Maybe. So, we would eliminate the US Environmental Protection Agency, the US Department of the Interior, and the US Natural Resource Conservation Service, and all related state agencies, and all private organizations concerned with Spaceship Earth systems (e.g., the Sierra Club, unless they, too, were able to engage in buying and selling within the new Market), to list a few. Self-interest expressed in Markets will solve all. Reason is: Private property owners will husband their property, being naturally moral and ethical in the order of things, so they will just naturally sustain it. And, the private property owner is all-knowing, we might surmise having been willing to spend a substantive part of the profit made from owning the Spaceship to

G. D. Lynne, *Metaeconomics*, Palgrave Advances in Behavioral Economics, https://doi.org/10.1007/978-3-030-50601-8_12

do the scientific research essential to sustaining it? Really. Where is that occurring? In any case, being private property ensures husbanding and sustaining, the knowledge on how to do so must come from somewhere. We might guess, it is the Invisible Hand, once again. So, there will be no Tragedy.

And, the empirical reality is that private property owners do not always manage the resource in sustainable ways, often because the Market sends a bad signal. Also, it is not clear that every private property owner is aware of all the science needed to so sustain the system. So, Metaeconomics points to how a Market can produce its own kind of *Tragedy of Over-privatization*: A Market can also destroy a Spaceship Earth System, again, because of excessive Greed.

Also, a huge presumption: All value V arising in Other Forums would now have to be translated into price P in the new Markets. Everyone in the Other Forums would need plentiful money to compete with the money capacity of entities who are normally in the Market. The vehicle for expression of value V of the Spaceship Earth would be shifted dramatically.

As Metaeconomics makes clear, if we are to form private property, at minimum it must be a highly attenuated right, a right reflecting the shared Other-interest in long-term sustainability. An attenuated private property right is a right that arises out of an Empathy-based moral and ethical system. An attenuated private property right tempers the Self-interest into using the property in more reasonable ways, onto a happy and efficient path 0Z, rather than self-interest only path 0G. It is about balance in private&public. Importantly, based on the empirical evidence on Spaceship Earth Systems that are being operated sustainably, good mixes of private&public-property can happen, resulting in avoiding the Tragedy, even without Government taking any action (see Ostrom 1990, 1992).

Also, as important aside: Starting at about the time of Enlightenment, the propriety of conduct on path 0Z turned into encouraging a heavy dose of Common Law-based private property. The older idea of propriety, which was all about the appropriate and good conduct of a person, led to the idea of (private) property (see Smith and Wilson 2019, esp. pp. 13–14, on how propriety is the essence of property, as it first evolved). Said property came out of an exercise in Empathy leading to sympathy-based reflection (as Smith and Wilson 2019 make clear, a theme in *The Theory of Moral Sentiments* book, Smith 1759/1790) about the good and bad of it. The moral and ethical basis for Common Law, and especially for what came to be an attenuated private property right, came from walking-in-the-shoes-of-others, going in every direction. The Market needed that kind of an attenuated property right in order to avoid injustice, and, avoiding all the other bad things from not living with the other virtues represented on path 0M. To operate on path 0Z is to operate in good conduct and with propriety, as Smith (1759/1790) saw as essential to a good property system. Metaeconomics sees a good capitalism needing (attenuated) private property in good balance with public property, with attenuation focused on bounding and stopping foul play in the Markets.

Figure 12.1 helps in understanding the broad issues. The figure is a variant on one first presented in Zimmermann (1933/1951), who as an InstiEcon with an understanding of thermodynamics made the earliest argument for the notion that we live on an inexorable Arrow of Throughput. The economy is all about transforming the Neutral Stuff,

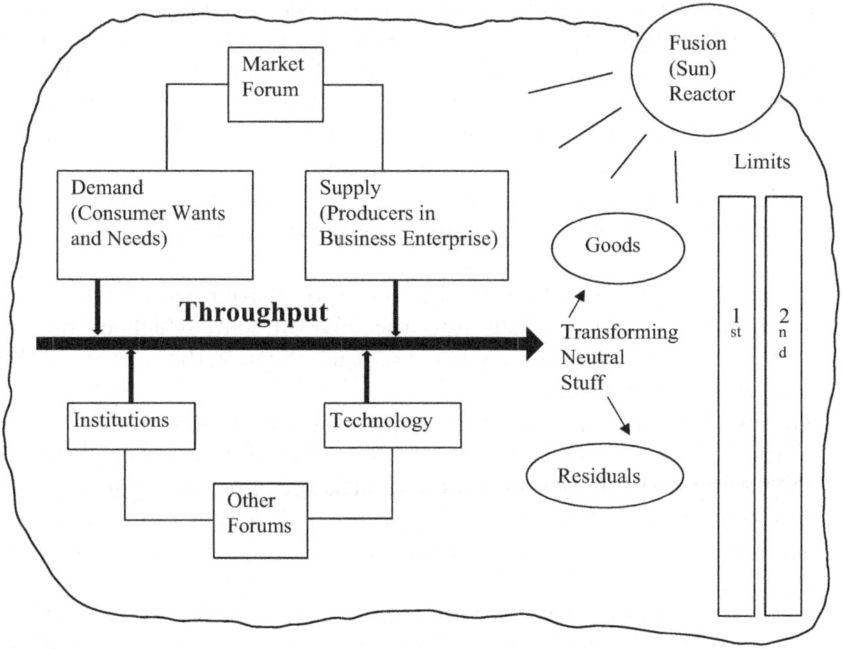

Fig. 12.1 Thermodynamic reality in metaeconomics: throughput paced by balance in market and government with first law (residuals) and second law (entropy) limits. (Source: Author's creation, inspired by Zimmermann (1933/1951))

represented in energy and material from the Spaceship, into products and services, which also inherently produces wastes and residuals (1st Law working here). Overall, the Sun drives the Throughput (2nd Law working here). And, the Market is embedded within the Spaceship Earth System, with all of it powered by the Sun.

The overall physical context is a closed Spaceship powered by the Sun. Market-based Wants and Needs (Demand) above the Arrow are the main force, and are served by Business Enterprise (Supply). Technology, under the Arrow, is both a driving and dampening force, the latter in managing residuals. Institutions (represented especially in Government, but in Community in general) are also drivers, but mainly serve in the role of tempering and conditioning, perhaps bounding, the Arrow. Technology and Institutions (laws, rules, regulations, customs, culture) resolve in a variety of Other Forums. Said Forums are largely Government (Administrative, Legislative, and Judicial) but also generally involve a variety of Private Organizations (e.g., the Sierra Club, a local Hunting Club) who also affect the pace of the arrow. Value V emerges below the Arrow; price P emerges above it. Eventually, the Arrow reaches the limits as described in 1st and 2nd Law Thermodynamics, the 2nd Law pointing to the Sun, which is a fusion reactor, burning out.

As Einstein argued it: The Thermodynamic Laws are the most irrefutable scientific laws of all, and will likely never be over-turned:

1st Law: Neither matter nor energy can be destroyed, so, therefore, we continually release residuals into the environment, which eventually cannot hold and process anymore. We reach the wall, the capacity of the Spaceship Earth system.

2nd Law: The capacity to do further work is continually lost, as we move from the low entropy situation represented in abundant carbon-based (including fossil and plant sourced) fuels and nuclear (including the Sun) fuels toward ever higher entropy, and, then, eventually to a state of maximum entropy on the Spaceship.

So, we might suppose that if every person in the Market acted in accordance with 1st and 2nd Law, and the basic ideas in Fig. 12.1, it could be possible for a Market to achieve sustainability. The pace of the Arrow would be determined by the magical Invisible Hand. Empirical evidence, please.

The Throughput Arrow metaphor also helps us see that sustaining the Spaceship Earth system through such things as shifting to renewable energy, which would also dampen the residuals load (reduce the amount of carbon going to the atmosphere and pollutants entering land and water sinks), does not stop the Arrow. We ultimately hit the Walls: There are limits. We can only influence the trajectory, pace and, thus, the time, at which it happens, dependent on the balance in Market&Government.

Carbon Taxes and Carbon Markets

The 1st Law is especially relevant to the challenge of carbon. The Spaceship Earth System has finite capacity to hold and process greenhouse gases, with carbon dioxide the main one. Metaeconomics points to addressing both the value *V* and price *P* of that capacity, as in "pricing carbon."

One possibility for evolving a price *P* would be for the Government to use a Carbon Tax to simulate it. In effect, the tax reflects the value *V* of sustainability held in the shared Other-interest sense, an approach favored by Progressives. Another approach would be to convert some or all the public property in the atmospheric capacity into private property. Seemingly said approach would be more favored by Conservatives.

Government Prices for the Capacity to Hold and Absorb Carbon Emissions

To help in highlighting what is at issue, we consider the *Wall Street Journal* article titled "Economists' Statement on Carbon Dividends" (Commentary 2017). It is coming mainly from the NeoClassEcon, Microeconomics frame of reference. To a lesser extent, the NeoInstiEcon way of thinking, with some representation from BehavEcon and EconPsych is also in the mix. The economists and psychologists behind the proposal suggest that the carbon pricing (they refer to it as a carbon tax) option is the best approach; each proposition is considered, *with a Metaeconomics assessment of each in italics*:

> Global climate change is a serious problem calling for immediate national action. Guided by sound economic *(Note: mainly Neoclassical Economics)* principles, we are united in the following policy recommendations.
>
> I. A carbon tax offers the most cost-effective lever to reduce carbon emissions at the scale and speed that is necessary. By correcting a well-known

market failure, a carbon tax will send a powerful price signal that harnesses the invisible hand of the marketplace to steer economic actors towards a low-carbon future.

On it being a serious problem, in fact, it is a Tragedy of the Commons that is on the near horizon. And, it is a massive market failure to not be mindful (no Empathy) of the capacity of the Spaceship Earth System to absorb and recycle carbon. The Market Failure can only be alleviated by recognizing the shared Other-interest. The Invisible Hand (questionable there is even such a thing, see Samuels, Johnson, and Perry 2011*) is failing. It is also a massive Government failure, in that the capacity of the atmosphere is a public property, being treated like a common property. So, calling for the Market to pay the price P, simulated with a carbon tax T, to better reflect the true value V of the atmosphere is one way to help avoid the Tragedy. The Visible Hand needs to be brought into play, to upset the flawed Moral Order operating in the Markets. The Invisible Hand is often insufficient to the task of solving pollution (overusing the capacity makes greenhouse gases, including carbon dioxide, a pollutant) problems (Altman* 2012, *loc 3668).*

II. A carbon tax should increase every year until emissions reductions goals are met and be revenue neutral to avoid debates over the size of government. A consistently rising carbon price will encourage technological innovation and large-scale infrastructure development. It will also accelerate the diffusion of carbon-efficient goods and services.

Metaeconomics sees the tax T being adjusted through time to reflect changes in the value V coming out of the Other Forums in community and Government. It would reflect the moral and ethical community. Through tax T acting as a price P, incentives are in place to stir innovative ways to use less carbon. It could be revenue neutral if other taxes are reduced.

III. A sufficiently robust and gradually rising carbon tax will replace the need for various carbon regulations that are less efficient. Substituting a price signal for cumbersome regulations will promote economic growth and provide the regulatory certainty companies need for long-term investment in clean-energy alternatives.

It is in effect a calling for Government to not only set the cap but to also do the trade (i.e., *evolve the Tax = Price through time that in effect achieves the cap). And, sure, faced with paying a price for the capacity, minimum cost ways are found to produce products with lower carbon content. It is demonstrated in Fig. 4.1, in that recycle content goods generally have lower carbon content, as do the conservation inputs considered in Fig. 8.1. It is about recognizing the shared Other-interest in sustaining Spaceship Earth systems.*

IV. To prevent carbon leakage and to protect US competitiveness, a border carbon adjustment system should be established. The system would enhance the competitiveness of American firms that are more energy-efficient than their global competitors. It would also create an incentive for other nations to adopt similar carbon pricing.

Metaeconomics, because it sees Spaceship Earth as a system affecting all Travelers, sees pervasive interdependence. That is, there is no such thing as an externality, because everything is internal too, and interdependent with everything else. So, Metaeconomics would point to a universal price P across the entire Spaceship. It would reflect the reality that the Spaceship Earth capacity to handle carbon emissions (and, all other greenhouse gases) is a joint issue for everyone; the price P needs to be set by a Spaceship Earth wide value V system, perhaps involving entities like the United Nations, and not be set by each country based on nationalistic, tribal identities.

V. To maximize the fairness and political viability of a rising carbon tax, all the revenue should be returned directly to US citizens through equal lump-sum rebates. The majority of American families, including the most vulnerable, will benefit financially by receiving more in "carbon dividends" than they pay in increased energy prices.

A carbon dividend suggests all the Travelers on the Spaceship do own the capacity to hold and absorb carbon in the atmosphere, including the ecosystem capacity to recycle it: It is indeed a public property. So, sure paying the public property owners for use of said property has some sense to it. And, a lump-sum rebate is simple. It would also serve to work against the extreme inequality of income and wealth that is causing all manner of social and public health problems, including problems caused by overloading the atmosphere of the Spaceship Earth with carbon dioxide.

The other way to solve the greenhouse gas problem: Move some or all the public property rights in greenhouse (especially carbon dioxide) gas holding, absorbing, and recycling capacity over to a set of limited, attenuated private property rights.

Market Prices for the Capacity to Hold and Absorb Carbon Dioxide

Massive Government failure has been at work for some time. It appeared a few years back in the failure in the US Legislative Branch to facilitate the formation of carbon markets. It has failed in the US Administrative branch, albeit the US Environmental Protection Agency has tried to address the greenhouse gas problem without much success because of political push back. It has failed in the US Judicial system. Intriguingly, despite all the

Government failure, there has been some trading in emissions allowances and greenhouse gas offsets.

The voluntary trade&cap (Note: Normally referred to as cap&trade, but reversed here to mirror the Metaeconomics notion of Market&Government) approach asks that each individual firm and industry on their own recognize the scarce capacity of the atmosphere to absorb carbon and other greenhouse gases and to set their own caps. The Chicago Climate Exchange (CCX) developed several pilot projects in order to help industry learn how such a system might work for carbon. Emissions allowances at one point were trading in the vicinity of $3–4 in contrast to $10–15 in Europe (late 2006) where caps are closer to reflecting actual atmospheric capacity/scarcity. By late 2010, the CCX market had collapsed, with allowance and offset prices <$0.50/metric ton, because of the stalemate in the US Senate, and the US Administration also moving away from pushing for a trade&cap system. In contrast, the European Climate Exchange is still quite active (see European Commission https://ec.europa.eu/clima/policies/ets_en) although it lagged a bit in 2012–2014. Here in the US, the northeastern states Regional Greenhouse Gas Initiative (see RGGI Staff https://www.rggi.org/) is an active trade&cap system. California is also actively implementing a trade&cap system (see Center for Climate and Energy Solutions https://www.c2es.org/content/california-cap-and-trade/), which was started in late-2011.

The mystery remains as to why the current overall path in the US is toward the carbon-driven tragedy on the horizon, rather than to a carbon emissions Market. We can only speculate the Conservatives on the Right Isle did not see sustainability as part of the shared Other-interest. The latter is more of a Progressive Left Isle notion, with many on that Isle wanting a sustainable Spaceship Earth. It may also have been from misunderstanding of trade&cap approaches. In any case, the intriguing Metaeconomics question is: Why would the Conservatives stop a Market solution to the problem?

A main reason might be the hype of the climate deniers, the science deniers, based on a very narrow, shared Other-interest, and often reflecting a taking ideology. Deniers, in consort with the oil, gas and coal industries who profit from denying, apparently plan to take as much wealth out of the production of carbon products as they can, before they are stopped, and, the ultimate stop point is when the tragedy arrives. The climate deniers, and the distortion by the industry, have been ignoring the thermodynamic realities about the true costs to the economy from excessive carbon emissions (and other greenhouse gases). Importantly, they have prevailed/lobbied in both Administrative and Legislative Branches, and, to some extent in the Judicial Branch as well, including influencing both elections and who is appointed to positions in the Government. The Market has been stopped, ironically, by Conservatives in the Right Isle, we must presume because science and facts play a lessor role: Table 6.1 points to how the Conservative sensibility is to downplay science. Go figure.

In light of the series of events leading to stopping the evolution of a free Market in carbon allowances, it is also ironic that the first experiment in using a Market approach, one based in a Government set cap, was touted and encouraged by a leading Conservative politician. President H.E.W. Bush, on the Conservative Right Isle (again, see Table 6.1), drove the evolution of the US emissions allowance market related to acid rain.

Market Prices for the Capacity to Hold and Process Sulfur Dioxide

Just like greenhouse gas science overwhelmingly points to essential action, the science of acid rain was also compelling. The Administrative Branch of Government (in particular, the U.S. Environment Protection Agency) moved to action based on the scientific finding that burning high sulfur coal, especially in the midwestern US, was leading to (literally) acid rain in the northeastern US. Forests were being denuded, and ecosystems were being damaged as the acid came down with the snow and rain. It was literally raining, snowing sulfuric acid, H_2SO_4 (as well as Nitric acid) as the H_2O (water) integrated with SO_2 (sulfur dioxide) from the high sulfur coal emissions coming out of the smokestacks. So, what was to be done?

The Clean Air Act was amended in 1990 (Title IV was added), establishing a maximum of 8.95 M tons of sulfur emissions as the cap: The cap is the Government, the Progressive part. In addition, Title IV also created an emissions market to facilitate trade in the allowances to emit sulfur: A Market could now evolve, the Conservative part. So, as Metaeconomics would support, there was an integration across the Isles, with a Conservative&Progressive outcome represented in the trade&cap approach.

Each allowance represents one ton of sulfur emissions, also defined by Government, the unit of trade in the Market. The allowances associated with the cap were distributed among the electric power utilities. It was done through Government using the latest science to set the cap and then moving out of the way of the Market to allocate the capacity (for the details on how it was accomplished, see Ellerman et al. 2000). As initially designed, there were potentially 8.95 M allowances, the cap, with each utility given an initial allocation, which could be freely traded in the Market as the utilities deemed appropriate.

Another outcome of the Market&Government, Conservative& Progressive-plan was to enhance what came to be a substantial increase in the Market for low sulfur coal, with a major source of such coal available in Wyoming. That is, even if the coal burning, electricity-generating utilities could not improve their technology, they could reduce emissions by burning low sulfur coal, which freed emission allowances for selling on the Market. Wyoming continues to be a main supplier of low sulfur coal, with huge financial payoffs not only to Wyoming but to the railroad industry from running 100 car coal trains on newly built, double tracks. Full trains go east to the coal burning electric utilities in the Midwest; empty cars go west to the Wyoming mines. Trains run 24/7, with upward of 1–2 or more trains passing through every hour.

There were roughly 17.5 million tons of sulfur being emitted in 1980. The goal was to cut it in half by the year 2000. So, while the emissions were initially capped at 8.9 million tons in 1995, the cap has varied somewhat overtime from as high as 10 million tons in 2000, to as low as 7.4 million tons in the late 1990s. It settled into around 9.5 million tons in the mid-2000s.

Overall results were to reduce SO_2 emissions by over 5.5 million tons from 1990 levels, or about 35% of total emissions from the power sector. Compared to 1980 levels, SO_2 emissions from power plants have dropped by more than 7 million tons, or about 41%. It also resulted in cutting NOx emissions by about 3 million tons from 1990 levels, so that emissions in 2005 were less than half the level anticipated without the program. Other efforts, such as the NOx Budget Trading Program in the eastern US, also contributed significantly to the reduction.

Ellerman et al. (2000) points to how trading can work; politics do not matter much: The allowances Market has performed well; Markets can develop largely on their own, once given context from the Government; trading handles surprises well; opt-in provisions tricky: perhaps gave away too many allowances at the outset; and, extrapolate with care. Not everything learned in the sulfur allowances market could be used directly in a carbon allowances market, but we do have considerable experience, which is a key point in Metaeconomics: Build on experience, on empirical-based reality, rather than Conservative and Progressive, Right and Left ideology, and status quo, Invisible Hand claims that nothing needs to change.

There are also much grander proposals, such as that outlined in "Who Owns the Sky?" (Barnes 2001), wherein the capacity of the entire atmosphere surrounding Spaceship Earth is viewed as an asset owned jointly by all Travelers. It is a massive public property. Thus, each Traveler could also then be paid a dividend from its use. Barnes calls for a world-wide Market in carbon (and other greenhouse gas) allowances, although it seems he has in mind that Government would sell the allowances. Another variant on the Sky Trust idea is that each Traveler would be given an allotment of emission allowances, given some private property in the atmospheric capacity at birth, reflecting their natural right share in the ownership of the Spaceship Earth. Said allowances could then be traded on a Market not unlike the sulfur emissions market operating here in the US, and the carbon markets in Europe. Metaeconomics would point to a path 0Z outcomes rather than the tragedy of the commons outcome on the vertical axis of excess Greed, and hitting the thermodynamic walls, which is where the systems is currently headed.

Green New Deal

In early 2019, the US Green Party proposed what is referred to as the Green New Deal, playing on the notion of the New Deal coming out of the 1930s' financial crisis and depression. The Green New Deal is to bring us beyond the 2008 crisis, and build a more resilient, viable, moral and ethical community, and a science-based future. Several on the Left Isle adopted part or all the ideas into their platforms for the 2020 election. Many on the Right Isle immediately labeled it pejoratively as "socialism." Neither Left nor Right seems to be attuned to the possibility that we could move toward a better, joint, sustainable, thermodynamically based good capitalism. It would avoid both socialism and all the varieties of bad capitalism, especially the crony capitalism. So, can Metaeconomics help make sense of what a good capitalism might entail?

Propositions Under a Green New Deal: Toward Sustainability

The Deal is about nudging the conversation about moving onto a sustainable path 0Z. The list is from the Green Party website (See Green Party

Staff https://www.gp.org/green_new_deal; also, see L. Friedman 2019), *with Metaeconomics-based commentary added*:

Right now, our federal government subsidizes the rich agribusiness corporations and the oil, mining, nuclear, coal and timber giants at the expense of small farmers, small business, and our children's environment. We spend tens of billions every year moving our economy in the wrong direction. The Green New Deal will instead redirect that money to the real job creators who make our communities healthier, sustainable, and secure at the same time.

Metaeconomics sees many empirical questions in the statement, especially as relating to the extent to which crony capitalism is operant. Do we have a Taking rather than Making capitalism at work? Are said industries acting in consort with powerful politicians and bureaucrats, perhaps with carbon industry ties, working together to keep profits higher? Is it leading to a denigrated environment, especially for the small farmer, small business operation, and our children and grandchildren who will have to deal with it in the future? If any of the questions are answered "yes," then using Metaeconomics, pointing to a new moral and ethical community in the Other-interest, is the task, putting the system on a path 0Z.

With the passage and implementation of the program, We the People will (i.e., *all Travelers on the Spaceship Earth, within the boundaries of the US, at least, together will build a new shared Other-interest*):

Invest in green business by providing grants and low-interest loans to grow green businesses and cooperatives, with an emphasis on small, locally based companies that keep the wealth created by local labor circulating in the community rather than being drained off to enrich absentee investors.

Metaeconomics sees green business is an Empathy-tempered business. Cooperatives could easily be favored after an empirical analysis guided by Metaeconomics. Cooperatives embed a capitalism-based business within the community, within the Spaceship, working to find balance in Self&Other-interest.

Move to 100% clean energy by 2030: Prioritizing green research by redirecting research funds from fossil fuels and other dead-end industries toward research in wind, solar, and geothermal, we will invest in research in sustainable, nontoxic materials and closed-loop cycles that eliminate waste and pollution, as well as organic agriculture, permaculture and sustainable forestry.

Metaeconomics recognizes the thermodynamic reality of the need for developing closed-loop production and consumption systems to handle the waste issue (1st Law) and the need to move to renewable energy (2nd Law). And, Metaeconomics would likely find that it could well take perhaps 100 years, maybe even several 100 years, not 10 years, to make the transition. It is time to start.

Provide green jobs by enacting the Full-Employment Program, which will directly provide 16 million jobs in sustainable energy and energy-efficiency retrofitting, mass transit and "complete streets" that promote safe bike and pedestrian traffic, regional food systems based on sustainable organic agriculture and clean manufacturing.

Metaeconomics has nothing directly to say about a Full-Employment Program, per se, *other than it highlights the humane aspect of employment,* that is, *"if I were in that un- or under-employment situation, how would I wish to be treated." It is essential to find a way to Make the miracle of wealth happen in some form for everyone, including each person being involved through employment and otherwise engaged in Making it.*

Propositions as Socialism, Bad Capitalism, or Enlightened Good Capitalism?

As made clear by Ecological Economics (see Daly and Farley 2011; Hayes and Lynne 2004, 2013), the current Newtonian way of characterizing the Spaceship Earth leads to unsustainable outcomes. The Green New Deal, by using a Thermodynamics frame, could indeed guide the path to sustainability. It is not about socialism; it is about achieving sustainability. It is about moving away from bad capitalism. Metaeconomics makes it clear that the current high carbon path is not sustainable. Sustainability is essential to a good capitalism. And, Empathy (again, sorry, as Brown et al. 2019, have made abundantly clear) is the key to achieving it.

References

Altman, M. 2012. *Behavioral Economics for Dummies.* Kindle ed. Mississauga: John Wiley and Sons Canada, Ltd.

Anderson, Terry L., and D.R. Leal. 2001. *Free Market Environmentalism.* Revised ed. New York: Palgrave Macmillan.

Barnes, Peter. 2001. *Who Owns the Sky? Our Common Assets and the Future of Capitalism.* Washington: Island Press.

Brown, K., W. N. Adger, P. Devine-Wright, J. M. Anderies, S. Barr, F. Bousquet, C. Butler, L. Evans, N. Marshall, and T. Quinn. 2019. Empathy, Place and Identity Interactions for Sustainability. *Global Environmental Change* 56: 11–17.

California Cap and Trade. https://www.c2es.org/content/california-cap-and-trade/. Accessed 23 March 2020.

Commentary. 2017. Economists' Statement on Carbon Dividends. Opinion/ Commentary, *Wall Street Journal*, January 17. https://clcouncil.org/economists-statement/?utm_source=GDPR&utm_campaign=30d8264894-EMAIL_CAMPAIGN_2019_02_22_02_28&utm_medium=email&utm_term=0_7c51e322b7-30d8264894-. Accessed August 14, 2020.

Daly, Herman E., and Joshua Farley. 2011. *Ecological Economics: Principles and Applications*. 2nd ed. Washington, DC: Island Press.

Ellerman, A.D., P.L. Joskow, R. Schmalensee, J.-P. Montero, and E.M. Bailey. 2000. *Markets for Clean Air: The U.S. Acid Rain Program*. Cambridge, MA: Cambridge University Press.

Eu Emissions Trading System. https://ec.europa.eu/clima/policies/ets_en. Accessed 23 Mar 2020.

Friedman, Lisa. 2019. What Is the Green New Deal? A Climate Proposal, Explained. *New York Times* (New York), February 21.

Green New Deal. https://www.gp.org/green_new_deal. Accessed 23 March 2020.

Hardin, G. 1968. The Tragedy of the Commons. *Science* 162 (3859): 1243–1248.

Hayes, W.M., and G.D. Lynne. 2004. Towards a Centerpiece for Ecological Economics. *Ecological Economics* 49 (3): 287–301.

———. 2013. The Evolution of Ego and Empathy: Progress in Forming the Centerpiece for Ecological Economic Theory. In *Building a Green Economy: Perspectives from Ecological Economics*, ed. Robert B. Richardson, 107–118. East Lansing: Michigan State University Press.

Lynne, G.D., N.V. Czap, H.J. Czap, and M.E. Burbach. 2016. Theoretical Foundation for Empathy Conservation: Toward Avoiding the Tragedy of the Commons. *Review of Behavioral Economics* 3: 245–279.

Ostrom, Eleanor. 1990. *Governing the Commons: The Evolution of Institutions for Collective Action*. New York: Cambridge University Press.

———. 1992. *Crafting Institutions for Self-Governing Irrigation Systems*. San Francisco: ICS Press.

Samuels, Warren J., Marianne F. Johnson, and William H. Perry. 2011. *Erasing the Invisible Hand: Essays on an Elusive and Misused Concept in Economics*. Kindle ed. New York: Cambridge University Press.

Smith, Adam. 1759/1790. *The Theory of Moral Sentiments*. Edited by D.D. and A.L. Macfie Raphael. Indianapolis, Indiana: Liberty Fund, Inc.

Smith, Vernon L., and Bart J. Wilson. 2019. *Humanomics: Moral Sentiments and the Wealth of Nations for the Twenty-First Century*. Cambridge Studies in Economics, Choice, and Society. New York: Cambridge University Press.

The Regional Greenhouse Gas Initiative. https://www.rggi.org/. Accessed 23 March 2020.

Zimmermann, E.W. 1933/1951. *World Resources and Industries*. New York: Harper and Brothers.

CHAPTER 13

Tax Policy: Pay the Price

Taxes are the price we pay in order to obtain many of the outcomes pursued in the shared Other-interest. So, Metaeconomics in contrast to Microeconomics gives a substantive analytical system for dealing with the tax question, because of recognizing the Other-interest. Metaeconomics clarifies that taxation is about paying for, and thus bringing forth the payoffs from that which we share, like recording deeds and titles to private property; enforcing property rights, which is essential to a Market; licensing, registering, and enforcing patents; military, police, and fire services; road and harbor construction and maintenance; dams and reservoirs to provide for water in the desert Southwest US and for flood control in the humid Eastern US; safety nets for the poor; helping people transition to a new job; public education; scientific research that provides new equipment and techniques, and new drugs; environmental quality and sustaining Spaceship Earth Systems and the free work done by same; providing safe and reliable water supplies, and waste water management, and, yes, helping with pandemics, to list a few: All have a price.

Sales Taxes

Neoclassical Microeconomics always leads to concluding that any kind of a tax is in some sense a distortion, in some sense not conducive to achieving efficiency. Metaeconomics, in contrast, points to the reality that a tax is often essential to achieving efficiency, and, happiness.

G. D. Lynne, *Metaeconomics*, Palgrave Advances in Behavioral Economics, https://doi.org/10.1007/978-3-030-50601-8_13

Thinking back to the recycle case demonstrated in Fig. 4.1 as a case in point: Lowering the sales tax on a recycle content good would move the price from $p_e^{'}$ to p_e^o. Why would we ever lower (or raise) the sales tax on one good, relative to another? We might do so in the case of a recycle content good in that the real value *V* suggests it, the sense of right versus wrong in the amount of recycle content good we purchase.

Lowering the sales tax on the recycle content good (or, raising it on the other good) would send a signal that it is in our shared Other-interest to shift purchases in that direction. Result? The now lower price p_e^o would cause a shift in the entire system from path 0G and point *A*′ toward path 0Z and point B. Ironically, point B is also a happier place to be, brought by a relative change in the sales tax. So, in what sense is a shift to a happier and efficient path 0Z driven by using a sales tax to stir the move, a distortion? A MetaEcon would argue it is efficient. A NeoClassEcon claims it is a distortion. Empirical question.

Anticipating a Microeconomics critique here: So, is not just having a sales tax, at all, lead to eliminating all distortion? Well, if one believes that anything keeping one from maximizing only the Self-interest is a distortion, the answer is "yes." So, for the Econ among us, yes, a sales tax is a distortion. For a Human (and most everyone is a Human), the answer is "no." Why? Well, it is because a Human also needs payoff in the Other-interest, and the tax can bring it about. Why is it a distortion to provide for the Other-interest of the Human? Empirical question.

Estate Taxes

It first needs to be understood that very few estates in the US ever pay any estate tax. Exemptions have been increased rather dramatically over time, for example, going from $5.49 M in 2107 to $11.18 M in 2018 (data from Wikipedia). In addition, estates can give money to federally approved charities, for another $5 M+. Exemptions plus estate tax free donations lead to the fact that only about 2000 people in the US, at the current time, are currently liable to pay the price/tax on the estate upon death. Only about 0.00006 percent of the population will be paying any estate tax.

The reality is missed often in the political conversation. The framing comes from what Right Isle claims that there is an inherent "natural right" in not paying any estate taxes, at all.

Microeconomics analysis would likely support the Right Isle, and suggest that an estate tax is not efficient, and, therefore, is an unnecessary impediment (although the empirical support for such a claim is lacking) on the economy, even if it involves only 0.00006 percent. Metaeconomics, in contrast, can clearly point to cases where an estate tax is not only beneficial, but essential. Another way of saying it: If Self-interest only is to be maximized, as Microeconomics presumes, the estate tax needs to be eliminated, because it impedes 0.00006 percent of the people in maximizing their Self-interest.

In contrast, as Metaeconomics suggests, there could well be a shared Other-interest pointing to tempering how the wealth is used, on moral and ethical grounds, after the death of the person. The shared Other-interest, especially if representing a humane ethical system, would not likely favor the creation of dynasties of wealth, which is encouraged, if not ensured, without an estate tax. Such dynasties seemingly are more about taking and keeping, than in making wealth? Empirical questions.

And, there is substantive empirical evidence that encouraging dynasties does not work. An especially dramatic case in point is Versailles in France, before the Revolution. The monarchy squandered wealth in gold-plated rooms of a summer home while the people starved. Off with their heads. So, reasonable, empirically based sense of the shared Other-interest would seem to suggest that the wealth clock, in effect, needs to be reset each generation. If not, wealth would be concentrated for no reason other than the fact a relative who was good at making (i.e. entrepreneurs) or taking (i.e., most Monarchies) wealth did it. Good reason? Empirical question.

In fact, by thinking here about the shared Other-interest, the ethical system as it were, whether it was the result of taking, keeping, or making, might affect how it is taxed. So, the taxing might be different for the estate of a Henry Ford who created the first pragmatic car and truck that anyone could afford, and, paid the labor on his wealth-making production line enough to own one of them. So, if the Ford legacy of making and sharing through paying good wages was continued, the estate tax might justifiably be lower? Perhaps the family would carry-on the legacy, and do more of said kind of making?

There are several notable cases wherein only limited dynasties were created, with plentiful wealth left for descendants, but also substantive parts dedicated to help the economy and society. For example, John D. Rockefeller who was noted for maximizing Self-interest, in the end worked to acknowledge a shared Other-interest and created the Rockefeller Foundation. Other notable cases in recent times include the Gates Foundation, and related participation by Warren Buffet, with both Gates and Buffett already deciding that upon their deaths, the bulk of their estate will fold into foundations. Both Gates and Buffett have made it clear that the wealth is to be used for increasing opportunities spread widely among travelers, to help with health and social issues, and generally creating opportunity for entrepreneurs to make new wealth. Seemingly the intent is to serve a more widely shared Other-interest.

There is also a potential dark side to such efforts, however, as in the various Foundations and groups created by wealthy people to buy politicians (MacLean 2017). Metaeconomics would suggest, due to focusing on both empirical and ethical considerations, such political contributions need to be transparent.

And, it seems the estate tax could increase happiness, not only from reducing dark money activities, but also keeping people who might squander an inheritance away from the egoistic-hedonistic path 0G. Having less wealth, especially when used to produce things in the shared Other-interest, could well put them on happiness path 0Z. Empirical questions.

Property Taxes

Henry George may have had it about right, when he made the claim that one of the fairest taxes was that on property, which in his time meant a tax on land owned in private property. The proposition implicitly recognizes the thermodynamic reality that the Spaceship Earth System helps make a substantive part of the wealth. So, a Henry George frame is to tax the dollar wealth produced by that System. Also, the materials and services provided by that system (e.g., minerals, water, and waste-cleaning services provided by ecosystems) were legitimately owned as a public property, in the Henry George frame, by all the travelers: So, why not tax the Market for using it?

Ironically, real estate taxes, the tax rates paid by real estate developers, were recently reduced. Proposals to reduce property taxes are regularly brought before state legislatures, a continual Right Isle proposition. Intriguingly, said property taxes are usually the main if not the only source of tax revenue for public schools, local roads, and many other public services including police and fire. What is reducing property taxes all about? Metaeconomics would suggest it is about taking and keeping, not about making.

Overall, taxing away just that portion of wealth contributed by the Spaceship cannot have a distorting effect on the Market, as the Spaceship is not in the Market. Makes sense?

Progressive Income Taxes

On income taxes in general, and specifically for progressive income taxes, Metaeconomics would ask the empirical question: Just how much income do you really need in order to have a reasonably good experience throughout your life, achieving happiness? Throwing life and liberty in for good measure, what is the best entropic path 0Z, as a Spaceship Earth Traveler? Everyone eventually reaches maximum entropy (death). What is the best path to it? And, while the number would likely be a matter of considerable dialogue and debate, it would likely be agreed, eventually, from the perspective of a moral and ethical community, that not all the income one earns, especially on the higher rungs, is essential or even good for that trip.

So, Metaeconomics might find, even strictly looking at the matter only empirically and pragmatically, that progressive income taxes indeed make substantial sense. Reason? Well, if one earns large amounts of income, well beyond the level needed to enjoy a good trip as a Traveler on the Spaceship, paying a bit more could better serve the need for balance. Recall that Metaeconomics points to the happiness path 0Z, which means some sacrifice in Self-interest. The progressive income tax is especially effective in producing said balance and, thus, producing more happiness, by shifting the person away from the Self-interest only path.

Recall the selfish&selfless analysis of Greed in Fig. 7.1. A tax level of 10 percent puts the economy at point A. At said point, little in the way of products and services are coming from the public sector, which is generally where the shared Other-interest arises. The result is the low level of shared Other-interest outcome on I_M^1 at point A. As the tax moves from 10 percent toward 30 percent, the system moves toward $I_M^2 > I_M^1$, with a bit of sacrifice in the Self-interest with $I_G^2 < I_G^1$. Intriguingly, in the Nordic economy (see Lakey 2016), the tax rates are somewhere between 50 and 70 percent, which tends to move the system toward $I_M^3 > I_M^2 > I_M^1$. Is happiness increased or decreased from said move?

Well, based on the surveys of people in the Nordic countries, it seems moving toward point C results in people being happier than are US residents who operate close to point *A*. And, what would determine whether the tax is 10 or 30 percent, or even higher? Well, the value *V* from Fig. 7.2 would determine it: It depends on how people value *V* the balance in

Self-&Other-interest. It is clear the Nordic countries put more value *V* on the shared Other-interest.

As McCloskey (2019) would have it, a humane and liberal capitalism, a happier capitalism, is the goal. Perhaps it is not possible at the Other-interest only (socialism?) point C? Perhaps it is not possible at the Self-interest only (bad capitalism?) point A? Maybe a happier, due in the main from being a more humane, capitalism is possible in the vicinity of point B? Empirical questions.

Taxes Are Not a Distortion

So, again, to emphasize: In what sense are Taxes a distortion, as Neoclassical Microeconomics always claims? As noted, it is true that Taxes distort the pursuit of Self-interest: Microeconomics has that Right, and, people on the Right Isle generally agree. The question is: Why is being happier a distortion? And, why is not paying for that which arises out of the shared Other-interest not a distortion?

Taxes, paying the price of Government, works to help attain the outcomes of a shared Other-interest, even in such mundane things as roads, police and fire services, public health (Corona virus management, anyone?), water supply, and the military. Paying for the shared Other-interest might also mean higher quality public schools, better ensuring people can participate in and contribute to a truly humane and liberal, democracy-based capitalism. Such investments in shared Other-interest make the Market work better. Could such shared efforts make you happier? Sure. So, again, sorry to keep asking, but in what sense is a tax a distortion?

Importantly, Metaeconomics does not inherently favor either the Right or Left, Conservative or Progressive position on the matter of Taxes. It just asks, what leads to happiness? And, could taxes serve to increase happiness, by producing a better balance in Self&Other-interest? Empirical questions, indeed.

References

Lakey, George. 2016. *Viking Economics: How the Scandinavians Got It Right – And How We Can, Too.* Brooklyn, New York: Melville House Publishing, Kindle ed.

MacLean, Nancy. 2017. *Democracy in Chains: The Deep History of the Radical Right's Stealth Plan for America.* New York: Penguin Books.

McCloskey, D.N. 2019. *Why Liberalism Works: How True Liberal Values Produce a Freer, More Equal, Prosperous World for All.* Kindle ed. New York: Yale University Press.

CHAPTER 14

Income and Wealth Policy: Toward Optimal Inequality

Lucas (2004), who was the president of the American Economic Association, a NeoClassEcon, and a Nobel Prize in Economics awardee, said it: "Of the tendencies that are harmful to sound economics, the most seductive, and in my opinion the most poisonous, is to focus on questions of distribution" (quoted in Stiglitz 2019, p. 33). So, considering distribution questions is harmful to economics? The MetaEcon find the contention, a standard position taken by a NeoClassEcon, highly questionable. Metaeconomics, instead, focuses attention on finding the best level of inequality, the best distribution as related to what is in our shared Other-interest: Empathy-based ethics, please. Distribution becomes a focus, a core concern. The Lucas view is a contention with which Adam Smith (1759/1790) would also, we might reasonably surmise, have disagreed. Adam Smith would have fully acknowledged that extreme inequality was not conducive to a good capitalism, on many fronts.

Inequality as a Public Health and Social Issue

Metaeconomics points to how the degree of inequality of wealth and income as represented in the balance in Self&Other-interest can influence expressions of Self-interest, and, even the ability to express Self-interest at all, in that the currency of a Market is money; so, Metaeconomics has pointed directly at acting on the moral and ethical side of inequality, to ensure everyone has some reasonable amount of money, which is

G. D. Lynne, *Metaeconomics*, Palgrave Advances in Behavioral Economics, https://doi.org/10.1007/978-3-030-50601-8_14

essential to participating in the Market. Payne (2018) would likely not disagree but is pointing to another part of the moral dimension.

Payne (2018) sees inequality as not only a moral (and ethical) issue but leading to a worsening public health and social problem. Tension and stress are at an all-time high, which is a major driver in the opioid crisis, as well as all manner of related crime and violence (especially as associated with the illegal drug trade). Feeling left behind on the wealth ladder, as Stiglitz (2019, p. 44) notes few ever overcome, potentially leads to severe mental health and stability issues. People just give up, operating on ever shorter planning horizons represented in unrestrained hedonistic drives expressed at young ages, becoming too sexually active too early; using alcohol and drugs; and taking high risk, often criminal paths in the attempt to become rich quick. The result is little hope for anything on a Higher Plane of value *V*. Intriguingly, extreme inequality also causes public health and social problems on the upper rungs of the ladder, too, as confirmed in research by Piff (2015).

Metaeconomics would predict such outcomes. On the lower rungs, inequality reduces people to the primal path 0G, hedonistic-based survival-only modes. People simply stop trying, and instead move toward feeling entitled to that monthly welfare or fraudulent disability check, and/or go into other illegal, not ethical, activities. Intriguingly, the move to entitlement thinking on path 0G is also common at the upper end of the income and wealth spectrum, too (Piff 2015; Piff, Kraus, and Keltner 2018), which is also unethical. On path 0G, everyone enters a "dog-eat-dog" environment of just getting by for the people who are on the lowest rungs, and running on a materialistic treadmill that runs faster and faster for a person on the higher rungs. Empathy (and the ethic of it all) plays little to no role in said states of mind, as Ego-based entitlement takes over. The result is few that are truly happy, especially for the people on the middle rung, the middle-class, who pay for the extremes on both ends: Bad capitalism is the outcome. Socialism on the Left and Fascism on the Right, one or both tend to appear on the scene, promising to fix it all.

The health and social problems reason for moving instead toward path 0Z choices in the US becomes clear with respect to an analysis by Wilkinson and Pickett (2006, 2010) as pointed to in Payne (2018, Fig. 2.3, p. 51). The Nordic countries and Japan rank the best: The US ranks as the worst. The Travelers within the US area of the Spaceship reflect the most severe health and social problems driven by extreme income and wealth inequality. And, it is not getting better (trickle-down, anyone?): The ratio of the share going to the top 20% divided by the share going the bottom 20%

continues to increase. Ironically, given how wealthy the US is overall, in gross domestic product terms, happiness has become elusive for virtually the entire US Population—top, bottom, and everyone in-between.

Payne (2018, Fig. 2.3, p. 52) also points to a huge variability among US states (again, drawing on Wilkinson and Pickett 2006, 2010). Intriguingly, my first 18 years were spent as a Traveler within the part of the Spaceship known as North Dakota, which ranks well. It was a relatively peaceful, happy time for me: Now I know one of the main reasons. Along with Minnesota, Vermont, New Hampshire, Iowa, and Utah, it has minimal health and social problems mainly because of far less inequality in income and wealth. Mississippi, Louisiana, and Alabama do the worst.

So, reducing inequality is a key aspect of a viable economy. Moving to path 0Z would produce a larger proportion who are happy. It is also the way to reduce political chaos.

Inequality as a Political Issue

Payne (2018, Chapter 4, esp. pp. 106–107) makes a convincing case that inequality is the major driver in political turmoil, in that inequality causes people to identify with and connect ever more with the narrow, shared interests within their own Tribes (i.e., racial, religious, gender, heterosexual, LGBT, urban, rural, political, and, overall, income, and wealth). It leads to a tendency toward pointing to other Tribes as the cause of the problems. For example, it is currently popular to blame immigrants for all manner of economic and social ills, which has little in the way of empirical reality to it. It is clear the extreme inequality drives populism, especially if Tribes see the elite and wealthy taking and keeping. Populism also emerges when people on the lower rung are viewed as taking something they are perceived as not deserving (e.g., poor immigrants receiving food stamps, or Government funded medical care, as well as Social Security and Medicare). As perhaps mentioned too many times, there is also the failed notion of trickle-down wealth. The reality is that trickle-down wealth has never worked, and cannot work (see Stiglitz 2019, p. 38). Metaeconomics clarifies why: The more primal Econ, even if essential to Making, just naturally evolves to Taking and Keeping too much, as excessive Greed takes over.

In the Populist environment, the Right Isle blames the Left, and the Left Isle blames the Right. The Right Tribe or Left Tribe cheers when it "wins," albeit there no winners, overall. Some politicians have capitalized on the opportunity, making it the approach to stirring the Tribes to continue in their narrow views, as then nothing has to be done: The politician who stirs the discord can then maneuver in the background as the Tribes fight. Distraction works great, when people are in a populist mood: Fascism at work.

Also, on Right and Left, there is a lot of history here, we might say entrenched history, which is not going to be easy to change. Payne (2018, pp. 82–83) claims the framing of Right and Left, with inequality always a major feature of it, goes back at least to the time leading up to the French revolution: Again, sorry, but is a very powerful example, gold plated walls at Versailles (a must see for the Paris visitor) and "off with their heads," which is not something we want to see, but it stirs thinking. People with religious and political power, who were also generally the wealthier, took positions to the Right of the King. People who were part of what was coming to be understood as Enlightenment (originally, both humane and liberal, now distorted to leave out the humane) thinking stood to the Left. The Left included a person dedicated to rational, empirical science-based framing and discussion, not always accepting the authority of the Church or the Monarchy supported by that Church or the Business People intertwined with both (so, especially, could see the rampant cronyism, making it Visible). People seeing some merit in both Right and Left went to the Center, represented in the Moderates, the Independents.

So, people who wanted to keep things the same, the (Invisible Hand) status quo, were about preserving current traditions embedded in their narrowly defined Other-interest, were on the Right. At that time, it meant preserving extreme inequality in both wealth&power. People who were experiencing the inequality, or otherwise wanted to temper it, were to the Left. In Metaeconomic terms, the Left wanted to modify the content of that Other-interest, and make Visible Hand–based progress to new content in a new Other-interest. As Pinker (2018, p. 85) further clarifies, the Right is also concerned about maintaining civil order, so the military is on the Right, too, a tradition pretty much intact (ironic, as the military is a kind of socialism, with all equipment and material owned and controlled by the Government, and hierarchically run: Little room for free expression of Self-interest, except at the top of the command).

Also, the Left does not generally want to change everything, but rather only the things working poorly. It seems it would rely on empirically based humane reasons to find the best path to making things work better only for things that need to be fixed, like extreme inequality: Socialism, anyone? Well, people wanting change on the Left will be labeled that way by the Right, whether it is or is not, and whether it is leading to good or to bad outcomes. The status quo, even if bad, is preferred.

Metaeconomics suggests it is not either Right or Left. Metaeconomics proposes we really need to be searching for the Right&Left-Isle integrated on path 0Z. Payne (2018) makes it clear that the inequality question is not resolved by taking positions on either side of the Isle, which often results in doing nothing, or, even worse, one Political Tribe wins.

As Pinker (2018, p. 85) emphasizes, the Right simply believes in, and accepts, inequality as a kind of natural order of things, perhaps even a natural right (also a claim of Will 2019; see Table 6.1). On the Right, the Other-interest is only in the moral order, hidden away in the Invisible Hand. The Invisible Hand is always presumed, without empirical test, to be a good hand. Is it, really? Need to take an empirical look at it, make it a Visible Hand, to know for sure?

For the Left, the notion of a moral order needs to be replaced with a moral and ethical community. Reason is: The moral order of the Right generally deteriorates into "monopolies, old-boy networks, institutional racism and sexism, and cycles of advantage and disadvantage that shape people's outcomes for reasons that have nothing to with individual virtues" (Pinker 2018, p. 86). So, it is not necessarily moral (nor is it ethical). Metaeconomics sees said outcomes as primal, coming out of the Self-interest only frame.

As Metaeconomics makes clear, Prudence pursued with Self-interest is encouraged on both Right and Left; the Left, however, puts less credence in the Invisible Hand adequately representing the Other-Interest. Rather, the Left favors a Visible Hand to ensure good doses of temperance, justice, courage (fortitude), faith, hope, and love (charity) are at work in the Invisible Hand. The Left is especially concerned with less than adequate temperance and fortitude associated with expression of Self-interest only; the Right believes it is only through Self-interest that one will act on temperance and fortitude (again, see Table 6.1), and that both are naturally and inherently present in the Invisible Hand of the Market. Maybe. I suppose it is possible, if every person in the Market regularly goes to the Station of the Impartial Spectator before a Market decision is made. Empirical questions.

So, in the view of the Left, the fact the poor get poorer and the rich get richer needs to be monitored by the Visible Hand. The Left often sees the need for some kind of outside intervention focusing on the context, the system for making wealth, the operant Other-interest that affects the pursuit of Self-interest, and, then, the primal tendency to inequality. On the Right, it is just natural and perfectly fine for the rich to get richer, and the poor are to aspire to the same shared Other-interest in being richer, creating incentives to make wealth to become richer. It is the presumption that anyone can do it, as in the old "rags to riches" story. Payne (2018) puts empirical holes in that story, as Metaeconomics framed analysis would likely do as well, speaking instead of income traps from which one cannot escape, no matter how hard one tries.

As Payne (2018, p. 88) describes it, both Right and Left see that "individual responsibility, talent and hard work are important factors in achieving success, and they agree that context matters." Metaeconomics points to actively molding the context, picking the balance, we might say the "best level of inequality," based on what works best, pragmatically speaking. And, entitlement at both ends is not part of an optimal inequality.

Inequality as an Economic Issue

Chief Executive Officer (CEO) pay, and generally the sharing of wealth between management and labor, who both contribute to Making that wealth, immediately comes to mind. Huge disparities in compensation packages reflect the excessive Greed that brings economies down into depression. In fact, in some ways, said realization was the impetus for Metaeconomics, growing out of conversations with Gerald Cory. One of the first times Gerald Cory and I discussed the fact we had both come to see the role of the dual nature of human nature in economic choice, the conversation immediately turned to the matter of balance in taking&making of wealth, as represented in Ego&Empathy. Cory (1999) points to how mental stability in the personality requires such balance, and relayed how he had observed it in CEOs and the businesses they ran. Without balance, he had found, the result will be tension, stress, and mental disorder, represented in health and social issues in the family. Without balance in how companies dealt with the taking&making of wealth, economic issues would also arise for the company, which drives the same matters at the larger community and social scale. The jointness needed to be recognized and the balance struck.

Cory (1999) had come to see the need for balance, in comparing CEOs in Japan and the US. Cory found a tendency for the Japanese CEO to be oriented more toward Empathy at work, with Japanese companies often operating in familial ways. The CEO was expected to walk-in-the-shoes-of-others, the CEO putting a huge amount of their energy on any given day into being mindful. The Japanese CEO was expected to act on the empathy-sympathy-compassion path with respect to employees. As a result, from having been out of balance all day, Japanese CEOs would go home at night with a wide shift in the direction toward the Egoistic tendency, with the result being all manner of difficulties at home. Japanese CEOs were prone to domestic abuse, poor relationships with children and other family, and generally also not connecting with and contributing to their communities.

In contrast, the typical US CEO was found to be Egoistic at work, using little in the sense of mindfulness on an Empathy path. The same US CEO was found to take the wide shift, but now in the other direction, over to a more Empathy-based behavior at home. The shift to Empathy resulted in much better relationships with the significant others in their lives, including being actively engaged in their communities. Cory had confirmed what his Ego&Empathy model suggests: Both the typical Japanese and US CEO would be personally better-off, as would their families and communities, and their companies would be more functional, productive, better places to work, if there is a more appropriate balance in Ego&Empathy: Happier CEOs in happier companies, with happier families and happier communities, and, we might suggest, happier (not depressed, no economic depressions) economies.

The same imbalance was represented in CEO compensation packages. US companies have much higher CEO/Labor ratios in pay. Japanese CEOs make significantly less money than do US CEOs, resulting in dramatically lower ratios of CEO pay relative to worker pay, perhaps too low. And, it is not only pay that is the issue: A company with a less than optimal level of inequality is also a less productive company.

Payne (2018) confirms the reality that companies with higher inequality are less productive, and produce lower quality product. We might logically expect the same to true for companies without enough inequality. Both extremes point to the need to find the optimal level of inequality. It would be expected that moving toward better balance in the CEO relative to the employee compensation packages would lead to more viable, productive companies. It would also likely contribute to fewer and less severe economic depressions writ large. The Payne research would suggest inequality needs to be reduced in the US and increased in Japan, with gains in productivity and happiness in both countries.

As Payne (2018) suggests, extreme inequality was a major contributor to the 1930s' Great Depression, as well as to the recent financial crisis in 2008. Why? Well, extreme inequality follows from excessive Greed, causing economic systems to become depressed (out of balance stirs depression) to crash. Anti-diversity is generally the next step, as others are blamed for the inequality.

And, it can happen at either end: Toward the far left end, the promise of more equality led to authoritarian capitalism under communism (e.g. Soviet Union, China) and under socialism (e.g. Venezuela), with even more inequality and intolerance. Both have also emerged on the right in every attempt at a free for all, no holds barred capitalism in both Britain and the US. Also, at the far right end, we find inequality and anti-diversity from authoritarian capitalism in nationalism-fascism (like that in Germany and Italy in the 1930s), a continual lure. It is being demonstrated right now in Hungary, Israel, France, Poland, Britain, and the US (Applebaum, 2020, p. 3). Metaeconomics points to the extremes as always producing bad capitalism.

The current extreme inequality and predictable anti-diversity in the US has its origins in the early-1980s, when politicians changed the narrative, consistent with the story from the NeoClassEcon (ala Milton Friedman and other NeoClassEcon) that the Market can do only good, and from Public Choice Economics (ala Buchanan et al.) that the Government can only do bad. It shifted the economic narrative (see Shiller 2019) toward Market-only framing. It was perhaps an overreaction to the Great Society associated with President Johnson, which came about shortly after the Civil Rights Act of 1964. Both frames brought considerable Government nudging and some control into the Market. The moral and ethical compass was re-focused, toward righting the wrongs over 300–400 years of slavery, and especially the wrongs under Jim Crow framing for almost 100 years after the Civil War, into the 1960s. It is as though all the Political Isles suddenly converged: The barbarism of Jim Crow was to be eliminated, as per the Conservatives; the oppressed were to be given opportunity, as per the Progressives; the coercion was finally to be removed, as per the Libertarians; and, perhaps even the globalization of the more Cosmopolitan-oriented person came to force further clarifying that segregation was out of fashion.

Unfortunately, it was all rather short-lived. It starts in the early-1970s, and by the early-1980s, the supply-side narrative (which emerged again in about 2016) reduced regulations, laws, and other efforts to supposedly right the wrongs, even if said efforts were doing a good job. The narrative became, largely without empirical support, that both fewer regulations and lower taxes at the upper end of the income and wealth ladder supposedly would stir economic growth and prosperity for everyone. It was the start of the trickle-down idea. Wealth would naturally increase at all levels, every boat would float higher, it was said.

As Stiglitz (2019) makes clear, and Metaeconomics supports the narrative, supply-side economics, with supposed trickle-down, simply does not work, unless some bounds, tempering is also included in the mix. It is about good regulations, and, sure, the bad regulations need to be removed: Tempering and bounding Government is needed just as much as tempering and bounding of the Market. A viable economy cannot evolve (empirical tests confirm it) unless excesses in both the Market and the Government are tempered, hopefully by a humane and liberal Own-self. Ignoring the reality of the more primal excess of the Econ, however, nudges the system toward "too little investment in people, infrastructure, and technology, too much faith in the ability of markets to solve all of our problems, too little regulation where we need it, combined with too much regulation where we don't" (Stiglitz 2019, pp. 25–26). Also, many of the successes from the path struck in the mid-1960s have been lost since the mid-1980s. We might guess too much control on the Government side can also be counterproductive.

Ironically, while the trickle-down of the 1980s diverted attention from the other virtues and shifted almost exclusively to prudence, the Great Society of the 1960s notion perhaps also did not put enough attention to the other virtues in providing the conditions for strong expressions of Self-interest. The 1960s narrative perhaps did not place enough emphasis on making wealth with hard work and determination. Metaeconomics would suggest that both narratives—the Great Society and the Trickle-Down Society—failed by not putting enough attention to ensuring strong families could emerge, and to building community, characterized by faith, hope, and charity within. Frameworks and tools like that developed in Etzioni (1993), which is all about building the community, the shared Other-interest, needed to be integrated with the financial side of both narratives.

Inequality as Market and Government Failure

Both Market-failure and Government-failure have contributed to extreme inequality. The failure is measured by not moving people onto happiness path 0Z. In Metaeconomic terms:

1. Market-failure means (a) the failure to facilitate and adjust to a new, progressive Other-interest consistent with a reasoned, enlightened, empirically based moral and ethical community that works for everyone; for example, the Market failed to fix the ongoing condition prior to the Civil Rights Act of 1964 and prior to the legislation made part of the Great Society narrative in 1965, and/or (b) the failure to facilitate the expression of Self-interest (it requires money to express Self-interest in Markets, and, the less you have, the less you can influence the Market) except by the few who have managed to accumulate large amounts of wealth and are already earning a substantive level of income, for example, the situation for substantive numbers of Americans prior to the Great Society–based transfer of income and wealth that took place leading up to the early-1980s.
2. Government-failure means (a) the failure to temper and restrain the more primal tendency of people in the Market to excessive Greed, leading eventually to Taking (and Keeping) as much wealth as possible, without contributing much to Making. The substantive income transfer to the lower rungs of the ladder during the mid-1960s to early-1980s created a generation of takers, who came to believe they were entitled. Similarly, starting in the early-1980s the Government-failure to temper and bound Greed on the upper end of the income and wealth ladder also created a whole generation of takers who are extremely wealthy, and also believe themselves entitled, and/or, (b) the failure to not adequately represent the shared Other-interest of everyone; Self-interest may be at play in Government, too, with the administrative branch operating on the Self-interest in power, accomplished by favoring only narrow Self-interest of the favored tribes; the Legislative branch maximizing a Self-interest in power, by the politician, in being re-elected; Judicial Branch maximizing the Self-interest of narrow ideological views.
3. Market&Government-failure arises simultaneously when the more primal Self-interest dominates in both the Market and the Government, a prime example being cronyism, the ultimate in joint failure. Fixing failure is about tempering the excesses of Self-interest in every domain. Extreme inequality in income and wealth is just a symptom of the underlying tendency to excessive Greed. And, it comes from not addressing, with the Visible Hand, just what would be an optimal amount of inequality? Empirical question.

Inequality Is Bad and Equality Is Bad: So, What Is a Good Level of Inequality?

Both Conservative and Progressive liberalism has failed to deal with inequality, being diverted to other more peripheral matters. Metaeconomics suggests the reason why both have failed to address inequality: It is about tempering Self-interest while working not to control it, more about a humane liberalism, the kind described in McCloskey (2019). Such a humane liberalism would also reflect a more optimal inequality. Insights on what it might look like come from the study of compensation levels in professional sports.

Payne (2018, p. 188) highlights the main findings in said inequality research, pointing to professional baseball, which has been intensely studied due in part to a deep and wide set of data on how teams and individuals on said teams perform:

1. Teams with lower inequality performed better than teams with higher inequality
2. Superstars on higher inequality teams performed worse than superstars on lower inequality teams
3. Superstars perform better with higher pay, but only to a point where resentment among team members starts to affect the superstar incentive (and ability) to play at ever higher levels
4. Higher inequality creates resentment that works to reduce cooperation and teamwork, which is the reason the higher inequality teams performed at a lower level
5. Fan and media attention increase as inequality increases (although there is some anecdotal evidence that some fans leave, because of rising resentment; need more research here), the attention stirred by the large compensation packages for the superstars
6. Team owner revenue increases as inequality increases (although, as noted, it needs more empirical attention, as anecdotal evidence suggests at least some fans stop following the team due to finding it unreasonable to pay a few so much, which dampens increases in revenue), creating an incentive for team owners to move to ever greater inequality
7. Too equal pay across all athletes reduces team performance, especially superstar performance if pay is too low

8. Team owners are faced with the challenge of finding the optimal amount of inequality, which needs consideration of both fans and players (Note: Metaeconomics points to the finding the best content for the shared Other-interest, widely shared across all persons affected)
9. Higher pay works well to drive performance in solo sports like golf and singles tennis, and motor sports, but only to a point

Clearly incentives matter, as the NeoClassEcon, Conservative Liberal, and especially the Libertarian claims: Higher relative pay for the better players can lead to both higher player and team performance. Yet, if a person is paid too much relative to the pay to others, productivity goes down, consistent with the NeoInstiEcon and Progressive Liberal understanding. Finally, if inequality is too low, productivity also suffers. Metaeconomics points to said realities as empirically based, not just ideological. So, Metaeconomics clarifies it is about balance in owner&player, and superstar&typical-player compensation, perhaps even the degree of inequality in the arena of superstar&fan. Said lessons seemingly need to be influencing the balance in pay and compensation in both the Market and in the Government, and most importantly, in joint Market&Government.

Also, we know that even in the sole athlete case, an extreme level of compensation does not buy happiness: Payne (2018, pp. 203–204) points to happiness increasing with income, but leveling off at about $80,000; in fact, a person earning in the range of $80,000 to $8M was about equally happy to a person at $80,000. As Payne (2018, p. 204) notes, it leaves a lot of ground for increasing happiness, through reducing both health and social problems in the US, as the median income is around $54,000. It also points to the lack of empirical reality to the contention that extremely high incomes are essential to stir innovation and hard work; the Nordic countries that have much flatter distributions in compensation are also quite innovative. As a case in point, Norway has more entrepreneurs per capita than the US (Lakey 2016, loc 1005).

As Payne (2018, p. 188) shows, the performance pattern not only exists in sports. For example, higher paid truck drivers, due to more or less solo work, perform at higher levels as pay increases. Computer programmers do, too, until the point is reached where team effort is needed to complete the task. Payne (2018, 189) also points to studies of companies, factories with production lines: The greater the pay inequality, the lower the quality of the products coming out of said lines, and the "more team-like a workplace is, the more likely it is that the harmful effects of resentment over inequality will negate the motivating effects of incentives."

Resentment leads to all manner of bad behaviors, with sabotage and theft common. Increasing the CEO and upper management compensation package ever higher makes it ever worse, and, if every CEO eventually is paid upward of 300–400 times or more the average pay, we eventually arrive at a situation widely spread, "enough to insult the sense of fairness of most" (Payne 2018, p. 194). And, then, overall lower levels of economic performance, in the entire system. Bad capitalism, anyone?

Intriguingly, studies have found that most believe that CEOs are at a ratio of 10, and that most point to a reasonable ratio of CEO compensation is 4–5, relative to the average worker (Payne 2018, p. 193). So, something like 4–10 times the average worker pay fits the shared Other-interest by workers. Obviously, there is a long way to go, not only in making transparent that the ratios are not 10 but 30–40 times. It will be quite a challenge, taking a lot of Self-control, nudging, and perhaps control, in moving from ratios of 300–400 back toward 4–10.

Boards of Directors in the US are often composed of former CEOs, and, are also often paid extremely well to be on said board: The shared Other-interest within the board and the CEO is to favor extreme inequality. So, without any vehicle to temper the Greed between the boards and the CEOs, it continues to drive an extreme, ever increasing inequality. Stockholders also seem oblivious to just how much the CEO is actually paid; stockholders could perhaps influence their Boards of Directors. Based on the company performance studies, stockholders would likely be better off with more optimal inequality: The apparent belief (being it is tolerated by shareholders) that extremely high CEO pay leads to extremely high performance, and thus higher stock prices, has no grounding in empirical reality.

Only 5 percent of the variation in company performance is from differences in CEO performance (Payne 2018, p. 194). In fact, about 70 percent of the variation in company performance is from chance events, alone. At best, 5–20% of the variation in company performance is from the CEO alone (Payne 2018, p. 195). So, to enhance performance, balance must be sought in the compensation packagers for the CEO&labor: Extremes need to be avoided.

Balance in Wage, Salary, and Compensation: The Gravity Payment Case

An especially direct and relatively easy way to address then overall extreme inequality problem in the US comes with putting a more reasonable balance in the wage, salary, and compensation packages. Said packages could be rebalanced from within, freely chosen from within every company, every government agency, every situation. A case in point is demonstrated in the headline "The $70000-a-Year Minimum Wage" with the subtitle "A small Seattle company shows that capitalism can have a heart" (Kristoff 2019). Metaeconomics would say: A capitalism with heart is a humane capitalism influenced by Empathy.

While several employees had been in the $30,000–40,000 range of salary, Dan Price, one of the owners of Gravity Payment, a company that processes credit card transactions for small business, decided to raise compensation for each person to a minimum of $70,000. It was accomplished in part by Dan Price reducing his own salary from $1.1M to $70,000. Intriguingly, Seattle also passed an ordinance, about the same time, that raised the minimum wage for all workers in the city to a minimum of $15/hour, suggesting there was a wider shift, beyond just the one company, in the nature of the Other (shared with others regarding wage and salary compensation packages)-interest in the Seattle area at the same time.

The Gravity case raised a firestorm of reaction in the extreme political elements associated with the Right Isle. As Kristoff (2019) notes, on Fox Business, Dan Price was labeled the "lunatic of all lunatics," and Rush Limbaugh declared, "I hope this company is a case study in M.B.A. programs on how socialism does not work, because it's going to fail." Intriguingly, such statements would also find support in the outcome of research and analysis using Neoclassical Microeconomics based analysis, as well. So, what is going on? Is Dan Price a lunatic? Is the case a study in socialism, which inherently will fail? Or, is it something more akin to the Kristoff implicit claim that capitalism could have a heart, acting with Empathy and not just Ego, that is, be something more like what Metaeconomics might call a good capitalism, coming out of a humane liberalism?

While you may not like mathematics used as language, we will do a bit of it here, because it helps us to be more precise. From Eq. A.23 in the Appendix, we find the demand for employees, workers in the credit card payment processing company described by (just hang with me, mathematics can be helpful; we will also refer to the figures in the chapters, and talk about the equation in words):

$$X_1^D = X_1^D\left(\kappa_1 r_1, \kappa_2 r_2, p, I_G, I_M, R\right)$$

That is, the number of employees at Gravity Payment, the disciplined demand, D, disciplined by the moral dimension, leading to a balance in the dual interest, is determined by the salary paid the employees r_1, the prices/costs of all other inputs to the company r_2, and the capital available to the company R. If we assumed the two moral, ethical dimension multipliers κ on the prices were 1, and I_G, I_M were not in the equation, we would have the Microeconomics-based single interest, Self-interest only theory version of the demand (but not a disciplined demand in the sense of balanced interests, but disciplined to maximize Greed). It would follow that raising r_1, the price/cost of labor would put a strain on capital R, with the company having to cut back their efforts to Make wealth.

If it worked to strain investment, we suppose it could be considered a kind of lunatic-driven socialism, as the Right Isle claims. Clearly less labor would be hired, and capital would be exhausted, with the business not being able to compete. Profits would decline below acceptable levels, so Gravity Payment would go out of business. The Fox Business and Rush Limbaugh position is that every company is to operate on path 0G in Fig. 8.1: To help make sense of the claim, think of input e in Fig. 8.1 as a more humane compensation plan and input *d* as the Greed-based compensation plan.

So, the Limbaugh plan is at best a kind of moral order that is Selfish: No Spectator, no selfless influence, from Smith (1759/1790), at work here. The Invisible Hand of Greed guides the company to maximum profit at point A, or, even onto the vertical axis with no regard for what is shared with the Other. The Single Interest Theory demand curve would evolve along path 0G in Fig. 8.1 with supply and demand crossing at point A.

We also need to understand what happens to the supply of the product. Again, bear with me, regarding some mathematics, but the precision of it is helpful, from Eq. A.24 in the Appendix:

$$I_G^D = I_G^D\left(\kappa_1 r_1, \kappa_2 r_2, p, I_M, R\right)$$

The disciplined (D) supply of the credit card payment service I_G^D is affected by the costs/prices paid for labor r_1, the costs/prices paid for all other inputs r_2, the price charged for credit card payment services p and the capital available to produce the service R. Again, if we assumed the two moral, ethical dimension multipliers κ on the prices were 1, and I_M were not in the equation, then Microeconomics-based Single Interest Theory would say it: The greed-driven version of supply suggests that the company would have difficulty supplying the service with costs of production so high (not competitive with other companies providing similar services). It would exhaust the capital, and, again, the company would go out of business, giving support for the Limbaugh claim that lunatic socialism does not work. Under excessive Greed capitalism, as touted by Fox Business and Limbaugh, it is all about Self-interest, and one is a lunatic who tries to do anything else, acting on any kind of moral and ethical dimension. Forget humane and liberal capitalism. Again, using Fig. 8.1, the supply, too, would evolve along path 0G, with supply of the credit card payments services equaling the demand at point A.

Using the full set of parameters and other variables suggested by Metaeconomics leads to a quite different story. Gravity Payment decided that the shared Other-interest is such that $\kappa_1 > 1$. Also, I_G, I_M variables are prominent here: Gravity Payment sees the need to re-balance Self&Other, tipping the balance away from Self-interest I_G toward Other (shared sense of reasonable inequality)-interest I_M, moving from a point A toward a point B in a Fig. 4.2 now associated with Fig. 8.1. Gravity Payment was shifted from point A to point B in Fig. 4.2, causing it to move to path 0Z in Fig. 8.1.

There is now some sacrifice in profits from that at point A in Fig. 8.1, and some sacrifice in the ethical, moral side too, as compared to point C, but maximizing across both interests at point B gives a happy and efficient outcome. Both the demand and the supply evolve on path 0Z in Fig. 8.1, with balance in the company, balance for all employees. In the Fox Business frame, Dan Price is a lunatic for not taking every advantage of the situation. Dan Price is a lunatic for leaving dollars on the table for the lower income employees in his company to use, rather than taking them in his Self-interest.

What happened? Well, we do not have enough data, information to do a thorough empirically based analysis, but Metaeconomics points in some intriguing directions, so we can speculate in a different way about what is going on. First, the owner reduced his salary from \$1.1 M per year to \$70,000 per years, which helped maintain R, with \$1.03 M coming out of the "pay owners" account and into the "pay employees" account: It is possible the R^0R^0 capital line illustrated in Fig. 8.1 did not move at all. He was willing to leave some money on the table, seeing it was not going to detract from Gravity Payment doing just fine. That is, if the typical salary for the lower echelon in the wage structure was around \$30,000, shifting the \$1.03 M to the employee account means about 25 employees could be paid out of the salary savings at the top, that is, \$1,030,000/\$40,000 = 25–26 with higher pay, without reducing the capital that could be used in the business for other things. We don't know from the Kristoff article how many were increased to \$70,000, but we can use the number to clarify that R probably did not change as much as the lunatic socialism analysis would claim.

It is true that a couple of the higher paid, upper employees became concerned about losing ground relatively speaking, for example, someone earning say \$100,000 not getting a raise while many were now making \$70,000, and left the company (Kristoff 2019). We might guess that the people were eventually replaced (employee count increased overall from 120 to 200, so a reasonable guess), we might assume at about the same pay scale as people who left. It would be a piece of data we would want to collect, as perhaps it would have been necessary to scale up the entire salary range? In addition, several new hires arrived on the scene looking for employment by the fact they shared in the I_M introduced by the owner, Dan Price, moving toward point B in Fig. 4.2. New arrivals and hires wanted to work for a company that shifted the balance a bit away from Self-interest toward more orientation to a shared Other-interest, to a more reasonable salary sharing situation, and to a better working environment because of it. As Kristoff (2019) says it:

> Tammi Kroll, a Yahoo executive, took an 80 percent pay cut to move to Gravity, where she is now chief operating officer …. "My whole goal when I went to school was to make more money," said Kroll, who comes from a working-class background. But as she rose in the corporate world and her taxable income topped \$1 million, she had an epiphany: "Money doesn't make you happy, doesn't make you a better person." When she heard about Gravity, her heart leapt—and so did she.

So, rebalancing I_G, I_M toward the I_M clearly worked for her; path 0Z, like Adam Smith (1759/1790) suggested, can bring happiness (and, peace-of-mind; perhaps the bad capitalism is the place for the lunatic).

On the supply side, notice that a larger I_M, more attention to the shared Other-interest, could result in more product being produced, more credit card payment services, which is exactly what happened. Payment services increased in volume from \$3.8 B before the wages were increased to \$10.2 B at the current time. Why did the services business increase? Well, we do not have enough data and information to know exactly why it increased so much, but Metaeconomics does suggest, again, it could be about the new I_M, the ethic, the new Moral, new Ethical Dimension represented in the company by its owner. As Kristoff (2019) notes:

> Jody Hall … who worries about income inequality, owns a nearby cafe, Cupcake Royale. She chooses Gravity to process her payments, admires what (the company) has done and offers her own employees health care.

Businesses who shared I_M views with Gravity on just what the shared Other-interest needs to be regarding salary distribution, gave Gravity more business. Are these lunatics?

For Dan Price, the moral dimension represented in I_M is part of his business, again from Kristoff (2019):

> He grew up in rural Idaho in an intensely Christian family and spent three hours a day listening to Limbaugh and two hours memorizing Scripture. He's less religious today, but he says ethics remain deeply important to him.

It is ironic that Rush Limbaugh may have nudged Dan Price into acting the opposite from what Limbaugh saw as best for Gravity, instead bringing the moral and ethical dimension into the company.

We have to suggest, albeit it is an empirical question, that Metaeconomics would point to asking: It appears that Fox Business and Limbaugh prefer bad capitalism, excessive Greed capitalism and see it superior to anything that considers ethics, moral community, and tempering Greed on the way to good capitalism? Also, employees of Gravity presented a brand-new Tesla to Dan Price (Kristoff 2019); his \$70,000 salary had him driving an old car that needed to be replaced. Empathy, and the shared Other-interest it produces, goes both ways, which Smith (1759/1790) also makes clear.

The intriguing empirical question coming out of Metaeconomics is: What would happen to the health and social problems index; the political turmoil; and the stability of the US economy, if Dan Price styled-changes were made throughout the entire Market&Government system? Could we finally say the Enlightenment was bearing the kind of fruit that Smith (1759/1790, 1776/1789) envisioned, represented in a good capitalism, representing a kind of humane liberalism?

Intriguingly, changing the distribution of compensation in a business in a dramatic way has been tried before. Again, so, it is not real breaking news, recall that Henry Ford raised the factory line worker pay from $1 to $5 a day over 100 years ago, encouraging hard work, giving pride, raising productivity on the line, and making it possible to buy a Model-T Ford. The action still endears some to buying Fords (me included), and companies others than Gravity Payment are doing some similar things today. Metaeconomics suggests the important question: What if every company moved to a kind of shared Other-interest involving more reasonable mix in the compensation, still unequal, but not extremely so? Would such Ego-&Empathy-based action lead to a better capitalism?

Minimum Wage: Seattle Case

The more common approach to reducing inequality as pushed from the Left Isle, and abhorred, resisted at every turn, on the Right Isle, is to directly reduce poverty on the lower rungs. The minimum wage is one way to apply a Visible Hand at helping the lower rungs.

As noted, Seattle did increase the minimum wage to $15/hour, for the entire city, about the time that Dan Price set the minimum salary in Gravity Payment at $70,000. And, just like Fox Business, Limbaugh and other Right Isle elements would generally argue, we would likely arrive at the same place: Raising the minimum wage is lunatic socialism. The Right, as does NeoClassEcon, claims it raises unemployment, it damages the economy, and is not good capitalism. What would Metaeconomics have to say?

One part of the answer is clear: The outcome is affected by the source of the money used to pay a higher minimum wage. One of the main reasons it worked to raise the bottom wages at Gravity is that Dan Price gave up a substantial amount of his income in order to not only set a standard about the shared Other-interest, but to demonstrate the alternative shared Other-interest with action. It freed up a considerable amount of cash, for a company with only 120 employees. Shifting most of his $1 M+ salary to the lower paid group really made a difference, and, probably did not cost the firm much, as it came out of the profits. We can only speculate on what shifting salary, compensation from the higher levels in corporate US would do, but the numbers are substantive, considering CEOs alone average about $12 M per year, with some making upward of $300 M and more. It would make for paying a lot of $70,000 salaries at the lower levels in the companies, and, yes, perhaps employees would perhaps reciprocate with a gift of a Tesla, too.

In contrast, the story on the Right Isle, as supported by Neoclassical Microeconomics, is that only the bottom pays the costs. If the minimum wage is increased, fewer low wage workers are hired, because of capital constraints. But, from the above analysis, it is true only if people at the high end do not sacrifice anything to pay the higher minimum wage. If the salary structure is changed, an I_M, a shared Other-interest involving more of the (sorry, here it comes again) "we are all in it together" framing could evolve: Moving some money out of the upper end of the compensation packages could produce plenty of resources to hire the same or even more of the lower end employees after the minimum wage was increased. If it comes out of the high end of the compensation range, it is doubtful it would have any of the dire consequences predicted by Neoclassical (and Libertarian) Microeconomics. Makes (Metaeconomic) sense, right?

Admittedly, it is an empirical question, but a question driven by the 250-year-old philosophy from Smith (1759/1790), as noted earlier: Capitalism was to be profitable&humane, and each depended upon the other. Seattle is trying, just seeing the need for some re-balancing, to Be Lovely.

Gravity Payment, the company in Seattle is also trying to Be Lovely (be a Human). Payne (2018), through pointing to a wide arena of solid empirical findings in the behavioral and social sciences supporting a move to optimal inequality is pushing for more to try the move to Be Lovely. Metaeconomics-based questioning suggests that if every city and community, and every company, and government shift the focus to finding the optimal inequality the entire Market&Government could Be Lovely. And, by tempering, one could also Be Loved (Profitable).

Social Security

Another arena of concern about the minimum wage, and optimal inequality, pertains to the elderly, as represented in social security and Medicare. In general, the elderly face extreme challenges in making everything work in a Market as they become ever less able to make wealth through their own, daily efforts. The minimum wage of social security and Medicare is the currency of retirement in a Market economy, so what is to be done?

As a prominent Conservative thinker associated with the Right Isle would have it "the nation's most ominous governance problem is the unsustainable trajectory of the entitlement state because of the unfunded promises that have been made regarding pensions and medical care" (Will 2019, loc. 318). Ironically, however, the biggest drain on the capitalistic economy is generally at the upper rungs of the income and wealth ladder, not the lower, as the super wealthy come to believe they are entitled to it all (Ryan 2019, esp. p. 188). So, the extraordinary tax right offs, and tax avoidance strategies, for the super wealthy seemingly need to be tempered.

Social security was originally designed, starting in 1935, to provide a minimum wage, a minimum amount of income to support people in their old age, whether they had worked or not (pushpins or poetry) while younger. People contribute to the funds while working, through FICA (Wikipedia, *Federal Insurance Contributions Act*) and SECA (Self Employed Contributions Act) taxes, indexed to how much one earns. Also, working people in addition contribute to Medicare plans while working, and, pay a premium for Medicare insurance after they retire. Yet, as pointed out on the Wikipedia site, even for people who have paid in more: "Social Security has always been primarily a retirement, disability and spousal insurance policy for low wage workers and a poor retirement plan for higher salaried workers who hopefully have a supplemental retirement plan unless they want to live on significantly less after retirement than they used to earn." It has always been essential that the eventual retiree also have a private investment plan in order to have anywhere nearly adequate level of retirement income. Also, a supplemental health insurance plan is essential as Medicare does not pay the entire cost of medical treatment.

So, in Metaeconomic framing, the social security and Medicare health plan for the retiree has always represented a Market&Government approach, with the Government playing a larger role for the lower income person. Intriguingly, the mix of Market&Government is a quintessential question on the US Political scene, with the Right Isle pushing for total responsibility by each person to cover all costs from birth to death, including the retirement years, on path 0G trajectories. In contrast, the Left Isle has historically pushed for a larger role for shared responsibility on path 0M trajectories, with the actual outcomes, going back to 1935, on various trajectories represented in path 0Z.

Is the move to jointness in Market&Government since 1935 without problems? Of course not. We can rest assured that some are taking advantage of Government, and not paying enough attention to saving enough money to cover old-age needs, a common theme on the Right Isle. Such programs can have a perverse effect on human incentives, because of the primal drive of Ego-only Self-interest at work in everyone. It is an empirical question, however, as to the extent it is a serious problem, as the Right Isle proclaims without empirical evidence. At the same time, also without empirical evidence, the Left Isle is also often ready to transfer even more money over to help increase the income of the retiree, perhaps depending too much on the Empathy-based Other-interest for making decisions about such matters. Metaeconomics asks for empirical evidence of whether it is better to be more oriented to path 0G or path 0M trajectories, pointing to the empirical reality that we will virtually always (based on four decades of empirical testing of Metaeconomics, albeit it has not been tested directly in the realm of pensions and health care) find some path 0Z better than either path touted by Right or Left Isle. Rather, we would likely find a balanced path Right&Left as, pragmatically speaking, the best choice.

And, perhaps most importantly: The Right Isle argument that people need to save more money while they are working is without empirical substance when there is insufficient money being earned. The Left Isle would claim, and a Metaeconomics guided empirical analysis would likely support it: If wages and salaries were more balanced, a more optimal inequality existed throughout the working life of every individual, perhaps social security and Medicare would not be so essential? Perhaps it is more about how the wealth being made is shared between the CEO&labor? Metaeconomics proposes changing the frame of the conversation away from the tired old debate about transfers from the rich to finding optimal inequality. Instead, shift the focus to an Empathy-tempered look at salaries, wages, compensation packages, return on investments, as well as to paying taxes to cover the price *P* of the shared Other-interest (which might also pay more attention to shared costs of education and health care, as well as sustaining the Spaceship). People cannot save money for retirement unless they make enough money while working: Optimal inequality throughout a lifetime, anyone?

References

Applebaum, A. 2020. *Twilight of Democracy: The Seductive Allure of Authoritarianism.* New York: Knopf Doubleday Publishing Group, Kindle edition.

Cory, G.A. 1999. *The Reciprocal Modular Brain in Economics and Politics.* New York: Kluwer Academic/Plenum publishers.

Etzioni, A. 1993. *The Spirit of Community: Rights, Responsibilities and the Communitarian Agenda.* New York: Crown Publishing Group.

Kristoff, Nicholas. 2019. The $70000-a-Year Minimum Wage. *New York Times* (New York), March 30, Opinion.

Lakey, George. 2016. *Viking Economics: How the Scandinavians Got It Right – And How We Can, Too.* Brooklyn, New York: Melville House Publishing, Kindle ed.

Lucas, Robert E. 2004. *The Industrial Revolution.* Minneapolis: Federal Reserve Bank.

McCloskey, D.N. 2019. *Why Liberalism Works: How True Liberal Values Produce a Freer, More Equal, Prosperous World for All.* Kindle ed. New York: Yale University Press.

Payne, Keith. 2018. *The Broken Ladder: How Inequality Affects the Way We Think, Live, and Die.* New York: Penguin Books.

Piff, P.K. 2015. Wealth and the Inflated Self: Class, Entitlement and Narcissism. *Personality and Social Psychology Bulletin* 40 (1): 34–43.

Piff, P.K., M.W. Kraus, and D. Keltner. 2018. Unpacking the Inequality Paradox: Psychological Roots of Inequality and Social Class. *Advances in Experimental Social Psychology* 57: 53–124.

Pinker, Steven. 2018. *Enlightenment Now: The Case for Reason, Science, Humanism, and Progress.* New York: Penguin Random House LLC.

Ryan, Christopher. 2019. *Civilized to Death: The Price of Progress.* New York: Simon and Schuster.

Shiller, Robert J. 2019. *Narrative Economics: How Stories Go Viral and Drive Major Economic Events.* Princeton: Princeton University Press.

Smith, A. 1759/1790. *The Theory of Moral Sentiments,* ed. D.D. Raphael and A.L. Macfie Raphael. Indianapolis: Liberty Fund, Inc.

———. 1776/1789. *An Inquiry into the Nature and Causes of the Wealth of Nations.* ed. E. Cannan. New York: Random House.

States: Income and Wealth Inequality. http://ebookassets.penguinrandomhouse.com/ebookassets/features/brokenladder/graphic-51.pdf. Accessed 1 Apr 2020.

Stiglitz, Joseph E. People. 2019. *Power and Profits: Progressive Capitalism for an Age of Discontent.* New York: W. W. Norton and Company.

Wikipedia. 2020. Federal Insurance Contributions Act, March 28. Encyclopedia. https://en.wikipedia.org/wiki/Federal_Insurance_Contributions_Act_tax

Wilkinson, R.G., and K.E. Pickett. 2006. Income Inequality and Population Health: A Review and Explanation of the Evidence. *Social Science and Medicine* 62: 1768–1784.

———. 2010. *The Spirit Level: Why Greater Equality Makes Societies Stronger*. New York: Bloomsbury.

Will, George F. 2019. *The Conservative Sensibility*. Kindle ed. New York: Hachette Books.

CHAPTER 15

Saving Capitalism: Bring Empathy into Mind and Action

We have alluded to the role of the economic narrative. A focus on Self-interest only characterized the narrative started in the early 1980s (the Reagan-Thatcher Narrative; see Shiller 2019), without enough attention to the essential role of the shared Other-interest in Government. The narrative pointed to Government can do no good, going viral by the mid-1990s through the current time (as represented in Gillespie and Schellhas 1994, again, see Shiller 2019). Perhaps the narrative from the 1960s that the Market has done bad and the Government will fix it, led to the backlash? Empirical question.

Being the 1980s narrative is back in force here in the early-2000s, let me get it straight, trying to be an empirical MetaEcon here: All the bad people go to work in Government so Government does only bad and all the good people go to work in the Market so the Market does only good? Maybe. It seems such narratives are what is bad and have led to a great deal of bad capitalism and bad government, as Stiglitz (2019) and others have documented. Overall, the question is, can capitalism be saved, especially with both good and bad people in both Market&Government? And, like Commons (1934a) said, it is fundamentally about "... trying to save capitalism by making it good" (quoted in Whalen 1993).

G. D. Lynne, *Metaeconomics*, Palgrave Advances in Behavioral Economics, https://doi.org/10.1007/978-3-030-50601-8_15

Metaeconomics Helps Make Sense of Political Economic Turmoil

Before we start to weave the story, we need to first understand that in contrast to Neoclassical Economics with Microeconomics, Metaeconomics is not about market fundamentalism and neoliberalism, which just naturally leads to bad capitalism, a non-sustainable capitalism. It is also not about a liberalism devoid of the shared Other-interest represented in community, which is *Why Liberalism Failed*, why an unfettered capitalism fails, as Deneen (2019a, b) makes clear.

Metaeconomics is also not the same as Neoinstitutional Economics, especially not the New Institutional Economics (e.g., Coase 1960; North 1990; Williamson 1975). New Institutional Economics sees Self-interest driving the evolution of institutions. It is also not about the close relative in Public Choice Economics (e.g., Buchanan and Tullock 1967), which sees Government, too, driven only by Self-interest. And, again, apparently only bad people work in Government, so it cannot do good things. Maybe.

While perhaps being a bit presumptuous and audacious to even consider it, in what sense could Metaeconomics serve to guide saving, and then building a good capitalism, for which the other main frameworks have failed to do so? Well, it actually gains its' potential to do the job from being more akin to Classical Economics as in Smith (1759/1790, 1776/1789), and to Classic Institutional Economics as in Commons (1934b/2017; see Bromley 2006) both which saw the essential role for the shared Other-interest in tempering the Self-interest. Ayres (1944), too, as represented in seeing Value as instrumental, contributes to the Metaeconomics proposition of valuing the balance in Self&Other-interest on a Higher Plane. Such valuing comes out of Empathy. As in Metaeconomics, Ayres (1944) went well beyond the notion of value revealed in a price evolving from a Self-interest only Market.

Metaeconomics is consistent with the Commons (1934a) contention about saving capitalism by making it good, through a Visible Hand consideration of the moral and ethical dimension: It is the only way to do so. Unethical capitalism is a bad capitalism. Making it good is about evolving an Empathy-based Other-interest with content about the Right Thing to Do. So, if we integrate neoclassical&neoinstitutional economics, we are in effect about integrating Ego&Empathy, Self&Other-interest, which is the Metaeconomics frame. We bring the Visible Hand into action. We set aside the narrative of a magical Invisible Hand. We use the Dual Interest Theory as the analytical engine.

Current Status of Capitalism

As noted in the earlier discussion about finding balance through optimal inequality, the Economic Narrative started to change in the late-1960s into the early-1970s, as popularized in articles like Friedman (1970). The narrative gained traction in the Reagan-Thatcher era in the early-1980s. The Narrative contributed to all manner of bad things, including but not limited to: Far fewer high-paying jobs for what used to be the middle-class. Communities shattered as factory doors slam. Families disintegrating as parents work two to three jobs, having no time for family. Children without dads and moms, young men without wives, and young women without husbands, and others without stable relationships with a significant other. Opioid addiction. Drug addiction. Waves of immigrants clinging to their own culture rather than integrating into a widely shared culture, and the door slammed on trying to enter. Fraud and deception, an entrenched sense of entitlement, at both ends of the income and wealth ladder. Disability claims on the lower rungs, while at the top, cronyism of the worst sort, like the bankers and traders who crashed the economy, in effect demanding the taxpayer bail them out, and then taking millions in bonuses because they are the entitled elite. Spaceship Earth system pollution and destruction as represented in excessive loading of the atmosphere with greenhouse gases (e.g. too much carbon dioxide) and loss in species diversity. Politicians bought by the extreme wealth of the extremely, absurdly rich: Crony capitalism. Top 0.1 percent enjoying a raise of 227 percent raise since 1980. CEOs pay at upward of 300–400 times the median wage. Rampant growth in narcissism, hedonism and the focus on the Ego-only frame.

As the title of a recent book (Goldberg 2018) proclaims, we now risk the *Suicide of the West*. Capitalism is in danger from ever more ignoring the Empathy-based Other-interest, in not addressing just what it is that everyone can go along with. Even the optimism of Pinker (2018) has come under fire: Bartlett (2019) argues the Enlightenment has not been as successful as Pinker claims. McCloskey (2019) seems to agree, while clarifying that it really is a humane liberal democracy-based capitalism that is needed. What is a humane liberal frame all about? In a word, Empathy. Hedges (2018) sees America through the lens of a *Farewell Tour*, self-destructing as it goes along.

Stiglitz (2019), too, sees a kind of self-destruction at work and the need to put Market&Government back together. It seems that the political tribes just want to win, focusing on reinforcing their identity, rather than accomplishing anything of much substance, at least not overall, for everyone: It emboldens the rebel politician, the populist, the one who pays little attention to law and custom. Also, as the real message of the Enlightenment taught us, the way to solve the problem is once again to have a community-wide fact-based conversation about democracy, freedom and liberty, and what good capitalism brings. It is about evolving the kind of moral and ethical community essential to a good capitalism.

Goldberg (2018) refers to it as building a "civil society," something sorely missing in the contemporary narrative. Also, smaller tribes representing smaller factions, in many smaller communities, are not all bad. Good coalitions among them can create good super communities. Yet, there is also danger: As conservative political commentator George Will (2019, loc 701) makes clear, the "tyranny of the majority" can be a problem in democracies, if the majority is unreasonable, off on some non-sustainable tangent not recognizing true conditions. A case in point is ignoring the limited capacity Spaceship Earth atmosphere and ecosystem to handle pollutants. A majority can lead to bad things, bad capitalism.

Intriguingly, Deneen (2019b), a seeming detractor of Enlightenment thinking, argues that it is the liberty and freedom of autonomous people that is causing the populism, tribalism, nationalism, and identity politics. We might ask, though, just how autonomous? Metaeconomics, through recognizing the key role of the Other-interest, also sees the autonomous person operating without bounds as the challenge if not the problem, and the need to build civil society which includes homonomy. A civil society is an essential part of each person, on their own, achieving balance in the dual interest. And, a civil society also plays a role when Self-control fails.

It is essential to keep in mind that the Enlightenment always had its detractors (pointed out by Stiglitz 2019, esp. pp. 14–15), represented by people opposed to findings in science, not seeing the need for science, even working to distort and misrepresent science, absolutely breaking science&ethics, as in the "deniers" frame; against innovation on many fronts, including the essential need to continually reform religions and social mores; and opposed to forming new social and community, and even more so, governmental, organizations, common laws and essential regulations, to make things work better.

We are experiencing said kinds of resistance to Enlightenment thinking today, in a slowdown in the progress toward tolerance for racial and gender differences; distrust of basic science and universities; distrust of traditional news sources, including the essential investigative journalism that helps keep light on democracy; and religious as well as social conservatives increasing skepticism about classical liberalism, because of the focus on the autonomous person, again as highlighted in Deneen (2019b). And, perhaps more than anything, we have reverted to the extreme inequality of income and wealth that was the standard in the pre-Enlightenment period. We have replaced the powerful monarchy and religious, along with their business cronies, with a new kind of entitled elite as represented in the extremely rich and the politicians they buy. Such people often have little regard for anyone, including other elites (as argued in Ryan 2019; James 2012).

Making Sense of Ongoing Issues in Capitalism

As is now clear, Metaeconomics suggests the most important reason for the current problems, deterioration in capitalism, arises from the current bad balance in Ego&Empathy. As Piff (2015) and many others have demonstrated, the shift in recent years has been away from Empathy as narcissism has grown, with ever more focus on Self-interest only. Narcissism is in vogue (also see James 2012), made even worse by a deterioration in Self-control.

Like Goldberg (2018) and the notion of building civil society, conservative commentator Brooks (2019), too, sees the need to move toward facilitating "A Nation of Weavers" who are "building community… weaving the social fabric" and thus moving away from the current "culture of fear, distrust, tribalism, shaming and strife" of Market-dominated choices… and "we don't just have a sociological problem; we have a moral problem." Metaeconomics points in the same direction: It is time to build a moral and ethical community.

In contrast to the play of the Enlightenment, which brought Empathy (and, then, the moral and the ethical) as a force, suggesting a kind of humane liberalism, Ego has now come back to dominate. As alluded to earlier, the ancients argued that Desire could dominate Thymous, the Horse of Ego dominating the Horse of Empathy with the Chariot Driver losing control, which is the current situation. Several other contemporary writers have proclaimed that it is the time for Empathy to once again play a more substantive role in addressing the excesses of Ego (see DeWaal 2009; Obama 2006; Rifkin 2009; Brown et al. 2019). Humane liberalism (after McCloskey 2019), here we come: It is the key to producing the true wealth of every nation on the Spaceship.

Miracle of Wealth Arises in Good Capitalism

Capitalism has facilitated Making wealth, and people in capitalistic systems now enjoy a standard of living, never thought possible prior to the Enlightenment. Saving capitalism is about building upon the miracle of wealth that humans have experienced only in the past few hundred years, since the time of the Enlightenment (again, see Pinker 2018). Saving capitalism also requires ensuring everyone has access to that wealth through being paid higher wages and salaries for contributing to Making of it, and thus avoiding extreme inequality. As Hedges (2018, p. 200) says it:

> The conflict will not end until followers of the alt-right and the anticapitalist left are given a living wage and a voice in how we are governed. Take away a person's dignity, agency, and self-esteem and this is what you get.

The middle is full of resentment, as many in the middle follow either the anticapitalist left or the alt-right, especially apparent in the recent phenomenon of the cosmopolitan-nationalist continuum. Also, in fact, unbounded wealth accumulation is not even good for people who are doing it, with people enjoying said "good fortune" often deteriorating, becoming isolated, perhaps even paranoid, hiding behind locked gates, often with armed guards (Piff 2015; Ryan 2019). Metaeconomics sees the condition behind locked gates as the natural outcome of too much Ego without enough Empathy (recall the Cory finding about CEOs in Japan vs. in the US).

As Metaeconomics clarifies, we now know that wealth is not really a miracle, but rather is because of significant shifts in both the way we think about and otherwise frame the interaction in Market&Government, balance in Ego&Empathy. On the Market side, we dramatically changed how we thought about the business community, and the role of the freedom to choose. The talk reframed the positive role of the bourgeois, in the shared Other-interest, and pointed to a visible, conscious look at the character of good business (McCloskey 2006; for a review, see Khachaturyan and Lynne 2006). Business, industry, and trade in truly competitive Markets (involving hundreds, perhaps thousands of producers, not rule-of-three concentrated and monopolized Markets) gradually came to be valued more highly by not only the larger population, but also its leaders, the good ones being of high character. It was an ethical bunch of bourgeois at work; it appears the ethical side has been lost. Also, on the

Government-side, the monarchy became subject to the rule of law, driven by recognizing freedom and liberty for each person as essential, and that no one was born into the privilege of power over others, as had been the divine monarchy. Political and religious leaders had to be of high character, as well. Ethics, again. Wealth is a miracle only with a good, ethical Other-interest operating in the background of the Self-interest pursued through liberty and freedom for all people: Everyone needs a living wage, voice, dignity, and agency, and, an ethic driven by Empathy can produce same.

Money Became Wealth

The other dramatic shift at the beginning of the miracle was the evolution of money as the measure of wealth. In an earlier time, land was that measure, which greatly limited not only the magnitude of the wealth, but especially who could be wealthy. Money lubricated the Market for thousands of potential sellers and buyers, rather than for just a few who had the land-based wealth. Money facilitated developing production capacity to Make wealth, not bounded by land, and, perhaps most importantly, not just creating dollars for the Taking. Making wealth, with it widely spread across all the Travelers, is a main feature of good capitalism. Yet, the money cannot be mainly accruing to, and being held in, the hands of a few. There is the essential need for Visible Hand attention to finding the optimal inequality that works in a widely shared Other-interest.

Role of Private&Public-Property

Metaeconomics suggests the need to find the best combination of private-&public-property. Stiglitz (2019, p. xxiii) is saying much the same thing here:

> Capitalist economies have always involved a blend of private markets and government—the question is not markets *or* government, but how to combine the two to best advantage. (Stiglitz 2019, p. xxiii)

It is saying essentially the same thing in that the primary feature of a Market is private property, and of a Government is public property. The two must be combined in such a way as to get the best outcomes, pragmatically speaking.

It follows that any plan to move to a Market-only Spaceship Earth, often touted on the Right, means moving to ever more private property. Taken to the extreme, it means the waterways represented in the rivers, lakes, and even the ocean would be privately owned; the atmosphere would have to be privatized, and, the air we breathe subjected to the price of a market (coins operating air tight breathing masks, perhaps); all of the ecosystem of Spaceship Earth would have to be privatized, as would all the minerals, oil and otherwise; all the fish would be privately owned; every piece of land, both that under and above water, would have to be privatized; all the roads, fire and police services, education, safety nets for the poor, health care, as well as the military, all would need to be owned in private property, exchanged in Markets, and operated for profit. All the research efforts and educational services would also be provided by private entities; we might guess, too, that every college and high school football and other sports teams would likely be privately owned teams. Pure capitalism would have "no taxes, no price ceilings, no price floors, no public parks, no central banks, no wars of aggression, no immigration restrictions" (Munger and Villarreal-Diaz 2019, p. 351, quote from Labeit 2009). Ironically, a tendency toward pure capitalism is also a tendency to producing bad capitalism. It also works counter to saving capitalism, as pure capitalism would lead to massive Market-failure.

Intriguingly, the other extreme is equally unworkable: The most fundamental characteristic of a Government-only frame is public property, often more favored on the Left Isle. The view suggests, by birthright, being born and now a Traveler on the Spaceship, we own the Spaceship together, that is, the water, oil, coal, minerals, atmosphere, ecosystem, and all the land, both under and above water. We also would own, together, the capacity to produce fire, policy and military services. We also would own the capacity to provide a safety net, to take care of the poorest of the poor; to help people who lose jobs with unemployment coverage and job retraining opportunities; and own all the production of health care.

In the pure version of Government-only property, decisions about it would be ongoing strictly in a variety of legislative, judicial, and administrative forums. The currency of exchange is voting, political power, and the smooth talker in the administrative, legislative and judicial branches of Government. Everything available would be supplied out of the Government. The Spaceship Earth Travelers owning the property together would also be running the Government together, and traveling together provisioning each other on Spaceship Earth. In the extreme, all means of production, and all supply of goods, would come out of the production capacity owned as a public property. We would arguably have a kind of pure socialism, or even more extreme, a pure communism, at work. Pure public involvement would lead to massive Government failure.

The absurdity of either extreme end of the Public Property–Private Property continuum (recall Table 5.1) quickly becomes apparent. A balance shifted to either extreme is not viable nor stable, as reflected in the empirical reality, the actual experience for hundreds of years. It just does not fit human nature, which needs balance in Ego&Empathy, Self&Other-interest. As Munger and Villarreal-Diaz (2019, 351) say about pure capitalism, which is also true for pure socialism (or, even more extreme, pure communism), each "is a definition of something that does not exist and cannot exist." Empirical evidence supports balance, as either extreme in the property regime will fail. The only thing that works is good balance in private&public-property, Market&Government.

Balance in Private&Public-Property Is Decided in Law

The question of the best balance in private&public-property to save capitalism comes to play in the law. As noted, the huge step forward in law came in the early part of the Enlightenment, as well, wherein the private law of the Monarch, generally always favoring the monarch and the small circle of supporters with the same shared Other-interest as the monarch, was eventually replaced with the Common Law of the people. In the Common Law, everyone had a say, referring here specifically to English Common Law. It made the Government subject to the people, not the opposite. The monarch-styled Government could easily be pejorative, who in consort with favored religious and business cronies made the law without recourse for people. Common Law, in contrast, asked the basic question: "How would I wish to be treated, in law, if I were the person being subjected to the matter in question?" Empathy, as represented in walking-in-the-shoes-of-the-other, has always been the first step on the way to a law that works for everyone. It was about what everyone could go along with.

For example, we have historically answered the question of "just who should have access to the water produced by the Spaceship Earth's hydrologic system" as "everyone," with such access determined, together, through public property. We use Other Forums within the US Government (legislative, administrative, and judicial) rather than the Market Forum for the allocation of water. Even in the US, wherein private property in land is the dominant mode, even the land under the lakes and rivers (and the ocean) as well as the corpus of water itself is still retained largely in public property ownership.

Intriguingly, too, finding the balance in private&public-property is largely about finding community. Tempering the more primal drive to private property is tantamount to finding the basis for a moral and ethical community of shared Other-interest in attenuating the rights, and, then, keeping a substantive amount of influence and control on the Market with public property. And, while Neoclassical Economics (and its Microeconomics engine) presumes mainly private property (else there can be no Market), and Neoinstitutional Economics sees a perhaps greater role for public property than is essential, Metaeconomics sees the need to find balance in private&public. At least, that is empirical question: What balance works best?

Free Markets, Socialism, and All That

Not much changes: In the current time, the socialism word is thrown at proposals to build a lower carbon economy; ensure access to health care for all (we might even suggest in dealing with pandemics, in that budgets have been cut, and those without adequate health care in the past are more likely to die from the virus); help with Medicare and sustaining social security; environmental regulation; fuel-efficiency standards and renewable fuel subsidies; labor unions, minimum wages, CEO compensation guidelines, and other attempts to address extreme income and wealth inequality; and, perhaps the most important, public education, to list a few. So, anything that focuses on the shared Other-interest in such things as environmental sustainability and a healthy, educated population, or reasonable sharing of the wealth produced by capitalism, is about socialism? Metaeconomics proposes instead that it is about Empathy, and, even more importantly, about balance in Ego&Empathy, which is how we save capitalism.

Three Essential Roles for Government in Order to Facilitate a Good Capitalism

Saving capitalism requires recognizing the Metaeconomic contention that Government has three pragmatic and major roles. The three roles are represented in being protective, productive, and, yes, even at times facilitating predatory "rent-seeking" (always a pejorative-only notion in Buchanan/Public Choice Economics) choices.

It is protective in the broadest possible sense in providing for the national defense; it also provides for police services, fire services, and general safety net protection for citizens. Being protective includes bringing the latest science to bear, helping make choices that work to ensure a sustainable Spaceship Earth on which we travel. It is protective in dealing with public health issues, like pandemics. It is protective of the freedom and liberty of each person, keeping outside control at bay, and only used sparingly when Empathy fails through lack of Self-control. It is protective in dealing with the inherent jointness and interdependence, especially as pertaining to use of the natural resources and avoiding the Tragedy of the Commons, which is really a Tragedy of Excess of all kinds, excessive Greed at work, on the Spaceship.

Government can also be protective in addressing fairness, tolerance, opportunity, and, yes, in ensuring democracy itself (after B. Friedman 2006, p. 7). Yet, there is always the possibility of going too far, resulting in Government-failure to facilitate enough expression of Self-interest, about which the Market must be aware, and work to temper. As Will (2019) convincingly argues, Government sometimes creates perverse incentives to cheat, defraud, and otherwise Take wealth from others, at both ends of the wealth spectrum, albeit, as noted, Will seemingly only sees it at the lower rungs. Perhaps most importantly, Government plays a key role in being protective of private property rights, essential to the Market, as along as said rights appropriately reflect the shared Other-interest. Again, saving capitalism is about finding the best balance in private&public-property.

Government is also productive in providing at least a minimal, basic education for everyone, essential to saving capitalism. A well-funded, widely supported public education system better ensures the opportunity for everyone to make wealth. Government has also been especially productive in funding and sometimes even directly doing the basic research, for example, in NASA; US National Science Foundation; and, especially key and real to my four decades of experience, actually my experience going back as long as I can remember, the public-funded agricultural/food research in the US Land Grant Universities. The Government support of the latter, historically (not so much anymore, as the narrative has been moved evermore to privatization), along with Market partners, helped make agriculture and the food industry economically viable. Public-funded research formed the foundation for filling the supermarkets with a wide-variety of high-quality foods, while using ever fewer resources from the Spaceship Earth. Another case in point is Silicon Valley, wherein most if not all of the electronic technology, for example, in smart phones (see Mazzucato 2018, who makes it clear that the basic technology behind Apple's iPhone was developed in Government based research efforts), used by everyone has been, and continues to be, influenced by the productive work of the Government.

Saving capitalism is also about ensuring that the truly public goods are produced and otherwise provided. True public goods cannot be reliably and economically produced by the private sector. Public goods are represented in such things as dams and reservoirs for water supply and flood control; road and other transportation lines navigation (the classic pure public good represented in the light house example being a case in point, but also such things as air traffic control); food and drug safety; public health information and services; and environmental quality. Such goods serve the shared Other-interest, and, without them, it is impossible to operate on the happiness path 0Z.

Government can also provide for some good predation, good rent seeking, for example, in helping a startup industry, perhaps an industry involved in providing for essential national security, or for such things as developing the technology for renewable energy produced with wind towers or solar panels, essential to the long survival of Spaceship Earth. The rent-seeking of the agricultural and food industries (e.g., Government-subsidized crop insurance; conservation payments) is also another example where it can be good. Ensuring a steady, reliable food supply from an industry so tied to the vagaries of weather and other natural happenings in the Spaceship Earth is essential: Everyone needs to eat.

Overall, as both Mazzucato (2018) and Stiglitz (2019) make clear, and Metaeconomics supports, the Government is essential to Making wealth, which Smith (1759/1790) also understood. And, it is in the shared Other-interest to do so. And, the bottom-line: Government, overall, plays the most important and essential role in questioning the status quo, hidden in the Invisible Hand. Government needs to be a clear and active player in the Visible Hand, to ensure entrenched power and influence does not prevail, indefinitely. The US Declaration of Independence, the US Bill of Rights, and the US Constitution must be continually reconsidered, and a new Visible Hand implemented, as needed. All people are represented by a good Government, with all considered as being created equal and endowed with unalienable rights. Good Government is about Empathy.

Material and Moral Economic Growth

Saving capitalism is also, then, about a deeper understanding of the nature of good economic growth. Said growth is material&moral. So, is it necessary to keep increasing the Gross Domestic Product every year? Recall Fig. 12.1: There are thermodynamic limits. Continual, infinite growth denies limits. So, with Material-only framing, and infinite, no limit reframing, we would not recycle, and we would tend, as B. Friedman (2006, p. 7) says it, to "over-produce pollution, noise and congestion." We would also tend to produce a more subtle form of "externalities" as represented in the form of less fairness, tolerance, democracy, and opportunity (B. Friedman 2006, p. 7). As B. Friedman (2005, 2006, p. 8) points to, and about which Metaeconomics can provide new insights:

> Someone who cares more about material concerns believes that he or she should be for economic growth, while someone who places greater emphasis on the moral dimensions of life instead is led to conclude that he or she should resist economic growth, and should oppose policies likely to spur growth.

Metaeconomics sees the material group on path 0G, and the moral group on path 0M. B. Friedman (2005, 2006, p. 8) goes on:

> Economic growth brings benefits in the form of opportunity, tolerance, democracy and fairness ... (as well as ways to resolve other externalities) .... It is wrong, therefore, to structure the debate over economic growth as one of balancing purely material benefits versus purely moral drawbacks. The benefits are, importantly, moral as well. Similarly, the mapping of a person's location on the spectrum from material concerns to moral concerns into his or her indicated stance in either favoring or resisting economic growth, and hence either supporting or opposing growth related policies, is a false mapping.

So, using Metaeconomics, there is payoff in both domains of interest with no simple tradeoff (as believed in Microeconomics) between the material (pushpins) and the moral (poetry); they cannot be separated into two separate sets of isocurves. Rather, the material&moral arise jointly on happiness path 0Z (Figs. 4.1, 7.1, and 8.1). The two dimensions are joint, nonseparable entities, because of the nonallocable feature of material&moral between the two interests.

Both can also be enhanced, at an increasing rate, as in possibility frontiers becoming ever further apart. Increases in both the material&moral emerge as we move along path *OZ*, a symbiotic sum greater than the sum of the parts (as illustrated in Fig. 7.2). The inherent jointness of the material&moral is also a theme in Hirschfeld (2018), who also sees the same jointness as the essential feature of a humane economy, much like that in the humane liberalism-based capitalism envisioned by McCloskey (2019). And, Metaeconomics would suggest that focusing only on growth without the moral and ethical dimension of it, especially not paying enough attention to reasonable compensation for everyone who helps Make it, is to build a Potemkin Village "any construction (literal or figurative) whose sole purpose is to provide an external façade to a country which is faring poorly" (from Wikipedia)" Assuring it is moral and ethical, as well as scientifically and empirically based, avoids the façade of the Potemkin Village.

Saving Capitalism Is Not About Strong-Leader-Based Fascism

Both Fascist Politics and Fascist Religion are reoccurring phenomenon, especially when bad capitalism emerges, as though we never learn. Neither one honors the contention that every person is created equal, and endowed at birth with certain unalienable rights, as the US Declaration makes clear:

> We hold these truths to be self-evident, that all men are created equal, that they are endowed by their Creator with certain unalienable Rights, that among these are Life, Liberty and the pursuit of Happiness (US Declaration of Independence)

It frames what both politics and religion are to mean in the US, and that frame is not Fascism. A humane liberal democracy is inconsistent with Fascism, but why bring it up here, in a book on Metaeconomics? Also, Mark Twain said it, "It is easier to fool people than to convince them they have been fooled." Fascism works at fooling people: Metaeconomics, as a science&ethics-based analytical system, can be used to work at convincing them they have been fooled.

Unfortunately, the moment that bad capitalism appears, it is always just a short time before Fascism arises, and promises through fooling people, to save it. So, due to the claim herein that Metaeconomics as an analytical system can serve to help save capitalism, it is necessary to explain how Metaeconomics is so profoundly different.

First, in contrast to the economic framing and theory in Fascism, Metaeconomics is based in empirical reality, built on facts, not conjecture about things that may have at best only a bit of truth content. Fascist myths use bits. Second, Metaeconomics is built on the foundation that every person is created equal, and has unalienable rights: It is the most fundamental ethic, and, there are others arising out of Empathy. To emphasize: Metaeconomics is about science&ethics, while both Fascist Politics and Fascist Religion create and rest on myths, fooling people, rather than being based on empirical reality and science. Fascism works unethically to serve only the favored few.

Fascist Politics

In contrast to Fascist Politics, Right&Left-Isle Politics have in the past both generally recognized, and worked to abide by, the overall frame from the US Declaration of Independence (as well as the US Bill of Rights and the US Constitution). The fundamental documents undergirding US Democracy are about every person's inherent equality and rights. Senator Moynihan said it, referring to the political conversation in the US: "Everyone is entitled to their own opinion, but not to their own facts." Politics is to have a fact and reality base, not just ideology-based largely on opinion or myths. It requires a willingness to go do the hard work to dig out the facts, and, then, use them.

So, Metaeconomics could, then, be used by both the Right&Left. Metaeconomics could be put to productive use in both the Conservative-&Progressive-Isles. Why? Well, it is based on a reality economics: Go, ask the questions. Find out what really works. Stay consistent with a focus on true liberty and freedom for each person, that person being created equal with unalienable rights.

Fascist Politics fails on both fronts. Fascist Politics takes bits of fact, if facts at all, and builds a mythical story. The story is opinion at best, and outright propaganda at worst. The 1930s were characterized by such myths, promises from now infamous strong-leader Fascists like Hitler and Mussolini, in Germany and Italy, respectively. Fascism gained traction arising out of desperate times after the 1929 economic crash of capitalism, with their promise to, in general, save capitalism. Be careful. Fascism has again come to the fore, stirred by the 2008 crash. Actually, it all starts with the early-1980s, again with largely empty, smoke-and-mirror, emperor-has-no-clothes styled promises, leading to a kind of Potemkin populism.

Stanley (2018, loc 85) points to several strategies used by the Fascists in selling the myths. Generally, the Fascist (drawing also on Wolff 2019) works to stop immigration, or to favor only certain groups; stop globalization; eliminate "unnecessary" regulation, anything that aims at tempering excesses; stir old tensions between races and ethnic groups, with a favorite group always in mind. The Fascist cons everyone into joining in, driving buy-in to myths that are designed to serve the strong-leader and supporters. Fascism spreads the propaganda it produces, turning it into "facts" as all credible sources are discredited. Fascism leads to a kind of cult-like behavior in the favored group, everyone ready to drink the Kool-Aid on command.

A kind of authoritarian populism, a close relative, also emerges. As Hedges (2018, pp. 5–6) describes it:

> The acceleration of deindustrialization by the 1970s created a crisis that forced the ruling elites to devise a new political paradigm … trumpeted by a compliant media, shifted its focus from the common good to race, crime, and law and order. It told those undergoing profound economic and political change that their suffering stemmed not from corporate greed, but from a threat to national integrity. The old consensus that buttressed the programs of the New Deal and the welfare state was attacked as enabling criminal black youth, welfare queens, and social parasites. The parasites were to blame. This opened the door to an authoritarian populism … (starting in the early-1980s) … which supposedly championed family values, traditional morality, individual autonomy, law and order, the Christian faith, and the return to a mythical past, at least for white Americans. … (more recent politicians, with not only authoritarian populist but also fascist tendencies, especially in not acknowledging empirically based, sound facts) … capitalized on this perceived threat to national integrity and authoritarian populism to take power.

So, Government is moved away from helping the "parasites" and redirected, usually using borrowed money, increasing the national debt, to help finance (often directly subsidize) the bad capitalism. Increasing the federal debt is a guaranteed way to ensure that the excess Greed is served well. It is then argued that any kind of program to serve the widely shared Other-interest like public education, public health, social security, and sustaining Spaceship Earth systems now needs to be cut.

The main underlying theme, though, is to cleanse the system. Only the selected few are deemed to have been created equal, and to have unalienable rights. Keep out immigrants (unless they buttress the selected group), narrowing the focus to the ethnic group, religious group, culture, or skin color favored by the Fascist. Nationalism is used as the way to disguise the cleansing, the Fascism favoring the ethnic, favored skin color of the strong-leader. Disguised as a call to patriotism it is really a move to Fascism. The strong-leader is stepping in, to save the nation, somehow returning to a greater time, a time which was magically great, like the Fascist period of the 1930s? The Jim Crow era which operated well into the 1960s? The era when the Cayuga River in Cleveland burned for three days and the air in Los Angeles was unfit to breath? The time before electric cars, CFL and LED light bulbs, and low flush toilets?

Still another focus of Fascist Politics: Work to eliminate all criticism of the strong-leader, through threatening and bullying, discrediting anyone who risks raising questions. So, discredit and work to silence investigative journalists, making fun of same, claiming long standing and highly reputable news organizations produce fake news, when in fact the fake news comes from the propaganda machine of the strong-leader. Science is also framed as biased, not to be trusted, unless it serves the strong-leader and supporters who benefit from not dealing with scientific realities that put in question the bad capitalism economic activities: The essential need for science&ethics is broken.

Trade unions are discouraged and eliminated when possible, and minimum wage laws are debunked. Why? Well, trade unions work for a more reasonable compensation for all involved in the Making of the wealth, and, even more disturbing to the Fascist, to bridge gaps among all people in the union. A good union (and, naturally, empirically it could also occur, there could be a bad union, too) sees every union member created equal and having the same unalienable rights. A union member is to be treated the same no matter one's gender, race, or sexual preference, and every other thing that distinguishes a person from another person. The equality and unalienable right arises in the diversity within the good union. A Fascist does not approve of said framing, in that only a certain few are so created and have unalienable rights, so it is essential to downplay the role of the union. The same is true for discrediting cooperatives, especially worker cooperatives, and, any kind of suggestion that perhaps labor, or other stakeholders like people wanting to sustain Spaceship Earth systems, needs voice on the board of directors.

Also, without enough money, better ensured with low wages and few education opportunities, shored up by not having a minimum, life-supporting wage, people can be kept out of influencing the direction of the Market. A person needs money in order to express value in a Market Forum. So, keep wage power down; the value V coming from low-wage people will be minimal, as it can only be expressed through price P, and that takes money. So, minimize the amount of money for each person, pay them as little as possible. Excessive Greed prevails. Also, with low wages, a person has to work perhaps two to three jobs simultaneously, so there is no time to participate in a liberal and humane democracy-based political process, which is exactly what Fascist Politics wants to accomplish: Eliminate democracy, especially the humane version of it.

A fully functioning liberal and humane democracy-based capitalism also requires everyone have access to education, to learning, in order to help them do the homework and process the content of facts. Education is essential to making sense of the reality in which a person lives, learning especially about how a good system would operate. Education positions everyone to participate, to truly work to save and build a good capitalism. So, Fascists purposely work to eliminate public education, especially if it dares to treat every student as though they are created equal and have unalienable rights, and, even more so if it presents scientific information that does not square with the Fascist agenda. Extreme inequality in access to education is a good thing. Private schools, which can easily accommodate people with agendas favored in Fascist Politics, and, in Fascist Religion, a close relative, are encouraged. Private schools are to even be funded with public tax dollars, now redirected to teaching based on the myths. No science please. Starve the public education, which is designed to represent the widely shared Other-interest, into extinction.

Also, the strong-leader Fascist claims to be all about eliminating "socialism," elimination accomplished through branding, calling, framing, bullying anything, and anyone that asks for tempering or bounding bad capitalism. The strong-leader in Fascist framing does it in order to frighten people into believing efforts to save capitalism by tempering the excesses are attempts to bring Pure Communism and Pure Socialism to the fore. The approach is to divert attention to the extreme end of the spectrum, which may be laudable if such extreme systems were a real threat. Generally, it is not. Such distraction keeps attention away from what really is needed to save capitalism by tempering the Greed, and, even worse, distracts from what the Fascist is really doing. Fear keeps people distracted, and, in line. In such manner, the strong-leader can eliminate the people who protest against bad capitalism. Making others fearful of the protestors, rather than addressing what they are really protesting about, is in general the Fascist way.

Finally, some of the most invidious strong-leader framing is to pretend to protect religious rights, build up a strong military and police force to ensure law and order to protect the people (which is more about ensuring Fascist power and control, than about protecting the people), and build strong families, among other ostensibly good things. It all sounds good, and many people get wrapped into the empty rhetoric, while the favored rich and powerful go to the bank with the strong-leader. A close relative of Rightish Liberal Statism emerges, especially shorn up by the Fascist Religion that supports it. On the religion front, the reality that the strong-leader is generally also not only Ego-based but also usually extremely hedonistic, and often also narcissistic (albeit an empirical question, but highly likely), is also lost on religious people who really believe they are being protected. By an Egoist? Empathy-sympathy-compassion needs to be the main feature of religion, in that it is necessary to recognize each person is created equal and endowed with unalienable rights. The Ego leads to an empty rhetoric about protecting the rights to do religion, even if bad religion is at work.

The ostensible representation of and support for Empathy through supporting religion is instead of the dark type. The Fascist uses a form of dark Empathy: Studying, learning about, and knowing people who are not considered equal and not to have rights. Such a capacity is extremely useful in making the subject miserable, and in extreme cases, perhaps even torturing with precision, and killing, as in the Dark Empathy of Hitler and Mussolini. Dark Empathy ensures surgical precision can be brought to bear, to hurt people being denied rights and are deemed unequal. And, Dark Empathy has no sympathy or compassion, so there is no regret. It is a sad, sorry system, and, one might ask, where are the good religious people?

Fascist Religion

By definition, Fascism in general, whether in Politics and/or in Religion, cannot put people and systems onto a Metaeconomic path 0Z, which is about happiness. Why? Well, the answer is clear: Fascism, in addition to being not reality and not fact based, is also not a system consistent with a widely accepted moral and ethical community. It is above the law, above the ethical system that created the law, and above the US Constitution. It is above any sense of what is an ethical religion, too. Recall, again, the created equal and unalienable rights frame, which is discounted in Fascist Politics. The same is true in Fascist Religion: Only the in-group is created equal and has unalienable rights.

So, what are the main tenets of a Fascist Religion? How do the tenets relate to a moral and an ethical community, writ large? Empirical questions. Also, we focus here on Fascist Religion that selectively uses premises and claims associated with Christianity, fully realizing there are other kinds of Fascist Religion (the extreme, fundamentalist elements of the Muslim religion as a case in point) at work in various areas of Spaceship Earth.

Perhaps the following is a place to start. Hedges (2007, p. 5) notes:

> There is enough hatred, bigotry and lust for violence in the pages of the Bible to satisfy anyone bent on justifying cruelty and violence ... the Bible has long been used in the wrong hands—such as antebellum slave owners in the American South who quoted from it to defend slavery—not to Christianize the culture, as those wielding it often claim, but to acculturate the Christian faith.

Hedges (2007) goes on to make the case that selective interpretation and use of passages and themes from the bible is common in Fascist Religion, a kind of culture formed to serve a narrow shared Other-interest. Use what serves the strong-leader and followers, ignore the rest. So, even the overall empathy-sympathy-compassion frame, even though the fundamental frame of Christianity, can be selectively applied only to the favored few.

In general, a Fascist Religion sees the proposition that "all men are created equal, that they are endowed by their Creator with certain unalienable Rights" is somehow applicable only to certain kinds of Christians. It also applies literally to men, not to women, and certainly not to anyone on the continuum between the two. Said persons are a select few, "the believers." Heterosexual men favoring hierarchical control over women are especially favored. Certain skin colors are favored: Turn Jesus into the favored color. Liberty and freedom are given only to true believers of the Fascist Religion version of Christianity. Fascist Religion–based liberty and freedom is not the same as that coming out of the Enlightenment, which originally was a truly humane liberalism. And, the Founding Fathers had a humane liberalism in mind as represented in the US Declaration of Independence, the US Bill of Rights, and the US Constitution.

The counter-argument is usually that: "Well, the founding fathers were Christian, and built the foundation for a Christian nation." Well, maybe, although there is little in the way of empirical evidence that the founding fathers had in mind building a Christian nation, at least not for a narrowly defined special group of "Christians." Rather, it was about all people, no matter their creed, race, religion, color, ability, and any number of other things in the list that describe all people in the sense of created equal.

In fact, many if not most of the founding fathers were Deists, so it was quite possible, in their framing, that every person could be created equal and endowed by a Creator with unalienable rights. On the matter of religion, that was about it, albeit some of the Deist framing did suggest believing in a kind of eternal life (As an aside: Thermodynamics does suggest matter and energy cannot be, and is never, destroyed. Humans are matter and energy, and perhaps have a soul, which is an empirical question; in any case, the matter and energy in a human just changes form at and after the point of maximum entropy, the point of death, so, sure, why not).

So, what does it have to do with the brand of Christianity touted in Fascist Religion? Seeing the key role of empathy-sympathy-compassion, applied universally to all people, in the teaching of Christ seems consistent with being created equal with unalienable rights. It seems the universal application of the principle to all people could be quite defensible, based on empirical reality about what Christ did, day-to-day. And, it is not just in Christianity within which Empathy plays a role; in a speech reaching out to the moderate and reasonable Muslim world, Obama (2009) noted:

> It's easier to see what is different about someone than to find the things we share. But we should choose the right path, not just the easy path. There's one rule that lies at the heart of every religion — that we do unto others as we would have them do unto us...This truth transcends nations and peoples.

Read the "right path" as the peaceful, peace-of-mind, happiness path 0Z pointed to in Metaeconomics. It is part of our natural and social evolution. It is reflected in religions, and perhaps even in our genetics, our evolutionary code. It is not what Fascism is about. Christian framing is about finding peace and happiness, freely chosen.

Using Metaeconomics, the most bothersome feature of Fascist Religion is the lack of appreciation for the essential need for Empathy. It is Empathy that facilitates the freedom for each person to pursue their Own-interest. In the US Constitution, it is characterized in general as life, liberty and the pursuit of happiness. In contrast, in Fascist Religion, the "freedom" to pursue life, liberty, and happiness is given only to people who believe in a "mythical Christ" (see Hedges 2007, p. 15) who demands, more like a Critical (strict, disciplinarian) Parent commanding an Adaptive Child (which is the predisposition for authoritarianism) obedience at all cost. Such compliance with outside control can make a person quite unhappy: Rightish Liberal Statism, again. In contrast, the actual Christ, at least an empirical reading of the framework used by Christ, requiring own homework, had a large Free Child (he enjoyed a glass of wine with his friends, and encouraged us to do the same in communion with him and church friends), and preferred to be a Nurturing Parent to all people. Christ nurtured lepers, prostitutes, even Empathized with the money lenders and others into extreme Greed (although he did not have much sympathy or compassion for same: The matter of a camel going through the hole in a needle comes to mind). It was all about grace, as Martin Luther reminded everyone a few hundred years later. Fascist religion is not about grace; it is about control. It is not about seeking the Own-interest on a happy path 0Z.

Also, it perhaps cannot be emphasized enough: The US Founding Fathers, while seeing a key role for an Empathy-based religion to affect and better ensure building a humane system, also saw the need to separate Church and State. The founders saw the dangers of religious dictums, as it would be impossible for a system with too much influence from religion, especially of the Fascist type, to be both humane and liberal.

Empirical Evidence That Fascist Politics and Fascist Religion Are Both Myths

Looking at reality, history illustrates that strong-leader-based Fascist systems, both Political and/or Religious, have never worked. Germany and Italy tried it in the 1930s through the end of World War II, with massive failure, destroying and not saving capitalism. Such a system can never work, no matter what new strong-leader, secular or religious, emerges. Reason: Distortions in science and ethics. Metaeconomics, due to being based in science&ethics, can be used to help stay away from ever producing the ground in which a strong-leader Fascist system can set a foothold.

Saving Capitalism Is About Keeping Power in Balance

Offsets represented in building power in opposition to bad capitalism can come in several forms. One of the best forms is represented in the historically successful, but now a shadow of the power it carried, the labor union. Another way to counter excess is in cooperative structures, such as the farm cooperatives referred to in the Preface. Still another is more worker and other stakeholder (community, consumers, suppliers, sustaining Spaceship Earth) involvement in corporate boards of directors, bringing principles of democracy to bear in influencing corporate direction, especially compensation policy. It is unlikely CEOs would be paid 300–400 times the average worker if compensation was influenced by a labor union, a democracy influenced board of directors, or a cooperative. It is unlikely that practices which ignore the limits of Spaceship Earth systems would be continued.

The Nordic model especially as represented in Norway and Sweden, which started evolving in the late-1800s through the 1920s to eliminate poverty, and then gained even more ground in the 1930s to offset Fascism, is one model to consider. The Nordic Model (also including Denmark and Iceland) is pragmatic, resting in balance in ambition&community, which is in parallel with Ego&Empathy, Market&Government.

Looking back at the early pragmatism in what became the Nordic Model, Hedges (2018, pp. 261–262) clarifies how in the 1930s Fascists favoring the Right in Norway and Sweden tried to stir the Progressives and others on the Left into conflict and violence with the Right, which would benefit the Fascists. The Fascists could take power while everyone was distracted by the two extremes, in effect, while the more reasonable where not looking. As Hedges (2018) points out, the Nazis did it in Germany and the Fascists in Italy, on their way to taking absolute power. Why does it work? Well, the people in the Middle, between the Right&Left, do not want the violence, so they tolerate, perhaps even implicitly encourage the police and military being brought in by the strong (Fascist)-leaders. Gaining control through the police and military was the goal in the first place, in order to eventually take absolute control, so mission accomplished. The Fascist strategy did not work in Norway and Sweden because the Left, even though taunted by the extreme Right, did not play their game (Hedges 2018, p. 261); it simply was not pragmatic.

Instead, offsetting power by the people was built through massive strikes, boycotts and demonstrations, which involved most everyone on the Left, in the Middle, and substantive numbers on the moderate Right. Even the Independent and Right-tending farmers would refuse to participate in auctions of farms being foreclosed by the large banks, who could not, then, gain any benefit from the foreclosure. It was Empathy in action. The result is the Nordic form of capitalism, which is all about finding balance in Self&Other-interest. It is functioning notably well (see Lakey 2016): Empathy influenced pragmatism at work. The building of offsetting power through Empathy was also a fundamental feature of the Civil Rights movement in the US, as associated with Martin Luther King (see Hedges 2018, p. 260). Metaeconomics, anyone?

Cooperatives, which to this day play substantive roles in the Nordic economies, may be especially useful to building offsets to power. Cooperatives, by being based on principles of democracy, an Empathy-influenced capitalism, can be key players in making wealth. Cooperatives can be a vehicle for finding that optimal amount of inequality. I suppose my Norwegian and Swedish roots, and my early years among transplanted, in the northern US, immigrants from Norway and Sweden because of bad capitalism, may also be at work here. The Norwegians and Swedes of North Dakota (and others that joined in, from other parts of the Spaceship Earth also having bad capitalism in the "old country") used cooperatives, regularly, at least in the early years: balanced ambition&community, Ego&Empathy, Self&Other-interest at work.

Virtually all of that has been lost. I barely recognize my home state, especially with the loss of most of the cooperatives among losses in other offsetting forces to power. Regarding the Farewell Tour of America, as described in Hedges (2018), which is largely about the loss of offsets, North Dakota is now on the list. It surprises and disappoints as to how the historical commitment to balance (it was there, once upon a time, see Shoptaugh 2019) in ambition&community has been lost. Such balance is in the Nordic Roots.

As Shoptaugh (2019) makes clear, the North Dakota of the early 1900s was about the farmers forming an offset to the power of the monopoly railroads, the large milling companies (North Dakota at that time was all about wheat), and the large banks, but especially the milling companies who bought all the wheat. So, the Nonpartisan (That is correct: All Political Isles were invited) League was formed, and actually made some huge strides for a decade or so toward bringing the jointness of Conservative&Progressive into practice. It was all about fostering a better balance in the Market&Government, a balanced power, as it pertained to food and agriculture. It was about a more balanced profit (Shoptaugh 2019): "Sons of the wild jackass—leaders of the Nonpartisan League—questioned everything, argued constantly, and developed a political platform demanding more profits for the farmer." How did they do it?

For one thing, a Government-owned bank was established, using tax dollars to Pay for a shared Other-interest in what happened in the credit Markets. A Government-owned mill and elevator was established, too, again, Paying for the shared Other-interest in competing with the privately own mills and elevators in the wheat processing Market. We might guess an eye was also put to railroad rates. It was Nonpartisan League pragmatism directed at bringing an offset to power, and, thus to encourage a price *P* reflecting the shared value *V* in a stable and sustainable agriculture, helped through tempering the price *P* in the credit, grain, and rail transport markets.

Unfortunately, tribal tendencies of the Political Isles eventually re-emerged, as well as too much in the way of Ego-driven leaders from within, and the Nonpartisan League went down (again, see Shoptaugh 2019, esp. starting on p. 159, who describes in great detail how things fell apart). Yet, the legacy of the Nonpartisan League, and other less dramatic but still effective farmers movements since that time, are still bringing more reasonable balance to the Market&Government of agriculture. The balance is represented in the stability, sustainability, and safety of the US food and agricultural system. Also, North Dakota (Government) still operates both the State Bank and the State Mill and Elevator, and both are quite profitable, both still working in offset to power (Market). Pragmatically, it can work.

Using the Kling (2019) characterizations of political continuums (and others in Table 5.1), and the reason North Dakota as well as virtually every other US State is on the Farewell Tour list, it seems the move has been too far toward the tribal extremes, with the huge swings back and forth on the political continuums. The most recent swing that Hedges (2018) has documented seems to suggest the extreme move toward the civilization end of Conservatism; toward the oppressor end of Progressivism; toward the liberty end of Libertarianism; and, most dangerously, toward the Nationalist end of the Cosmopolitan-Nationalist continuum (again, see Table 5.1). Such extremes give rise to Tribal Wars, and cannot work. The questioning and arguing needs to lead to joint and productive outcomes, not just tribal wins. It seems the only Hope is to go to something more akin to a non-tribal, joint Conservative&Progressive, joint across all political isles, issue focused Nonpartisan League style political system. And, it is needed not just for the food system, but also in jointly addressing matters like pandemics, the public health challenge, drawing on what each does best.

The Farewell Tour in America (and, in many other areas of the Spaceship Earth, perhaps the exception being the Nordic economies), especially with respect to the need to rebalance and offset power, can still be averted with the help of Metaeconomics. Averting would include such things as more support for labor unions and cooperatives, anything that returns the principles of a humane and liberal democracy into business and commerce, and brings better balance in power. Yet, a cautionary note: In the process of building offsets to power, as demonstrated in the case of the Nonpartisan League, such entities must also build in safeguards to ensure Self-interest does not overwhelm said organizations. The classic labor union boss is a case in point: Labor union leaders, too, with several examples from the past (what did happen to Jimmy Hoffa?), can also succumb to Ego-based excesses in Self-interest. And, cooperatives can act like they have been "MBAed (run strictly for profit, not for profit&community)." Be careful.

References

Ayres, Clarence E. 1944/1978. *The Theory of Economic Progress*. Kalamazoo: New Issues Press, Western Michigan University.

Bartlett, Tom. 2019. Why Do People Love to Hate Steven Pinker? *Chronicle of Higher Education*, March 7.

Bromley, D.W. 2006. *Sufficient Reason: Volitional Pragmatism and the Meaning of Economic Institutions*. Princeton: Princeton University Press.

Brooks, David. 2019. A Nation of Weavers. Opinion, *New York Times*, February 18 2019.

Brown, K., W.N. Adger, P. Devine-Wright, J.M. Anderies, S. Barr, F. Bousquet, C. Butler, L. Evans, N. Marshall, and T. Quinn. 2019. Empathy, Place and Identity Interactions for Sustainability. *Global Environmental Change* 56: 11–17.

Buchanan, James M., and Gordon Tullock. 1967. *The Calculus of Consent*. Ann Arbor: University of Michigan Press.

Coase, Ronald H. 1960. The Problem of Social Cost. *The Journal of Law and Economics* III (October): 1–44.

Commons, John R. 1934a. *Myself (Autobiography)*. New York: Macmillan.

———. 1934b (reprinted 2017). *Institutional Economics: Its Place in Political Economy, with New Introduction by Malcolm Rutherford*. New York: Routledge.

Cory, G.A. 1999. *The Reciprocal Modular Brain in Economics and Politics*. New York: Kluwer Academic/Plenum Publishers.

Deneen, Patrick J. 2019a. A Defense of Conservatism That Veers toward Liberalism. Opinion, *Washington Post* (Washington, DC), June 21 2019, Digital.

———. 2019b. *Why Liberalism Failed*. Kindle ed. New Haven: Yale University Press.

DeWaal, F. 2009. *The Age of Empathy*. New York: Harmony Books.

Friedman, Benjamin M. 2005. *The Moral Consequences of Economic Growth*. New York: Alfred A. Knopf.

———. 2006. The Moral Consequences of Economic Growth: The John R. Commons Lecture, 2006. *The American Economist* 50 (Fall, 2): 3–8.

Friedman, Milton. 1970. The Social Responsibility of Business Is to Increase Its Profits. *The New York Magazine*, September 13.

Gillespie, E., and B. Schellhas, eds. 1994. *Contract with America: The Bold Plan by Representative Newt Gingrich, Representative Dick Armey, and the House Republicans to Change the Nation*. New York: Random House.

Goldberg, Jonah. 2018. *Suicide of the West: How the Rebirth of Tribalism, Populism, Nationalism, and Identity Politics Is Destroying American Democracy*. New York: Crown Publishing Group.

Hedges, Chris. 2007. *American Fascists: The Christian Right and the War on America*. New York: Free Press.

———. 2018. *America: The Farewell Tour*. Kindle ed. New York: Simon and Schuster.

Hirschfeld, Mary L. 2018. *Aquinas and the Market: Toward a Humane Economy*. Cambridge, MA: Harvard University Press.

James, Aaron. 2012. *Assholes: A Theory*. New York: Doubleday.

Khachaturyan, Marianna, and Gary D, Lynne. 2006. *Review of Mccloskey, D. N. The Bourgeois Virtues: Ethics for an Age of Commerce*. Chicago: The

University of Chicago Press, 616 pp. *Journal of Socio-Economics* 23 (October 2010): 610–612.

Kling, Arnold. August, 2019. *The Three Languages of Politics: Talking across the Political Divides.* 3rd ed. Cato Institute: Washington, DC.

Labeit, Michael. 2009. Explaining the Difference between Capitalism and Corporatism to Michael Moore. *Economic Policy Journal.* http://www.economicpolicyjournal.com/2009/11/explaining–difference–between.html

Lakey, George. 2016. *Viking Economics: How the Scandinavians Got It Right – And How We Can, Too* (Kindle ed). Brooklyn, New York: Melville House Publishing, 2017, 2016.

Mazzucato, Mariana. 2018. *The Value of Everything: Making and Taking in the Global Economy.* New York: Hachette Book Group.

McCloskey, D.N. 2006. *The Bourgeois Virtues: Ethics for an Age of Commerce.* Chicago: The University of Chicago Press.

———. 2019. *Why Liberalism Works: How True Liberal Values Produce a Freer, More Equal, Prosperous World for All.* Kindle ed. New York: Yale University Press.

Munger, Michael C., and Mario Villarreal-Diaz. 2019. The Road to Crony Capitalism. *Independent Review: A Journal of Political Economy* 23 (3): 331–344.

North, D. 1990. *Institutions, Institutional Change, and Economic Performance.* New York: Cambridge University Press.

Obama, B. 2006. *The Audacity of Hope: Thoughts on Reclaiming the American Dream.* New York: Three Rivers Press.

———. 2009. Obama's Speech in Cairo. *Wall Street Journal*, June 4.

Piff, P.K. 2015. Wealth and the Inflated Self: Class, Entitlement and Narcissism. *Personality and Social Psychology Bulletin* 40 (1): 34–43.

Pinker, Steven. 2018. *Enlightenment Now: The Case for Reason, Science, Humanism, and Progress.* New York: Penguin Random House LLC.

Rifkin, J. 2009. *The Empathic Civilization: The Race to Global Consciousness in a World in Crisis.* New York: Jeremy P. Tarcher.

Ryan, Christopher. 2019. *Civilized to Death: The Price of Progress.* New York: Simon and Schuster.

Shiller, Robert J. 2019. *Narrative Economics: How Stories Go Viral and Drive Major Economic Events.* Princeton: Princeton University Press.

Shoptaugh, Terry L. 2019. *Sons of the Wild Jackass: The Nonpartisan League in North Dakota.* Fargo: North Dakota State University Press.

Smith, A. 1759/1790. In *The Theory of Moral Sentiments*, ed. D.D. Raphael and A.L. Macfie Raphael. Indianapolis: Liberty Fund, Inc.

———. 1776/1789. In *An Inquiry into the Nature and Causes of the Wealth of Nations*, ed. E. Cannan. New York: Random House.

Stanley, Jason. 2018. *How Fascism Works: The Politics of Us and Them.* New York: Random House.

Stiglitz, Joseph E. 2019. *People, Power and Profits: Progressive Capitalism for an Age of Discontent.* New York: W. W. Norton and Company.

Whalen, Charles J. 1993. Saving Capitalism by Making It Good: The Monetary Economics of John R. Commons. *Journal of Economic Issues* 27 (4): 1155–1179.

Will, George F. 2019. *The Conservative Sensibility.* Kindle ed. New York: Hachette Books.

Williamson, Oliver E. 1975. *Markets and Hierarchies: Analysis and Anti-Trust Implications. A Study in Economics of Internal Organization.* New York: Free Press.

Wolff, Richard D. 2019. *Fascism: An Analysis for Today.* Podcast Audio. Economic Update, 2019.

CHAPTER 16

Conclusion

We might ask, as we leave the book: Just where does Metaeconomics fit, as one reviewer asked, in the "broader economic tool-box?" Formally, the answer is: Metaeconomics starts at the same point as Neoclassical Microeconomics, and, at the same point as Neoinstitutional Economics. For the former, focus on the individual, who is an Econ. For the latter, focus on the person and the people, the Human in community, including the larger Spaceship Earth community. Metaeconomics sees both the Human and the Econ within. And, most importantly, through seeing the Human, Metaeconomics brings the moral (and ethical) dimension, the moral sentiments as Adam Smith referred to it, back into focus. Bringing the sentiments—that which people can go along with—back into economics is also the plan of Humanomics.

Metaeconomics demonstrates no fundamental difference in the formal structure of Microeconomics, except now there are two overlapping indifference curves (at least two: actually, there may be several) and two overlapping isoquants (and, again, could be several). The overlapping isocurves move the frame from single interest and independence to dual interest and interdependence. An Econ has a single, Self-interest; a Human has a dual interest, working to integrate Self&Other-interest, and working to maximize Own-interest. An Econ has only Ego. A Human has the capacity for both Ego and Empathy. Empirical tests of Metaeconomics suggest Ego-only choices may not describe reality. The same tests point to one expecting that Empathy plays a role, too. As a result, Metaeconomics not only

G. D. Lynne, *Metaeconomics*, Palgrave Advances in Behavioral Economics, https://doi.org/10.1007/978-3-030-50601-8_16

holds the potential for supplementing, but at times, for some issues, can even be a more productive framework and theory than either Neoclassical Microeconomics or Neoinstitutional Economics. While Ego or Empathy are considered, Metaeconomics shifts the attention to the balance in Ego&Empathy. So, it seems that both the NeoClassEcon and the NeoInstituEcon have got it partly right, but are missing the key role of balance, as decades of testing by the MetaEcon suggest.

Due to seeing the interdependence, Metaeconomics, much like does Neoinstitutional Economics, also then sees the role of culture, moral, and ethical systems, institutions representing how one Human relates to another Human, and the law. It is the institutional (not organizations, but institutions like culture, regulations, law, social capital, all coming out of fellow-feeling) context that forms the underlying reality of the choices to not only the Econ, but to the Human. It also, then, directly addresses the matter of excessive Greed, seeing that often it is essential to temper, and perhaps bound it, in institutional context.

Metaeconomics integrates across the columns of Neoclassical Self-interest and Neoinstitutional Other-interest (recall Table 2.1). The integration is made possible through drawing on empirical science, as in Behavioral (and, to some extent, Experimental, but not much the Neoclassical version of it) Economics: The selection from both columns of Table 2.1 for insertion into Metaeconomics depends upon whether it stands scientific, empirical testing, both with significance and substance. It is especially essential that the integration across the two columns be subjected to ethical reflection, that it meets a standard in the moral and ethical dimension of the economy. It is about science&ethics.

As a result, Metaeconomics also can be used as an analytical engine to help integration across the Conservative&Progressive-Isles as characterized in Tables 5.1 and 6.1. It focuses attention on the fact that a good politics is also an ethical politics; it is also a fact-based, an empirical evidence-based politics, focused on real problem solving rather than protecting tribal territory. Also, there is some overlap with the integration in the political economic sciences, in that main propositions on each of the Conservative and Progressive Isles are often supported on each of the Neoclassical and Neoinstitutional Economics Isles.

Metaeconomics is also much intertwined with Behavioral Economics, by using and contributing to the empirical findings represented therein. Metaeconomics is, in a sense, a kind of Behavioral Economics. Also, in that Behavioral Economics does not have its own framework and theory, metaeconomics offers a possibility for serving that role, especially as an analytical engine. Metaeconomics can also be such an engine for Buddhist, Humanistic, Humane, Feminist, and Ecological Economics, as well as for Humanomics.

So, as audacious, and perhaps presumptuous as it sounds, it is my current view that Metaeconomics holds great potential as a major player in the toolbox of Economics. Please join in the quest to help it be so, or, if not, please explain why it cannot be so.

On a less formal, but perhaps the most important final note: There is a reason we have stories like *A Christmas Carol,* the Ghost Story of Christmas, all about Ebenezer Scrooge (Capitalist) and Bob Cratchit (Labor). Scrooge was an Econ. Scrooge was prone to excessive Greed. The Ghosts stirred Empathy, and out came a humane Scrooge, as in Scrooge&Ghosts. He awoke on Christmas morning as a more moral and ethical Scrooge, a Scrooge who was better balanced in Self&Other-interest. Both the Market and the Government need to awaken in the same way. Perhaps waking-up with Empathy, writ large in joint Market&Government, can also Save Capitalism, so we do not have to wave Farewell. Good ghosts like that should not be busted.

Appendix: Formal Structure of Dual Interest Theory

This Appendix is about adding the powerful analytical machinery of mathematics. It is about the mathematics of a Dual Interest Theory. It formalizes the idea of a joint, nonseparable, interdependent Self&Other-interest arising because of nonallocable inputs in production and supply, and nonallocable goods in consumption and demand. It brings ethics and the moral dimension back into a formal mathematical model through representing same in the shared other-interest.

A key feature to be demonstrated is interdependence: Consumers are interdependent with other consumers. Producers are interdependent with other producers. Both consumers and producers are interdependent with nature, as well as with each other. So, supply and demand are also interdependent. The interdependence arises from (1) the reality described in thermodynamics on the production side: Every human production system is embedded within, and is nonseparable from, interdependent with, the natural system on Spaceship Earth, and (2) the reality of Self&Other-interest being operant, and nonseparable within the Own-self, the mind/brain, on the consumption side. As result, a person can influence the relative outcomes but cannot separate the interests out for individual consideration.

Microeconomics misses the essential point of interdependence. It misses interdependence from not seeing the essential role played by the Impartial Spectator. Going to the Station of the Impartial Spectator is to form the shared Other-interest. Said Other-interest holds the content of

G. D. Lynne, *Metaeconomics*, Palgrave Advances in Behavioral Economics, https://doi.org/10.1007/978-3-030-50601-8

the moral dimension, the moral and ethical system. It sees only independent and separable producers and consumers (both within each category, and between producers and consumers), and, by ignoring the moral dimension, is at best an amoral theory. It ignores ethics and the ethical system essential in an economy system. Each person acts on their own without ever walking-in-the-shoes-of-the-other, not Empathizing: No role for the moral sentiments. Happiness is generally not possible.

Granted, Microeconomics is often "patched" to consider externalities, and other rather flawed ways (like interdependent utility) to account for the other in the economy. The patch, however, is generally not the best way to handle the reality of jointness and interdependence, nonseparability. The patch really does not represent what is really going on. The patch also does not help in achieving happiness.

And, in fact, for such obvious joint processes as represented in the classic example from Frisch (1965), a sheep internally allocates grain and hay between wool and mutton, Production Microeconomics cannot address the case in a meaningful way. It presumes the sheep rancher can choose (presumes complete control over) how the sheep allocates the grain and hay. Similarly, Consumption Microeconomics presumes that the purchase of a good that has recycle content is producing only Self-interest payoff, and has no reasonable, believable way to represent the reality that such goods simultaneously produce Other-interest payoff.

Also, Metaeconomics posits that humans are inherently challenged in finding the best balance in the Self&Other-interest arising from problems in Self-discipline and Self-control. Drawing on Behavioral Economics, empirical research, it sees a wide array of human fallacies and shortcomings in the decision process. The problem of Self-control is especially well documented in Behavioral Economics, especially the economic psychology and psychological economics branches (see Altman 2012; Tomer 2017). There is always a tendency to slip back to the more hedonistic, Self-interest only path of choice, doing what we want to do, including ignoring what the systems in Spaceship Earth are doing in the background. It is simply more primal. And, it is often done unconsciously, even when one attempts to be mindful of the Other-interest (the moral dimension, the moral community, the ethical system, the conscience, the Impartial Spectator, the natural system) in the background. Being mindful of the Other-interest is essential to doing the right thing for one's Own-self.

The Microeconomics-trained reader will recognize the visual depiction of Ego-based Self-interest only indifference curves in set I_G of Fig. 4.1, and the Ego-based Self-interest only isoquants in set I_G of Fig. 8.1. In contrast, the Dual Interest Theory suggests there are always overlapping indifference and isoquant curves represented by the I_M set(s), overlapping the I_G set in each figure. We now turn to the formal mathematics.

Appendix A: Indifference Between Nonallocable Goods

As noted, Frisch (1965) stirred the imagination about how jointness in production arising from the reality of nonallocable inputs could also perhaps exist in consumption as arising from the real possibility of nonallocable goods. The Lynne (1995) paper was the first to suggest how it might work, with two sets of overlapping indifference curves, as illustrated in Fig. 4.1. We can also represent that which is illustrated in Fig. 4.1 with a formal mathematical model on the mathematics of indifference, first presented in Lynne (2006a).

Thinking about payoff represented in Eq. (A.1), Microeconomics sees the payoff as utility. After Etzioni (1986), we might consider the arguments as pleasure utility *G* and moral utility *M*. Metaeconomics prefers thinking of payoff in the Ego-based Self-interest *G* and Empathy-based Other-interest *M*, both contributing to a Higher Plane of value *V*. Said *V* is different from price *P*, and akin to the instrumental value of Ayres (1944). The value *V* serves to balance Self&Other-interest. We show how value *V* is subject to an income constraint *y*. Equation (A.1) also demonstrates only one Other-interest I_M, while there are generally several; we live in a complex web of interdependence with every person and every system on Spaceship Earth, where the value *V* reflects the moral and ethical system giving context to the economic choice:

$$\phi = V\left(I_G, I_M\right) + \lambda\left(y\right) \tag{A.1}$$

where

$$I_G = I_G\left(q_1, q_2\right) \tag{A.2}$$

$$I_M = I_M\left(q_1, q_2\right) \tag{A.3}$$

Notice that q_1 and q_2 are nonallocable goods; that is, the same quantity of the same, identical.

Good is in both Eqs. (A.2) and (A.3). In words, people cannot place the payoff in their two interests into separate accounts. The goods are nonallocable as between the two interests, in direct contrast to Microeconomics. In Microeconomics, we would be allocating parts of each good to each interest. Microeconomics would add an i, like in q_{1i} where the i represents the Interest, under the presumption of independence, complete separability. Also, generally, only Self-interest is presumed, so there is no Other-interest I_M Eq. (A.3).

It perhaps cannot be emphasized enough: It is the fundamental nonallocable feature of each good q that leads to jointness in the interests. The Human brain is incapable of separating payoffs from the good into separable parts. The brain is intertwined, overlain, absolutely nonseparable as to "wiring" between the Ego&Empathy-based Self&Other-interest (the "&" used to indicate that wiring).

The budget constraint for the consumer also takes on a different flavor, because of the Metaeconomics contention that value V is often different from price P in the Market, as represented by a subjective element κ:

$$y = \kappa_1 p_1 q_1 + \kappa_2 p_2 q_2 \tag{A.4}$$

Bringing it all together, we seek to maximize the Own-interest arising out of the nonseparable interest, pertaining to value V on a Higher Plane, as illustrated in Fig. 4.2. The maximization of Own-interest is influenced by price P in the Market Forum. The maximization of Own-interest is also influenced by the value V coming out of Other Forums, in community and Government. As usual, the maximization is subject to the income y, budget constraint. The formulation also recognizes that maximizing Own-interest entails some sacrifice in both domains, that is, not being on either the Self-interest path 0G or the Other-interest path 0M. It leads to the following set of first order conditions on path 0Z in Figs. 4.1 and 4.2:

$$\frac{\partial \phi}{\partial q_1} = \frac{\partial V}{\partial I_G}\frac{\partial I_G}{\partial q_1} + \frac{\partial V}{\partial I_M}\frac{\partial I_M}{\partial q_2} - \lambda \kappa_1 p_1 \tag{A.5}$$

$$\frac{\partial \phi}{\partial q_2} = \frac{\partial V}{\partial I_G}\frac{\partial I_G}{\partial q_2} + \frac{\partial V}{I_M}\frac{\partial I_M}{\partial q_2} - \lambda \kappa_2 p_2 \tag{A.6}$$

$$\frac{\partial \phi}{\partial \lambda} = y - \kappa_1 p_1 q_1 - \kappa_2 p_2 q_2 \tag{A.7}$$

So, the happiness path 0Z, which entails a bit of sacrifice in both domains of interest, is defined by:

$$\frac{\frac{\partial V}{\partial I_G}\frac{\partial I_G}{\partial q_1} + \frac{\partial V}{\partial I_M}\frac{\partial I_M}{\partial q_1}}{\frac{\partial V}{\partial I_G}\frac{\partial I_G}{\partial q_2} + \frac{\partial V}{\partial I_M}\frac{\partial I_M}{\partial q_2}} = \frac{\kappa_1 p_1}{\kappa_2 p_2} \tag{A.8}$$

Keep in mind that the $\frac{\partial V}{\partial I}$ derivatives have both I_G and I_M arguments, for commonly used forms (e.g., Cobb-Douglas, Constant Elasticity of Substitution, Quadratic with interaction terms) leading to the path 0Z equation:

$$q_2 = q_2\left(\kappa_1 p_1, \kappa_2 p_2, q_1, I_G, I_M\right) \tag{A.9}$$

It means that when we use the path equation to find the demand curve, the interests I_G and I_M arguments do not drop out, as they would in Microeconomics derivations. It is about the need to also do maximizing on the Higher Plane of value *V*, as illustrated at point *B* in Fig. 4.2. Weighing the interests on a Higher Plane of value, and because of the jointness in the goods, the interests need to be quantified in order to estimate the demand for a good, like in the case for good q_1:

$$q_1^D = q_1^D\left(\kappa_1 p_1, \kappa_2 p_2, I_G, I_M, y\right) \tag{A.10}$$

with the "D" referring to a "disciplined" demand. Self-control is influencing Self-interest with the shared Other-interest. It reflects value *V* on the Higher Plane (see Fig. 4.2), so *V* influences the price *P*. So, if the interests are representing utility, we would have to go back to seeing utility as quantitative and measurable, as did Bentham. We need to think about finding balance in that utility (as in balancing pleasure and moral utility, as in Etzioni 1986).

The mathematics of the Higher Plane of value tradeoff frontier in Fig. 4.2 starts with first solving the budget constraint Eq. (A.4) as follows:

$$q_1 = \left(y - \kappa_2 p_2 q_2\right) / \kappa_1 p_1 \tag{A.11}$$

Next, substitute (A.11) into (A.1):

$$V = V\left\{I_G[\left(y - \kappa_2 p_2 q_2\right) / \kappa_1 p_1, q_2], I_M[\left(y - \kappa_2 p_2 q_2\right) / \kappa_1 p_1, q_2]\right\} \tag{A.12}$$

Now, substitute (A.9) and (A.10) into (A.12):

$$V = V\left(I_G, I_M, \kappa_1 p_1, \kappa_2 p_2, y\right) \tag{A.13}$$

Equation (A.13) traces the value frontiers of Fig. 4.2. Notice it is not just a simple tradeoff between the interests, but instead represents the complex interplay of the Ego&Empathy, Self&Other-interest along the budget constraint, for example, along RR^o in Fig. 4.1. It goes well beyond price P to also include the influence of value V. Also, we may have incommensurable values, as in pushpins having a P and poetry having a V.

Appendix B: Isoquants Between Nonallocable Inputs

For greater details regarding the formal, mathematical version of jointness arising from nonallocable inputs, and the resulting overlapping isoquants, see Lynne (2006b), and Frisch (1965, Chapters 14–15). The essence of the formal model as developed in Lynne (2006b) starts with the value V function (which is not part of the Frisch 1965, development of the framework, using only prices P). It suggests production outcomes have a higher value V than just that represented in the prices P of the products produced, as illustrated in Figs. 4.1 and 4.2. We now think of the value V arising from a production rather than a consumption process, with overlapping isoquants as in Fig. 8.1. The value function, including a constraint on resources R is:

$$\Phi = V\left(I_G, I_M\right) + \lambda\left(R\right) \tag{A.14}$$

where the production functions show nonallocable inputs:

$$I_G = I_G\left(X_1, X_2\right) \tag{A.15}$$

$$I_M = I_M(X_1, X_2) \quad \text{(A.16)}$$

There are no allocating subscripts like X_{1j}, always there in Microeconomics. A Microeconomics subscript presumes complete control, the power of the manager to control the allocation of X_1, which is not possible when there is jointness in the products (the sheep does it, not the rancher; the Spaceship Earth system does it, not the producer).

To illustrate the formal framework, we take a simple form (leaving out the squared terms of a common quadratic, and there are many other possibilities) of an overall value function:

$$\Phi = \iota p I_G(X_1, X_2) + \tau I_M(X_1, X_2) + \gamma(I_G)(I_M) + \lambda(R - \kappa_1 r_1 X_1 - \kappa_2 r_2 X_2) \quad \text{(A.17)}$$

where the r_1, r_2 are input prices, and p is the Market-generated price for the Egoistic interest in providing a Market product. There is only value V associated with I_M, no Market price: In an agricultural situation, the I_M might reflect the shared other-interest in wildlife that also depends on the same land as does the corn I_G being produced on it. Notice the subjective elements: κ_1, κ_2 for input cost; ι from Ego; τ from Empathy, the latter about walking-in-the-shoes of employees, input suppliers, consumers, community, and the Spaceship Earth System within which the production is embedded.

First order conditions are:

$$\frac{\partial \Phi}{\partial X_1} = (\iota p + \gamma I_M)\frac{\partial I_G}{\partial X_1} + (\tau + \gamma I_G)\frac{\partial I_M}{\partial X_1} \underline{\underline{set}}\, \kappa_1 r_1 \quad \text{(A.18)}$$

$$\frac{\partial \Phi}{\partial X_2} = (\iota p + \gamma I_M) + \frac{\partial I_G}{\partial X_2} + (\tau + \gamma I_G)\frac{\partial I_M}{\partial X_2} \underline{\underline{set}}\, \kappa_2 r2 \quad \text{(A.19)}$$

$$\frac{\partial \Phi}{\partial \lambda 2} = R - \kappa r_1 X_1 - \kappa r_2 X_2 \,\underline{\underline{set}}\, 0 \quad \text{(A.20)}$$

Least-cost is achieved where:

$$\frac{(\iota p+\gamma I_M)\frac{\partial I_G}{\partial X_1}+(\tau+\gamma I_G)\frac{\partial I_M}{\partial X_1}}{(\iota p+\gamma I_M)\frac{\partial I_G}{\partial X_2}+(\tau+\gamma I_G)\frac{\partial I_M}{\partial X_2}}=\frac{\kappa_1 r_1}{\kappa_2 r_2} \tag{A.21}$$

Notice how in Microeconomic $\iota = \kappa_1 = \kappa_2 = 1$ and $\tau = \gamma = 0$. The expansion path 0Z in Fig. 8.1 from (A.21) is:

$$X_2 = X_2(\kappa_1 r_1, \kappa_2 r_2, p, I_G, I_M, X_1) \tag{A.22}$$

Leading to the derived demand D for X_1

$$X_1^D = X_1^D(\kappa_1 r_1, \kappa_2 r_2, p, I_G, I_M, R) \tag{A.23}$$

Notice how Empathy I_M (D, or "disciplined by the moral dimension") affects input demand.

Substituting (A.23) and the demand for X_2^D into both (A.15) and (A.16), supply for the commercial product of interest is:

$$I_G^D = I_G^D(\kappa_1 r_1, \kappa_2 r_2, p, I_M, R) \tag{A.24}$$

The disciplined (D) supply is influenced by the Empathy I_M arising with employees, input suppliers, consumers, shareholders, and the Spaceship Earth system.

We can derive the Ego&Empathy frontier in Fig. 4.2, but now referring to production tradeoffs along RR^0 in Fig. 8.1. We insert both X_1^D and X_2^D into the value function (A.17), and staying on some budget line RR^o we can trace a curve in Fig. 4.2 of the form:

$$\Phi = \Phi(I_G, I_M, \kappa_1 r_1, \kappa_2 r_2, p, R) \tag{A.25}$$

Various measures of complementary, competitive and degrees of independence can be derived from using said production possibility frontiers: See Lynne (2006b) for details.

References

Altman, M. 2012. *Behavioral Economics for Dummies*. Kindle ed. Mississauga, ON: John Wiley and Sons Canada, Ltd.

Ayres, Clarence E. 1944/1978. *The Theory of Economic Progress*. Kalamazoo: New Issues Press, Western Michigan University..

Etzioni, A. 1986. The Case for a Multiple Utility Conception. *Economics and Philosophy* 2: 159–183.

Frisch, Ragnar. 1965. *Theory of Production*. Chicago: Rand McNally and Company.

Lynne, G.D. 1995. Modifying the Neoclassical Approach to Technology Adoption with Behavioral Science Models. *Journal of Agricultural and Applied Economics* 27 (1): 67–80.

———. 2006a. Chap. 6: On the Economics of Subselves: Toward a Metaeconomics. In *Handbook of Contemporary Behavioral Economics*, ed. M. Altman, 99–122. New York: M.E. Sharpe.

———. 2006b. Toward a Dual Motive Metaeconomic Theory. *Journal of Socio-Economics* 35: 634–651.

Tomer, John F. 2017. *Advanced Introduction to Behavioral Economics*. North Hampton: Elgar.

Index

G. D. Lynne, *Metaeconomics*, Palgrave Advances in Behavioral Economics, https://doi.org/10.1007/978-3-030-50601-8

The manufacturer's authorised representative in the EU is Springer Nature Customer Service Centre GmbH, Europaplatz 3, 69115 Heidelberg, Germany. If you have any concerns regarding our products, please contact ProductSafety@springernature.com

Printed and bound by CPI Group (UK) Ltd, Croydon, CR0 4YY
30/09/2026
02225451-0015